GW00502637

REVISION WORKBOOK

Land:
THE LAW OF REAL PROPERTY

Third Edition

PROFESSOR CEDRIC D BELL
LLB, LLM, PhD, Barrister
Chief Executive, Holborn College
Visiting Professor of Legal Practice, University of Hertfordshire

OLD BAILEY PRESS

OLD BAILEY PRESS
at Holborn College, Woolwich Road,
Charlton, London, SE7 8LN

First published 1997
Third edition 2004

© Holborn College Ltd 2004

All Old Bailey Press publications enjoy copyright protection and the copyright belongs to Holborn College Ltd.

All rights reserved. No part of this publication may be reproduced or transmitted in any form or by any means, electronic, mechanical, photocopying, recording or otherwise, or stored in any retrieval system of any nature without either the written permission of the copyright holder, application for which should be made to the Old Bailey Press, or a licence permitting restricted copying in the United Kingdom issued by the Copyright Licensing Agency.

Any person who infringes the above in relation to this publication may be liable to criminal prosecution and civil claims for damages.

ISBN 1 85836 554 6

British Library Cataloguing-in-Publication.

A CIP Catalogue record for this book is available from the British Library.

Printed and bound by CPI Antony Rowe, Eastbourne

Contents

Acknowledgement

Some questions used are taken or adapted from past University of London LLB (External) Degree examination papers and our thanks are extended to the University of London for their kind permission to use and publish the questions.

Caveat

The answers given are not approved or sanctioned by the University of London and are entirely our responsibility.

They are not intended as 'Model Answers', but rather as Suggested Solutions.

The answers have two fundamental purposes, namely:

a) to provide a detailed example of a suggested solution to an examination question; and

b) to assist students with their research into the subject and to further their understanding and appreciation of the subject.

Introduction

This Revision WorkBook has been designed specifically for those studying land law to undergraduate level or its equivalent. Its coverage is not restricted to any one syllabus but embraces all the core land law topics to be found in most university, college and institutional examinations.

Each chapter contains an introduction explaining the scope and general content of the topic covered. This is followed by detailed 'key points' which direct students to the material they must know if they are to fully understand the topic and a section entitled 'key cases and statutes' which identifies the most important cases and statutory provisions in the area in question from a student's perspective. Throughout the text there is an emphasis on contemporary developments including, in particular, the Land Registration Act 2002 which, came into force on 13 October 2003 (although not all of its provisions take effect immediately). The Act repeals the Land Registration Act 1925 and fundamentally changes the system of registered title in England and Wales.

A number of past examination questions are included to enable the student to focus on the examinable issues within each topic. These questions have been selected to cover a good range of the question variations that an examiner may set in each topic. Each question has a general comment and skeleton solution followed by a full suggested solution. Although students are not expected to produce a skeleton solution in the examination it can be a useful examination technique to adopt, and ensures a well planned, full and logical answer.

There are a number of references in the text to 'Cheshire' and 'Megarry and Wade'. The works referred to are Cheshire and Burn's *Modern Law of Real Property* (16th edition, 2000) and *The Law of Real Property* by Megarry and Wade (6th edition, 2002).

Studying Land Law

The study of land law should be directed to answering the two types of question found in the examinations – the essay question and the problem question.

The essay-type of question may be either purely factual in asking you to explain the meaning of a certain doctrine or principle, or it may ask you to discuss a certain proposition usually derived from a quotation. In either of these cases you must explain to the examiner the meaning and significance of the relevant doctrine, principle or proposition, its origin in common law, equity or statute and identify cases which illustrate its application in land law. A good land law essay answer will exhibit the following characteristics. First, it will be properly structured: opening/'scene set' (setting out where you are going), deal with all the relevant issues in a logical progression and have a clear conclusion. Second, it will focus upon the relevant principle/doctrine or proposition and will not be converted into a 'write all you know' answer about the general topic. Third, cases cited will be relevant and evaluated (in particular you should avoid citing a plethora of cases to illustrate the same point). Fourth, it will be an up-to-date answer including coverage of any recent case developments and/or of any proposals for reform of the area of law in question. Fifth, the answer will be thought-provoking and kept within the relevant time constraint (students frequently overrun on essay answers to the detriment of the final answer).

The problem-type question requires a different approach. You may well be asked to advise a client/party or merely discuss the problems raised in the question. In either case, the most important factor is to take great care in reading the question. By its nature, the question will be longer than the essay-type question and you will have a number of facts to digest. Time spent in analysing the question at the outset may well avoid you having a mid-answer crisis! It is important not to be put off attempting a problem question by its length as sometimes a long problem question can be comparatively straightforward. It is crucial to identify all the issues contained in a problem question at the outset (ie before starting to write an answer). Usually there will be three or four key points/issues in the problem (if you can only identify one point to discuss, the chances are that you are missing something and you would be well advised to select another question to answer). A good land law problem answer will exhibit the following characteristics. First, it will have a clear and recognisable structure (opening, body and conclusion). The opening will identify the issues to be discussed and if the student is sufficiently confident outline the conclusions to be reasoned towards. The body of the answer will discuss the issues relevant to the question and will apply the relevant legal principles to the facts. The conclusion will do what the rubric of the question asks – advise the party or parties specified or, if you are required to discuss the problem set, draw the strands of the answer together. Second, it will keep within the boundaries of the question set. There is an understandable temptation to want to demonstrate to an examiner the breadth of your knowledge of land law but if material is outside the parameters of the question set it will be of little avail including it in the answer and will be time lost. It is important to remember that the issues to be discussed in a problem question are set out therein and not infrequently the material to be covered in such a question is narrower than that in a ranging essay title. Third, it will apply the relevant law to the facts clearly, where necessary distinguish the facts of the problem from the leading cases, and if the current law is unsatisfactory explain why and endeavour to reach realistic conclusions. It will not always be the case that the question merits 'one conclusion'. Rather, alternative arguments may be appropriate and you should be alert to such possibilities. Fourth, while keeping within the boundaries of the question set, the opportunity will be taken to comment judiciously on proposals to reform the law in question and on any relevant journal literature. Such an 'extra dimension' is often the difference between a solid 2.2 answer and one which is of a 2.1 standard.

Always try to prepare a rough outline before embarking upon the formal answer. This will give you time to assemble your thoughts and organise your material. It may also help to ensure that you answer all the points you believe the examiner has raised. In developing a particular theme within the answer, it is very easy to overlook a matter which you had remembered in the initial review of the question. The suggested solutions in this Revision WorkBook use this technique by way of a skeleton solution which precedes the full suggested solution.

Finally, always leave sufficient time before the examination finishes so that you can better ensure that your answers read well, that any points missed out can be included and any mistakes dealt with (eg mixing up names of parties in a problem answer). Such a final revision can often bring a real bonus in terms of marks awarded.

The key to this approach is knowledge and the requirement to read the subject as often as time permits will bring the benefits when the examination is faced. The reading of the compulsory textbook is, therefore, an essential pre-requisite to a satisfactory result in the examination and is equally essential if full advantage is to be taken of the Revision WorkBook.

There are various ways of assembling land law for revision purposes. One method would be to divide the subject into the following four parts and devote revision time, in turn to each part:

Revision WorkBook

Part	Chapter	Chapter No.
1	1925 legislation	1
	Settlements of land	4
	Co-ownership	5
2	Registration	3
	Adverse possession	11

Revision and Examination Technique

Revision Technique

Planning a revision timetable

In planning your revision timetable make sure you do not finish the syllabus too early. You should avoid leaving revision so late that you have to 'cram' – but constant revision of the same topic leads to stagnation.

Plan ahead, however, and try to make your plans increasingly detailed as you approach the examination date.

Allocate enough time for each topic to be studied. But note that it is better to devise a realistic timetable, to which you have a reasonable chance of keeping, rather than a wildly optimistic schedule which you will probably abandon at the first opportunity!

The syllabus and its topics

One of your first tasks when you began your course was to ensure that you thoroughly understood your syllabus. Check now to see if you can write down the topics it comprises from memory. You will see that the chapters of this WorkBook are each devoted to a syllabus topic. This will help you decide which are the key chapters relevant to your revision programme, though you should allow some time for glancing through the other chapters.

The topic and its key points

Again working from memory, analyse what you consider to be the key points of any topic that you have selected for particular revision. Seeing what you can recall, unaided, will help you to understand and firmly memorise the concepts involved.

Using the WorkBook

Relevant questions are provided for each topic in this book. Naturally, as typical examples of examination questions, they do not normally relate to one topic only. But the questions in each chapter will relate to the subject matter of the chapter to a degree. You can choose your method of consulting the questions and solutions, and for your assistance three suggestions (strategies 1–3) are set out below. Each of them presupposes that you have read through the author's notes on key points and key cases and statutes, and any other preliminary matter, at the beginning of the chapter. Once again, you now need to practise working from memory, for that is the challenge you are preparing yourself for. As a rule of procedure constantly test yourself once revision starts, both orally and in writing.

Strategy 1

Strategy 1 is planned for the purpose of quick revision. First read your chosen question carefully and then jot down in abbreviated notes what you consider to be the main points at issue. Similarly, note the cases and statutes that occur to you as being relevant for citation purposes. Allow yourself sufficient time to cover what you feel to be relevant. Then study the author's skeleton solution and skim-read the suggested solution to see how they compare with your notes. When comparing consider carefully what the author has included (and concluded) and see whether that agrees with what you have written. Consider the points of variation also. Have you recognised the key issues? How relevant have you been? It is possible, of course, that you have referred to a recent case that is relevant, but which had not been reported when the WorkBook was prepared.

Strategy 2

Strategy 2 requires a period of three hours in which to practise writing a set of examination answers in a limited time-span.

Select a number of questions (as many as are normally set in your subject in the examination you are studying for), each from a different chapter in the WorkBook, without consulting the solutions. Find a place to write where you will not be disturbed and try to arrange not to be interrupted for three hours. Write your solutions in the time allowed, noting any time needed to make up if you are interrupted.

After a rest, compare your answers with the suggested solutions in the WorkBook. There will be considerable variation in style, of course, but the bare facts should not be too dissimilar. Evaluate your answer critically. Be 'searching', but develop a positive approach to deciding how you would tackle each question on another occasion.

Strategy 3

You are unlikely to be able to do more than one three hour examination, but occasionally set yourself a single question. Vary the 'time allowed' by imagining it to be one of the questions that you must answer in three hours and allow yourself a limited preparation and writing time. Try one question that you feel to be difficult and an easier question on another occasion, for example.

Misuse of suggested solutions

Don't try to learn by rote. In particular, don't try to reproduce the suggested solutions by heart. Learn to express the basic concepts in your own words.

Keeping up-to-date

Keep up-to-date. While examiners usually do not require familiarity with changes in the law during the three months prior to the examination, it obviously creates a good impression if you can show you are acquainted with any recent changes. Make a habit of looking through one of the leading journals – *Modern Law Review*, *Law Quarterly Review*, *Conveyanver & Property Lawyer*, *Solicitors' Journal* or the *New Law Journal*, for example – and cumulative indices to law reports, such as the *All England Law Reports* or *Weekly Law Reports*, or indeed the daily law reports in *The Times*. The *Law Society's Gazette* and the *Legal Executive Journal* are helpful sources, plus any specialist journal(s) for the subject you are studying.

Examination Skills

Examiners are human too!

The process of answering an examination question involves a communication between you and the person who set it. If you were speaking face to face with the person, you would choose your verbal points and arguments carefully in your reply. When writing, it is all too easy to forget the human being who is awaiting the reply and simply write out what one knows in the area of the subject! Bear in mind it is a person whose question you are responding to, throughout your essay. This will help you to avoid being irrelevant or long-winded.

The essay question

Candidates are sometimes tempted to choose to answer essay questions because they 'seem' easier. But the examiner is looking for thoughtful work and will not give good marks for superficial answers.

The essay-type of question may be either purely factual, in asking you to explain the meaning of a certain doctrine or principle, or it may ask you to discuss a certain proposition, usually derived from a quotation. In either case, the approach to the answer is the same. It is necessary to give the examiner the meaning or significance of the doctrine, principle or proposition and its origin in common law, equity or statute, and cases which illustrate its application to the branch of law concerned. Essay questions offer a good way to obtain marks if you have thought carefully about a topic, since it is up to you to impose the structure (unlike the problem questions where the problem imposes its own structure). You are then free to speculate and show imagination.

The problem question

The problem-type question requires a different approach. You may well be asked to advise a client or merely discuss the issues raised in the question. In either case, the most important factor is to take great care in reading the question. By its nature, the question will be longer than the essay-type question and you will have a number of facts to digest. Time spent in analysing the question may well save time later, when you are endeavouring to impress on the examiner the considerable extent of your basic legal knowledge. The quantity of knowledge is itself a trap and you must always keep within the boundaries of the question in hand. It is very tempting to show the examiner the extent of your knowledge of the subject, but if this is outside the question, it is time lost and no marks earned. It is inevitable that some areas which you have studied and revised will not be the subject of questions, but under no circumstances attempt to adapt a question to a stronger area of knowledge at the expense of relevance.

When you are satisfied that you have grasped the full significance of the problem-type question, set out the fundamental principles involved.

You will then go on to identify the fundamental problem (or problems) posed by the question. This should be followed by a consideration of the law which is relevant to the problem. The source of the law, together with the cases which will be of assistance in solving the problem, must then be considered in detail.

Very good problem questions are quite likely to have alternative answers, and in advising a party you should be aware that alternative arguments may be available. Each stage of your answer, in this case, will be based on the argument or arguments considered in the previous stage, forming a conditional sequence.

If, however, you only identify one fundamental problem, do not waste time worrying that you cannot think of an alternative – there may very well be only that one answer.

The examiner will then wish to see how you use your legal knowledge to formulate a case and how you apply that formula to the problem which is the subject of the question. It is this positive approach which can make answering a problem question a high mark earner for the student who has fully understood the question and clearly argued their case on the established law.

Examination checklist

a) Read the instructions at the head of the examination carefully. While last-minute changes are unlikely – such as the introduction of a compulsory question or an increase in the number of questions asked – it has been known to happen.

b) Read the questions carefully. Analyse problem questions – work out what the examiner wants.

c) Plan your answer before you start to write.

d) Check that you understand the rubric before you start to write. Do not 'discuss', for example, if you are specifically asked to 'compare and contrast'.

e) Answer the correct number of questions. If you fail to answer one out of four questions set you lose 25 per cent of your marks!

Style and structure

Try to be clear and concise. Fundamentally this amounts to using paragraphs to denote the sections of your essay, and writing simple, straightforward sentences as much as possible. The sentence you have just read has 22 words – when a sentence reaches 50 words it becomes difficult for a reader to follow.

Do not be inhibited by the word 'structure' (traditionally defined as giving an essay a beginning, a middle and an end). A good structure will be the natural consequence of setting out your arguments and the supporting evidence in a logical order. Set the scene briefly in your opening paragraph. Provide a clear conclusion in your final paragraph.

Table of Cases

Table of Statutes

Chapter 1

Basis of Land Law

1.1   Introduction

1.2   Key points

1.3   Key cases and statutes

1.4   Questions and suggested solutions

1.1 Introduction

Although many examiners neglect this area of land law it remains important to understand the fundamental principles that underpin the subject. In particular no candidates should go into a land law examination without a working knowledge of s1 of the Law of Property Act 1925 and knowing the difference between the doctrine of tenure and the doctrine of estates and the practical significance of the doctrines today. Candidates should appreciate that in theory there is no such thing as 'owning land' in England and Wales (all land being held of the Crown), but that in reality the freeholder is to all intents and purposes 'the owner' and therefore it is important to know what the freeholder can and cannot do with 'his' land. The ability to give definitions of the two legal estates will be particularly useful as, also, is a knowledge of the contents of s205(1) LPA 1925 (the definition section).

1.2 Key points

Introductory

Nature of land – s205(1)(ix) LPA 1925

History

Legal definition of land – s205(1)(ix) LPA 1925

Tenures and estates

Doctrine of tenure – quality of the holding – sets out the terms on which the land is held

a) Military tenures

   i)   knight's service;

    ii) grand serjeanty;

    iii) petty serjeanty.

b) Agricultural tenures

    Common socage.

c) Spiritual tenures

    i) frankalmoign;

    ii) divine service.

d) Unfree tenure – copyhold: s128 and 12th Schedule LPA 1922.

e) Effect of 1925 legislation – Cheshire states 'A conception of merely academic interest it no longer restricts the tenant in his free enjoyment of the land.' Of little practical importance today.

Doctrine of estates – quantity of the holding – describes for how long the land is held

a) Original freehold estates

    i) fee simple;

    ii) fee tail;

    iii) life estate;

    iv) Estate – pur autre vie.

b) Original estates less than freehold

c) Estates and interests since 1925 – they continue to be of importance.

    i) It is important to study in detail the reduction in legal estates and interests made by LPA 1925, s1(1), (2) and (3), and to know why the reductions took place – legal rights are binding in rem therefore the more legal estates and interests in existence the greater the risk that a purchaser would buy land subject to such an estate or interest.

    ii) Fee simple absolute in possession: see s205(1)(xix) LPA 1925.

    iii) Term of years absolute: see s205(1)(xxvii) LPA 1925.

    iv) Modified fees – compare the determinable fee simple with the conditional fee simple.

c) The estate in fee simple

    Method of creation:

    i) at common law;

ii) wills;

iii) s60(1) LPA 1925 – will pass the fee simple or whatever estate is presently held of the vendor;

iv) corporations;

v) registered land:

- s19(1) LRA 1925 – title must be completed by registration;

- ss6 and 7 LRA 2002 – title is void if not submitted for registration within two months. Period for compulsory registration is the same as under the LRA 1925. Relevant transaction becomes void so far as the transfer, grant or creation of a legal estate is concerned, ie the legal estate remains vested with the transferor.

Extent of ownership

a) Cujus est solum ejus est usque ad coelum et ad inferos (whosoever has the soil also owns to the heavens above and to the centre beneath)

Cheshire: 'The common law principle is that a tenant in fee simple is owner of everything in, on and above his land.'

Commissioner for Railways v *Valuer-General* [1974] AC 328, Lord Wilberforce: 'At most the maxim is used as a statement, imprecise enough, of the extent of the rights, prima facie, of owners of land.'

Megarry and Wade: 'The absolute freedom of the owner is qualified in many ways.'

Limitations:

i) overhanging objects;

ii) treasure trove: see Treasure Act 1996;

iii) chattels under or attached to land – fixtures: see below;

iv) wild animals;

v) minerals;

vi) flights over land: see s76(1) Civil Aviation Act 1982 and *Bernstein* v *Skyviews & General Ltd* [1977] 3 WLR 136, where Griffiths J stated:

'… the balance was best struck by restricting the rights of an owner in the airspace above his land to such heights as was necessary for the ordinary use and enjoyment of his land and the structures upon it, and declaring that above that height he had no greater rights in the airspace than any other member of the public.'

vii) fishing rights in non-tidal parts of rivers;

viii) water rights;

ix) bed of non-tidal river;

x) effects of legislation including security of tenure provisions.

b) More particularly, limitations should be noted as follows:

i) Rights over the land of another – rights in alieno solo.

ii) Rights in airspace:

Kelsen v *Imperial Tobacco Co Ltd* [1957] 2 QB 334;

Bernstein v *Skyviews & General Ltd* [1977] 3 WLR 136 and s76 Civil Aviation Act 1982;

Anchor Brewhouse Developments Ltd v *Berkley House (Docklands) Developments Ltd* (1987) 284 EG 625.

iii) Minerals – gold and silver – petroleum – coal.

iv) Treasure trove – gold/silver – found hidden in/on land – owner not known (the common law of treasure trove was replaced with a new regime introduced by the Treasure Act 1996).

v) Wild animals – res nullius – things without an owner.

vi) Water

- Common law:

Own land or flowing past – riparian rights

River – abstraction for ordinary purposes or extraordinary purposes

Swindon Waterworks v *Wilts & Berks Canal Navigation Co* (1875) LR 7 HL 697

Percolating water – unlimited amounts regardless of damage

Stephens v *Anglian Water Authority* [1987] 1 WLR 1381

Langbrook Properties Ltd v *Surrey County Council* [1970] 1 WLR 101

Palmer and Another v *Bowman and Another* [2000] 1 All ER 22

Drainage of natural water from higher land onto separately owned lower land could not exist as an easement – such drainage was an essential incident of land ownership

- Statute – Water Resources Act 1963 – licence required.

vii) Liability in tort – trespass – nuisance – negligence. Duty of care on landlord: s4 Defective Premises Act 1972.

viii) Statute – Megarry and Wade: '… during the last 70 years there has been much legislation imposing on landowners restrictions and liabilities in the public interest'.

Town and Country Planning Acts – Housing Acts – Public Health Acts – security of tenure provisions.

c) Fixtures

i) Definition – goods annexed to land in such circumstances that the law assumes that they are now to be treated as land.

ii) Why is the question of fixtures important? Who now owns the goods?

iii) Explain the two tests applied to fixtures: (a) degree of annexation; (b) purpose of annexation.

iv) Is test (a) conclusive? No, rebut by showing intention of person who affixed.

v) Evidence of rebuttal? Object merely resting on land or better enjoyment of object. What benefits – the land or the object?

vi) Why was test (b) required? Limitations of test (a).

vii) Which areas of land law are affected by 'fixtures'?

Landlord and tenant: trade: domestic: agricultural.

Tenant for life – remainderman: *D'Eyncourt* v *Gregory* (1866) LR 3 Eq 382; *Leigh* v *Taylor* [1902] AC 157.

Mortgagor – mortgagee: *Hobson* v *Gorringe* [1897] 1 Ch 182; *Reynolds* v *Ashby* [1904] AC 466.

Vendor – purchaser: *Berkley* v *Poulett* [1977] EGD 754; *Dean* v *Andrews* (1985) The Times 25 May.

1.3 Key cases and statutes

- *Berkley* v *Poulett* [1977] EGD 754
  Fixtures – purpose of annexation

- *Bernstein* v *Skyviews & General Ltd* [1977] 3 WLR 136
  Rights of freeholder as to airspace above his land

- *Chelsea Yacht & Boat Club Ltd* v *Pope* (2000) The Times 7 June
  A boat on the river was not on land or anything like land

- *D'Eyncourt* v *Gregory* (1866) LR 3 Eq 382
  Fixtures – purpose of annexation

- *Elitestone Ltd* v *Morris and Another* [1997] 2 All ER 513
  Fixtures – chalet resting on concrete pillars with no physical attachment to land a fixture, not a chattel

- *Leigh* v *Taylor* [1902] AC 157
  Fixtures – purpose of annexation

- Law of Property Act 1925, ss1(1), (2), (3) and s205(1)(ix)
- Treasure Act 1996

1.4 Questions and suggested solutions

Analysis of questions

As indicated in the Introduction, a working knowledge of s1 LPA 1925 is essential. Every land law paper will provide students with opportunities to display their understanding of this crucial provision. Students may be asked to explain the doctrine of tenure and the doctrine of estates and assess the contemporary significance of each. As to leases, sometimes questions focus upon the requirement that the duration of a lease must be certain for it to be a legal lease and the related statutory provisions.

A further area for questions could be the 'cujus' maxim. Of these the problems of air space, rights over water and fixtures are of importance.

QUESTION ONE

a) 'There are thus two fundamental doctrines in the law of real property ... tenure answers the question "upon what terms is it (land) held"?: estates answers the question "for how long"?' (Megarry and Wade, *The Law of Real Property*).

   Explain this statement.

b) What interests, if any, are created by each of the following transactions?

   i) A conveys Blackacre to B in fee simple, imposing covenants and reserving a right of re-entry on breach of covenant.

   ii) C, lessee of Whiteacre, sublets to D for the remainder of the term without asking for the consent of X, the landlord, as provided in the lease.

University of London LLB Examination
(for External Students) Land Law June 1985 Q1

General Comment

A question to remind the candidate that all examinations are based on a syllabus and the examiner is entitled to select questions from any part of that syllabus. Part (a) emerges from the first substantive paragraph of the syllabus and is a welcome encouragement to those tutors who advise students that an understanding of land law is always helped by an appreciation of fundamental areas such as this.

Part (b) reminds candidates that leases effectively feature twice in the syllabus being part of the general debate on s1 LPA 1925 and subsequently as a separate area of study in their own right.

Skeleton Solution

a) Describe tenure: quality of holding – feudal pyramid (diagram) – forms of tenure (diagram) – tenures today.

Describe estate: quantity of the holding – types of estate before 1926 (diagram) – the legal estate today (s1(1) LPA 1925) (diagram) – conclusion – the estate today.

b) i) 'Conveys': indicates fee simple absolute in possession – 'absolute' where a right of re-entry exists – effect of Law of Property (Amendment) Act 1926 on s7(1) LPA 1925.

   ii) Is this a sub-lease or an assignment? – illustrate distinction – qualified covenant applies, depending on terms, to both sub-lease and assignment – effect of s19(1)(a) Landlord and Tenant Act 1927 on such a qualified covenant – response of C (s53 Landlord and Tenant Act 1954): interpretation of reasonableness in this context.

Suggested Solution

a) This statement of Megarry and Wade summarises the rules which formed the basis of land law.

Tenure answered the question 'upon what terms' was the land held. This described the quality of the holding and, in particular, referred to the early rules of subinfeudation by which the grantee held 'land' in return for services. This concept of subinfeudation emerged after the Norman Conquest and represented the rewards given by the King to those who had supported him. This created a form of holding which acquired the title of the feudal pyramid because all 'land' was held either directly, or indirectly through intermediaries, from the King himself. This may be represented by the following diagram of freehold tenures:

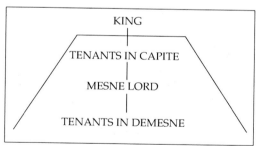

Thus each intermediary would grant an interest in land in return for some service and in this way the fabric of feudalism was created. It did not last for many years in that it became much easier to pay for services than provide them directly. As a consequence the doctrine of subinfeudation was brought to an end by the statute of Quia Emptores in 1290. The major effect of the statute was to replace subinfeudation by substitution. This is described in Megarry and Wade as follows:

'Quia Emptores marked the victory of the modern concept of land as alienable property over the more restrictive principles of feudalism. For no new tenures in fee simple could thenceforth be created except by the Crown.' This is followed by a suitable epitaph to the feudal pyramid: 'After 1290 the feudal pyramid began to crumble. The number of mesne lordships could not be increased, evidence of existing mesne lordships gradually disappeared with the passing of time, and so most land came to be held directly from the Crown.' In the words of the statute itself:

> 'Our Lord the King ... at the instance of the great men of the realm ... ordained, that from henceforth it shall be lawful to every freeman to sell at his own pleasure his lands and tenements, or part of them; so that the feoffee shall hold the same ... fee, by such service and customs as his feoffor held before.'

The forms of tenure may be described as the quality of the holding. This quality was varied by the nature of the services to be provided by the grantee. A popular diagram of the forms of tenure is as follows:

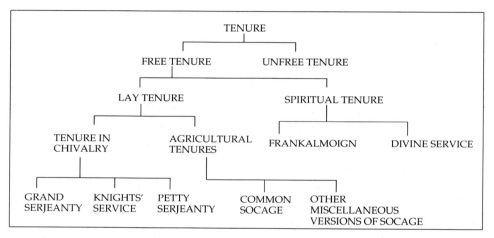

Of these forms of tenure the most significant was, probably, knights' service. This contained many 'incidents' which formed the basis of the tenure and included relief, escheat, wardship and marriage. Most of the forms of tenure had ended before they were abolished by the Tenures Abolition Act 1660: some, including frankalmoign and the services incident to grand and petty serjeanty, survived until 1925. From the 1st January 1926 the only surviving form of tenure is socage now known as freehold tenure. The consequence is neatly summarised by Cheshire:

> 'The result is that though the general theory of tenure is still a part of English law in the sense that all land is held by a superior and is incapable of absolute ownership, yet the law of tenure is both simpler and of less significance than it was before 1926. It is simpler because there is now only one form of tenure: namely socage. It is of less significance because all the tenurial incidents (including escheat) which might in exceptional cases have brought profit to a mesne lord have been abolished ... We can,

in fact, now describe the theory of tenure, despite the great part that it had played in the history of English law, as a conception of merely academic interest. It no longer restricts the tenant in his free enjoyment of the land.'

Estate deals with the duration of interest and describes the quantity of the holdings. It is, again, possible to demonstrate this by way of a diagram in which it will be noted there are two major categories of estate – the freehold and the less than freehold estate. Unlike tenures, the concept of estates remains with us today and formed the essential part of s1(1) of the Law of Property Act 1925. The types of estate that existed before 1926 may be shown diagrammatically as follows:

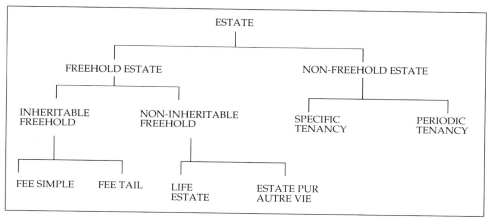

Of these estates the fee simple and the non-freehold estate remain as legal estates under s1(1) LPA 1925. They are now, respectively, the 'fee simple absolute in possession' and the 'term of years absolute'. The fee tail and the life estate also continue but are now equitable interests known, respectively, as the entailed interest and the life interest. However, the Trusts of Land and Appointment of Trustees Act 1996 (which came into force on 1 January 1997) prevents the creation of any more entailed interests (Sch 1, para 5). A feature of the estate is that several could exist concurrently and this is retained by s1(5) LPA 1925 which provides: 'A legal estate may subsist concurrently with or subject to any other legal estate in the same land.' The effect today is the possibility of the fee simple, leases and sub-leases all being separate estates in the same land.

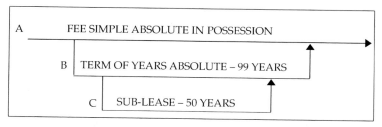

It will be seen that 'estate' is not the land itself. The estate is a conceptual matter which has been separated from the land. It is the estate that is the subject of conveyance, lease or assignment whilst the land itself remains in the ownership of the Crown as a further reminder of the feudal origins. Cheshire defines 'estate' as '… the right to possess and use the land for the period of time for which it has been granted'.

Most authors recognise the unique quality of the estate and the right of seisin which represents the present right to enjoy the possession of the land by an owner of the freehold estate holding for freehold tenure. A fitting conclusion is provided by Cheshire:

> 'In conclusion, it may be said that this doctrine of the estate has given an elasticity to the English law of the land that is not found in countries outside the area of the common law.'

b) i) The use of the word 'conveys' indicates that A holds the fee simple absolute in possession in Blackacre and he conveys the freehold estate to B. The conveyance includes covenants which mean that A will retain an interest as covenantee and will be able to enforce the covenants, whether they are positive or negative, as a matter of contract against B. The question which arises is whether B has an 'absolute' fee simple when A may re-enter if any of the covenants are broken. This clearly is a restriction on the 'absolute' nature of the estate as the word 'absolute' is defined in general usage. This problem was recognised, belatedly, by the draftsmen of the 1925 legislation and the following words were added to s7(1) LPA 1925 by the Law of Property (Amendment) Act 1926: '… and a fee simple subject to a legal or equitable right of entry or re-entry is for the purposes of this Act a fee simple absolute'. The effect of this addition to s7(1) is that B does hold a 'fee simple absolute in possession', a legal estate, even though A has a right of re-entry if any of the covenants are broken.

ii) Every sub-lease requires the sub-lessor to retain a reversion even if it is just for one day. The effect of this transaction may be seen:

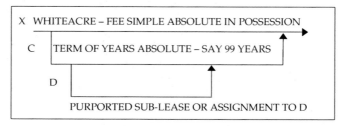

The effect of this transaction will be to assign to D the residue of the term of years presently vested in C. D will become the tenant of X and C will cease to have any interest whatsoever in Whiteacre except that he will continue to be bound to X by privity of contract if X and C were the original landlord and tenant respectively and the lease was entered into before 1 January 1996. However, if the lease was entered into on or after 1 January 1996 (ie when the Landlord and Tenant (Covenants) Act 1995 came into force) C will be released from his covenants on the assignment of the term.

The original lease contains a requirement that C should obtain the consent of X before parting with possession of Whiteacre. The clause would presumably express the restriction in words such as:

> 'C shall not assign, underlet or part with possession of Whiteacre without the consent of X.'

If the covenant is expressed in these terms it is a qualified covenant and C will be liable to X.

The assignment itself will still be effective and any notice to quit would have to be served on the assignee D: see *Old Grovebury Manor Farm Ltd v W Seymour Plant Sales & Hire Ltd (No 2)* [1979] 1 WLR 1397.

Because the covenant is qualified by requiring the consent of X reference must also be made to s19(1)(a) of the Landlord and Tenant Act 1927 which provides:

> '(1) In all leases whether made before or after the commencement of this Act containing a covenant condition or agreement against assigning, underletting, charging or parting with the possession of demised premises or any part thereof without licence or consent, such covenant condition or agreement shall, notwithstanding any express provision to the contrary, be deemed to be subject –

> (a) to a proviso to the effect that such licence or consent is not to be unreasonably withheld ...'

Section 22 of the Landlord and Tenant (Covenants) Act 1995 amends s19 of the 1927 Act by inserting a new s1A into it. This enables a landlord and tenant to detail in the lease what terms or conditions must be satisfied for the landlord to give his consent to an assignment. If thereafter the terms or conditions are not satisfied and the landlord does not consent to the assignment, his consent will not be regarded as having been unreasonably withheld. However, the amendment to s19 of the 1927 Act cannot apply to residential premises. It only applies to business premises. For the purposes of the question, it is assumed that Whiteacre is a residential property.

If C does not apply to X for consent he will be liable in damages. The risk to D is that the lease would also become liable to forfeiture for breach of covenant. If X unreasonably refuses consent C may apply to court for a declaration that the consent has been unreasonably withheld, in which case C could then assign the residue of the term to D. The jurisdiction is in the county court: s53 of the Landlord and Tenant Act 1954. The burden of proof is placed on the landlord by ss1 and 2 of the Landlord and Tenant Act 1988.

There are problems over the nature of the test of reasonableness. Cheshire states:

'It is submitted that the question must be approached objectively, and that, as it has been aptly put, the landlord's mental processes and uttered words are irrelevant.' The question was further discussed by Balcombe LJ in *International Drilling Fluids Ltd* v *Louisville Investments (Uxbridge) Ltd* [1986] 2 WLR 581, although the matter must now be further considered in the light of ss1 and 2 of the 1988 Act.

Megarry and Wade conclude: 'The test, however, is not subjective but objective, and so depends on what a reasonable landlord would think.'

QUESTION TWO

'The principle that a term must be certain applies to all leases and tenancy agreements. A term must either be certain or uncertain. It cannot be partly certain because the tenant can determine it any time and partly uncertain because the landlord cannot determine it for an uncertain period.'

Explain this statement and indicate the ways in which statute has intervened to give effect to leases that would otherwise fall foul of this principle.

University of London LLB Examination
(for External Students) Land Law June 1994 Q8

General Comment

Determining what this unattributed statement actually means as a matter of plain English is not without difficulty. However, the author has assumed that the central issue is the *Lace* v *Chantler* point that the duration of a lease must be certain. The question provides students well-versed with this essential requirement for a valid lease and the related statutory provisions with a fairly straightforward opportunity to display their knowledge and understanding.

Skeleton Solution

Essential requirements of a lease – term or duration must be certain – *Lace* v *Chantler* – *Ashburn Anstalt* v *Arnold* – *Prudential Assurance Co Ltd* v *London Residuary Body* – periodic tenancies – leases for lives – s149(6) LPA 1925 – leases for perpetuity – s145 LPA 1922.

Suggested Solution

Since 1 January 1926, there are only two estates which are capable of existing at law: the fee simple absolute in possession and the term of years absolute or lease: see s1(1) Law of Property Act (LPA) 1925. For there to be a valid legal lease four requirements must be satisfied. First, the premises must be sufficiently defined. Second, the tenant must have been granted exclusive possession of the property, ie the tenant can exclude everyone including the landlord from the property for the duration of the term. Third, both the commencement date and the duration of the term must be certain or capable of being ascertained at the outset of the term: see s205(1)(xxvii) LPA 1925. Fourthly, any relevant formalities must be complied with. For example, a lease in excess of three years must be granted by deed: see ss52(1) and 54(2) LPA 1925. This question concerns the third requirement.

In order for a lease for a fixed term to be valid it must have a certain duration. In *Lace v Chantler* [1944] KB 368 a lease granted during the course of the Second World War for the duration of the war was void. However, subsequently several Court of Appeal decisions cast some doubt on this principle. For example, *Re Midland Railway Company's Agreement* [1971] Ch 725 decided that the landlord could bar himself from determining the lease. This case was applied by the Court of Appeal in *Ashburn Anstalt v Arnold* [1989] Ch 1. However, the principle of *Lace v Chantler* was reaffirmed by the House of Lords in *Prudential Assurance Co Ltd v London Residuary Body* [1992] 3 WLR 279. There their Lordships held that a lease 'until land was required for widening the road' was void because the period was uncertain. Lord Templeman said of *Re Midland Railway Company's Agreement* that if it was correctly decided it would make it unnecessary for a lease to be of a certain duration. However, their Lordships held that it had been wrongly decided and it was overruled (*Ashburn Anstalt v Arnold* was also overruled on this point).

The rule that a lease must be certain or capable of being made certain at the outset of the term applies also to periodic tenancies (tenancies from month-to-month, year-to-year etc). In *Prudential Assurance Co Ltd v London Residuary Body*, Lord Templeman explained how a yearly periodic tenancy could be certain. He said that:

'... a tenancy from year-to-year is saved from being uncertain because each party has power by notice to determine at the end of any year. The term continues until determined as if both parties made a new agreement at the end of each year for a new term for the ensuing year.'

Accordingly, *Prudential Assurance Co Ltd v London Residuary Body* has brought about a welcome return to orthodoxy.

The requirement that the commencement date and duration of the term must be certain for a lease to be valid would mean that a lease for life and a lease for perpetuity would both fall foul of this principle and be void. However, in respect of both types of lease statute has intervened to prevent this happening. By virtue of s149(6) LPA 1925 leases at a rent for life or lives or until the marriage of the lessee are converted into leases for a term of 90 years determinable after the end of the life or lives or on the marriage of the lessee, as the case may be, by the giving by either party of not less than one month's notice expiring on one of the quarter days, applicable to the tenancy. It is important to note that this provision only applies to a lease at a rent or fine. A term determinable with life at no rent might prior to the coming into force of the Trusts of Land and Appointment of Trustees Act 1996 have come within s20(1)(iv) Settled Land Act 1925 and so created a strict settlement.

A perpetually renewable lease is one which gives the lessee the right to renew the lease for another period as often as it expires. They are converted by s145 and Sch 15 LPA 1922 into terms of 2,000 years determinable only by the lessee by not less than ten days' notice expiring on any of the old renewal dates. Basically, if the covenant for renewal is part of a separate obligation then there is no perpetually renewable lease: see *Marjorie Burnett Ltd* v *Barclay* [1980] 258 EG 642. However, if the lease is to be renewed on the existing terms, including the covenant for renewal, then there will be a perpetually renewable lease: see *Parkus* v *Greenwood* [1950] Ch 644.

Finally, for a lease to be valid its duration must be certain in the sense that there is either a definite limit to the length of the term (period fixed at the outset) or the limit can be set by either party in a clearly defined way (periodic tenancy).

Chapter 2

Acquisition of a Beneficial Interest in Land

2.1 **Introduction**

2.2 **Key points**

2.3 **Key cases and statutes**

2.4 **Questions and suggested solutions**

2.1 Introduction

A very important subject which underpins much of land law. Two types of question can arise. First, a question which is concerned solely with acquisition of a beneficial interest in land, and which could either be an essay or problem question. Second, a question which has an acquisition element, but which goes on to deal with protection of that interest against third parties, or the alienation of it.

2.2 Key points

There are four methods of acquiring an interest: express trust, resulting trust, constructive trust and proprietary estoppel.

Express trust

a) Where stated? – in conveyance or will.

b) Effect? – conclusive (in the absence of fraud or mistake) of the party's beneficial interest: *Goodman* v *Gallant* [1986] Fam 106.

Resulting trusts

a) Elements – common intention and contribution.

b) Common intention:

 i) Purchase by two or more and conveyance not into all their names.

 ii) Inferred from contributions: *Gissing* v *Gissing* [1971] AC 886; *Pettitt* v *Pettitt* [1970] AC 777.

iii) Not inferred from a gift or loan: *Re Sharpe (A Bankrupt)* [1980] 1 WLR 219.

c) Contribution:

    i) to deposit;

    ii) to mortgage instalments;

    iii) to legal costs;

    iv) effect – beneficial interest proportionate to contribution (but see *Midland Bank plc* v *Cooke* [1995] 4 All ER 562).

Constructive trusts

a) Basis – express informal agreement and detriment *or* imputed agreement based on conduct.

b) Express informal agreement and detriment:

    i) At time of acquisiton or exceptionally later: *Lloyds Bank plc* v *Rosset* [1990] 2 WLR 867.

    ii) Cogent evidence: *Eves* v *Eves* [1975] 1 WLR 1338; *Cooke* v *Head* [1972] 1 WLR 518; *Hammond* v *Mitchell* [1992] 2 All ER 109.

    iii) Detriment: *Hammond* v *Mitchell* [1992] 2 All ER 109.

    iv) Effect – size of share determined by agreement.

c) Imputed agreement based on conduct:

    i) Direct financial contributions: *Lloyds Bank plc* v *Rosset* [1990] 2 WLR 867.

    ii) Other contributions: *Lloyds Bank plc* v *Rosset* [1990] 2 WLR 867; *Hammond* v *Mitchell* [1992] 2 All ER 109.

    iii) Effect – courts seemingly adopt a broad brush approach to determining the respective shares of the parties *Drake* v *Whipp* (1995) The Times 19 December.

Proprietary estoppel

a) Elements: *Willmott* v *Barber* (1880) 15 Ch D 96; *Taylor Fashions Ltd* v *Liverpool Victoria Trustees Co Ltd* [1982] QB 133; *Grant* v *Edwards* [1986] Ch 638; *Hammond* v *Mitchell* [1992] 2 All ER 109.

b) Detriment:

    i) Expenditure: *Inwards* v *Baker* [1965] 2 QB 29.

    ii) Other: *Greasley* v *Cooke* [1980] 1 WLR 1306.

c) Expectation

Present or future interest: *Re Basham (Deceased)* [1986] 1 WLR 1498.

d) Reliance

Detriment as evidence of reliance: *Coombes* v *Smith* [1986] 1 WLR 808.

e) Satisfying the equity

Determination of remedy: *Crabb* v *Arun District Council* [1976] Ch 179; *Pascoe* v *Turner* [1979] 1 WLR 431; *Inwards* v *Baker* [1965] 2 QB 29; *Dillwyn* v *Llewellyn* (1862) 4 De GF & J 517.

2.3 Key cases and statutes

- *Burns* v *Burns* [1984] Ch 317
  Woman not on legal title who made no financial contribution to acquisition but who performed domestic duties and carried out interior redecorating failed to establish beneficial interest

- *Cooke* v *Head* [1972] 1 WLR 518
  Unmarried couple – man said woman's name should not appear on the title deed of house as it might prejudice her pending divorce – statement evidence of an intention that woman should have a beneficial interest

- *Drake* v *Whipp* (1995) The Times 19 December
  There is a difference between acquiring a beneficial interest under a resulting trust as opposed to a constructive trust

- *Eves* v *Eves* [1975] 1 WLR 1338
  Unmarried couple – woman not on legal title made substantial work contribution to the house – beneficial interest established

- *Gissing* v *Gissing* [1971] AC 886
  There was no special regime applicable to matrimonial and quasi-matrimonial property – rather, the matter was subject to the law of trusts

- *Grant* v *Edwards* [1986] Ch 638
  Party not on legal title claimed a share of beneficial interest based on an indirect contribution to acquisition of the home – 'intention approach' governed the imposition of a constructive trust in such cases

- *Greasley* v *Cooke* [1980] 1 WLR 1306
  Proprietary estoppel – nature of detriment – expenditure of money not an indispensable element of estoppel

- *Inwards* v *Baker* [1965] 2 QB 29; [1965] 1 All ER 446
  Proprietary estoppel – estoppel licence could bind a third party

- *Lloyds Bank plc* v *Rosset* [1990] 2 WLR 867
  Title to registered land in husband's name alone – wife made no financial contribution to acquisition but made a work contribution – wife had no beneficial interest – application of s70(1)(g) LRA 1925

- Law of Property Act 1925, s53(2)

- Land Registration Act 1925, s70(1)(g)

- Land Registration Act 2002, Schs 1 and 3

2.4 Questions and suggested solutions

Analysis of questions

Questions which are solely on the acquisition of a beneficial interest in land require an application of the four methods outlined above. In particular, the overlap between constructive trusts and proprietary estoppel is usually apparent.

Other questions involve a brief and preliminary discussion of the acquisition of an interest, for instance, co-ownership questions (Chapter 5) and registration questions (Chapter 3).

Note that the suggested solutions in respect of Questions 1–3 refer to s70(1)(g) of the Land Registration Act 1925, which was applicable at the time the questions were set. However, references to that subsection must now be read in light of Schs 1 and 3 of the Land Registration Act 2002.

QUESTION ONE

When Stella decided to buy a farm, she invited her lover, Paul, to come and live with her and help her run the farm. Stella paid the whole purchase price and the farm was conveyed into her sole name. When Paul asked why it had not been conveyed into their joint names, Stella told him that there was no need for him to worry as he would get a half-share when they got married and as she was going to leave him her London apartment in her will anyway. Stella and Paul never married but they worked hard on the farm for several years, sharing the profits equally, and as a result the value of the farm doubled. Recently Stella has died leaving all her estate to her mother. Paul now claims both the farm and the London apartment.

Advise Stella's mother.

University of London LLB Examination
(for External Students) Land Law June 1993 Q6

General Comment

A standard question on the acquisition of interests in land dealing with resulting trusts, constructive trusts and proprietary estoppel. A knowledge of the decision in *Hammond v Mitchell* would be useful.

Skeleton Solution

Conveyance – *Goodman v Gallant* – resulting trust – constructive trust – informal agreement – *Lloyds Bank plc v Rosset* – *Eves v Eves* – detriment – *Hammond v Mitchell* – estoppel – *Re Basham* – *Grant v Edwards*.

Suggested Solution

The main issue here is whether Paul has any interest in the farm or London apartment.

As both the farm and apartment were vested in Stella's sole name, clearly Paul has no legal interest in them. Furthermore, there is no evidence to suggest that conveyances contained a trust in favour of Paul (contra: *Goodman v Gallant* [1986] 1 All ER 311). In the circumstances, if Paul is to have an interest he must have acquired it by way of resulting or constructive trust or by way of proprietary estoppel.

Farm

As regards the farm, Stella paid the whole of the purchase price thus ruling out any form of direct financial contribution by Paul to its acquisition (a direct contribution to acquisition would have resulted in Paul acquiring a beneficial interest by way of resulting trust).

In order to claim an interest under a constructive trust Paul would have to argue that there was either an express informal agreement between the parties which he acted upon to his detriment, or that an agreement should be imputed between them giving him an interest: see Lord Bridge in *Lloyds Bank plc v Rosset* [1990] 2 WLR 867.

As for the former, it might be argued that Stella's excuse for not putting the farm into joint names was evidence of an agreement between the parties that he should have an interest, in much the same way as in *Eves v Eves* [1975] 1 WLR 1338, *Cooke v Head* [1972] 1 WLR 518 and *Grant v Edwards* [1986] Ch 638. It does not matter that such an agreement came into existence after the acquisition of the farm, for as Lord Bridge stated in *Rosset*, in exceptional cases the agreement could come into existence at a later date. In any event Paul would have to produce cogent evidence of the agreement. If Paul can establish the existence of the agreement he also needs to show that he has acted to his detriment in reliance upon it. Clearly, Paul participated fully in the farm business and it may be argued that his involvement in the commercial venture was enough to give him an interest in the land: see *Hammond v Mitchell* [1992] 2 All ER 109. Alternatively, it could be said that there was no agreement that he should have an interest and the share of the profits was his only reward.

As regards the latter, the court would analyse the subsequent conduct of the parties to see whether they are sufficient to spell out some presumed intention on the part of the parties. Clearly, Paul's hard work would indicate that he should have some share, but it could be argued that it should be limited to a share in the profits only. If a constructive trust arises in favour of Paul, his actual occupation coupled with the interest under the trust would give him an overriding interest in land under s70(1)(g) Land Registration Act 1925, which would be binding on Stella's mother: *Williams & Glyn's Bank* v *Boland* [1981] AC 487.

If Paul's claim to an interest under a constructive trust were to fail, he could rely on estoppel as in *Grant* v *Edwards*. In order to do so, he would have to show the existence of a representation and reliance as in the case of a constructive trust (indeed in *Lloyds Bank* v *Rosset* they were recognised as being very similar doctrines). As described above, Stella's statement to Paul could be seen as the representation. As in the case of the constructive trust, Paul's wholehearted participation in the commercial activities on the farm could be seen as a detriment and evidence that he had acted consistently with the representation: *Hammond*.

If an estoppel arises in favour of Paul, the task for the court will be how best to satisfy it, and the court will do the minimum necessary to do justice to the estoppel: *Crabb* v *Arun District Council* [1976] Ch 179. The precise remedy appears largely to depend on the representation in that the applicant gets what he has been promised, be that the transfer of fee simple (*Pascoe* v *Turner* [1979] 1 WLR 431) or a life interest: *Inwards* v *Baker* [1965] 2 QB 29. On this basis, if the representation is that Paul will get a one half share that may well be what the court will award.

Apartment

The same principles as discussed above in relation to the farm are relevant when considering the claims to the apartment. As in the case of the farm, Paul has made no direct financial contributions which would justify an interest by way of resulting trust.

Furthermore, such acts as he has done to his detriment appear to relate exclusively to the acquisition of an interest in the farm and not the apartment. Those activities were not of a nature which would justify the inference of an intended proprietary interest in his favour in the apartment: see *Hammond*.

As far as proprietary estoppel is concerned, whilst it is possible for a promise of a future interest to found an estoppel (see *Re Basham* [1986] 1 WLR 1498), the problem for Paul here is largely the same as that connected with constructive trusts, viz, his acts are acts of detriment connected to the farm not the apartment: *Hammond*.

In the circumstances, it appears that Paul will have a better prospect of claiming an interest in the farm, be it by constructive trust or proprietary estoppel, than he will in the apartment.

QUESTION TWO

When Tim married Janet, Barbara, Tim's mother, bought a house for the couple to live in. Barbara paid the whole of the purchase price and the house was registered in her sole name. The couple agreed to be responsible for repairs and other outgoings and they insisted, against Barbara's wishes, on paying her a token monthly 'rent'. A few years later the marriage broke down and Tim moved out of the house. Janet continued living in the house, doing the repairs and paying the rent. Finding herself short of cash, Barbara decided to sell the house and, while Janet was away on holiday, she sold it to a local building company. As the new registered proprietor, the company seeks possession of the house with a view to redeveloping the site.

Advise Janet.

University of London LLB Examination
(for External Students) Land Law June 1995 Q7

General Comment

A mixed question which touches upon several areas of land law including matrimonial property, licences, leases and aspects of registration. It provides students well-versed in the relevant areas with a fairly straightforward opportunity to display their knowledge and understanding. Not a question for students who had only revised some of, but not all, the areas covered.

Skeleton Solution

Legal estate in one party – acquisition of a beneficial interest – indirect contributions, constructive trusts – overriding interest under s70(1)(g) LRA 1925 – periodic tenancy – contractual licence: *Errington* v *Errington* – estoppel licence.

Suggested Solution

In view of the fact that Barbara provided all the purchase money for the house, and had it registered in her sole name, it is necessary to see if Janet can establish an interest in the property which will be binding on the building company to whom Barbara subsequently sold the house. Having regard to the facts of the question, it would seem appropriate to consider whether Janet has acquired a beneficial interest, a periodic tenancy or a licence.

A person not on the legal title can acquire a beneficial interest in a variety of ways including by way of resulting or constructive trust. For example, a direct contribution to acquisition of the property (contribution to purchase price or mortgage instalments, paying legal costs, etc) will give rise to a resulting trust with the size of the shares being proportionate to the parties' contributions. Here, since Barbara paid the whole of the purchase price, this rules out any form of direct financial contribution by Janet to the acquisition of the house. While a direct contribution to acquisition is clearly sufficient to acquire a beneficial interest, the position as to indirect contributions is much more difficult. In essence Janet is relying upon indirect contributions, ie 'repairs and other outgoings'. Formerly the courts sometimes took a liberal approach to indirect contributions: *Hazell* v *Hazell* [1972] 1 WLR 301. However, that approach has now been rejected. For example, in *Burns* v *Burns* [1984] Ch 317 a woman whose contribution amounted to paying for the housekeeping and some bills, as well as buying some electrical appliances and furniture, was held not to have a beneficial interest. In *Lloyds Bank plc v Rosset* [1990] 2 WLR 867 the House of Lords laid down guidelines concerning indirect contributions and constructive trusts (which traditionally has been the mechanism used to give effect to a beneficial interest arising by indirect contributions). Where there is an express oral declaration or agreement between the legal title owner and the other party (which does not meet the requirements of s53 Law of Property Act (LPA) 1925) then for a constructive trust to be imposed the other party has to have relied on the agreement to his/her detriment (ie there has to be common intention and detrimental reliance). Detrimental reliance is shown by significant contributions in money or money's worth which need not be direct: *Grant v Edwards* [1986] Ch 638. In *Lloyds Bank v Rosset* the claim of Mrs Rosset to a beneficial interest based on her interior decorating and supervision of builders carrying out renovation work was unsuccessful. Lord Bridge said that what Mrs Rosset was relying upon as a contribution, when set against the cost of the property which exceeded £70,000, was 'so trifling as to be almost de minimis'. Here it is submitted that Janet will be unlikely to be able to establish a beneficial interest in the house – the facts are not supportive of any common intention between Barbara, Tim and Janet to share the beneficial interest, nor are contributions to repairs and other outgoings likely to be regarded as significant contributions in money or money's worth for purposes of detrimental reliance.

Since this is registered land, if Janet could establish an equitable interest in the house she might be able to claim an overriding interest under s70(1)(g) Land Registration Act (LRA) 1925. Overriding interests bind a purchaser without appearing on the register and even though he has no knowledge of them. There are three aspects to establishing an overriding interest under s70(1)(g). First, the claimant must have a proprietary interest in the property (eg an equitable interest). Second, the claimant must be in actual occupation of the land prior to completion of the transaction: *Abbey National Building Society v Cann* [1990] 2 WLR 832. Whether a person is in actual occupation is a question of fact and degree. There must be some degree of permanence and continuation, not a mere fleeting presence. It is submitted that Janet could show a degree of permanence and continuity as to her occupation, and this would not be destroyed just because she was temporarily absent on holiday at the time Barbara sold the house to the building company. Third, if an enquiry is made by a prospective purchaser and the right is not disclosed (because of active concealment on the part of the person claiming an overriding interest under para (g)), then the purchaser will take free of that right. Here Janet's main problem with claiming an overriding interest under s70(1)(g) LRA 1925, which would be binding on the new registered proprietor, is that, as previously mentioned, she is unlikely to be able to show that she has an equitable interest in the house.

Next, it is necessary to see if Janet has a lease as she is paying a token monthly rent and after the marriage breaks down she continues to do so. A periodic tenancy (from week to week or month to month) can be created, either by express agreement or by inference – such as that arising from the payment and acceptance of rent measured by reference to the period in question (week or month, etc). In this case there is obviously no express agreement as the payments are against Barbara's wishes. Nevertheless, if Barbara accepted these payments from Janet, then it is submitted that Janet could have a monthly periodic tenancy by inference. However, a monthly periodic tenancy is not very advantageous to Janet vis-à-vis the new registered proprietor, since such a tenancy can be brought to an end by the tenant being given a month's notice to quit (subject to any contrary agreement between the parties).

Finally, it is necessary to consider whether Janet has a licence which would be binding on the building company.

A contractual licence is one granted for valuable consideration (ie Janet has to show that she has given value for it). Clearly, Janet could show she has given value because she is paying rent and is responsible for repairs and other outgoings. If Janet has a contractual licence would it bind the building company? Originally, contractual licences were seen as personal transactions between the parties and not creating any interest which would be enforceable against a third party: *Clore* v *Theatrical Properties Ltd* [1936] 3 All ER 483. However, in *Errington* v *Errington and Woods* [1952] 1 KB 20 the Court of Appeal held that a contractual licence was binding on a third party except a purchaser for value without notice. Thereafter there was much uncertainty as to whether a contractual licence could bind a third party or not, with cases going either way. The position was substantially clarified in *Ashburn Anstalt* v *Arnold* [1988] 2 All ER 147 when the Court of Appeal (albeit obiter) held that a contractual licence did not bind a third party and that *Errington* v *Errington and Woods* had been wrongly decided on this point. Accordingly, establishing that Janet has a contractual licence will not avail her much since it is not likely to be binding on the building company.

The other possibility for Janet in respect of licences is to try to show that she has an estoppel licence. Such a licence arises as follows. If a landowner (Barbara) allows another person (Janet) to spend money or alter her position to her detriment in the expectation that she will enjoy some privilege or interest in the land, then the owner will be prevented (ie estopped) from acting inconsistently with that expectation. In essence the requirements of an estoppel licence are representation, reliance and detriment. The main attraction for Janet in establishing an estoppel licence is that such a licence is capable of binding a third party (ie the building company). The possible problem for Janet in this regard is showing that Barbara made an appropriate representation, or created an expectation in Janet vis-à-vis the house, since the facts given are not really conclusive of this matter. Janet can certainly show expenditure of money on the house, and the expenditure of money is the usual evidence of detriment relied upon in such cases. Further, since this is registered land, for a third party to be bound by the estoppel licence it has to be protected by the entry of a notice or caution on the register, unless it is an overriding interest under s70(1)(g) LRA 1925, in which case he is bound because it is an overriding interest. Here, as discussed previously, it is unlikely that Janet will be able to establish a para (g) overriding interest, and therefore it seems that if there is an estoppel licence the question whether it is binding on the building company will turn on whether or not it has been entered as a notice or caution on the register. Finally, if Janet has an estoppel licence there is no certainty as to what relief will be granted by the court to satisfy the equity (ie what remedy she will get). In this regard, the courts have shown great flexibility (remedies used include transfer of fee simple to licensee; life interest for licensee; and reimbursement of licensee's expenses). However, this in turn has produced uncertainty because it is difficult for practitioners to anticipate how the equity will be satisfied in a given case.

In conclusion, it seems that Janet's best hope for resisting the building company's effort to gain possession of the house would be to try to establish an estoppel licence. However, it is by no means certain that such a licence can be found here.

QUESTION THREE

When Henry inherited some money from his uncle, he decided to buy a house for himself, his girlfriend (Pamela) and their daughter (Lily) to live in together. Henry paid the whole of the purchase price and the house was registered in his sole name. When Pamela suggested registering it in their joint names, Henry replied, 'Of course the house is as much yours as mine, but my lawyer advises me that for the moment it is better to have it in my name alone'. For the following two years Pamela stayed at home looking after Lily and spending much of her time and most of her savings refurbishing the house. Recently Henry died leaving his estate to his mother, Wilma. Wilma has now written to Pamela asking her to vacate the house and in the meantime to pay Wilma an occupational rent. Pamela is not sure whether Wilma wants to sell the house or to occupy it herself.

Advise Pamela.

University of London LLB Examination
(for External Students) Land Law June 1997 Q4

General Comment

The question is concerned with a 'family home' and a number of matters usually encountered in examination questions in respect of the same including acquisition of a beneficial interest in land and estoppel. Students should include coverage of the relevant sections of the Trusts of Land and Appointment of Trustees Act 1996.

Skeleton Solution

Legal estate in one party – acquisition of a beneficial interest: direct contribution; resulting trusts; express declaration of intention; indirect contribution (domestic caring, refurbishment); constructive trusts – implied trust of land under Trusts of Land and Appointment of Trustees Act 1996 (TOLATA) – overriding interest under s70(1)(g) LRA 1925 – payment of rent by beneficial interest holder not on legal estate: *Dennis v McDonald* – powers of court under ss14 and 15 of TOLATA 1996 – estoppel.

Suggested Solution

In view of the fact that the house is registered in Henry's sole name, it is necessary to see if his girlfriend Pamela can establish a beneficial interest in the property and then to consider how any such interest would affect her position vis-à-vis Wilma.

A person not on the legal title can acquire a beneficial interest in a variety of ways. On the facts, it is necessary to consider whether Pamela has acquired a beneficial interest by virtue of Henry's excuse for not putting the title to the house in their joint names, by staying at home and looking after their daughter Lily and by spending most of her time and most of her savings refurbishing the house.

A direct contribution to the acquisition of the property by the person not on the legal title (eg contribution to purchase price, deposit, legal costs or mortgage instalments) will give rise to a resulting trust with the size of the shares being proportionate to the parties' contributions. Here, since Henry paid the entire purchase price for the house, there is obviously no possibility of Pamela acquiring a beneficial interest by way of resulting trust since she has not made a direct contribution to the acquisition of the house.

Pamela suggested that the house should be registered in their joint names. However, to avoid so acting Henry gave the following excuse to her 'of course the house is as much yours as mine, but my lawyer advises me that for the moment it is better to have it in my name alone'. An excuse, as here, as to why the property is registered in the man's name alone will be treated as an express declaration of an intention to share the beneficial ownership. In *Cooke* v *Head* [1972] 1 WLR 518 – a case concerning an unmarried couple – the man said that the woman's name should not appear on the title deeds as it might prejudice her pending divorce. In *Eves* v *Eves* [1975] 1 WLR 1338 – which also concerned an unmarried couple, the house purchase was financed by the man and it was conveyed into his name alone. However, he told the woman that had she been 21 it would have been put into their joint names as it was to be their joint home. In both cases, the Court of Appeal concluded that the statements/excuses were evidence of an intention that the woman should have a beneficial interest. In *Eves* v *Eves*, Lord Denning MR put the matter thus: 'In view of his conduct it would ... be most inequitable for [the defendant] to deny her any share in the house.'

However, in order to succeed in this regard Pamela has to establish not only the existence of an agreement between them that she should have a beneficial interest in the house but also that she acted to her detriment in reliance upon it. The most common form of detriment is a material sacrifice in the nature of financial contributions or improvements to property. In *Cooke* v *Head* the woman made a work contribution in the form of physical labour on the property (she demolished a building, removed hardcore and rubble, worked the cement-mixer and painted) and accordingly a constructive trust was imposed on the man to provide her with a one-third beneficial interest. In *Eves* v *Eves* the woman did a great deal of work to the property and cared for the man and their children. She obtained a quarter-share in the house. Here for a period of two years after the acquisition of the house Pamela spent 'much of her time and most of her savings refurbishing the house'. Although there is no precise quantification as to how much she spent on the house, it is submitted that Pamela may well be able to satisfy the 'detriment' requirement. Accordingly, it is submitted that Henry's excuse for not putting the house into the joint names of himself and Pamela is evidence of an agreement between them that Pamela should have a beneficial interest in the house which Pamela relied upon to her detriment by 'spending much of her time and most of her savings in refurbishing the house'. Finally, any beneficial interest acquired by Pamela in this way would arise under a constructive trust.

Pamela has also, in the two years after acquisition of the house, stayed at home and looked after their daughter Lily. The issue here is whether such domestic caring would rank as an indirect contribution to acquisition so as to give rise to a beneficial interest (or in view of the above an enlarged beneficial interest) under a constructive trust. After much uncertainty it is now clear that 'wifely services' that is domestic duties cannot be referable to the acquisition of property: *Burns v Burns* [1984] Ch 317.

It is submitted that Henry is holding the legal title on trust for himself and Pamela in equity. The trust would be a new trust of land under the Trusts of Land and Appointment of Trustees Act 1996 (by virtue of s1(1)(a) of that Act the new regime applies, inter alia, whenever equitable interests in land arise by way of resulting or constructive trusts). This is so irrespective of when Henry bought the house because under the 1996 Act all trusts for sale in existence prior to the Act coming into force on 1 January 1997 are automatically trusts of land. Under the 1996 Act trustees of land hold the legal estate on trust with a power to sell and a power to retain the land: s4.

On Henry's death, the legal title to the house passes to Wilma. If, as seems likely, there is a constructive trust in favour of Pamela, her actual occupation coupled with the interest under the trust would give her an overriding interest in the land under s70(1)(g) LRA 1925 which would be binding on Wilma: *Williams and Glyn's Bank v Boland* [1981] AC 487.

As to whether Wilma can require Pamela to pay an occupational rent the position is somewhat uncertain. In *Dennis v McDonald* [1982] 1 All ER 590 an occupational rent was ordered to be paid when one co-owner evicted the other. There a man was violent to a woman as a result of which the woman left the house taking the children with her while the man remained in the house. The man was required to pay rent for his sole occupation of the house. However, it is submitted that the current scenario is quite distinguishable from the aforementioned case.

Wilma has written to Pamela asking her to vacate the house and it is assumed that Pamela wishes to remain in occupation. In such circumstances and since Pamela is a person with an interest in property subject to a trust of land she can apply to court for an order under s14 of the Trusts of Land and Appointment of Trustees Act 1996. Under s14 of the 1996 Act the court can make orders for sale or preventing sale, etc. Section

15(1) of the 1996 Act contains a statement of factors which the court is to have regard to in making an order under s14. The factors include:

a) the settlor's intentions;

b) the purpose for which the property subject to the trust is held;

c) the welfare of any minor who occupies the trust land; and

d) the interests of secured creditors.

The use of the word 'include' in s15(1) demonstrates that the list is not intended to be exhaustive. Relating the facts of the question to s15(1) of the 1996 Act it is most unlikely that the court would order Pamela to vacate the house – it was bought as a family home for Henry, Pamela and their daughter Lily to live in. The welfare of Lily (who is assumed to be a minor since Pamela stayed at home to look after her) who occupies the house with her mother would be relevant and there are no secured creditors to take account of. The court is likely to make a declaration that Pamela has a beneficial interest under a constructive trust or an estoppel (see below). In the event of Wilma trying to sell the house Pamela should seek an injunction to stop her from so acting. If Wilma did sell the house Pamela's overriding interest would be binding on any purchaser from Wilma and since only Wilma is on the legal title there would be no overreaching of her overriding interest (for an overriding interest to be overreached purchase monies must be paid to two trustees).

The facts are also supportive of Pamela establishing an estoppel licence. Such a licence arises as follows: if a landowner (Henry) allows another person (Pamela) to spend money or alter her position to her detriment in the expectation that she will enjoy some privilege or interest in the land then the owner will be prevented (ie estopped) from acting inconsistently with that expectation. In essence the requirements of an estoppel licence are representation, reliance and detriment. Here the representation is Henry's assertion 'Of course the house is as much yours as mine, etc' while Pamela spending much of her time and most of her savings refurbishing the house can be seen as a detriment and evidence that she had acted consistently with Henry's representation. A key reality in this regard is that an estoppel licence is capable of binding a third party (ie Wilma).

If, as seems likely, an estoppel arises in favour of Pamela, the task for the court will be to decide how best to satisfy it and the court will do the minimum necessary to do justice to the estoppel: *Crabb* v *Arun District Council* [1976] Ch 179. The courts have shown great flexibility in this regard; remedies used include transfer of fee simple to licensee (*Pascoe* v *Turner* [1979] 1 WLR 431), life interest for licensee (*Inwards* v *Baker* [1965] 2 QB 29) and reimbursement of licensee's expenses/outgoings: *Dodsworth* v *Dodsworth* (1973) 228 EG 1115. However, this in turn has produced uncertainty because it is difficult for practitioners to anticipate how the equity will be satisfied in a given case. It seems that the remedy granted in cases of estoppel licence is largely dependent on the representation made (ie the applicant gets what she has been promised). Here, given that Henry said to Pamela that 'the house is as much yours as mine', there is a realistic prospect that the court might transfer the fee simple to her. Indeed, on the facts, the least she could expect to satisfy the equity would be the right to stay in the house until Lily's schooling is completed.

In conclusion, it is submitted that Pamela has a strong case and that she would not have to vacate the house whether the court found a constructive trust or an estoppel licence in her favour.

QUESTION FOUR

Karl and Fozia became lovers and decided to set up house together. In 1990 they purchased a small house for UKP200,000 and it was registered in Karl's sole name. Karl paid UKP160,000 of the purchase price, Fozia paid UKP30,000 and Fozia's mother, Janice, contributed UKP10,000 as a gift to the couple. On one occasion, when Fozia asked Karl why he did not register the house in both their names, he replied 'Don't worry! You know that what's mine is yours and what's yours is mine.' They lived happily together for two years and in 1994 Fozia paid a further UKP20,000 for the building of an extension to the house for her study. In 1995 Karl lost his job and began to fall into debt. Instead of sharing all the household expenses, Fozia now paid them all. Karl and Fozia began to quarrel and on 1 March 1997, after a heated argument, Fozia moved in with Janice for two months, but then returned to the house. While she was away Karl arranged to mortgage the house to the Fixquick Bank for UKP100,000. The mortgage was completed on 15 April and registered on 15 May. Subsequently, Karl defaulted on his mortgage repayments and the bank now seeks possession of the house with a view to selling it.

Advise Fozia as to her position. If the house were sold, how would the proceeds of sale be divided?

University of London LLB Examination
(for External Students) Land Law June 1999 Q1

General Comment

To answer this question candidates must be prepared to discuss not only resulting and constructive trusts, but also the distinction between them, particularly in relation to the question. Nor must the application of the Trusts of Land and Appointment of Trustees Act (TOLATA) 1996 be ignored. The question further requires a grasp of the complexities of s70(1)(g) LRA 1925.

Skeleton Solution

Resulting trust in favour of Fozia – s36(4) SLA 1925 – TOLATA, Sch 3 – bank's position with regard to Fozia; s70(1)(g) LRA 1925 – Fozia's occupation – s14 TOLATA – the value of Fozia's share – Fozia could consider a constructive trust to obtain a greater share.

Suggested Solution

Karl was registered as sole proprietor of the house although he was not the only contributor to the purchase price, both Fozia and Janice having made contributions. Fozia's contribution could give rise to an equitable interest in the house, while Janice's contribution gives rise to no such interest because it was intended as a gift to both Karl and Fozia.

The purchase was made in 1990. As a consequence of Fozia's direct contribution to the purchase price, a resulting trust was created in equity under which Karl held the legal estate in the house on trust for himself and Fozia as beneficiaries in equity to the extent of their respective shares: *Bull v Bull* [1955] 1 QB 234. They became co-owners in equity, and because their contributions were of unequal shares they became tenants in common. Following *Bull v Bull*, s36(4) SLA 1925 applied giving rise to a trust for sale.

When TOLATA came into force on 1 January 1997 it altered the position of trusts for sale (under ss34 and 36 LPA 1925); trusts for sale could no longer be implied (as they previously were). Under s5 and Sch 2 of TOLATA, these would now become trusts of land, and would be governed by the provisions of the Act. Moreover, these provisions are made to operate retrospectively: Sch 2, para 3(6) (as regards s34 LPA) and para 4(4) (as regards s36 LPA).

However, *Bull v Bull* was decided under s36(4) SLA as previously noted. That section has been amended to produce a trust of land instead of a trust for sale (Sch 3, para 11), but there is nothing in the third schedule to indicate that this amendment is retrospective, which means that the trust for sale implied in this case by s36(4) SLA in 1990 remains a trust for sale. Whether this omission by the legislature was by design or accident is not clear, but the trust for sale falls within the definition of a trust of land as defined by s1(2)(a) TOLATA and is subject to the provisions of the Act. As far as the facts of this case are concerned Fozia's holding as a beneficiary under a trust for sale will be of no consequence.

A resulting trust is based on the presumed intentions of the parties unless there is any evidence of rebuttal, and none is apparent here. In 1994 Fozia paid for the extension, increasing the value of her share to a total contribution of UKP50,000.

We may now pass to the subsequent events where Karl mortgaged the house in Fozia's absence, and it is important to notice the chronological order of events as being relevant to Fozia's position with the bank. Fozia was absent from 1 March 1997 for two months, presumably returning at the end of April. Completion of the mortgage was on 15 April, but it was not registered with the land registry until 15 May, by which time she had resumed occupation. Can the bank argue that it is entitled to possession as against Fozia?

Fozia could argue that the bank took the mortgage subject to her equitable interest in the house. The mortgage monies were advanced to Karl as sole trustee and therefore no question of overreaching arose. Fozia must look to the provisions of s70(1)(g) LRA 1925 and argue that her equitable interest is a 'right' under that provision and, as such, constitutes an overriding interest binding on the bank. The paragraph protects the rights of persons in 'actual occupation'. The rights in question must constitute an interest in land and must not be merely personal. Fozia's right clearly is an interest in land falling within the provision: *Williams & Glyn's Bank* v *Boland* [1981] AC 487, but was she in actual occupation at the relevant time? To answer this we must turn to the judgment of Lord Oliver in *Abbey National Building Society* v *Cann* [1991] 1 AC 56. To understand his remarks, it must be appreciated that in registered land a property transaction occurs in two stages: completion followed by registration of the transaction at the land registry, which must be effected not more than two months later. Lord Oliver pointed out that 'the relevant date for determining the existence of an overriding interest ... is the later date of registration', but went on to further state that the relevant date for actual occupation is the earlier date of completion. Thus, in order for Fozia to claim the benefit of s70(1)(g) she must prove that she was in actual occupation on 15 April, the date of completion. At that time she was living with Janice, which may present Fozia with difficulties. Actual occupation is a matter of fact and not law: *Williams & Glyn's Bank* v *Boland*. The difficulties this can present may be seen from the judgment of the Court of Appeal in *Lloyds Bank plc* v *Rosset* [1989] Ch 350 where Nichols and Purchase LJJ thought Mrs Rosset was in occupation while Mustill LJ thought that she was not. In *Chhokar* v *Chhokar* [1984] FLR 313 Ewbank J held that a wife who was in hospital having a baby continued to be in actual occupation. Her absence was temporary and she intended to return.

It is probable that a court would hold that Fozia had not ceased to be in occupation as, on the facts, she did not intend to depart for good. However, her position cannot be entirely certain. If she cannot claim the protection of s70(1)(g), the bank will be entitled to possession against her.

The bank wishes to sell the house to recover its loan and may apply to the court for an order for sale under s14 of TOLATA. What is Fozia's position if she is able to establish that she has an overriding interest? Unfortunately for her, it would appear from the decision in *Bank of Baroda* v *Dhillon & Another* [1998] 1 FLR 524 that this overriding interest would not be an effective defence to the bank's application for an order for sale. *Dhillon* was decided under s30 LPA 1925, but s14 has replaced s30, and the cases decided under that earlier section continue to be relevant to applications for sale brought under s14. In *Dhillon* sale was ordered despite the wife's overriding interest and that decision is likely to be followed in this case. However, Fozia's interest in the proceeds of sale would be unaffected. To summarise, although Fozia's overriding interest (if she has one) would protect her against any claim for possession by the bank, it would not help her when the bank sought an order for sale as opposed to possession.

An evaluation of Fozia's share under the resulting trust must now be made. In cases where there is an implied trust of land, any declaration by the parties on the quantum of their respective shares is conclusive (*Clough* v *Killey* (1996) 72 P & CR D22; *Hembury* v *Peachey* (1996) 72 P & CR D47), but there is no declaration to that effect in this case and we must now consider how a court is likely to assess her share.

We have seen that her total contribution amounted to UKP50,000. She is also entitled to claim a half share in Janice's gift of UKP10,000 adding to her share another UKP5,000 making a final total of UKP55,000. The house's value was originally UKP200,000 which has now increased by UKP20,000 as a result of the value of the extension. Thus the figures are as follows:

Value of house	UKP220,000
Karl's share	UKP165,000
Fozia's share	UKP55,000

On these figures therefore Fozia is entitled to one quarter of the proceeds of sale. It will be recalled that she held under a resulting trust and the orthodox view is that she would be entitled to a share in the proceeds of sale in direct proportion to her share, namely one quarter: *Springette* v *Defoe* (1992) 65 P & CR 1.

However, the reasoning behind this type of valuation has become somewhat muddied by the decision of the Court of Appeal in *Midland Bank plc* v *Cooke* [1995] 4 All ER 562. In that case there was a resulting trust, with the husband providing the bulk of the funding. The house was conveyed into his sole name. The wife made no direct contribution herself but the husband's parents made a wedding gift to the couple which went towards the purchase price of the house. The gift was £11,000 and the county court judge held that half of that figure, £5,500, represented the wife's only contribution, which he concluded gave her a 6.74 per cent share of the house's value.

The Court of Appeal adopted a more flexible approach. It recognised that the couple had never discussed what their shares should be and that there was no available evidence as to their intentions on the issue. It thought the correct approach was to make an assessment of their respective proportions on the basis of what they are presumed to have intended, looking at the whole course of dealing between them, taking into account factors which in the past had not been considered (see *Burns* v *Burns* [1984] 1 All ER 244), such as the wife providing a home for the family, improving the house and garden, paying the household bills and assisting with the payments of a second mortgage. Waite LJ concluded 'one could hardly have a clearer example of a couple who had agreed to share everything equally'. The Court of Appeal awarded the wife a half share of the house. This was a complete departure from the orthodox approach adopted in *Springette* v *Defoe*. Fozia could certainly invoke *Midland Bank plc* v *Cooke*, but whether on the facts another court would follow it or revert to the orthodox approach is speculative.

Bearing in mind that Fozia may well find that by relying on a resulting trust she may only be awarded a quarter share, she should consider as an alternative that she is a beneficiary under a constructive trust, because in cases of constructive trusts the court adopts a more flexible approach in assessing quantum. To establish a constructive trust, she must prove that although the house was registered in Karl's sole name, there was a common intention that she should have a beneficial interest in the house and that, in reliance on that common intention, she acted to her detriment: *Lloyds Bank plc* v *Rosset* per Lord Bridge.

Fozia could argue that Karl's words 'what's mine is yours and what's yours is mine' is evidence of a common intention, although they were spoken after the date of purchase. However, Lord Bridge states that there must be an agreement or understanding that the property is to be shared equally, and while saying that normally that agreement or understanding must be made prior to the acquisition of the property, he did say it could be made 'exceptionally at some later date'. This leaves a loophole to enable Fozia to rely on Karl's words. The fact that she made a direct financial contribution at the outset could also be pleaded as evidence of common intention.

In discussing the situation where there was no evidence to support a finding of an agreement, Lord Bridge observed that in those cases the conduct of the parties may be relied upon to prove both common intention and detrimental reliance, and thus establish a constructive trust. He concluded 'in this situation direct contribution to the purchase price by the party who is not the legal owner whether initially or payment of mortgage instalments will readily justify the inference necessary to the creation of a constructive trust'.

Thus Fozia's initial contribution could serve to establish common intention and detrimental reliance. The role of her expenditure on the extension is more problematical since it occurred some time after the purchase, but that expenditure would be relevant in assessing her share in the value of the house.

Lord Bridge's words are somewhat puzzling, because although it is clear from the context that he intends to deal only with constructive trusts, he does not refer to the fact that a direct financial contribution is the classic method of creating a resulting trust.

The difference in the courts' approaches as to quantum in respect of resulting trusts and constructive trusts is well illustrated by *Drake* v *Whipp* [1996] 1 FLR 826. In the county court the judge held that the claimant was a beneficiary under a resulting trust and was entitled to a share based on her percentage contribution to the purchase and conversion of a barn, which had been purchased in the sole name of the legal owner. On this arithmetic he awarded her 19.4 per cent of the barn's value.

The Court of Appeal disagreed with the judge's finding of a resulting trust and held that on the facts she was a beneficiary under a constructive trust: there was proof of common intention to share beneficially and she had acted in reliance thereon to her detriment by making monetary payments towards the costs of the purchase of the barn and its subsequent conversion. There was an express common intention as to the value of the parties' individual shares, but that was no deterrent to the Court in making its own assessment. It considered the claimant's fair share in the barn's value to be one third.

The Court took the opportunity to note that in the past some judges had not always recognised the difference between resulting and constructive trusts, and went out of its way to emphasise the importance of the distinction, particularly in relation to the assessment of quantum. The court is more flexible in the case of constructive trusts as *Drake* v *Whipp* illustrates.

It may well be to Fozia's advantage to try to establish a constructive trust, since she may succeed in obtaining more than a quarter share in the house.

QUESTION FIVE

When James, a wealthy widower, fell in love with Lucy, he suggested that she should come and live with him in his country house. 'Sell your flat and give up your job', he told her, 'you will have a roof over your head and no financial worries during my lifetime and on my death you will inherit the house and the rest of my estate'. Lucy sold her flat for a good price, left her job and went to live with James and look after the house. James made a will leaving all his estate to Lucy. After six years the relationship broke down and James then fell in love with Mady. James has now told Lucy to leave the house and he has made a new will leaving everything to Mady.

Advise Lucy.

University of London LLB Examination
(for External Students) Land Law June 2000 Q2

General Comment

This is a question on proprietary estoppel and requires an analysis of that doctrine and its application to the facts. *Gillett* v *Holt and Another* must be discussed and applied and the question as to how Lucy's equity should be satisfied should be examined.

Skeleton Solution

No formal arrangement between James and Lucy – can Lucy claim under proprietary estoppel? – requirements for proprietary estoppel – James' assurances sufficient to found a claim? – detrimental reliance by Lucy? – what constitutes detrimental reliance? – on balance Lucy has probably provided sufficient detrimental reliance – how is Lucy's equity to be satisfied? – difficult question: variation in court's approach – James' promise that Lucy would inherit his estate – wills have no binding force until testator's death: *Gillett* v *Holt and Another*.

Suggested Solution

James has told Lucy to leave the house after having lived with him for six years and at first sight she appears to be in a precarious position, since James is the owner of the house and there is no formal arrangement between them defining her rights in the house or indicating how long she was entitled to stay.

These informal arrangements, which is what they were in this case, can give rise to serious difficulties for persons in Lucy's position but, nevertheless, such persons can sometimes find protection in the doctrine of proprietary estoppel.

Has Lucy acquired an equitable interest in the house arising from proprietary estoppel? It is necessary first of all to examine the requirements necessary to establish proprietary estoppel. The doctrine may be summarised as follows: where an owner of land (O) allows another (E) to spend money on that land or otherwise act to his detriment in respect of it under an expectation created or encouraged, or acquiesced in by O, that he (E) will be allowed to remain on the land or acquire an interest in it either now or at some future time, then equity will restrain O from defeating that expectation and denying E's right to remain on the land or acquire an interest in it.

Proprietary estoppel differs from promissory estoppel in that the latter is a defence or, as it has been described, a shield. It is not a cause of action. Proprietary estoppel, by contrast, may constitute a cause of action resulting in the claimant acquiring an equitable interest in the land which is proprietary in nature and capable of binding third parties.

It can be seen that there are two principle elements necessary for proprietary estoppel: first, conduct of the landowner, and second, detrimental reliance on that conduct by the claimant. They will be examined in turn.

Take first the conduct of the landowner. There must be some conduct by that owner, either taking the form of a positive representation or acquiescence, which induces the claimant to believe that he has rights in the land or will acquire rights in it at some time in the future. *Inwards v Baker* [1965] 2 QB 29 was an illustrative case. A father owned land and when told by his son that he (the son) was contemplating purchasing land on which to erect a bungalow, suggested that the son should build the bungalow on his (the father's) land instead. The son accepted that suggestion and did so. Several points should be noted: there was no contract between the parties; it was an informal family arrangement consisting of the father's promise and the son's acceptance. Nor did the father convey any land to his son. The son built the bungalow on his father's land, and in law the ownership of it vested in the landowner father.

The son clearly acted to his detriment in spending money on the construction of the bungalow. Many years before the events occurred, the father had made a will leaving the land to a third party. The father died in 1951. The third party could have ordered the son to leave but she did not do so. When, however, she died, her trustees did. The son claimed a licence by estoppel and the Court of Appeal agreed. The son was allowed to remain in the bungalow for the rest of his life. In his judgment Lord Denning MR said:

> 'If the owner of land requests another, or indeed allows another, to expend money on the land under an expectation created or encouraged by the landowner that he will be able to remain there, that raises an equity in the licensee such as to entitle him to stay.'

The expectation created in the claimant's mind is not confined to existing rights but may relate to an expectation to acquire rights in the future. Such was the case in *Re*

Basham (Deceased) [1986] 1 WLR 1498. In that case the claimant acted as she did, without payment on the belief, induced by the promise, that she would inherit the promisor's land. He died intestate and she had no claim on the estate. It was held that she had acted to her detriment in reliance on the promisor's promise that she would acquire his estate when he died and that she was therefore entitled to the whole estate.

The assurances must be sufficient to found a claim in proprietary estoppel. The representations by the landowner must not be too vague. In *Orgee* v *Orgee* [1997] EGCS 152 the court held that the representations were not 'sufficiently concrete'.

We must now examine the assurances which James gave to Lucy. He not only promised her immediate and continuing benefits, but also that on his death she would inherit the house and the rest of his estate. Given these assurances there can be no doubt that they are sufficient to satisfy the first requirement for the establishment of proprietary estoppel.

We must now turn to the second requirement and ask if Lucy has relied on these assurances, and in relying on them acted to her detriment to a sufficient degree.

The detriment need not involve the expenditure of money. In *Greasley* v *Cooke* [1980] 3 All ER 710 the claimant (in 1938) went to work in the household of a widower, his three sons and a handicapped daughter as a maidservant. In 1946 she commenced living with one of the sons, K, as man and wife. From 1948 onwards she ceased to be paid any wages, but she nevertheless continued to look after the household. From time to time she had been given assurances by K, although expressed in vague terms, that she could live in the house as long as she wished. K died in 1975. The house then vested in one of the other sons and the daughters of another son, and they claimed possession of the house. In resisting the claim, the claimant claimed a licence by estoppel and she succeeded. The Court of Appeal held that:

a) the assurances she had been given were sufficient to found a claim in proprietary estoppel; and

b) that gave rise to a rebuttable presumption, that the claimant acted as she did on reliance of those assurances; the burden of proof of rebutting that presumption passed to those who contended that there was no proprietary estoppel; and

c) although the claimant must establish detriment in reliance on the assurances that need not consist of the expenditure of money.

The Court of Appeal held she could stay in the house as long as she wished.

In *Brinnand* v *Ewens* (1987) The Times 4 June Nourse LJ summarised the requirements necessary to establish a claim under the doctrine:

a) the claimant must show that he had prejudiced himself or acted to his detriment; and

b) he must have acted in the way he did because he believed he had an interest in the property or would acquire one at some future time; and

c) the belief must have been induced by the landowner.

Whether the claimant has acted to his or her detriment is a question of fact which it is not always easy to decide. If a claimant gives up her flat and job to move into rent-free accommodation provided by her boyfriend, can she be said to be acting to her detriment? In *Coombes v Smith* [1986] 1 WLR 808 it was held that the claimant, on having a child, moving away from her husband, redecorating and not trying to provide otherwise for herself, did not show that she was acting to her detriment. Her actions were either due simply to a desire to live with the defendant or done as an occupier of the property.

Lucy sold her flat at a good price but at the same time relinquished her home and independence and instead became dependent on James to provide her with a roof over her head. She also left her job, making her more dependent on James in that she lost her income. On the other hand she acquired rent-free accommodation and a comfortable life style. She did look after the house, but this can be discounted. It involved no capital expenditure on the house and was probably no more than an occupier would do anyway: *Coombes v Smith*.

On balance it is probable that her conduct, in reliance on James' assurances, has been sufficiently detrimental to enable her to found a successful claim under proprietary estoppel.

The next and more difficult question is: what are the extent of her rights as a licensee by estoppel? To use of the language of the courts: how is the equity to be satisfied? The answer to that question is at the discretion of the courts, to be applied to the facts of individual cases. The flexibility of approach adopted by the courts makes the outcome difficult to predict. Sometimes the courts decide that the expectation created in the claimant's mind should be the criterion for deciding the extent of the claimant's interest. Did the claimant expect to remain on the premises permanently or for a limited time? Sometimes the courts take the view that the appropriate criterion is the amount of detriment the claimant has suffered, to be quantified in monetary terms. Some decisions reflect neither approach.

In Lucy's case she was entitled to believe that not only was she to be secure in the house for life, but that she would become its owner on James' death. To what extent can she rely on James' assurance in the latter respect? He followed through his assurance of inheritance by making a will in her favour. However, in itself this provides no security for Lucy because a testator is always entitled to revoke a will. A will acquires no binding force until the testator's death. This problem arose in the case of *Gillett v Holt and Another* [2000] 2 All ER 289. In that case H made repeated promises and assurances to G over many years to the effect that he intended to transfer his farm by will to G. Following a new will in favour of the second defendant and excluding G completely, G sought equitable relief on the basis of proprietary estoppel (he claimed that H was bound by proprietary estoppel to bequeath substantially the whole of his estate to him). At first instance, G's action was dismissed. Carnwath J held that to establish proprietary estoppel it was necessary to show words and conduct going beyond a mere statement of intention and amounting to an irrevocable promise. G appealed. In allowing the appeal, the Court of Appeal emphasised that at the heart of proprietary estoppel was the fundamental principle that equity was concerned to prevent unconscionable conduct. It was necessary to look at a given claim 'in the round'. The assurances of H had been repeated over a long period of time and were unambiguous. They were intended to be relied upon and were relied upon by G to his detriment. Further, it was not necessary for them to be irrevocable. Equity could intervene to render an assurance irrevocable when the claimant had relied on the representations and suffered detriment in consequence. In the result the assurances gave rise to an enforceable claim based on proprietary estoppel.

In his judgment Walker LJ quoted an article by W J Swadling in *Restitution Law Review* (1998) which summarises the position very neatly:

> 'The whole point of estoppel claims is that they concern promises which since they are unsupported by consideration, are initially revocable. What later makes them binding, and therefore irrevocable, is the promisee's detrimental reliance on them. Once that occurs there is simply no question of the promisor changing his or her mind.'

The key question to be asked here is whether James' change of mind would constitute unconscionable behaviour. Given the fact that Lucy has acted to her detriment the answer is almost certainly in the affirmative. A court following *Re Basham (Deceased)* would probably hold that on James' death she would be entitled to his entire estate. However, what of Lucy's entitlement in the meantime? The most likely solution would appear to be that adopted in *Pascoe v Turner* [1979] 1 WLR 431, namely to order James to transfer the fee simple in the house to her with immediate effect. That would provide her with the security she was promised and is anticipating her future ownership on James' death.

Chapter 3

Registration

3.1   **Introduction**

3.2   **Key points**

3.3   **Key cases and statutes**

3.4   **Questions and suggested solutions**

3.1 Introduction

This is a comprehensive area of land law with two clearly distinct spheres of operation. In registered land the rules of the Land Registration Acts must be seen both in their own right and as possibly coming within questions relating to settlements, co-ownership, easements, mortgages or adverse possession. In unregistered land the effect of the Land Charges Act 1972 on the equitable doctrine of notice is of particular importance.

When applying these rules the first question to ask is: 'Which system or doctrine to apply?' Use the following sequence.

a) i)   Is title registered? [registration of title].

    ii) Consider use of direct words – 'title to which is registered', or indirect – by reference to owner as 'registered proprietor'.

b) If so – apply Land Registration Act 2002 (prior to 13 October 2003 it would have been the Land Registration Acts 1925–1997). Under the 'old' (pre 2003) registered land system all interests in land were categorised as 'registerable', 'overriding' or 'minor'. Do not use the doctrine of notice: Lord Wilberforce: *Williams and Glyn's Bank Ltd* v *Boland* [1980] 3 WLR 138.

c) i)   If title not registered: [registration of land charges/incumbrances] Does the Land Charges Act 1972 apply? Section 2 LCA 1972.

    ii) Class C(i)   Puisne mortgage   Class D(ii) Restrictive covenant
        Class C(iii) General equitable charge   [created after 1925]
        Class C(iv) Estate contract   Class D(iii) Equitable easement

    iii) Void against a purchaser if not so registered: s4 LCA 1972.

    Midland Bank Trust Co Ltd v *Green* [1980] Ch 590.

d) If interest not capable of entry on land charges register then apply the equitable doctrine of notice. Is the person a bona fide purchaser for value of the legal estate without notice?

Pre-1926 restrictive covenants or licence by estoppel – proprietary estoppel.

Ives (E R) Investments Ltd v *High* [1967] 2 QB 379.

e) Examination context

It is crucial to ascertain whether an examination question in this field concerns registered or unregistered land. Most titles are now registered.

However, if nothing is said in the particular question then assume the title to the land is not registered.

3.2 Key points

Note meaning of 'registration' in the context of both registered and unregistered land. The purpose of the LRA is to register title to land at the Land Registry to create a 'mirror' of the land itself.

Registration of title

Up to 13 October 2003, the Land Registration Acts 1925–1997 applied. The Registration of Title Order 1989 completed the extension of registration of title to the whole of England and Wales. From 1 December 1990 the whole of England and Wales is now subject to compulsory registration of title at the next appropriate transaction.

Introduction

Essential characteristics of registered title may be summarised as follows.

a) Abolishes need for repeated examinations of title.

b) Establishes a record of proprietors.

c) Provision for altering and correcting the register – Land Registration Rules 2003, rr126–130.

d) Provision of reliable plan.

e) Issue of land certificate to registered proprietor to replace title deeds.

f) Provides short, simple forms as transfers, mortgages or other dealings.

g) Search system to check entries on the register.

h) Quick detection of conveyancing mistakes.

i) Insurance fund to compensate for mistakes.

j) Open Register – since 3 December 1990 the Land Registry has, subject to the payment of an appropriate fee, been open to inspection by the public: s1 LRA 1988.

But Cheshire concludes: 'Registered conveyancing is not … a new system of land law.'

In other words, the normal substantive law of real property applies to registered land.

Advantages of system

a) Cheaper by reducing legal costs for dealing with registered land.

b) Simplicity.

c) State guarantee of the title to the land.

Conclusion

Cheshire: 'The conveyancing of registered land is different in principle and practice. Once the title to land is registered, its past history is irrelevant. The title thenceforth is guaranteed by the state, and a purchaser can do no other than rely on it.'

Megarry and Wade (5th edition, 1984): 'Its great merits are that it eliminates repetitive and unproductive work in conveyancing and provides financial compensation in some cases where otherwise an innocent party would suffer loss.'

Pre Land Registration Act 2002

Principles of registration – registered land only

a) Classification of rights – registered interests – overriding interests – minor interests.

b) The register – three parts – property – proprietorship – charges.

c) When registration necessary – s123 LRA 1925 – freehold or grant/assignment of lease over 21 years. However, the new s123 LRA 1925 substituted by s1 LRA 1997 made first registration compulsory in a number of new situations. The new triggers included conveyance by way of gift and first legal mortgage of freeholds or leaseholds having more than 21 years to run. There were 2 months to register – fail to register and vendor held as bare trustee for purchaser.

d) Classes of registered title:

    i) absolute;

    ii) qualified;

    iii) possessory;

    iv) good leasehold.

e) Conversion of titles – s1 LRA 1986.

Classification of interests

a) Overriding interests: a 'crack in the mirror' LRA s70(1) – note, in particular:

b) Section 70(1)(a) – *Celsteel* v *Alton House Holdings Ltd* [1985] 2 All ER 562; revsd in part [1986] 1 All ER 608.

c) Section 70(1)(f) – Limitation Act 1980.

d) Section 70(1)(g) –*Williams & Glyn's Bank Ltd* v *Boland* [1980] 3 WLR 138 and *Lloyds Bank plc* v *Rosset* [1990] 2 WLR 867 and *Abbey National Building Society* v *Cann* [1991] 1 AC 56 (a person claiming an overriding interest under para (g) had to be in occupation prior to *completion of the transaction*).

e) Section 70(1)(k) – *City Permanent Building Society* v *Miller* [1952] Ch 840 and s4 LRA 1986 – had to be granted.

f) Minor interests – notice – caution – inhibition – restriction.

g) Rules of notice were not applied to registered land – *Peffer* v *Rigg* [1978] 3 All ER 745.

Indefeasibility of title

a) Rectification of title: s82 – note s82(3) to give effect to an overriding interest.

b) Compensation: by s83 LRA 1925 (as substituted by s2 LRA 1997) a person who suffered loss by reason of rectification or non-rectification of the register, or 'by reason of the loss or destruction of any document lodged at the registry for inspection or safe custody' (s83(3) or inaccurate searches), might claim compensation.

But see *Re Chowood's Registered Land* [1933] Ch 574 as to the limits of the availability of this compensation.

Post Land Registration Act 2002

Introduction

a) Act came into force on 13 October 2003.

b) Not all its provisions take effect immediately.

c) Electronic conveyancing regime unlikely to become operative until 2007/2008.

d) Repeals LRA 1925.

Objectives

a) The principal objective of the 2002 Act 'is that, under the system of electronic dealing with land that it seeks to create, the register should be a complete and accurate reflection of the state of the title to land on line with the absolute minimum of additional enquiries and inspections': para 1.5 'Land Registration for the Twenty-First Century: A Conveyancing Revolution' (2001) Law Com No 271.

b) Rationale for this objective is to make conveyancing 'quicker, easier and cheaper'.

c) Principal objective cannot be fully achieved because law allows certain rights and interests in land to be created informally, eg leases granted for three years or less.

Electronic conveyancing

a) Act establishes the requisite framework to move from the current paper based system of conveyancing to one which is wholly electronic.

b) Land Registry will provide an electronic communications network so that conveyancing can be conducted on line.

c) Network will be secure and limited to authorised solicitors and licensed conveyancers.

d) Anticipated that registration will take place at the same time as completion (currently registration can be up to three months after completion).

e) Land Registry under a duty to provide assistance to private individuals carrying out their own conveyancing.

First registration

a) Compulsory first registration is extended to leases with more than seven years to run (rather than the 21 years under the old regime) and to the assignment of leases with more than seven years to run (rather than the 21 years under the old regime).

b) Possible to effect voluntary first registration in respect of profits à prendre in gross (eg shooting or fishing rights) and franchises (eg the right to hold a market) provided they are held for an interest equivalent to a fee simple absolute in possession or a lease with at least seven years left to run.

Overriding interests

a) Role of such interests is significantly reduced.

b) Some interests are abolished outright, some will lose their overriding status after ten years and some others are narrowed in scope.

c) Guiding principle – an interest should only rank as an overriding one if it is not reasonable for it to be protected in the register.

d) What has to be determined is whether the transaction said to be affected is a first registration of title (Sch 1 of the Act applies) or a disposition of an already registered title (Sch 3 of the Act applies).

e) There are some differences as between these two Schedules.

f) The main differences/points to note are as follows.

  i) Schedule 3 interests are more precisely and narrowly defined than those in Sch 1.

ii) Equitable easements and profits are excluded from both Schedules.

iii) Schedule 3 denies overriding status to certain legal easements, eg those not exercised within one year before the transaction.

iv) In contrast to s70(1)(g) LRA 1925 'the receipt of rent and profits' will not give rise to overriding status under either Schedule.

Adverse possession

a) New substantive system put in place in respect of registered land only.

b) Now more difficult for a squatter to obtain title to registered land because a registered proprietor's title is not lost through mere lapse of time.

c) Onus on squatter to take action if he wants to obtain title to registered land.

d) Requires an application to be registered as proprietor after ten years' adverse possession (ie there is a separate limitation period of ten years for registered land).

e) Upon receipt of such an application the Land Registry will notify the registered proprietor and other interested parties of it and they can object by serving a counter notice within a prescribed period.

f) If no counter notice is served, the squatter is registered as proprietor.

g) If counter notice is served the squatter's application is dismissed unless he can establish one of three limited grounds that could entitle him to be registered. See para 5, Sch 6 to the Act for these grounds.

h) If the application is rejected further application can be made if the applicant is in adverse possession for a further period of two years.

i) Law relating to unregistered land is not affected.

Protection of rights and interests

a) Subject to transitional arrangements cautions and inhibitions are abolished.

b) Only ways to protect rights and interests are by notice or restriction.

c) Interests under trusts of land and strict settlements cannot be registered.

d) Leases for less than three years and restrictive covenants in a lease cannot be registered.

e) No longer a category of interest known as 'minor interest'. Rather, there are interests that need to be protected by an entry on the register by way of the new style of notice.

f) Notice can be either an agreed notice or a unilateral notice – it is an entry in respect of the burden of an interest affecting registered land.

g) An agreed notice is registered either by the registered proprietor with his consent or where the Registrar is satisfied as to the validity of the entry. Otherwise it is a unilateral notice.

h) Proprietor can apply for cancellation of a notice. Registrar must give notice of any such application to the beneficiary of the notice. If the beneficiary does not object within the presented period the notice will be cancelled.

i) Restrictions are similar to those under the LRA 1925.

Crown land

a) The Crown can now grant itself a freehold estate so as to register it.

b) Aim – to better protect Crown land from adverse possession.

Independent adjudication

Lord Chancellor to appoint a new independent adjudicator to deal with disputes between individuals and the Land Registry concerning land registration matters.

Registration of incumbrances

Land Charges Act 1972 – *unregistered land only.*

Registration of land charges

a) Object – to enable a purchaser of land to discover easily the incumbrances affecting that land.

b) Matters registrable under the LCA 1972:

   i) Pending actions – action relating to land – five years and renewable – *Selim Ltd v Bickenhall Engineering Ltd* [1981] 1 WLR 1318.

   ii) Annuities – created before 1926.

   iii) Writs and orders affecting land – *Clayhope Properties Ltd* v *Evans* [1986] 1 WLR 1223, s6 LCA 1972.

   iv) Deeds of arrangement – control of debtor's property given for benefit of creditors.

   v) Land charges:

   Class A – charge imposed on application of person who has incurred expenditure relating to land.

   Class B – charge imposed automatically by statute.

   Class C

   • Puisne mortgage (C(i)) – legal mortgage/legal estate/no deeds.

- Limited owner's charge (C(ii)) – equitable charge of tenant for life who has discharged a liability out of his own funds.

- General equitable charge (C(iii)) – equitable mortgage/legal estate/no deeds.

  Effect of failing to register is that the charge is void against a purchaser for value – s4 LCA 1972.

- Estate contract (C(iv)) – contract to convey legal estate/option to purchase. *Pritchard v Briggs* [1980] Ch 338; *Midland Bank Trust Co Ltd v Green* [1981] AC 513; *Philips v Mobil Oil Co Ltd* [1989] 3 All ER 97.

Class D

- Charge of Commissioners of Inland Revenue (D(i)) – unpaid inheritance tax.

- Restrictive covenant (D(ii)) – created after 1925 and not between landlord and tenant.

- Equitable easement (D(iii)): *Shiloh Spinners Ltd v Harding* [1973] AC 691. Created after 1925 – construe narrowly.

  Effect of failing to register (Class C(iv) and Class D) is void against any purchaser of the legal estate for money or money's worth – s14(6) LCA 1972.

Class E – annuities created before 1926, registered after 1925.

Class F – rights of occupation under Family Law Act 1996 – confers rights of occupation on spouse who has no estate/interest in the property.

c) Effect of registration – s198 LPA 1925 – deemed *actual* notice. This is the only form of notice to use when the interest is capable of being registered: s199(1) LPA 1925.

d) Effect of failure to register – s4 LCA 1972 – see above – generally void against a purchaser.

e) Effect of search – conclusive in favour of a purchaser.

f) Unregistrable matters eg licences by estoppel – equitable doctrine of *notice*: *Ives (E R) Investments Ltd v High* [1967] 2 QB 379 and *Kingsnorth Finance Co Ltd v Tizard* [1986] 1 WLR 783. Consider actual notice, constructive notice, *Hunt v Luck* [1902] 1 Ch 428 and imputed notice – *Kingsnorth Finance Co Ltd v Tizard*.

Registration of local land charges: s1 Local Land Charges Act 1975

a) Location – district council/London boroughs.

b) Interests registrable – public rights – prohibitions on use of land. Only private matter is a light obstruction notice.

c) Effect of failure to register – purchaser bound by charge but is entitled to compensation from the local authority.

d) Effect of search: s10 Local Land Charges Act 1975 – search is no longer conclusive.

Companies Register

Land charge created by company for securing money.

3.3 Key cases and statutes

- *Abbey National Building Society v Cann* [1990] 1 All ER 1085
  Overriding interests – the relevant date for determining the existence of a s70(1)(g) overriding interest was the date of registration, but the relevant date for determining whether the claimant was in actual occupation for the purpose of para (g) was the date of completion of the transaction

- *City of London Building Society v Flegg* [1987] 2 WLR 1266
  Overreaching – there must be a minimum of two trustees or a trust corporation before an overreaching can take place

- *Clark v Chief Land Registrar* [1994] 4 All ER 96
  Entry of a caution to protect an interest in land did not confer priority on that interest over a subsequently registered charge

- *Hodgson v Marks* [1971] Ch 892
  Overriding interests – a person could be in actual occupation for the purposes of s70(1)(g) Land Registration Act 1925 even though this was not readily ascertainable from inspection of the property – inquiry of the vendor for the purpose of s70(1)(g) would not suffice, it had to be of the person 'in actual occupation'

- *Ives (ER) Investments Ltd v High* [1967] 2 QB 379
  Equitable right based on estoppel – acquiescence was not registrable under the Land Charges Act 1925 but was protected by the doctrine of notice

- *Lloyds Bank plc v Rosset* [1990] 2 WLR 867
  Confirmed the decision in *Abbey National Building Society v Cann* that the relevant date for determining 'actual occupation' for the purposes of s70(1)(g) Land Registration Act 1925 was the date of completion of the transaction

- *Midland Bank Trust Co Ltd v Green* [1981] AC 513
  In the case of registration of incumbrances under the Land Charges Act 1972 what was crucial was the state of the register not the state of the purchaser's mind – option to purchase required to be registered as a land charge – not registered – option void because of non-registration

- *Shiloh Spinners Ltd* v *Harding* [1973] AC 691
  Equitable right of re-entry for breach of a leasehold covenant was not registrable under the Land Charges Act 1972 but was covered by the doctrine of notice

- Land Charges Act 1972, ss2 and 4

- Land Registration Acts 1925–1997

- Land Registration Act 2002

3.4 Questions and suggested solutions

Analysis of questions

The questions appear in a number of guises. There may be specific questions on the protection of third party rights in registered and/or unregistered land. In the case of registered land it would be necessary to state that third party interests are protected in four ways (certain legal estates can be registered separately with their own title number, eg lease for more than 21 years; mortgage protected by registration of a charge in the charges register; entry of a minor interest; and overriding interests). In the case of unregistered land, it would be necessary to deal with overreaching; registration of incumbrances; and the doctrine of notice (emphasising in particular that the doctrine is of reduced significance today). Prior to 2003, there were often questions on overriding interests under the old s70(1)(g) LRA 1925. In such a question it was invariably necessary to deal in some detail with *Abbey National Building Society* v *Cann* [1990] 2 WLR 832 and to point out that as a result of that decision it became much more difficult for a claimant to establish a para (g) overriding interest. Questions on registered land may also form part of a question on another area of land law where the examiner adds this dimension by including a phrase such as 'would your answer differ if the title to the land were registered?'

Note: all the following suggested solutions are in respect of examination questions set before the coming into force of the Land Registration Act 2002 in October 2003 and must be read in light of that reality, particularly in respect of references to overriding interests under s70(1)(g) of the LRA 1925.

QUESTION ONE

'The purpose of section 70(1)(g) of the Land Registration Act 1925 was to make applicable to registered land the same rule for the protection of persons in actual occupation of land as had been applied in *Hunt* v *Luck*.'

Explain this statement and consider the extent to which it is accurate.

University of London LLB Examination
(for External Students) Land Law June 1992 Q5

General Comment

A question which requires candidates to state what the rule in *Hunt* v *Luck* is, how it applies and then to compare it with s70(1)(g). The similarities and the differences between the two principles should be teased out. This is not a question for the student who either does not know what *Hunt* v *Luck* says or is unable to analyse it.

Skeleton Solution

Explanation of *Hunt* v *Luck*: explanation of doctrine of notice – elements of s70(1)(g) LRA 1925 – need to investigate the land – enquiries of persons on the land – overreaching.

Suggested Solution

The rule in *Hunt* v *Luck* [1902] 1 Ch 428 is intimately connected with the common law doctrine of notice. At common law the purchaser of land was bound by any equitable interest in land of which he had actual, constructive or imputed notice. The rule in *Hunt* can be expressed as follows; a purchaser of land must make enquiries of any person in possession of the land and if he fails to do so then any title he acquires will be subject to that of the person in possession. In short, the purchaser would be caught by constructive notice. In its original formulation the rule was only applicable to the interests of a tenant in possession, but was later extended to cover the interests of any person in possession.

Section 70(1)(g) applies in the context of the Land Registration Act 1925 and is one of the categories of overriding interest. As such it will not appear on the land certificate thereby shattering the 'mirror principle', and, as an overriding interest it is capable of binding a purchaser. In order for s70(1)(g) to be made out a person must be in actual occupation of the land (see *Epps* v *Esso Petroleum Co Ltd* [1973] 2 All ER 465) with an interest in land capable of binding subsequent owners of the land, in other words, a proprietary interest as opposed to a personal one: *Williams & Glyn's Bank* v *Boland* [1981] AC 487. Additionally, he must not have concealed that interest upon enquiry being made of him.

In *Strand Securities* v *Caswell* [1965] Ch 958 Lord Denning described s70(1)(g) as carrying the rule in *Hunt* forward into registered land. Insofar as the person in actual occupation must have an interest in land, s70(1)(g) and *Hunt* are the same. Similarly, both recognise that the presence of the vendor on the land does not exclude the possibility of occupation by another. In *Hunt* the occupation was that of the lessee, in *Boland* it was that of the wife although Lord Wilberforce said that the rule could apply in favour of any person in actual occupation.

However, there are marked differences. Whereas *Hunt* is based on, and requires some investigation of the land, s70(1)(g) will bind a purchaser whether he knows of the existence of the right or not and whether he could have discovered it or not; it does not require any search or investigation of the land and is not in any way based on the doctrine of notice.

Second, like *Hunt*, if enquiry is made under s70(1)(g) and the rights are not disclosed (as a result of active concealment on the part of the person who claims them), the purchaser will take free of them. But, unlike *Hunt*, s70(1)(g) neither requires nor presupposes any enquiry being made in the first place.

Third, unlike *Hunt*, the overriding interests of a person in actual occupation of land under s70(1)(g) can be overreached by a purchaser. In order to do so the purchaser must comply with the provisions of s2 LPA 1925, viz, he must take a conveyance from trustees, the interest must be of a type which is capable of being overreached and he must pay the capital monies to *two trustees or a trust corporation*: see *City of London Building Society* v *Flegg* [1988] AC 54 and contrast *Boland*. The fact that s70(1)(g) is capable of being overreached serves to highlight the fact that a search or investigation of the land is not pre-supposed for the purposes of that section.

Fourth, s70(1)(g) protects not just the person in actual occupation but also the recipient of rents and profits from the land. In this respect it is wider than the rule in *Hunt*.

Therefore there is limited truth in the statement. Both *Hunt* and s70(1)(g) deal with the interests of a person in occupation, but the former is rooted in the doctrine of notice – the latter is not and is capable of being avoided by way of overreaching.

QUESTION TWO

'The system of registration of title is intended only to simplify conveyancing; it should not affect substantive rights.'

Discuss.

> University of London LLB Examination
> (for External Students) Land Law June 1996 Q5

General Comment

In compiling an answer to this essay title it is essential for students to demonstrate an awareness of the pre-1926 conveyancing problems in order to show how the registered land system simplifies conveyancing and to make clear that overriding interests do affect substantive rights.

Skeleton Solution

Aims of land registration system – pre-1926 conveyancing position – outline of the land registration system: three registers; registrable interests; overriding interests; minor interests and three principles – overriding interests: 'crack in the mirror'; s70(1)(g); *Abbey National Building Society* v *Cann* – rationale for overriding interests.

Suggested Solution

Registration of title was first introduced into England on a limited basis in the nineteenth century. However, the real impetus for the 'new system' of conveyancing came when registration of title was extended by the Land Registration Act (LRA) 1925, which came into force on 1 January 1926.

The purpose of the LRA 1925 was to simplify conveyancing by providing a safe, simple and economic system of land transfer.

The unregistered system of conveyancing (the pre-1926 system) was cumbersome, expensive and time consuming. It is a basic tenet of conveyancing that a vendor must be able to prove that he is entitled to the land before he can pass good title to a purchaser. Under the pre-1926 unregistered system of conveyancing, such proof was provided by the production of the title documents to the land (ie the conveyances or leases). The vendor had to be able to show the chain of ownership for the preceding 30 (now 15) years. A prospective purchaser then had to check these documents to confirm that the vendor was entitled to sell the property (ie he had to get the information he needed from a variety of sources – again cumbersome and expensive). Further, each time the land was sold all these documents had to be examined. This system involved a lot of repetitive work, and it was time consuming and thus expensive of solicitors' time. Finally, since proof of title was through documents held in private custody the system was susceptible to fraud.

The system of registration of title is designed to deal with the problems posed by unregistered conveyancing so that the conveyancing process could be simplified. Following the coming into force of the LRA 1925, compulsory registration of title was introduced by Order in Council gradually throughout England and Wales over many decades. An Order in Council would designate a particular area as one in which registration of title would be compulsory on sale. This meant that thereafter on the first occasion that land in the area was sold or granted on a long lease (21 years or more) application had to be made for the registration of the title to the land. If this was not done then the purchaser or tenant did not have a legal (ie marketable) title. Extending registration of title throughout the country was a slow process. For example, the coverage of the compulsory registration areas was a mere 14 per cent of the population of England and Wales in 1951. However, the programme to extend compulsory registration of title to the whole country was finally completed on 1 December 1990 (however, since registration only takes effect on 'sale' it will be quite some time before all titles are registered). The reason it took so long was primarily due to the fact that successive governments did not make the requisite resources available to achieve the goal earlier (no votes in giving public monies to the Land Registry!).

How does the registered land system simplify conveyancing? It does so by replacing the traditional title in unregistered conveyancing which, as already noted, has to be separately investigated on each purchase (prospective purchaser has to satisfy himself from the abstract of title, title deeds, etc that the vendor has the power to sell the land in question) with a single established title (ie one registered at the Land Registry) which in turn is guaranteed by the State. The 'big idea' is that investigation of title need only be done once, and it is done by the Chief Land Registrar. The end product is to create a register of title which, at any given time, acts as a mirror which accurately reflects all the interests existing in or over a given piece of land. Accordingly, when there is a prospective sale of a registered land property, the purchaser's solicitor applies to the Land Registry for an office copy entry of the vendor's title. Such document gives him a complete and accurate report on the current state of the title in question (he does not have to plough through several deeds to find out what he needs to know).

Each register of the title is made up of three registers. First, there is the property register. This gives the county or place where the land is situated and describes the property by reference to a filed plan. It also contains details of any rights over other land of which the registered land has the benefit, eg legal easement. Second, there is the proprietorship register. This tells you who owns the land and what title (absolute, good leasehold, etc) applies to the land. Third, there is the charges register. It contains encumbrances or charges affecting land – an interest which burdens it, eg a restrictive covenant.

All interests in land were recategorised by the LRA 1925 as 'registrable', 'overriding' or 'minor'. Registrable interests include fee simple absolute in possession and leases over 21 years. Overriding interests include leases of 21 years or less and all other interests listed in s70(1)(a)–(l) LRA 1925. Finally, minor interests include anything which is neither a registerable nor an overriding interest (ie all interests come within one category or another).

The system of registration of title comprises three main principles.

a) The 'mirror principle' – the register is designed to act as a mirror accurately reflecting the totality of estates and interests affecting the registered land in question. However, overriding interests (which are not usually entered on the register but bind the registered proprietor even though he may have no knowledge of them) constitute a major qualification to this principle.

b) The curtain principle – only the legal title is shown on the register. By virtue of the curtain principle all trusts are kept off the title as the beneficial interests behind the trust are overreached on sale.

c) The insurance principle – the State guarantees the accuracy of a registered title. An indemnity is paid out of public funds if a registered proprietor is deprived of his title or is otherwise prejudiced by the operation of the scheme.

Upon registration, the registered proprietor is given a land certificate which contains copies of the three parts of the register and a copy of the filed plan. However, the register, not the land certificate, is the document of title. The registered land system is much more secure than the unregistered system of conveyancing (if a land certificate is lost a replacement can be obtained upon payment of a small fee). Registration must take effect within two months of the transaction (ie the sale or granting of a long lease), failing which the grant will be void as to the legal estate unless an authorised extension has been granted by the Registrar: s123 LRA 1925. A purchaser of land subject to the registration scheme takes the land subject only to:

a) all entries on the register; and

b) any overriding interests existing at the time (overriding interests can appear on the register and if this happens they cease to be overriding interests and take their protection from the register).

The registered land system has unquestionably simplified conveyancing. It has established a safe, simple and economic system of land transfer. The quotation suggests it should not affect substantive rights. The reality is that it does in at least one important respect. As noted above, the register is intended to operate as a mirror accurately reflecting the totality of estates and interests affecting the registered land. However, overriding interests are a 'crack in the mirror' because although they are not usually entered on the register, they still bind the registered proprietor even though he has no knowledge of them. They are supposed to be readily discoverable by anyone who takes the trouble to go and look at the property. Further, the vendor/transferor is usually bound to disclose any overriding interests he knows about under the open contract rule and the standard conditions of sale.

Overriding interests are set out in s70(1)(a)–(l) LRA 1925. The subsection includes a multitude of rights. However, the most important overriding interests are terms of years of 21 years or less, legal easements and rights of persons in actual occupation of land under para (g).

Why does the land registration system have this 'crack in the mirror'? The answer is a mix of economic, policy and practical reasons as demonstrated by considering two of the aforementioned overriding interests – short leases and rights of persons in actual occupation of land.

It is submitted that the exclusion of short leases from the system was for economic and practical reasons. It would have been impracticable to require all short leases to be noted on the register. A very considerable increase in the Registry's resources would have been needed to facilitate their entry onto the register – resources which successive governments would not have been prepared to make available. Further, many leases which are not required to be by deed (see ss52(1) and 54(2) LPA 1925) are entered into comparatively informally, and it would have been unrealistic and unreasonable to expect a tenant to have protected his interest on the register.

Policy and practical considerations are the rationale for s70(1)(g) overriding interests – interests of persons in actual occupation of land. Paragraph (g) is drafted widely in order to protect people who from the standpoint of basic justice merit protection but whose interests (leaving aside the separate issue of whether their interests would be suitable for registration or not) are frequently created informally and are thus unlikely to be registered by lay people.

There are three aspects to establishing an overriding interest under s70(1)(g).

a) The claimant must have a proprietary interest in the property (eg an equitable interest).

b) The claimant must be in actual occupation of the land prior to completion of the transaction: *Abbey National Building Society* v *Cann* [1991] 1 AC 56. Prior to this decision there was uncertainty as to when the claimant had to be in occupation for the purposes of s70(1)(g). Was it the date of registration of the purchaser or mortgagee as proprietor or was it the date of completion of the purchase? The fact that the House of Lords in the *Cann* case ruled that the claimant had to be in occupation prior to completion of the transaction has had the effect of limiting most claims under para (g) to cases of second or later mortgages, as it is unusual for purchasers to be in occupation before completion.

c) If an enquiry is made by a prospective purchaser and the right is not disclosed because of active concealment on the part of the person claiming an overriding interest under para (g) then the purchaser will take free of that right.

In conclusion, the registered land system intends to and does simplify the conveyancing process. However, it does – through overriding interests – affect substantive rights. Indeed, it is submitted that if this 'crack in the mirror' had not been provided for the success of the whole initiative could have been jeopardised.

QUESTION THREE

Old Mrs Williams was persuaded ('for tax reasons') by her son, Jason, to sell him her house for £50,000 and Jason was duly registered as the proprietor. The purchase price was considerably less than the true value of the house, because Jason had agreed that his mother could stay in the house rent-free for the remainder of her life. Two years later Jason sold the house to David for £100,000, informing David falsely that he and his mother were intending to emigrate to Canada. David was registered as the proprietor of the house and Jason disappeared with the purchase money. David now seeks possession of the house from Mrs Williams, while she claims that she is entitled to be registered as proprietor in his place.

Discuss.

University of London LLB Examination
(for External Students) Land Law June 1994 Q2

General Comment

The question was probably a welcome one for many students because for the most part it deals with matters – proprietary estoppel, s70(1)(g) overriding interests – which are usually central aspects of most undergraduate land law courses. However, the tailpiece on rectification of the register may have caught some students out since this is an aspect of land registration which tends to receive only passing coverage in many undergraduate courses.

Skeleton Solution

Licences protected by estoppel or in equity: *Bannister* v *Bannister* – mirror principle: overriding interests (crack in the mirror) s70(1)(g) LRA 1925 – enquiries of persons on the land: *Hodgson* v *Marks* – when must a person be in occupation for the purposes of s70(1)(g)?: *Abbey National Building Society* v *Cann* – rectification of the register: s82 LRA 1925.

Suggested Solution

The question raises at least three main issues. First, what interest has Mrs Williams in the house after her son Jason is registered as proprietor? Second, has David purchased subject to Mrs Williams' interest? Third, can David obtain possession – will Mrs Williams be able to obtain rectification of the register? These questions will be considered in turn.

Mrs Williams sold her home to her son for a price considerably less than its true value on the understanding that she could remain in it rent-free for the rest of her life. The facts are very similar to *Bannister* v *Bannister* [1948] 2 All ER 133. There, a woman who owned two cottages orally agreed to sell them on the basis that the purchaser would allow her to remain in one of them rent-free for so long as she wished. The conveyance made no mention of this undertaking. Subsequently, when the purchaser tried to get the woman out, the Court of Appeal held that it would be a fraud to disregard the oral trust of land and the woman was entitled under a constructive trust to a life interest determinable on her ceasing to reside in the cottage. Similarly, in *Re Sharpe* [1980] 1 WLR 219 a constructive trust was found to enable an aunt who lent her nephew money to remain in the house until she was repaid. Subsequently, these cases were criticised mainly because the constructive trust was seen as too wide a remedy.

More recently reliance in such situations has been placed upon the doctrine of proprietary estoppel. This type of estoppel operates to prevent the revocation of a right affecting land which one party has been led by the other to believe to be permanent. For example, if A, the owner of land, allows B to spend money on that land or otherwise act to his detriment under an expectation created or encouraged by A that he will be allowed to remain on the land or acquire an interest in the land, then A will not be allowed to defeat that expectation and deny B's right to remain or to an interest in the land.

The courts have used the equitable doctrines of estoppel and the constructive trust to protect licensees where it would be contrary to justice to allow strict legal principles to be applied (in *Bannister* v *Bannister* the trust of land was not in writing as required by s53(1)(b) Law of Property Act (LPA) 1925).

Here Mrs Williams was persuaded to sell the house to her son at an undervalue because

Jason agreed that she could remain in it rent-free for the rest of her lif
seems that Mrs Williams has a licence which Jason would be estopp
during her lifetime.

Has David purchased subject to the interest of Mrs Williams? In t.
necessary to discuss s70(1)(g) of the Land Registration Act (LRA) 1925. ⎽ .egister is
designed to operate as a mirror accurately reflecting the totality of estates and interests
affecting the registered land. Overriding interests are an exception to this principle
(the mirror principle). They are not entered on to the register, yet they bind the
registered proprietor even though he may have no knowledge of them (a crack in the
mirror!). Overriding interests are set out in s70(1) LRA 1925. The most controversial one
is para (g) which deals with the right of a person in actual occupation. Mrs Williams
will be claiming that she has a para (g) overriding interest. To succeed she has to show
three things. First, her interest in the land must be proprietary in nature. Second, that
she is in actual occupation. In this regard it was held by the House of Lords in *Abbey
National Building Society v Cann* [1991] 1 AC 56 that the relevant date for occupation in
order to establish a right under para (g) was the date of completion of the transaction.
Third, that no enquiry was made of her. A purchaser of registered land is required to
inspect the premises and ask anyone in occupation the grounds on which they are
there: see *Hodgson v Marks* [1972] Ch 892. It is not enough to ask the vendor alone, it
must be the person 'in actual occupation': see *Hodgson v Marks*. Here Mrs Williams
has a proprietary interest in the house and she was in occupation before Jason sold the
house to David. Further, David accepted Jason's explanation and he made no enquiry
of Mrs Williams. Accordingly, he has bought the house subject to Mrs Williams'
overriding interest protected by her occupation.

A purchaser can take free of an otherwise overriding interest if he makes 'enquiry' of
the person who owns the interest and that interest is not disclosed.

Can David obtain possession of the house? In view of the protection of s70(1)(g) LRA
1925, Mrs Williams will be able to resist any claim by David for possession. The court
will invariably decide that she has a licence by estoppel. David has failed to make the
enquiry necessary under s70(1)(g) and he now has a property which he cannot occupy
or sell at full vacant possession market value because of the absolute requirement that
a purchaser of registered land must enquire of any person occupying the land, what
their interest is.

Finally, will Mrs Williams be able to obtain rectification of the register? Section 82 of the
Land Registration Act 1925 gives a wide discretion to rectify the register to both the
court and the Registrar in order to correct mistakes. There are eight grounds for
rectification, including fraud, mistake and consent (where all interested persons
consent). Here Mrs Williams is not the victim of fraud or mistake nor, presumably, does
David consent. She has received £50,000 from Jason and will probably be allowed by
the court to remain in the house for as long as she wishes. Accordingly, she will not
succeed in her claim to rectify the register.

QUESTION FOUR

When Dan retired from his job, he decided to sell his house and to go to live near Simon, his son. Simon, who owned a row of cottages, contracted to sell one of them (unregistered land) to Dan for £75,000. Dan paid the purchase-price to Simon and moved into the cottage. Two years later Simon, unknown to Dan, charged the cottage to the Bister Bank. Simon did not inform the bank about Dan's possession of the cottage, nor did the bank make any inquiries about it. When Simon defaulted on his mortgage repayments, the bank sought possession of the cottage.

Advise Dan. Would your advice be the same if the cottage had been registered land?

University of London LLB Examination
(for External Students) Land Law June 1997 Q2

General Comment

This question necessitates consideration of the position of a person not on the legal title but in occupation and with an interest in the land as against a mortgagee seeking possession both in relation to unregistered and registered land. In particular the effect of non-registration of a registerable land charge has to be addressed.

Skeleton Solution

Unregistered land

What interest does Dan have in the cottage? – Law of Property (Miscellaneous Provisions) Act 1989, s2: all dealings in land should be in writing – contract to sell: registerable land charge, void if not registered, s4 LCA 1972, *Midland Bank Trust Co Ltd* v *Green, Lloyd's Bank plc* v *Carrick*.

Registered land

What interest does Dan have in the cottage? – s123 LRA 1925 – overriding interests under s70(1)(g) LRA 1925 – overreaching requires two trustees, *Williams & Glyn's Bank v Boland, City of London Building Society* v *Flegg* – no overreaching: only one trustee – overriding interest binding on bank.

Suggested Solution

A key reality in this scenario is that Dan seemingly does not have legal title to the cottage he lives in. The fact that Simon was able to charge the cottage to the Bister Bank two years after Dan paid the £75,000 purchase price to Simon and moved in is supportive of that conclusion. Since Dan seemingly does not have the legal title it is necessary to consider if he has a beneficial interest in the cottage.

Simon who owned a row of cottages contracted to sell one of them (title to which was unregistered) to Dan for £75,000. Section 2 of the Law of Property (Miscellaneous Provisions) Act 1989 provides that:

'A contract for the sale or other disposition of an interest in land can only be made in writing and only by incorporating all the terms which the persons have expressly agreed in one document or, where contracts are exchanged, in each.'

This provision applies to contracts made on or after 27 September 1989 and requires the contract to be in writing not merely evidenced by writing. The aim of s2 of the 1989 Act is to prevent disputes about whether parties have entered into an agreement and what its terms are. It replaces s40 LPA 1925 under which a contract made prior to 27 September 1989 had to be either in writing and signed by the party to be charged (ie the defendant in any action on the contract) or evidenced by some written memorandum similarly signed or by an act of part performance. It is assumed that Simon's contract was entered into on or after 27 September 1989 and that it complies with s2 of the 1989 Act. However, if it does not so comply then the agreement between Simon and Dan would be void.

A contract to sell is equivalent to an option to purchase. In the case of unregistered land, a contract by the owner of a legal estate to convey (ie sell) a legal estate ranks as an estate contract which is a registerable encumbrance. It should be entered as a Class C(iv) land charge in the land charges registry. By virtue of s4 of the Land Charges Act 1972 failure to register a registerable encumbrance makes the interest void against a 'purchaser'. Registration is deemed to constitute actual notice to all persons for all purposes connected with the land. This means that a registered charge is binding on a purchaser whether he knew about it or not and an unregistered charge is not binding on a purchaser even if he had notice of it: see *Midland Bank Trust Co Ltd v Green* [1981] AC 513. Here Dan should have entered his estate contract as a Class C(iv) land charge in order to bind a purchaser for valuable consideration (ie the bank). However, he does not appear to have so acted and therefore it is submitted that his estate contract is not binding on the bank provided of course it is a legal mortgage: see *Lloyds Bank plc v Carrick* [1996] 4 All ER 630.

Accordingly, in the case of unregistered land Dan will not be able to prevent the Bister Bank taking possession of the cottage. These facts demonstrate vividly one of the principal shortcomings of the unregistered land system – its inability to protect people in occupation of land.

The advice to Dan would be significantly different if the title to the cottage had been registered. An application to transfer the title to the cottage to Dan must be made within two months of the date of the conveyance (if there was one) otherwise the conveyance is void: s123 LRA 1925. In practice an extension of time for such a transfer can be secured from the Land Registrar if an explanation for non-compliance with the two-month requirement is proffered. However, for the purposes of the question it is assumed that title has not been registered in the name of Dan.

Nevertheless Dan could have an overriding interest coming within s70(1)(g) LRA 1925. Overriding interests bind a purchaser without appearing on the register and even though he has no knowledge of them. There are three aspects to establishing an overriding interest under s70(1)(g). First, the claimant must have a proprietary interest in the property. A contract for the sale of land confers upon a purchaser an equitable interest in land: *Bridges v Mees* [1957] Ch 475. Secondly, the claimant must be in actual occupation of the land prior to completion of the transaction: *Abbey National Building Society v Cann* [1991] 1 AC 56. Whether a person is in actual occupation is a question of fact and degree. Satisfying this requirement causes Dan no difficulty since he was in occupation for two years before Simon charged the cottage to the Bister Bank. Third, if an enquiry is made by a prospective purchaser and the right is not disclosed (because of active concealment on the part of the person claiming an overriding interest under para (g)), then the purchaser will take free of that right. Here the Bister Bank made no inquiries about the cottage. Accordingly, it is submitted that Dan has an overriding interest under s70(1)(g) LRA 1925.

However, a s70(1)(g) overriding interest can be overreached by a purchaser. For this to happen the purchaser must comply with the provisions of s2 of the LPA 1925 one of which is that he must pay the capital monies to two trustees or a trust corporation. In *City of London Building Society v Flegg* [1988] AC 54 a legal charge was granted by two trustees for sale of registered land who were holding for tenants in common who remained in occupation but had no knowledge of the creation of the charge. The House of Lords held that the interest of the tenants in common was transferred to the equity of redemption held by the trustees and the capital monies raised by the charge and that the tenants in common could not claim an overriding interest under s70(1)(g) LRA 1925 to enable them to remain in occupation because their beneficial interest in the land was overreached by the legal charge, leaving nothing to which a right of occupation could attach. However, if a purchaser does not comply with s2 of the LPA 1925, eg because he only pays the capital money to one trustee there will be no overreaching, the overriding interest will prevail and the purchaser will be bound by the equitable interest: *Williams & Glyn's Bank v Boland* [1981] AC 487.

Here on the facts there is only one trustee – Simon (who charged the cottage to the Bister Bank). Therefore, applying the aforementioned cases, Dan's overriding interest cannot be overreached and the bank will not be able to repossess the cottage. Rather, it will have to pursue other means in order to recover the arrears.

QUESTION FIVE

Leslie was the registered proprietor of a house in London and in 1997 he divided the house into two flats, leasing the top flat to Tim and the bottom flat to Bob, each for a term of 15 years. Leslie granted Bob an option to purchase the freehold reversion in the house. In 1998, at a time when Bob had been posted abroad for two months, Leslie sold the freehold to Patrick, who was registered as proprietor. Bob now wishes to enforce his option against Patrick, whereas Patrick claims that he is not bound by any rights that Bob may have.

Advise Patrick. Would your advice have been different if the house had been unregistered land?

University of London LLB Examination
(for External Students) Land Law June 2000 Q1

General Comment

A somewhat searching question calling in particular for a detailed knowledge of s70(1)(g) Land Registration Act (LRA) 1925 and its case law. Candidates should notice that Bob is in occupation of only part of the house. Does this disqualify him from invoking s70(1)(g)? *Ferrishurst Ltd* v *Wallcite Ltd* should be discussed.

Care must be taken to distinguish between the relevant provisions of registered and unregistered land. In particular, notice that there is no equivalent of s70(1)(g) in unregistered land.

Skeleton Solution

Registered land: legal lease; overriding interest; s70(1)(k) LRA 1925; binds Patrick – option to purchase: minor interest; notice; caution – if not protected: is it overriding under s70(1)(g)? – s70(1)(g) meaning of rights – option to purchase: an equitable interest in land within para (g) – actual occupation: fact not law – two months' absence: has occupation ceased?; probably not – Bob only in partial occupation: may still claim s70(1)(g) applicable – *Ferrishurst Ltd* v *Wallcite Ltd* – timing under s70(1)(g): right must exist at time of registration by purchaser, and claimant (Bob) must prove he was in occupation at time of completion.

Unregistered land: legal lease; binds the whole world; Patrick automatically bound – option to purchase: equitable interest in land; Land Charges Act (LCA) 1972 – registrable as an estate contract – effect of registration: s198 Law of Property Act (LPA) 1925 – effect of non-registration: s4(6) LCA 1972 – vital difference between registered and unregistered land – in unregistered land, no equivalent of the s70(1)(g) safety net.

Suggested Solution

The basic question to be addressed is: when Patrick purchased the freehold of the house, did he take it subject to any rights that Bob might have or free of them? The starting point of the inquiry therefore is to ascertain what rights Bob has.

In 1997 Leslie, the freeholder, leased the bottom flat to Bob. It is necessary from the outset, when a lease is created, to declare if possible whether it is legal or equitable, as this is relevant to its binding effect on purchasers of the reversion. In this case we are not told if the lease was granted by deed or in writing. Given that it is a 15-year lease it is highly probable that it was made by deed. If this is the case it is a legal lease: s52 Law of Property Act (LPA) 1925, and the question will be answered on that basis.

The problem is set in the context of registered land and in deciding whether the lease is binding on Patrick a basic formula should be applied: is the lease an overriding interest or a minor one? If overriding, it will not appear on Leslie's register of title but will nevertheless bind Patrick. Section 70(1) Land Registration Act (LRA) 1925 contains a finite list of overriding interests and the next step is to see if the lease is to be found in that list. In performing that exercise s70(1)(g) LRA 1925 should be ignored for the time being, as it differs from the other overriding interests in s70(1) in that it constitutes a generality of interests and can be used as a safety net for unprotected minor interests, as will be demonstrated later.

A perusal of the list reveals that s70(1)(k) LRA 1925 will accommodate the legal lease in this case. Section 70(1)(k) defines any lease granted for a period not exceeding 21 years as an overriding interest. However, care must be exercised here as the word 'lease' may lead the unwary to assume that it includes both legal and equitable leases. This is not so. In *City Permanent Building Society* v *Miller* [1952] Ch 840 the court held that because the paragraph refers to leases that have been 'granted', its application was confined to legal leases. 'Granted' means granted by deed, and equitable leases (or agreements for leases) are not created in that manner. In this case Bob's lease, being legal, falls within para (k) and automatically bound Patrick when he acquired the reversion.

Since the lease is an overriding interest it is not necessary to proceed further. Had the lease not appeared in the list, say, for example, it had been an agreement for a lease, then it would have been a minor interest. In that case Bob, to ensure it bound a purchaser of the freehold, would have needed to protect it by entering a notice on Leslie's register of title. The basic rule to remember in the application of these principles is that a minor interest is an interest in land which is not in the list of overriding interests. The question of whether Patrick is bound by the option to purchase is more complex.

We start again by posing the question: is it overriding or minor? Then examine the list of overriding interests in s70(1) LRA 1925 passing over for the time being s70(1)(g). An option to purchase is not listed and accordingly it is a minor interest in land and requires an entry in the form of a notice on Leslie's register of title. It is at this point that Bob may encounter difficulties. To place a notice on Leslie's register of title, he will need to produce to the Registry Leslie's land certificate and Leslie may not be willing to cooperate. If he does so he will be facilitating the imposition of an incumbrance on his land. In the absence of Leslie's cooperation Bob can enter a caution on Leslie's register of title, but this is of little practical value. The caution simply obliges the Registrar, when he receives Patrick's application to register the assignment, to inform Bob that such application has been made.

Bob's option needs more effective protection than that and it is to be found in s70(1)(g) LRA 1925. This leads us on to a detailed examination of that paragraph and consideration of its application. The paragraph enacts that the rights of every person in actual occupation of land, or in receipt of rents and profits therefrom, save where enquiry is made of such a person and the rights are not disclosed, shall constitute an overriding interest. That means, as with the other overriding interests, that they do not appear on the register of title, which is subject to them, but nevertheless bind a purchaser of that land.

The key word in the paragraph is 'rights' for it is they which constitute an overriding interest, and it is the rights of persons in actual occupation of the land, or in receipt of rents and profits from it, which come within the paragraph. It is important to note that the paragraph does not protect occupation. The rights protected must subsist in reference to the registered land: s70(1) LRA 1925. That is to say they must constitute rights in land and not personal rights: *National Provincial Bank Ltd* v *Ainsworth* [1965] AC 1175 per Lord Wilberforce. The rights do not have to be legal rights. Equitable rights also fall within the paragraph: *Williams & Glyn's Bank* v *Boland* [1981] AC 487.

Does the option to purchase the reversion, which is a term of Bob's lease, fall within para (g)? The effect of such a covenant is to confer upon the tenant an equitable interest in the demised land: *London and SW Railway* v *Gomm* (1882) 20 Ch D 562. Such a right is capable of being an overriding interest under s70(1)(g): *Webb* v *Pollmount Ltd* [1966] Ch 584.

However, for Bob to claim that his option to purchase is binding on Patrick he must go on to prove that he was in actual occupation of the land. Several points have to be considered here: the meaning of 'actual occupation' and the relevant time of occupation.

Actual occupation is a matter of fact and not of law: *Williams & Glyn's Bank* v *Boland* per Lord Denning. This is not always an easy issue to resolve. For example, in *Lloyds Bank plc* v *Rosset*, two judges in the Court of Appeal held that Mrs Rosset was in actual occupation and the third decided she was not. In the problem we are told that, after Bob had been posted abroad for two months, Leslie sold the freehold to Patrick, who was registered as proprietor. That absence does not necessarily mean that Bob had ceased to be in actual occupation. The period was of short duration and he expected to return after two months. In *Chhokar* v *Chhokar* (1984) 14 Fam Law 269 a wife claimed that her equitable interest in a house under a trust for sale came within s70(1)(g) LRA 1925 and that, when her husband, who was the sole owner, sold the house her equitable interest was binding on the purchaser even though she was temporarily away at the time having a baby in hospital. Ewbank J held that she had not ceased actual occupation as her furniture was still in the house and she intended to return to the house on her discharge from hospital. We do not know if Bob had left his furniture in the house, although it is highly probable that he did. He would be most unlikely to have taken it with him for two months. Moreover, he intended to return at the end of that period.

There is a further point which the facts of this problem present. Patrick purchased the freehold of the whole house, but Bob was only in actual occupation of part of it – the bottom flat. For s70(1)(g) LRA 1925 to be applicable must a person claiming its protection be in occupation of all of the premises, or is it applicable if a person is in actual occupation of merely part of the premises, as is the case here? This point was considered in *Ferrishurst Ltd* v *Wallcite Ltd* [1999] 2 WLR 667. In that case the claimants were tenants of premises under a sub-underlease. That lease contained an option to purchase the underlease. Situated on the premises comprised in the underlease was a garage. The garage was occupied by a third party under a separate sub-underlease. Since the option was not protected as a minor interest, the claimants sought to exercise the option against all of the premises comprised in the underlease, although they were not in occupation of the garage. The Court of Appeal held that the claimants did not have to be in actual occupation of all of the land which was subject to the option, and consequently they were entitled to exercise the option against all the land comprised in the underlease. Thus the fact that Bob was only in occupation of part of the house would not preclude him from exercising the option to purchase the freehold. Patrick would be bound by the option.

We may conclude, therefore, with reasonable certainty that a court would decide that Bob had remained in actual occupation for the duration of the two-month period and that his partial occupation of the house would be no bar to him asserting a claim under s70(1)(g) LRA 1925. However, that is not the end of the matter. We must now consider when he is required to be in actual occupation for the paragraph to apply, and the paragraph gives no guidance on this point.

We must therefore turn to the authorities to decide the meaning of the paragraph. The principal one is *Abbey National Building Society* v *Cann* [1990] 2 WLR 832. The House of Lords held that where a purchaser acquires registered land which is subject to an overriding interest under s70(1)(g) LRA 1925, for a purchaser to take subject to it, it must be in existence at the time he is registered as the proprietor. It is only at that point that title to the registered land changes hands. Contrast this position with that in unregistered land. In that case title changes hands at the earlier date of completion. However, in the case of a s70(1)(g) LRA 1925 overriding interest the House of Lords imposed an additional requirement: namely, that the person claiming that an interest is binding on a purchaser by virtue of actual occupation under s70(1)(g) LRA 1925 must also prove that he or she was in actual occupation at the earlier date of completion.

Thus if Bob wishes to enforce his option against Patrick he must prove that first, he was in actual occupation; second, that the option was in existence at the date that Patrick was registered as proprietor, and third, that he was in actual occupation at the date of completion. On the facts it appears highly likely that he will experience no difficulty in establishing all three requirements. If the house had been unregistered land the answer is different.

Given that the lease is legal, it would automatically bind Patrick when he acquired the house at the date of completion. Legal estates bind the whole world; whether a purchaser knows of them or not is irrelevant.

As has been indicated before, the option to purchase the reversion conferred upon Bob is an equitable interest in the house. The question is: did Patrick take subject to it or not when he acquired the freehold of the house? This being unregistered land, the

Land Registration Act 1925 has no application and we must turn instead to the Land Charges Act (LCA) 1972 and consider whether it is registrable as a land charge under that statute. It is registrable as a land charge C(iv), known as an estate contract. This is defined by s2(4)(iv) LCA 1972 as 'a contract by an estate owner ... to convey or create a legal estate, including a contract conferring ... a valid option to purchase, a right of pre-emption or any other like right'. An option to purchase a reversion of a lease comes within the wording 'a valid option to purchase'.

To bind Patrick, however, Bob must have registered the option in the Land Charges Registry before Patrick acquired title. We are not told whether he has done so and we must therefore consider the two alternatives. If he did register the option then the effect of registration is 'deemed to constitute actual notice to all persons ... as from the date of registration': s198(1) LPA 1925. Thus Patrick would acquire the house subject to the option even if he did not know of its existence.

If, on the other hand, Bob did not register the option then the position is as enacted by s4(6) LCA 1972: 'an estate contract [C(iv)] ... shall be void as against a purchaser for money or money's worth ... of a legal estate in the land charged with it, unless the land charge is registered in the appropriate register before the completion of the purchase'.

Thus in the event of non-registration Patrick, who acquired the legal estate in the house and presumably paid for it, would take free of the option even if he had actual knowledge of it: *Midland Bank Trust Co Ltd* v *Green* [1981] AC 513.

It is important to notice a vital difference between registered and unregistered land in this context. In the case of registered land, if the option was not protected as a minor interest by a notice entered on Leslie's register of title, as has been seen, it could still bind Patrick as an overriding interest under s70(1)(g) LRA 1925. In that case s70(1)(g) LRA 1925 acts as a safety net to catch unprotected minor interests. There is no such safety net in the case of unregistered land. If the option is not registered as an estate contract under the LCA 1972 then, if Patrick is a purchaser of the legal estate in the house for money or money's worth, it is lost beyond revival.

Chapter 4

Settlements and Trusts of Land

4.1   **Introduction**

4.2   **Key points**

4.3   **Key cases and statutes**

4.4   **Trusts of Land and Appointment of Trustees Act 1996**

4.5   **Questions and suggested solutions**

4.1 Introduction

This area of land law has undergone very significant change with the coming into force on 1 January 1997 of the Trusts of Land and Appointment of Trustees Act 1996. The Act effected some of the most important reforms to real property law since the 1925 legislation. Accordingly, it is crucial for students to be familiar with the background to, and the effect of, the new legislation. In particular, it is important for students to grasp three important realities about the Act right from the outset. First, it created a new concept – the trust of land. Second, as a general rule no new strict settlement can be created since the coming into force of the 1996 Act. Third, all existing trusts for sale (ie those in existence before 1 January 1997) automatically became trusts of land (ie the Act is retrospective). Accordingly, since pre-1996 Act strict settlements can still exist it is still important for students to have an appreciation of the Settled Land Act 1925 regime.

4.2 Key points

Settlements under Settled Land Act 1925

a) Definition – s1 SLA 1925 – to provide for two or more persons in succession.

b) General effect – originally to keep land in the family and prevent it from being sold.

c) How it works – by re-settlement at each generation.

d) Where is the legal estate? With the tenant for life.

e) Definition of 'settlement' now in SLA s1 – emphasis on succession.

f) Creation of a strict settlement under the SLA 1925, ss4 and 5. Need for two documents – a vesting deed and a trust instrument.

g) The tenant for life and his powers:

    i) Definition of tenant for life: ss19 and 20 SLA 1925.

    ii) Definition of trustees of settlement: s30 SLA 1925.

    iii) Legal estate is vested in the tenant for life.

    iv) Statutory powers of tenant for life:

- power of sale – s38(1) SLA 1925;

- power of exchange;

- power to lease – ss41–48 SLA 1925;

- power to accept surrenders of leases;

- power to take leases of other lands;

- power to grant options;

- power to mortgage or charge – s71 SLA 1925;

- power to effect improvements – s84 and Sch 3 SLA 1925;

- power to sell timber ripe for cutting (and 'waste') – s66 SLA 1925;

- power to sell heirlooms;

- any transaction for benefit of settled land: s64 SLA 1925.

    v) Purported limitations on tenant for life's powers: s106 SLA 1925.

    vi) Court's jurisdiction under s64 SLA 1925: see *Hambro and Others v Duke of Marlborough and Others* [1994] 3 All ER 332.

    vii) Non-assignability of powers – remain in tenant for life, but note s24 SLA 1925.

    viii) Exercise of powers of disposition to the tenant for life.

    ix) Effect of failure to use correct machinery to create a strict settlement: see (h), below.

    x) Faulty conveyances: ss18(1) and 110 SLA 1925 – compare *Weston v Henshaw* [1950] Ch 510 and *Re Morgan's Lease* [1972] Ch 1.

h) Failure to use correct machinery to create a strict settlement. Section 13 SLA 1925 – paralysing section. Megarry and Wade: 'The policy of the Act is ... to make it impossible to deal with the land in any case where a vesting instrument ought to exist but does not.'

Where a tenant for life has become entitled to have a vesting deed/instrument executed no disposition of a legal estate can be made until a vesting instrument has been executed. Any purported disposition of the land inter vivos operates only as a contract to carry out the transaction after the necessary vesting instrument has been executed. Exceptions – where a sale may be effected without a vesting instrument:

i) Personal representatives in course of administration of estate.

ii) Section 13 does not apply if disposition made to a purchaser of the legal estate without notice of tenant for life entitled to vesting deed. After 1925 must register as land charge Class C(iv) – void if not registered (s4 LCA 1972).

iii) If settlement at an end before vesting deed made then no settlement still in existence: *Re Alefounders' Will Trusts* [1927] 1 Ch 360. Megarry and Wade: 'When the land ceases to be settled, the fetters of s13 fall away.'

iv) Where s1 of the Law of Property (Amendment) Act 1926 applies. This enables owners of land subject to family charges to sell land as if it was not settled with indemnity given by vendor. But purchaser is still subject to such charges with only the protection of this personal indemnity by vendor.

Note: it was the trustees of the settlement who had to execute the vesting deed – the settlor could not rectify his own mistake by executing the vesting deed himself: s9(2) SLA 1925. Megarry and Wade: 'The section … does not prevent the tenant for life from disposing of his equitable interest (eg his beneficial life interest) or exercising any equitable powers given to him by the trust instrument.'

i) Determination of a settlement – need for a deed of discharge?

j) Functions of Settled Land Act trustees.

k) Overreaching provisions under the Settled Land Act

s72 SLA 1925

The aim of overreaching is to allow land held subject to a settlement/trust to be sold to a purchaser free from the trust and beneficial interests even though he has notice of the trust.

On sale the interests of the beneficiaries transfer from the land to the purchase monies (ie they are overreached) and they have corresponding interests in the purchase monies.

'Family interests' are overreached.

'Commercial interests' are not.

Doctrine of conversion applied to trusts for sale.

The effect of overreaching may be demonstrated in the diagram below.

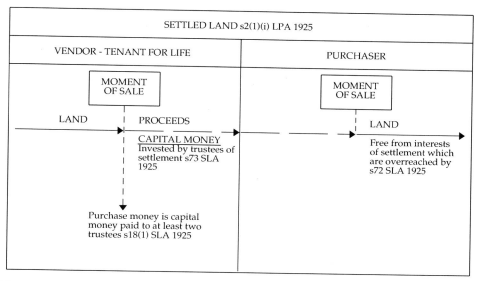

l) No new strict settlement can, as a general rule, be created after the coming into force on 1 January 1997 of the Trusts of Land and Appointment of Trustees Act 1996. However, pre-Act settlements and resettlements of settlements in existence at that date are still governed by the Settled Land Act regime.

Trusts of Land and Appointment of Trustees Act 1996

a) A new concept, the trust of land, is created.

b) Generally speaking no new strict settlement can be created under the Settled Land Act.

c) All existing trusts for sale are automatically trusts of land.

d) It is still possible to create an express trust for sale albeit as one type of the new trust of land.

e) In relation to trusts created on or after 1 January 1997, it is provided that where there would have been a trust for sale imposed by statute there is now a trust of land.

f) The doctrine of conversion is abolished.

g) Trustees are no longer under a duty to sell land. Rather they have a power to sell and a power to retain the land.

h) Additional rights for beneficiaries are created.

i) Wider powers for the court are provided.

j) Part II applies to trusts of personalty as well as those of land.

4.3 Key cases and statutes

- *Abbey National plc v Moss & Others* [1994] 1 FLR 307
  Trust for sale, secondary purpose still subsisting – no sale ordered under s30 LPA 1925

- *Citro (A Bankrupt), Re* [1991] Ch 142
  Trust for sale of matrimonial home – spouse with beneficial interest adjudicated bankrupt – interest of creditors prevailed over the interest of the other spouse beneficial interest holder and the children

- *Dent v Dent* [1996] 1 WLR 683
  Informal occupational arrangement effected by members of the same family gave rise to an irrevocable personal licence

- *Morgan's Lease, Re* [1972] Ch 1
  Protection of s110 SLA 1925 applied to a purchaser who was in fact dealing with a tenant for life even though he did not know it

- *Mortgage Corporation v Shaire and Others* [2001] Ch 743
  TOLATA 1996 was drafted with the aim of relaxing the old law so as to enable the court to have a greater discretion which could be exercised in favour of families and against banks and other chargees

- *TSB Bank plc v Marshall* [1998] 39 EG 208
  Case law developed under s30 LPA 1925 still relevant to ss14 and 15 TOLATA 1996 – the successor provisions – but note *Mortgage Corporation v Shaire* (above)

- *Weston v Henshaw* [1950] Ch 510
  Protection of s110 SLA 1925 only applied to a purchaser dealing with a person whom he knew to be a tenant for life

- Settled Land Act 1925, ss1, 13, 18(1), 19, 20, 30, 38(1), 106 and 110

- Trusts of Land and Appointment of Trustees Act 1996

4.4 Trusts of Land and Appointment of Trustees Act 1996

a) The Act came into force on 1 January 1997.

b) It effects some of the most important reforms to real property law since the 1925 legislation.

Background

a) Effectiveness of a strict settlement in keeping land within a family was broken by the Settled Land Acts 1882 and 1925 which, as a general rule, vest the legal estate to the settled land in the tenant for life, give the tenant for life the power to sell land and stipulate that this power cannot be expressly excluded by a trust instrument, ie you could not prevent a tenant for life possessed of the legal estate from selling it if he wanted to.

b) Strict settlements still arose – usually unintentionally, eg where a will was drawn up without professional advice which left a house to the testator's wife for her life and then to the testator's children absolutely.

c) Under a trust for sale, the beneficiaries were deemed to have an interest in the proceeds of sale into which the estate was to be converted rather than in the property itself. This was the position before the land had been sold.

d) There were significant differences between the strict settlement and the trust for sale as to how the legal estate was held and who had powers of management.

e) A primary catalyst for the Act was the 1989 Law Commission Report 'Transfer of Land: Trusts of Land' (Law Com No 181). The Law Commission concluded that there was a need for 'an entirely new system' in order to clarify and rationalise the law and that any new system should be based upon a new type of trust.

Trust of land

a) There is a new unitary system of holding land on trust.

b) 'Trust of land' is widely defined and includes any trust of property which consists of or includes land (s1(1)(a)).

c) The new regime applies as follows:

   i)   to all trusts of land whether the trust is created expressly or implied by statute;

   ii) to both concurrent and successive interests in land; and

   iii) whenever equitable interests in land arise by way of resulting or constructive trusts.

d) No new strict settlement can be created after the Act came into force.

e) The scheme of the Act applies to nearly all existing trusts and nearly all new trusts which include land. The exceptions are pre-Act strict settlements and land to which the Universities and College Estates Act 1925 applies.

Abolition of doctrine of conversion

a) Doctrine abolished for all trusts for sale (s3).

b) However, the overreaching of the equitable interests of beneficiaries on a sale of land remains unchanged (ie the conveyancing advantage is not lost).

c) There is one exception to the abolition of the doctrine – a trust created by will where the testator died before the commencement of the Act (s3(2)).

Power of sale and power to postpone sale

a) Trustees of land are to hold the legal estate in land on trust with a power to sell and a power to retain the land (s4).

b) A trust of land places no duty to sell the land on the trustees.

c) There is implied into every trust of land a power for the trustees to postpone sale and they are not to be liable even if they postpone selling for an indefinite period.

d) Power to postpone sale prevails over any wording in the trust instrument to the contrary.

General power of trustees

a) Trustees of land can convey land to beneficiaries (provided they are of full age, capacity and absolutely entitled to the land) even if such a conveyance has not been requested by the beneficiaries (s6(2)).

b) Trustees of land have a specific power to purchase a legal estate in any land in England and Wales (s6(3)). This power can be used for purposes of investment, to house the beneficiary or for any other reason.

c) Section 6 puts trustees of land in much the same position as an absolute owner.

d) Trustees of land have a specific power to partition trust land where the beneficiaries are of full age, capacity and absolutely entitled to the land (s7). They must obtain the consent of each beneficiary before exercising this power.

e) Only trustees can give a valid receipt for purchase money.

f) Powers conferred by ss6 and 7 can be excluded or restricted (see s8).

Power of delegation

a) Trustees of land can delegate any of their functions relating to the land to any beneficiaries of full age, capacity and entitled in possession to the land (s9).

b) Such a delegation may be for any period or indefinite (s9(5)).

c) Where trustees do so delegate they are not liable for any consequent acts or defaults by the beneficiaries unless they failed to exercise reasonable care in making the delegation.

d) Section 9 supersedes s29 LPA 1925.

e) A delegation can only be made to a beneficiary who is entitled in possession to the land.

Consents and consultation

a) Where a trust instrument requires the consent of two or more persons to the exercise by the trustee of any function relating to the land, the consent of any two such persons will suffice in favour of a purchaser (s10).

b) Section 10 is modelled to some extent on s26 LPA 1925 which is repealed by it.

c) Section 10 does not apply to charitable, ecclesiastical or public trusts – in such cases all consents must be obtained.

d) Trustees of land are required to consult with beneficiaries of full age and beneficially entitled to an interest in possession in the land before exercising any of their powers (s11). Obligation applies whether the interests are concurrent or successive.

e) Duty to consult can be expressly excluded by the trust instrument.

f) Requirement is only to consult 'so far as practicable' and only to act in accordance with the beneficiaries' wishes 'so far as consistent with the general interest of the trust'.

g) Duty to consult does not apply in respect of the power of trustees to convey land to beneficiaries absolutely entitled to the land irrespective of whether they want it (s6(2)).

Beneficiaries and occupation

a) Section 12 gives a right of occupation to certain beneficiaries.

b) Beneficiary entitled to an interest in possession in land has a right to occupy the property subject to a trust of land where:

   i) the purpose of the trust includes making the land available for the beneficiary's occupation (s12(1)(a)); or

   ii) the land is held by the trustees so as to be so available (s12(1)(b)).

c) Section 13 details the exclusions and restrictions which operate to restrict the right to occupation given by s12.

d) Where there is more than one beneficiary eligible to occupy the land the trustees have a discretionary power to exclude or restrict the right of occupation of any one or more, but not of all, of them.

e) The matters which the trustees are to have regard to in exercising this discretion are set out in s13(4).

f) Trustees may impose 'reasonable conditions' on any beneficiaries occupying land under s12 (s13(3)).

g) The aim of s13 is to help in co-ownership trusts of residential properties where there are frequently disputes as to occupation.

Powers of the court

a) A trustee or any person with an interest in property subject to a trust of land can apply to the court for an order under s14.

b) On such an application the court can make any order it thinks fit:

   i) relating to the exercise by the trustees of any of their powers (s14(2)(a)); or

   ii) declaring the nature or extent of any person's beneficial interest in the property subject to the trust (s14(2)(b)).

c) Under s14 the court can make orders for sale, preventing a sale, overriding a consent requirement, etc.

d) Section 15(1) contains a statement of factors which the court is to have regard to in making an order under s14. These factors include:

   i) the settlor's intention;

   ii) the purposes for which the property subject to the trust is held;

   iii) the welfare of any minor who occupies or might reasonably be expected to occupy the trust land; and

   iv) the interests of secured creditors.

e) There is no order of priority as to the matters listed.

f) Section 30 LPA 1925 is replaced by ss14 and 15.

g) Is the case law developed under s30 LPA 1925 still relevant today?

   i) Law Commission view;

   ii) *TSB Bank plc* v *Marshall* [1998] 39 EG 208;

   iii) *Mortgage Corporation* v *Shaire & Others* [2001] Ch 743.

Protection of purchasers

a) Section 16 deals with the protection of purchasers of unregistered land which is or has been held on trust. It absolves such a purchaser from the need to enquire whether there has been a breach of trust in various circumstances.

b) Further, it is provided that where trustees convey land to persons they believe to be beneficiaries of full age and capacity absolutely entitled to the land under trust, they are to execute a deed declaring that they are discharged from the trust in relation to the land (s16(4)).

Part II – appointment and retirement of trustees

a) Applies to all trusts (whether of land or personalty) whenever created.

b) Aims to give beneficiaries greater powers over the appointment of trustees.

c) Beneficiaries can now give trustees a written direction to retire from the trust or to appoint a particular person as a trustee (s19). This right, which is a new one, can be exercised at any time.

d) Decision in *Re Brockbank* [1948] Ch 206 is reversed.

e) There are a number of qualifying conditions to this right. It is only available if:

   i)   there is no person who is given power to appoint trustees in the trust instrument;

   ii) the beneficiaries are of full age and capacity; and

   iii) it has not been expressly excluded by the trust instrument.

f) Part II is inapplicable to discretionary trusts or where there are infant beneficiaries.

g) Section 19 takes effect subject to the restrictions imposed by the Trustee Act 1925 on the number of trustees (s19(5)).

Conclusion

a) The Act is an amending rather than a consolidating statute.

b) It removes the complication of the pre-Act system of two distinct ways of holding land in trust.

c) It is retrospective except as regards pre-Act strict settlements.

d) Aims to make the law more comprehensible to lay people.

4.5 Questions and suggested solutions

Analysis of questions

Prior to the coming into force of the Trusts of Land and Appointment of Trustees Act (TOLATA) 1996 a favourite question in this area was one which invited candidates to compare and contrast the strict settlement with the trust for sale. However, with the coming into force of the 1996 Act on 1 January 1997 such questions are now only likely to appear, if at all, in a legal history paper. Given the significance of the Act and the wide ranging reforms it introduced students should be prepared for the possibility of an essay question which invites them to (i) outline the background to the 1996 legislation; and (ii) identify and evaluate its key provisions. Accordingly, rather than reproduce several pre-1996 Act questions one such question is included as a backdrop to the 1996 Act and thereafter, given the aforementioned observation about the 1996 Act, an appropriate essay question is included below. A problem question is also included to demonstrate the retrospective effect of TOLATA 1996. In respect of the suggested solution to the latter question, references to s70(1)(g) LRA 1925 must now be read in light of the coming into force of the Land Registration Act 2002.

QUESTION ONE

'There is no justification today for retaining two methods of creating settlements of land.'

Discuss. If a single method is to be adopted, what form should it take?

University of London LLB Examination
(for External Students) Land Law June 1991 Q1

General Comment

Although this was not a difficult question for a reasonably well-prepared student, it was probably one which most students would have been better advised not to attempt. Essay questions are deceptively difficult to answer well in examination conditions and it is all too easy to spend a lot of time and words in saying very little of real significance. Certainly anyone who had not read the Law Commission paper on Trusts of Land should have chosen another question.

Skeleton Solution

What was the historical justification for two systems? – main characteristics of the SLA settlement – what are the main problems of the SLA? – was the trust for sale always appropriate? – conclusion: suggest single system based on the trust for sale but with some modifications.

Suggested Solution

The reason for the pre 1997 dual system of creating settlements of land was historical. The original idea behind a settlement under the SLA 1925 (and its predecessors) was to retain land in the family, in circumstances where the life tenant would be residing on the property and would require wide powers of management in order to deal with the settled land to the best advantage of all interested persons. The land was likely to be a large estate. By contrast, the idea behind the trust for sale was to create a mechanism for holding land as an investment pending a sale of the land. Considerable differences remained between the two systems but it was by no means clear whether the existence of these differences justified the retention of both systems prior to the coming into force of the Trusts of Land and Appointment of Trustees Act 1996.

The legal estate under an SLA settlement is held by the tenant for life and he will make all the management decisions concerning the property, including the decision whether or not to sell. It is impossible by s106 SLA to interfere with his exercise of these powers in any way. Under a trust for sale the legal estate was held by the trustees and they would make all the management decisions, although they might delegate the powers of leasing and management to the beneficiary. The pre-1996 Act legislation still gave priority to the SLA so that if no proper advice was taken, it was possible to have an SLA settlement by mistake – this was because if successive interests in land were created, there would be a settlement under the SLA unless an 'immediate binding trust for sale' was created, so that a home-made will which left a house to the widow for life and then to the children would have created an SLA settlement with its attendant expense and complexity. It seemed that a grant of a right of residence for life would also have created an SLA settlement: see *Bannister* v *Bannister* [1948] 2 All ER 133; *Binions* v *Evans* [1972] Ch 359.

The Law Commission identified several problems with the working of the SLA in their report on Trusts of Land. The system is complicated and expensive to administer with the requirement for two documents, a vesting deed and a trust instrument, and the need to take out a special grant of probate when the tenant for life dies. Further problems arise with settlements created accidentally under the SLA as these are bound to be improperly created without the required two documents. Conveyancing difficulties arose if it was not clear whether the settlement was under the SLA or a trust for sale as it was unclear whether the tenant for life or trustees should have executed the relevant documents. Further, there may well be a conflict of interest between the personal wishes of the tenant for life and the interests of the other beneficiaries and the latter are in a very weak position with no real right to object to the exercise of his powers by the tenant for life.

The conclusion of the Law Commission was that the strict settlement under the SLA 1925 be abolished. The recommendation was made on the basis that there was no longer sufficient justification in retaining two parallel systems. The historical reasons for two systems no longer applied and research undertaken by the Commission showed that hardly any new settlements were created under the SLA in any event. The mechanism was cumbersome and expensive and its only advantage was that in some cases it was more appropriate for the tenant for life than the trustees to manage the settled property. The Commission suggested granting an enhanced power of delegation to trustees instead. The old reason for a settlement under the SLA was to keep land in the family and this was easier to achieve pre the 1996 Act with a trust for sale by requiring consents to be obtained before sale.

However the Commission did not simply recommend that the trust for sale became the single possible system for creating trusts of land. The trust for sale was used in settlements with successive interests and when concurrent interests existed. In the latter case the trust for sale was an artificial concept. The Law Commission suggested that the type of co-ownership envisaged in 1925 would have been the situation of land being left to children in a will, when a sale would have resulted. In modern cases of co-ownership the land is purchased for occupation primarily rather than as an investment. The doctrine of conversion which applied to trusts for sale was incomprehensible to non-lawyers.

The recommendation was that the strict settlement and trust for sale should both be replaced by a new single system which would apply to all trusts of land, including bare trusts and concurrent interests. The land would be held by trustees with a power to retain and a power to sell. The doctrine of conversion would not apply. The powers of the trustees would be based on those of the absolute owner. The advantages of the new single system would be that it would remove the complexities inherent in a dual system and many conveyancing difficulties would disappear. In most cases it is more appropriate for the trustees to exercise the powers of management, but there would be improved delegation powers if it was wished that the life tenant should manage the property. The new system would be more in accord with the expectations and understanding of the lay person as it applied to co-ownership.

In conclusion, it was difficult to find any real justification for retaining the two systems of settling land and the scarcity of new SLA settlements in practice seemed to confirm this view. The historical reasons for the two systems no longer applied. Therefore in the interests of simplicity a single system was preferable. If a single system was to be adopted, the trust for sale was certainly the more appropriate choice than the strict settlement, which was really of little practical relevance today, but there were significant problems with the trust for sale itself. Therefore a new system based on the trust for sale with certain changes was suggested. The emphasis on the duty to sell and the doctrine of conversion would be abolished and the trustees given power both to retain the land and sell it. This system, as put forward by the Law Commission, would be closer to the layman's understanding of the position.

Note: this solution has been revised to take account of the coming into force of the Trusts of Land and Appointment of Trustees Act 1996.

QUESTION TWO

'The Trusts of Land and Appointment of Trustees Act 1996 has at last placed the law relating to settlements and trusts for sale of land on a rational and straightforward basis.'

Discuss.

University of London LLB Examination
(for External Students) Land Law June 1997 Q1

General Comment

A very typical essay question on the Act. A good answer would have succinctly summarised the shortcomings of the pre-Act law and outlined and evaluated the key provisions of the new legislation. Given the remit of the question answers should have focussed on Part I of the Act.

Skeleton Solution

Pre-1997 methods of holding land in trust – strict settlement and trust for sale – shortcomings of pre-Act law – Law Commission Report – scope of the Act – main provisions of the Act: the new trust of land; no new strict settlements after 1996; trusts for sale automatically trusts of land; doctrine of conversion abolished; trustees of land

have a power to sell and a power to retain land; and wider powers for the court –
evaluation.

Suggested Solution

The Trusts of Land and Appointment of Trustees Act 1996 received the Royal Assent on
24 July 1996 and came into force on 1 January 1997. It effects some of the most important
reforms to real property law since the 1925 legislation and it forms part of a clear
programme to review and revise the trust system which has remained substantially
unaltered since the 1925 legislation.

Prior to 1 January 1997, there were two distinct ways of holding land in trust either by
a strict settlement (related to successive interests in land) or a trust for sale (related
principally to concurrent interests in land although it could also relate to successive
interests as well). Each had a different rationale. The strict settlement was traditionally
used to keep ownership of land within a given family while under a trust for sale land
was held as an investment asset. The effectiveness of a strict settlement in keeping land
within a family was broken by the Settled Land Acts 1882 and 1925 which as a general
rule vest the legal estate to settled land in the tenant for life (s16(1) SLA 1925); give the
tenant for life the power to sell the land (ss38 and 39 SLA 1925) and stipulate that this
and other powers of the tenant for life cannot be expressly excluded by a trust
instrument: s106 SLA 1925. In view of these provisions, you would not have created a
strict settlement if your aim was to keep land within the family because you could not
prevent a tenant for life possessed of the legal estate from selling it if he wanted to.
However, strict settlements still arose usually unintentionally, eg where a will was
drawn up without professional advice which left a house to a testator's wife for life
and then to the testator's children absolutely. In contrast, a trust for sale was used to
convert property into cash which in turn could easily be distributed amongst the
beneficiaries. Under a trust for sale, the beneficiaries were deemed to have an interest
in the proceeds of sale into which the estate was to be converted rather than in the
property itself (the doctrine of conversion). This was the position even before the land
had been sold. Accordingly, in the case of a trust for sale land was held as an investment
asset rather than for long-term occupation (this explained why the trustees were under
a duty to sell).

In addition to the fact that the strict settlement and the trust for sale each had a different
rationale, there were also significant differences between the two systems as to how the
legal estate was held and who had powers of management. For example, in the case of
a strict settlement the legal estate was usually vested in the tenant for life (with the
settlement trustees in a more peripheral role) whereas in the case of a trust for sale the
legal estate was vested in the trustees.

A primary catalyst for the new legislation was the 1989 Law Commission Report
'Transfer of Land: Trusts of Land' (Law Com No 181). The Law Commission concluded
that there was a need for 'an entirely new system' in order to clarify and rationalise
the law and that any new system should be based upon a new type of trust. They

identified a number of weaknesses with the pre-Act law, four of which are particularly noteworthy. First, the existence of a dual system gave rise to a number of difficulties. Secondly, the settled land regime was unnecessarily complicated. Thirdly, it was possible to create a strict settlement unintentionally, eg a will drawn up without professional advice in the terms set out above. Fourthly, the trust for sale mechanism was not appropriate to the conditions of modern home ownership. In particular the duty to sell was artificial and inconsistent with the wishes of the majority of co-owners.

The Act is in three parts. Part I deals with Trusts of Land and derives substantially from the Law Commission Report. Some of the key provisions of Part I of the Act are outlined in the ensuing paragraphs.

A new concept, the trust of land, is created. The 'Trust of Land' is defined widely and includes any trust of property which consists of or includes land: s1(1). The new regime applies as follows: (i) to all trusts of land whether the trust is created expressly or implied by statute; (ii) to both concurrent and successive interests in land; and (iii) whenever equitable interests in land arise by way of resulting or constructive trusts. No new strict settlement can be created after 31 December 1996: s2(1). However, pre-Act settlements and resettlements of settlements in existence at the latter date are still governed by the SLA regime. In the case of such resettlements, the conclusion that they are to continue to be subject to the SLA regime can be avoided by an express statement in the creating instrument to the effect that this result is not intended (ie they can be converted to trusts of land). All trusts for sale in existence prior to 1 January 1997 are automatically converted into trusts of land. Further, in relation to trusts created on or after 1 January 1997, it is provided that where before that date a trust for sale would have been imposed by statute there is now a trust of land.

The effect of the doctrine of conversion was that where land was held on a trust for sale the interests of the beneficiaries were deemed to be in the proceeds of sale of the land even before it had been sold. Historically the aim of the doctrine was to ease conveyancing – since the beneficiaries had an interest in the proceeds of sale rather than in the land itself, a purchaser of the land took free of such beneficial interests. The doctrine is abolished by s3. However, the overreaching of the equitable interests of beneficiaries on a sale of land remains unchanged (ie the conveyancing advantage is not lost).

Before the Act, trustees for sale were under a duty to sell land. Further, such trustees had an implied power to postpone sale – although it was possible to expressly exclude the power to postpone sale. This regime was consistent with land being held as an investment asset rather than for long-term occupation. Under the Act, trustees of land hold the legal estate in land on trust with a power to sell and a power to retain the land (s4). Accordingly, the trust of land places no duty to sell the land on the trustees. The Act implies into every trust of land a power for the trustees to postpone sale, and they are not liable even if they postpone selling for an indefinite period.

Section 30 LPA 1925 has been replaced by ss14 and 15 of the 1996 Act. A trustee or any person with an interest in property subject to a trust of land can apply to the court for an order under s14. On such an application, the court can make any order it thinks fit: (i) relating to the exercise by the trustees of any of their powers (s14(2)(a)); or (ii) declaring the nature or extent of any person's beneficial interest in the property subject to the trust: s14(2)(b). Under s14 the court can make orders for sale, preventing sale, etc. In two respects, the powers of the court under s14 are wider than those it enjoyed under s30 LPA 1925. First, it can declare the nature or extent of a person's interest in the property subject to the trust. Second, the wording of s14(2)(a) is sufficiently wide to allow it to sanction a transaction which would otherwise be a breach of trust.

The Act is a modernising one. It unquestionably improves and rationalises the law as to the holding of land in trust. One of its main attributes is that it removes the complications associated with the old system of two distinct ways of holding land in trust. Not only is it advantageous that no new strict settlement can be created after 31 December 1996 (not least because of the complexities of the SLA regime) but the clear expectation is that pre-Act strict settlements will be phased out (how long this will take will depend upon how frequently on a re-settlement of a pre-Act strict settlement advantage is taken of the facility to convert to a trust of land). The new system now in place has many similarities to the trust for sale. However, the Act has removed those aspects of the trust for sale which were inappropriate to the conditions of modern home ownership, eg doctrine of conversion. It was clearly entirely artificial to have maintained under the old law that equitable joint tenants or equitable tenants in common had no interest in a house or flat held on trust for sale but had only an interest in the sale proceeds when no sale was actually contemplated.

Like the Law of Property (Miscellaneous Provisions) Act 1994 the 1996 Act aims to make the law more comprehensible to laypeople. However, time alone will tell whether that goal will be achieved.

QUESTION THREE

In 1995, Sam and Jim, who were brothers, bought a large house, 'The Gables', as a home for their families. The purchase price was paid by Sam and Jim from their savings and the house was registered in their joint names. At the time of the purchase they wrote to Arnold, their elderly father, inviting him to live with them at 'The Gables'. Arnold accepted the invitation, sold his flat and moved to 'The Gables'. The following year he spent part of the proceeds of the sale of his flat on having a bathroom built next to his bedroom in 'The Gables'. In 1998, while Arnold was away on a world cruise, the brothers mortgaged the house to Helpful Mortgages. Recently the brothers have defaulted on their mortgage repayments and Helpful seeks possession of the house with a view to selling it.

Advise Arnold. How, if at all, would your advice differ if Arnold had contributed to the purchase price of the house?

University of London LLB Examination
(for External Students) Land Law June 2001 Q1

General Comment

A question that requires an understanding of material drawn from various parts of the syllabus: implied trusts of land; proprietary estoppel; a good grasp of s70(1)(g) Land Registration Act (LRA) 1925. A case that must be mentioned is *Birmingham Midshires Mortgage Services Ltd* v *Sabherwal*, where the Court of Appeal decided that an equitable interest arising under proprietary estoppel can be overreached. Candidates should also notice that when the house was purchased in 1995 it became subject to a statutory trust for sale, but that as a result of the retrospective effect of the Trusts of Land and Appointment of Trustees Act (TOLATA) 1996 on ss34 and 36 Law of Property Act (LPA) 1925 the trust for sale was converted into a trust of land without any duty of sale.

Skeleton Solution

Implied trust for sale: ss34 and 36 LPA 1925; retrospective effect of TOLATA 1996; trust of land − Arnold's rights: proprietary estoppel; requirements; detrimental conduct by Arnold; is his right binding on the mortgagees?; s70(1)(g) LRA 1925 rights; actual occupation; time of occupation − can Arnold's rights under s70(1)(g) LRA 1925 be overreached?: direct contribution; resulting trust; beneficial interest overreached.

Suggested Solution

When Sam and Jim purchased 'The Gables' in 1995 the house was registered in their joint names, they having both contributed to the purchase price. As a result they are clearly co-owners of the property, and in 1995 this had to take effect behind either an express or statutory trust for sale. There is no evidence of an express trust for sale and, accordingly, a statutory trust for sale would have been created either under ss34 or 35 Law of Property Act (LPA) 1925, depending on whether they were joint tenants or tenants in common. In deciding what they were, the conveyance has to be examined to see if it describes them as joint tenants or tenants in common, but it appears to be silent on this point. The title was registered in their joint names but that was obligatory, since a legal tenancy in common was abolished by s1(6) LPA 1925 and the legal estate would have to be registered in that manner, whether they were joint tenants or tenants in common in equity. The fact of registration in their joint names is therefore no guide as to the nature of their equitable beneficial interests. Equity presumes a tenancy in common if they put up the purchase monies in unequal amounts, but again we are supplied with no information on that point.

We do not know whether their equitable interests under the trust for sale were those of joint tenants or tenants in common. We cannot therefore know under which section a statutory trust for sale was implied. Section 34 LPA 1925 was applicable if they were tenants in common; s36 LPA 1925 if they were joint tenants. However, whichever was applicable, the effect of either section would have been to vest the legal estate in both of them as joint tenants to hold it on a trust for sale as defined by s205(1)(xxix) LPA 1925 for both of them either as joint tenants or tenants in common in equity.

That would have been the position in 1995, but the Trusts of Land and Appointment of Trustees Act 1996, which took effect on 1 January 1997, amended the sections to produce, instead of a trust for sale, a trust of land without a duty to sell. The amendments were made to take effect retrospectively: s5 and Sch 2. Hence, the 1995 trust for sale was retrospectively converted into a trust of land.

The crucial point in the question relates to Arnold, whom we are asked to advise. Did he acquire rights in the house, and if so, did Helpful Mortgages take subject to those rights when they granted a mortgage to Sam and Jim? If they did so, then they cannot obtain a possession order against Arnold.

The first step is to ascertain whether Arnold obtained any rights in the house and there are two stages in this enquiry. The two brothers invited him to come and live in the house, presumably indefinitely, and he responded by selling his flat and moving into 'The Gables'. This prompts an examination of the doctrine of proprietary estoppel.

The doctrine may be summarised as follows: where an owner of land (O) allows another (E) to spend money on that land, or otherwise act to his detriment under an expectation created or encouraged, or acquiesced in by O, that he (E) will be allowed to remain on the land or later acquire an interest in it, then equity will restrain O from defeating that expectation and denying E's right to remain on the land or acquire an interest in it.

In *Willmott* v *Barber* (1880) 15 Ch D 96 the requirements necessary for the establishment of estoppel were expressed by Fry J in the form of five probandi, but these are no longer strictly applied, the courts having adopted a more flexible approach: *Electrolux Ltd* v *Electrix Ltd* (1953) 71 RPC 23. In that case Evershed MR observed:

> 'I think it is clear that it is not essential to find all the five tests set out by Fry J literally applicable and satisfied in every particular case.

> The real test, I think, must be whether upon the facts of the particular case, the situation has become such that it would be dishonest or unconscionable of the person having the right sought to be enforced, to continue to seek to enforce it.'

Goff LJ expressed agreement and went on to say 'the test is whether, in the circumstances, it has become unconscionable for the plaintiff to rely on his legal right'.

In *Taylor Fashions Ltd* v *Liverpool Victoria Trustees Co Ltd* [1982] QB 133 Oliver J, after an extensive review of the authorities, adopted the same approach.

The basis of a claim under the doctrine of proprietary estoppel must now be analysed. What must a claimant establish? The following two requirements can be deduced from the authorities.

a) In relation to claims in respect of land, there must be some conduct by the owner, either taking the form of a positive representation or acquiescence, which induces the claimant to believe that he has rights in the land or will acquire rights in it at some time in the future. *Inwards* v *Baker* [1965] 2 QB 29 was an illustrative case. A father owned land and when told by his son that he (the son) was contemplating purchasing land on which to erect a bungalow, suggested that the son should build the bungalow on his (the father's) land instead. The son accepted that suggestion and did so. Several points should be noted: there was no contract between the parties; it was an informal family arrangement consisting of the father's promise and the son's acceptance. Nor did the father convey any land to his son. The son built the bungalow on his father's land, and in law the ownership of it vested in the landowner father. The son clearly acted to his detriment in spending money on the construction of the bungalow.

Many years before the events occurred, the father had made a will leaving the land to a third party. The father died in 1951. The third party could have ordered the son to leave but she did not do so. When, however, she died, her trustees did. The son claimed a licence by estoppel and the Court of Appeal agreed. The son was allowed to remain in the bungalow for the remainder of his life. In his judgment Lord Denning MR said:

> 'If the owner of land requests another, or indeed allows another, to expend money on the land under an expectation created or encouraged by the landowner that he will be able to remain there, that raises an equity in the licensee such as to entitle him to stay.'

To apply this requirement to the facts of the instant case, we must ask if the landowners Sam and Jim have conducted themselves by making representations which induced Arnold to believe he was acquiring rights on the land. Whether they have done so is a matter of fact. Of itself inviting Arnold to come and live with them would not be enough. If, however, it was understood by all of the parties that this would involve Arnold in selling his flat, a court might conclude that by implication his sons were offering him the right to live in 'The Gables' for life. In the absence of more evidence, the matter cannot be taken any further and for the purposes of the question we will proceed on the basis that this requirement has been satisfied.

b) The claimant, relying on the representation or promise must have acted to his detriment. The detriment need not involve the expenditure of money. In *Greasley* v *Cooke* [1980] 3 All ER 710 the claimant (in 1938) went to work in the household of a widower, his three sons and a handicapped daughter as a maidservant. In 1946 she commenced living with one of the sons, K, as man and wife. From 1948 onwards she ceased to be paid any wages, but she nevertheless continued to look after the household. From time to time she had been given assurances by K, although expressed in vague terms, that she could live in the house as long as she wished. K died in 1975. The house then vested in one of the other sons and the daughters of another son, and they claimed possession of the house. In resisting the possession claim, the claimant contended that she had a licence by estoppel and she succeeded. The Court of Appeal held that:

i) the assurances she had been given were sufficient to found a claim in proprietary estoppel; and

ii) that gave rise to a rebuttable presumption that the claimant acted as she did on reliance of those assurances; the burden of proof of rebutting that presumption passed to those who contended that there was no proprietary estoppel; and

iii) although the claimant must establish detriment in reliance on the assurances that need not consist of the expenditure of money.

The Court of Appeal held she could stay in the house as long as she wished.

In *Brinnand* v *Ewens* (1987) The Times 4 June Nourse LJ summarised the requirements necessary to establish a claim under the doctrine:

i) the claimant must show that he had prejudiced himself or acted to his detriment; and

ii) he must have acted in the way he did because he believed he had an interest in the property or would acquire one at some future time; and

iii) the belief must have been induced by the landowner.

Whether the claimant has acted to his detriment is a question of fact which it is not always easy to decide. If a claimant gives up her flat and job to move into rent-free accommodation provided by her boyfriend, can she be said to be acting to her detriment? In *Coombes* v *Smith* [1986] 1 WLR 808 it was held that the claimant, on having a child, moving away from her husband, redecorating and not trying to provide otherwise for herself, did not show that she was acting to her detriment. Her actions were either due simply to a desire to live with the defendant or done as an occupier of the property.

Certainly we know that Arnold disposed of his flat, but his case clearly can be distinguished from *Coombes* v *Smith*. Balanced against the disposal of his flat must be the fact that he was acquiring rent-free accommodation for the rest of his life. It is difficult to predict whether Arnold has suffered a detriment sufficient to enable him to acquire an interest in 'The Gables' under the doctrine of proprietary estoppel. However, for the purposes of the question we will assume that he has.

His claim may be strengthened by spending some of the proceeds from the sale of his flat on having a bathroom built next to his bedroom. Here, he is making a positive contribution at his own expense to the value of the house with the full knowledge of his sons, who raised no objection. The fact that Arnold was not acting in that regard as a result of any representation made by his sons does not preclude a licence by proprietary estoppel arising in his favour. Such a licence can arise from the acquiescence of the landowner, as is illustrated by *Ives (E R) Investments Ltd* v *High* [1967] 2 QB 379. Lord Denning described how that came about in that case:

'The right arises out of the expense incurred by Mr High in building his garage with access only over the yard, and the Wrights standing by and acquiescing, knowing that he believed he had a right of way over the yard. By doing so the Wrights created in Mr High's mind a reasonable expectation that his access over the yard would not be disturbed. That gives rise to "an equity arising out of acquiescence".'

Thus it can be concluded with considerable confidence that the court would find that Arnold had acquired a right in the house founded on proprietary estoppel.

Would this right be binding on Helpful Mortgages? This leads on to the question as to whether it would be protected as an overriding interest under s70(1)(g) Land Registration Act (LRA) 1925. Is such a right one that is included in the word 'rights' in the paragraph, and was he in actual occupation at the relevant time? Only rights which are interests in land, as opposed to personal rights, come within para (g): *National Provincial Bank Ltd* v *Ainsworth* [1965] AC 1175. Does a licence arising from proprietary estoppel constitute an interest in land? In *Inwards* v *Baker* and *Ives (E R) Investments Ltd* v *High* (both unregistered land cases) the Court of Appeal confirmed that such licences conferred an equitable interest in land upon the licences which were capable of binding third parties.

Arnold's rights will only bind Helpful Mortgages as an overriding interest under para (g) if he was in actual occupation at the relevant time, and this point requires further examination. Firstly, the mortgage was created in 1998 while Arnold was away on a world cruise, and so he was not physically present at the time. Actual occupation is a matter of fact and not of law: *Williams & Glyn's Bank* v *Boland* [1981] AC 487. This is not always an easy issue to resolve and the decision in each case will depend on its particular facts. In *Lloyds Bank plc* v *Rosset* [1991] 1 AC 107 two members of the Court of Appeal held that Mrs Rosset was in actual occupation. The third member of the Court held that she was not. In *Chhokar* v *Chhokar* (1984) 14 Fam Law 269 a wife, who was in hospital at the relevant time, having a baby, claimed that she remained in actual occupation despite the fact that she was not physically present. She was claiming that her equitable interest under a trust for sale was binding on a purchaser of the house in which she had an interest under s70(1)(g) LRA 1925. The court held that she was in actual occupation: her furniture remained in the house and she intended to return. Arnold's absence was temporary; he would certainly have left his furniture behind and, most important, he intended to return. Although in these cases it is not always possible to predict how a court would rule, it appears probable that Arnold would be held not to have ceased being in actual occupation.

However, that occupation must subsist at the 'relevant time'. In *Abbey National Building Society* v *Cann* [1990] 2 WLR 832 the House of Lords made two important points about time as they related to s70(1)(g) LRA 1925. All overriding interests under s70(1) LRA 1925, if they are to bind a purchaser, must be in existence at the time the purchaser, which includes a mortgagee, is registered as the proprietor. This takes place sometime after completion (it should be within two months). It is only on such registration that the purchaser's title becomes effective. However, the Lords laid down a further requirement for the application of para (g), namely, that for it to be applicable the claimant must have been in actual occupation at the earlier date of completion.

It seems that both stages of the mortgage transaction occurred while Arnold was away, but as it is likely that a court would find that he was in actual occupation at the time of completion then his right to a claim under proprietary estoppel will fall within para (g).

Arnold wishes to resist Helpful Mortgages' claim to possession, and so far we are able to say that his rights in 'The Gables' bound the mortgagee when the mortgage was created for the reasons explained above. However, despite this there is nevertheless a major difficulty in his path. The mortgage monies were advanced to Sam and Jim as trustees of the trust of land, and this raises the issue of overreaching: s2 LPA 1925. It was established by *City of London Building Society* v *Flegg* [1988] AC 54 that a beneficial interest under a trust for sale could be overreached even though it was an overriding interest under s70(1)(g) LRA 1925. Sam and Jim hold the legal estate in 'The Gables' on trust to give effect to Arnold's rights under the doctrine of proprietary estoppel. Do the overreaching provisions apply to interests of that nature? If the overreaching provisions apply then Helpful Mortgages would have taken free of Arnold's rights. For overreaching to apply, the mortgagors' monies would have to be advanced to two trustees, and that is what happened here. Arnold could argue that the overreaching provisions were not intended to apply to an interest such as his and that such rights were exempt from those provisions. Unfortunately for Arnold, the Court of Appeal decided in *Birmingham Midshires Mortgage Services Ltd* v *Sabherwal* (2000) 80 P & CR 256 that interests arising from proprietary estoppel were not exempt from overreaching.

Thus Arnold's rights would have been overreached in 1998 when the mortgage was created despite s70(1)(g) LRA 1925, and he must be advised that the mortgagees are entitled to possession against him.

Would Arnold be advised differently if he had contributed to the purchase price of the house? Such a direct financial contribution would give rise, in equity, to a resulting trust in his favour. A resulting trust is based on the presumed intentions of the parties. It is a presumption that is rebuttable. It arises when one party, who is not on the title, makes a direct contribution to the purchase, which is what Arnold would have done here. There is nothing to suggest that the presumption has been rebutted. Even if there was no mention of Arnold in the conveyance, to comply with s53(1)(b) Law of Property Act (LPA) 1925 (declaration of trust must be manifested and proved by some writing) this would not matter as resulting trusts are exempt from those provisions.

Sam and Jim would hold on a trust of land as defined by s1 Trusts of Land and Appointment of Trustees Act (TOLATA) 1996 for themselves and Arnold as co-owner in equity either as joint tenants or tenants in common. We are not supplied with enough information to decide which Arnold's interest is. However, his beneficial interest would constitute an interest in land so as to come within s70(1)(g) LRA 1925: *Williams & Glyn's Bank* v *Boland*. We have seen that the question of occupation would not occasion him difficulty, but his equitable interest would be overreached when the mortgage was created: *City of London Building Society* v *Flegg*.

Finally, the mortgagees' rights must be briefly mentioned. They are entitled to possession 'before the ink is dry on the mortgage': *Four-Maids Ltd* v *Dudley Marshall (Properties) Ltd* [1957] Ch 317 unless they (the mortgagees) have expressly or impliedly excluded their right to do so: *Birmingham Citizens' Permanent Building Society* v *Caunt* [1962] Ch 883. Generally, mortgagees only seek possession with a view to sale because of default by the mortgagor, and in the case of domestic dwellings they must obtain a court order for possession. A measure of relief is afforded to defaulting mortgagors by the Administration of Justice Acts 1970 and 1973. This would not be available to Arnold, as he is not a mortgagor.

The provisions conferring a power of sale on the mortgagees are contained in ss101 and 103 LPA 1925. The power of sale must have arisen, eg has the legal date for redemption passed; has it become exercisable? It will have done so if Sam and Jim are at least two months in arrears with the mortgage interest.

Chapter 5

Co-ownership

5.1   Introduction

5.2   Key points

5.3   Key cases and statutes

5.4   Questions and suggested solutions

5.1 Introduction

This subject is one of the most popular with examination candidates. Co-ownership of land is present where two or more people hold an interest in land in possession concurrently (ie at the same time). Most married couples hold their homes in this way. A chronological problem question with annual changes to the facts is popular with examiners in this area. In relation to such questions it is essential to acurately diagnose at the outset of the answer how the equitable beneficial interest is held (joint tenancy or tenancy in common). If you do not make the correct diagnosis the answer starts to go wrong and may never give you the opportunity to rectify your mistake. The following diagram will help to overcome this problem of identification.

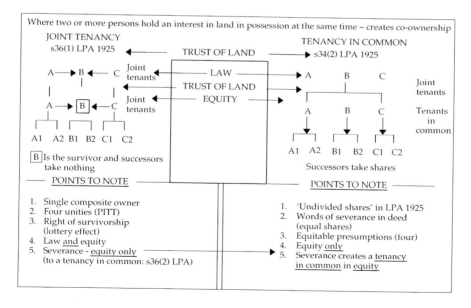

Effect on co-ownership of 1925 property legislation as amended by Trusts of Land and Appointment of Trustees Act 1996:

a) land held in trust (ss14 and 15 of the 1996 Act replacing s30 LPA 1925);

b) legal estate must be held as joint tenants;

c) equitable interests may be held as either joint tenants or tenants in common.

Distinguish several ownership – owner entitled in own right with no other person – and concurrent interest or co-ownership where owner and others have simultaneous interests in the land.

Cheshire: 'Land may be the subject of several, that is, separate ownership, or of co-ownership.'

5.2 Key points

a) *Joint tenancy* – where land is conveyed to two or more persons without *words of severance* indicating distinct shares, eg, 'in equal shares', 'share and share alike', 'equally'.

   i) Characteristics of joint tenancy:

      • survivorship – jus accrescendi – lottery effect;

      • the four unities:

         – unity of possession – all joint tenants;

         – unity of interest – same in quality;

         – unity of title – same document;

         – unity of time – vests at the same time.

   ii) Joint tenancy after 1925: s34(2) LPA 1925.

      No severance of legal joint tenancy to create a tenancy in common at law is possible: s36(2) and s1(6) LPA 1925.

b) *Tenancy in common* – no longer exists at law – s1(6) LPA 1925.

   i) Undivided shares.

   ii) Difference between tenancy in common and joint tenancy:

      • not subject to four unities – only unity of possession required;

      • no jus accrescendi – undivided shares pass to personal representatives for person entitled on will or intestacy in trust;

      • not necessarily in equal shares.

iii) Determination of tenancy in common

- Partition – each becomes sole owner of part.

- Sale – purchaser takes free of interests of co-owners – those interests continue in the purchase money.

- Acquisition by one tenant of the shares of his co-tenants.

iv) Presumptions in favour of tenancy in common

- Purchase money in unequal shares: *Bull* v *Bull* [1955] 1 QB 234 – s36(4) SLA 1925.

- Loan by co-mortgagees in equal or unequal shares.

- Partnership property: *Lake* v *Craddock* (1732) 3 P Wms 158; *Barton* v *Morris* [1985] 2 All ER 1032.

- Where grantees hold premises for their several individual business purposes: *Malayan Credit Ltd* v *Jack Chia-MPH Ltd* [1986] 1 All ER 711.

c) *Severance of joint tenancy* – equity only – s36(2) LPA 1925 – severance means conversion in equity from a joint tenancy to a tenancy in common.

Four methods:

i) inter vivos alienation;

ii) later acquisition of another interest in the land;

iii) agreement to hold as tenants in common – memorandum of severance on the original conveyance;

iv) Notice in writing: s36(2) LPA 1925 *Burgess* v *Rawnsley* [1975] Ch 429 – unilateral oral declaration may lead to severance. Look for 'a course of dealing'.

5.3 Key cases and statutes

- *Bull* v *Bull* [1955] 1 QB 234
  Presumption of an equitable tenancy in common when co-owners provide purchase money in unequal shares

- *Burgess* v *Rawnsley* [1975] Ch 429
  Severance of a beneficial joint tenancy could be effected by a course of dealing

- *Drake* v *Whipp* [1996] 1 FLR 826
  There was a difference between acquiring a beneficial interest under a resulting trust as opposed to a constructive trust

- *Draper's Conveyance, Re* [1967] 3 All ER 853
  Issuing a summons and supporting affidavit in divorce proceedings constituted

sufficient notice in writing for the purposes of s36(2) LPA 1925 to sever an equitable joint tenancy

- *Harris* v *Goddard* [1983] 3 All ER 242
  Prayer in a divorce petition relating to former matrimonial home not a notice of a desire to sever a beneficial joint tenancy under s36(2) LPA 1925

- *Jones* v *Challenger* [1961] 1 QB 176
  Sale ordered under s30 LPA 1925 where secondary purpose had come to an end

- *Lake* v *Craddock* (1732) 3 P Wms 158
  Presumption of an equitable tenancy in common when partners held co-owned property as part of partnership assets

- *Lloyds Bank plc* v *Rosset* [1990] 2 WLR 867
  Title to registered land in husband's name alone – wife made no financial contribution to acquisition but made a work contribution – wife had no beneficial interest – application of s70(1)(g) LRA 1925

- *Malayan Credit Ltd* v *Jack Chia-MPH Ltd* [1986] 1 All ER 711
  Presumption of an equitable tenancy in common where co-owners held for various business purposes

- *Mayo, Re* [1943] Ch 302
  Trustees for sale could only postpone selling the land if they all agreed to so act

- *Mortgage Corporation* v *Shaire and Others* [2001] Ch 743
  TOLATA 1996 was drafted with the aim of relaxing the old law so as to enable the court to have a greater discretion which could be exercised in favour of families and against banks and other chargees

- *TSB Bank plc* v *Marshall* [1998] 39 EG 208
  Case law developed under s30 LPA 1925 still relevant to ss14 and 15 TOLATA 1996 – the successor provisions

- Law of Property Act 1925, ss1(6), 30 (now repealed), 34(2) and 36(2)

- Law of Property (Joint Tenants) Act 1964

- Trusts of Land and Appointment of Trustees Act (TOLATA) 1996, ss14 and 15

5.4 Questions and suggested solutions

Analysis of questions

The links with other subjects, particularly trusts of land, are apparent in this area of land law. Problem questions are particularly popular with examiners. A typical question will involve a number of people buying a property with candidates being invited to trace developments after purchase (eg death of one of the co-owners) in respect of both the legal title and the equitable interest. A central issue in all such questions (which has to be addressed at the outset) is how the equitable interest is held – joint tenancy or a tenancy in common. Usually the equitable interest will be held on a joint tenancy since in such a situation the examiner will be able to bring severance of the equitable interest into play. Invariably the remaining co-owners will not be able to agree as to what to do with the land thus necessitating recourse to ss14 and 15 of the Trusts of Land and Appointment of Trustees Act 1996 (replacing s30 LPA 1925). Finally, in answering such a problem question students should include diagrams to show developments in respect of both the legal title and equitable interest. Questions may also contain a registered land element and a knowledge of the decision in *Williams & Glyn's Bank Ltd* v *Boland* [1980] 3 WLR 138 is always a useful base. In addition this is an area of change. Two changes in particular are worth noting. First, there is the impact on co-ownership of the Trusts of Land and Appointment of Trustees Act 1996. Second, whereas for many years three presumptions of an equitable tenancy in common were recognised they suddenly became four in *Malayan Credit Ltd* v *Jack Chia-MPH Ltd* [1986] 1 All ER 711 with the suggestion from the Privy Council that there may be others.

QUESTION ONE

In 1989 Henry inherited some money from his grandfather and he and his girlfriend, Ann, decided to buy a house together. The purchase price of the house was £100,000. Henry contributed £80,000 and Ann contributed £20,000, a gift from her mother. The house was conveyed to them as beneficial joint tenants. In 1990 Ann gave birth to twins. In 1992 after a series of violent rows it became clear to both Henry and Ann that they could no longer live together and Henry agreed to move out. He wrote to her offering to sell her his interest in the house and she wrote back agreeing in principle to his proposal but pointing out that she would have to approach her mother for a loan. Shortly thereafter Henry was killed in a climbing accident leaving his entire estate to his brother, Paul. Paul now wants to sell the house and he requires Ann to pay an occupation rent pending sale. Ann has spent money on necessary repairs to the house and wishes to continue living there with her children.

Advise Ann.

University of London LLB Examination
(for External Students) Land Law June 1994 Q1

General Comment

An interesting question on co-ownership which gives students a good opportunity to display their knowledge of the subject matter. The key point to note is that despite the fact that the purchase money for the house has been provided in unequal shares it was conveyed to the purchasers as beneficial joint tenants.

Skeleton Solution

Co-ownership trust of land ss34–36 LPA 1925 – legal title on a joint tenancy – beneficial interest on a joint tenancy – principle of survivorship – severance of beneficial interest: notice in writing; *Burgess* v *Rawnsley* – ss14 and 15 Trusts of Land and Appointment of Trustees Act 1996 (replacing s30 LPA 1925) – application for order of sale – secondary trust – *Jones* v *Challenger*.

Suggested Solution

A trust of land arises where there are concurrent interests in land (ie where there are more than one person holds interests in the land at the same time). Accordingly, the persons holding the interests are co-owners. Today, for all practical purposes, there are two types of co-ownership – joint tenancy and tenancy in common. In cases of co-ownership it is vital to distinguish between ownership at law and ownership in equity (ie beneficial ownership).

Since 1 January 1926, the legal estate in the case of co-owned land must be held on a joint tenancy: s1 Law of Property Act (LPA) 1925. Here the legal estate will be so held by Henry and Ann.

Although the legal estate must always be held on a joint tenancy the equitable interest can be held on either a joint tenancy or a tenancy in common. In determining how the equitable interest is held, the general rule is that a grant to two or more persons without words of severance (words in the grant which show that the tenants are each to take a distinct share in the property, eg 'share and share alike') creates a beneficial joint tenancy. To this general rule there are two qualifications. First, there are certain circumstances in which equity may presume that a tenancy in common was intended unless there is an express indication to the contrary. Secondly, a joint tenancy cannot exist without the presence of the four unities (time, title, interest and possession). On the facts there are no words of severance here. One of the circumstances in which equity may presume that a tenancy in common was intended is where, as here, the co-owners purchasing the property have put up the purchase money in unequal proportions. Here Henry and Ann have contributed £80,000 and £20,000 respectively to the cost of this £100,000 house. The presumption in such circumstances is that they intend to take interests in the property proportionate to their contributions. However, this presumption can be rebutted if there is an express indication to the contrary. Here there is such an indication – the house was conveyed to Henry and Ann 'as beneficial joint tenants'. Accordingly, on the facts the beneficial interest is held on a joint tenancy.

The aforementioned conclusions about the legal estate and the equitable interest can be repesented diagrammatically as follows:

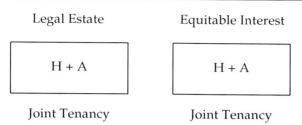

Legal Estate   Equitable Interest

H + A   H + A

Joint Tenancy   Joint Tenancy

One of the hallmarks of a joint tenancy is the principle of survivorship. On the death of one joint tenant his interest in the land passes to the other joint tenant by the right of survivorship. This right takes precedence over any disposition made by a joint tenant's will.

It is possible to sever the equitable joint tenancy without disturbing the joint tenancy of the legal estate. However, in view of the principle of survivorship such severance must be done during the joint tenant's lifetime. Severance is clearly relevant here because after Henry moves out he writes to Ann offering to sell her his interest and she writes back agreeing in principle to this proposal if she can borrow the necessary money. Severance can be effected in a variety of ways but on the facts it would be necessary to focus upon two in particular – notice in writing and course of dealing. By virtue of s36(2) LPA 1925 a joint tenancy can be severed by a joint tenant giving written notice to the other joint tenants. Any form of written notice will suffice provided it is given to all the other joint tenants and it shows a sufficient wish to effect an immediate severance. Henry writing to Ann could be so regarded. Further, severance may be effected by a course of dealing. A course of conduct will be sufficient to sever a joint tenancy if it indicates a common intention between the joint tenants that the joint tenancy should be severed. In *Burgess* v *Rawnsley* [1975] Ch 429 it was held that an oral agreement between two joint tenants was sufficient to evince an intention by them that the beneficial joint tenancy ought to be severed even though the agreement was unenforceable because of non-compliance with s40 LPA 1925. If the beneficial joint tenancy has been severed here a tenancy in common in equal shares will be created. On Henry's death, the legal title remains in Ann alone and if severance is deemed to have taken place (which henceforth is assumed) then Henry's share in the beneficial interest will pass to Paul.

Turning to Paul's desire to sell the house it is important to remember that co-owned land is now held on a trust of land. Prior to the coming into force of the Trusts of Land and Appointment of Trustees Act 1996 on 1 January 1997, the trustees (ie Ann) would have had a duty to sell with a statutory power to postpone sale and unless they all agreed on postponement the property would have had to have been sold (see *Re Mayo* [1943] Ch 302), ie the duty to sell took precedence over the power to postpone. Since the coming into force of the 1996 Act, the trustees have a power to sell and a power to postpone sale: s4 of the 1996 Act. However, Ann does not want to sell because she wants to continue living in the house with her young children. Accordingly, Paul is likely to seek the court's assistance under ss14 and 15 of the 1996 Act (replacing s30 LPA 1925). Any person with an interest in property subject to a trust of land (eg Paul) can apply to the court for an order under s14. The court can, under s14, make orders for sale preventing sale etc. The aim of the provision is to enable the courts to intervene in any dispute relating to a trust of land. Section 15(1) contains a non-exhaustive statement of factors which the court is to have regard to in making an order under s14 (it is based on how the courts have interpreted s30 LPA 1925). If Paul had gone to court before 1 January 1997 his application would have been under s30 LPA 1925 and the court would have looked for any 'secondary' or 'collateral' purpose to the trust – that is any reason for the purchase of the house other than sale. Here there is such a secondary purpose – Henry and Ann bought the house to live in it together with any children they might have. Where prior to 1997 the court found the existence of a secondary purpose and where that purpose was still – as here – subsisting the court would not usually grant a sale order: see *Jones* v *Challenger* [1961] 1 QB 176. Accordingly, on the facts it is likely that the court would have postponed a sale until Ann's children were much older – when they ceased to be of school age. How might he fare today under s14 of the 1996 Act? Much will depend on whether the case law developed under s30 LPA 1925 would still be regarded as relevant. At first sight it would appear to have little relevance to applications under s14 because s15(1) prescribes the matters that the court must take into account in exercisisng its discretion in determining applications under s14. However, the Law Commission's view was that there was much of value in that body of case law suggesting that it would remain influential despite the demise of s30 LPA 1925. In *TSB Bank plc* v *Marshall* [1998] 39 EG 208 a county court decided that the principles laid down in the case law developed under s30 LPA 1925 would still be regarded as relevant. However, a more cautious view was taken of the matter in *Mortgage Corporation* v *Shaire & Others* [2001] Ch 743. There the Court of Appeal concluded that the 1996 Act had been drafted with the aim of relaxing the old law so as to enable the court to have a greater discretion which could be exercised in favour of families and against banks and other chargees. In view of that conclusion, pre-1996 Act authorities, whilst still useful, should be treated 'with caution'. If the pre-1997 case law is followed then on the facts it is likely that the court will postpone a sale until Ann's children are much older – when they cease to be of school age.

Finally by virtue of s1(1) of the Law of Property (Joint Tenants) Act 1964 a survivor of a joint tenancy (Ann) shall in favour of any purchaser of the property be deemed to be solely and beneficially interested if she conveys as beneficial owner. One exception to this provision is a memorandum of severance endorsed on the conveyance. Accordingly, on the facts, Paul should endorse a memorandum of severance on the conveyance.

Note: this solution has been revised to take account of the coming into force of the Trusts of Land and Appointment of Trustees Act 1996.

QUESTION TWO

After the death of her husband, Brenda decided to go to London to live with her three unmarried daughters, Iris, Jill and Kirsten. Brenda purchased a large house for them all and, although she paid the whole purchase price, she agreed that it should be conveyed into the names of her daughters as beneficial joint tenants. It was understood that Brenda would live in the 'granny flat' in the basement for the rest of her life. Two years later Iris got married and moved out of the house; Jill and Kirsten agreed to buy her interest in the house but Iris was killed in a car accident before anything further was done. Jill has now been posted abroad and has suggested that the house should be sold. Brenda resists this suggestion.

Discuss. If the house were sold, how would the proceeds be divided?

University of London LLB Examination
(for External Students) Land Law June 1995 Q6

General Comment

This is a question primarily concerned with co-ownership. However, it is not a straightforward co-ownership question because it contains an additional dimension (Brenda). In terms of structuring an answer, it is probably better to look at the co-ownership issues first and then consider the position of Brenda.

Skeleton Solution

Co-ownership trust of land: ss34–36 LPA 1925 – legal title on a joint tenancy – beneficial interest on a joint tenancy – principle of survivorship – severance of beneficial interest: *Burgess* v *Rawnsley* – ss14 and 15 Trusts of Land and Appointment of Trustees Act 1996 (replacing s30 LPA 1925) – application for order of sale – secondary trust: *Jones* v *Challenger* – resulting trusts: *Dyer* v *Dyer*; *Bull* v *Bull* – presumption of advancement.

Suggested Solution

The question requires consideration of a number of issues concerning co-ownership. However, the situation is somewhat complicated by the position of Brenda in relation to the house. In the ensuing paragraphs the co-ownership issues are considered first and then the position of Brenda is evaluated. Further, the question requires not only a general discussion of the issues involved, but also consideration of how the proceeds would be distributed in the eventuality of the house being sold.

A trust of land arises where there are concurrent interests in land (ie where more than one person holds interests in the land at the same time). Accordingly, the persons holding the interests are co-owners. Today, for all practical purposes, there are two types of co-ownership – joint tenancy and tenancy in common. In cases of co-ownership it is vital to distinguish between ownership at law and ownership in equity (ie beneficial ownership). Since 1 January 1926, the legal estate in the case of co-owned land must be held on a joint tenancy: s1 Law of Property Act (LPA) 1925.

Here Brenda bought a large house for her three daughters and agreed for the house to be conveyed into the names of her three daughters as 'beneficial joint tenants'.

Accordingly, there are concurrent interests in land (ie co-ownership) and the legal estate is held on a joint tenancy by Iris, Jill and Kirsten.

Although the legal estate in co-owned land must always be held on a joint tenancy, the equitable interest can be held on either a joint tenancy or a tenancy in common. In determining how the equitable interest is held, the general rule is that a grant to two or more persons without words of severance (words in the grant which show that the tenants are each to take a distinct share in the property, eg 'share and share alike') creates a beneficial joint tenancy. To this general rule there are two qualifications. First, there are certain circumstances in which equity may presume that a tenancy in common was intended, unless there is an express indication to the contrary. Second, a joint tenancy cannot exist without the presence of the four unities (time, title, interest and possession). On the facts, there are no words of severance here. Further, there is nothing in the question to suggest that either qualification to the general rule is applicable here. Accordingly, it is submitted that Iris, Jill and Kirsten are holding the legal title on trust for themselves as beneficial joint tenants in equity (ie the beneficial interest is held on a joint tenancy). The aforementioned conclusions about the legal estate and equitable interest can be represented diagrammatically as follows:

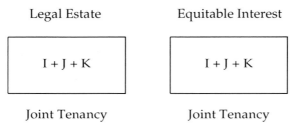

Legal Estate	Equitable Interest
I + J + K	I + J + K
Joint Tenancy	Joint Tenancy

One of the hallmarks of a joint tenancy is the principle of survivorship. On the death of one joint tenant his interest in the land passes to the other joint tenants by the right of survivorship. This right takes precedence over any disposition made in a joint tenant's will.

It is possible to sever the equitable joint tenancy without disturbing the joint tenancy of the legal estate. However, in view of the principle of survivorship such severance must be done during the joint tenant's lifetime. Severance is clearly relevant here. Iris has married and moved out of the house. Jill and Kirsten agree to buy her beneficial interest in the house, but before this can be effected Iris is killed in a car accident. The issue here is whether or not Iris severed her beneficial interest in the house before her death. In *Burgess* v *Rawnsley* [1975] Ch 429 the Court of Appeal unanimously held that an oral agreement between two joint tenants for one to buy the other's share was sufficient to evince an intention by them that the beneficial joint tenancy ought to be severed, even though the agreement was unenforceable because of non-compliance with s40 LPA 1925. (The significance of the agreement was not that it bound the parties, but that it served as an indication of a common intention to sever.) It was a course of dealing which was sufficient to effect a severance. On the strength of this case it could be argued that here the joint tenants had evinced an intention to sever. Iris had moved out and Jill and Kirsten agreed to buy her interest in the house. Here, since the agreement between the joint tenants was not 'made in writing' to satisfy s2 of the Law of Property (Miscellaneous Provisions) Act 1989 (which repealed s40 LPA 1925), the agreement between Iris, Jill and Kirsten is unenforceable. However, an intention to sever could be found, in which case Iris' one-third share henceforward would have been held on a tenancy in common, and on her death would have passed under her will or intestacy. On Iris' death the legal title remains in Jill and Kirsten.

Following Jill's posting abroad she suggests that the house should be sold. Brenda is opposed to selling (presumably because she wants to continue living in the 'granny flat' in the basement), and the question gives no indication as to Kirsten's view of the matter. As to Jill's desire to sell the house it is important to remember that now co-owned land is held on a trust of land. Prior to the coming into force of the Trusts of Land and Appointment of Trustees Act 1996 on 1 January 1997, the trustees (ie Jill and Kirsten) would have had a duty to sell with a statutory power to postpone sale and unless they all agreed on the postponement the property would have had to have been sold: see *Re Mayo* [1943] Ch 302. Since the coming into force of the 1996 Act, the trustees have a power to sell and a power to postpone sale: s4 of the 1996 Act. If Kirsten is not prepared to sell then Jill would seek a sale order under s14. By virtue of ss14 and 15 of the 1996 Act (replacing s30 LPA 1925) any person with an interest in property subject to a trust of land can apply to the court for an order under s14. The court can, under s14, make orders for sale preventing sale etc. The aim of the provision is to enable the courts to intervene in any dispute relating to a trust of land. However, if the trustees are prepared to sell the house then Brenda could be expected to take action under s14 of the 1996 Act. Upon an application under the old s30 LPA 1925 (which was repealed and replaced by ss14 and 15 of the 1996 Act) the court would look for any 'secondary' or 'collateral' purpose to the trust – that is any reason for the purchase of the house other than sale. Here there is such a secondary purpose – it was understood by all concerned that Brenda would live in the 'granny flat' in the basement for the rest of her life. Where prior to 1997 the court found the existence of a secondary purpose, and where that purpose was still, as here, subsisting, the court would not usually grant a sale order: *Jones* v *Challenger* [1961] 1 QB 176. The question is would a court be likely to take the same approach now that s30 LPA 1925 has been repealed? Much will depend on whether the case law developed under s30 LPA 1925 would still be regarded as relevant. At first sight it would appear to have little relevance to applications under s14 because s15(1) prescribes the matters that the court must take into account in exercising its discretion in determining applications under s14. However, the Law Commission's view was that there was much of value in that body of case law suggesting that it would remain influential despite the demise of s30 LPA 1925. In *TSB Bank plc* v *Marshall* [1998] 39 EG 208 a county court decided that the principles laid down in the case law developed under s30 LPA 1925 would still be regarded as relevant. However, a more cautious view was taken of the matter in *Mortgage*

Corporation v *Shaire & Others* [2001] Ch 743. There the Court of Appeal concluded that the 1996 Act had been drafted with the aim of relaxing the old law so as to enable the court to have a greater discretion which could be exercised in favour of families and against banks and other chargees. In view of that conclusion, pre 1996 Act authorities, whilst still useful, should be treated 'with caution'. If the pre-1997 case law is followed then on the facts it is likely that the court will postpone a sale until Brenda dies.

If the house were sold how would the proceeds be divided? It is here that the additional dimension of the question becomes particularly relevant. Brenda provided all the money to buy the house, but agreed to convey it into the names of her three daughters. Where land is conveyed to one person P, but the purchase money is provided by another, A, as purchaser, there is a resulting trust in favour of the person providing the purchase money, ie A: *Dyer* v *Dyer* (1788) 2 Cox Eq Cas 92. Likewise, where, as here, the legal estate is in the name of more than one person but where another – not holding the legal estate nor expressed to be a beneficiary – contributes, a resulting trust could arise: *Bull* v *Bull* [1955] 1 QB 234. However, these are only presumptions which can be rebutted, either by evidence that P (in the above example) was intended to benefit or by the presumption of advancement. Under the presumption of advancement, where a father or other person in loco parentis transfers property into the name of a child, the transaction does not create a resulting trust for the transferor but is an advancement or gift to the child, unless there is evidence of a contrary intention at the time of the transaction. Here, a mother (Brenda) transferred the property to her daughters. The traditional view is that the presumption of advancement would not apply to such a transfer. The courts currently seem to take the approach articulated by Jessel MR in *Bennett* v *Bennett* (1879) 10 Ch D 474:

> 'In the case of a mother … it is easier to prove a gift than in the case of a stranger: in the case of a mother very little evidence beyond the relationship is wanted.'

Thus the courts start from the position of a presumption of a resulting trust in favour of the mother which can be easily rebutted. Accordingly, if Jill and Kirsten can show that when their mother bought the house she intended them and Iris to benefit, then the presumption of resulting trust in favour of Brenda can be rebutted. If the presumption can be so rebutted then on a sale of the house the proceeds, it is submitted, would be divided one-third to those entitled under Iris' will or intestacy, with the remaining two-thirds going to Jill and Kirsten. However, if the presumption of resulting trust is not rebutted it could be the case that Brenda would be deemed to hold the entire beneficial interest in the house.

Note. this solution has been revised to take account of the coming into force of the Trusts of Land and Appointment of Trustees Act 1996.

QUESTION THREE

In 1996 Mary and her two daughters, Ros and Tina, bought a cottage for £200,000. It was conveyed to the three of them as beneficial joint tenants, Mary contributing £150,000,

Ros £30,000 and Tina £20,000. The following year Mary spent £1,000 landscaping the garden. Mary died in 1998 leaving her entire estate to Ros. In 1999 Ros moved out of the cottage and went to live with her boyfriend, Gary. She wrote to Tina offering to sell her her interest in the cottage for £100,000. Tina accepted the offer but pointed out that it would depend on her getting a loan from her bank. Soon afterwards Ros died in a car crash leaving her estate to Gary. Gary wants the cottage to be sold and he insists on Tina paying him rent pending sale. He also claims that he is entitled to occupy the cottage if he so wishes.

Advise Tina. If the cottage were sold, how would the proceeds of sale be divided?

University of London LLB Examination
(for External Students) Land Law June 2001 Q6

General Comment

A co-ownership question which is fairly straightforward and which requires a knowledge of the rules of severance. Candidates should notice that there is no express trust for sale or of land. They should also notice that the conveyance to the co-owners was executed in 1996, eg before the Trusts of Land and Appointment of Trustees Act (TOLATA) 1996 came into effect on 1 January 1997. Initially there would have been a statutory trust for sale under s36 Law of Property Act (LPA) 1925 but this would have been converted into a trust of land without a duty to sell by the retrospective provisions of TOLATA 1996.

A knowledge of the provisions of TOLATA 1996 relating to Gary's position is required: see ss12, 13, 14 and 15.

Skeleton Solution

Co-ownership in 1996: no express trust for sale; one implied by s36 LPA 1925; effect of s36 LPA 1925; co-owners; joint tenants in equity; retrospective provisions of TOLATA 1996 convert trust for sale into a trust of land – severance: no severance by will possible; right of survivorship operates on Mary's death; four methods of severance; does Ros' letter constitute severance?; s36 LPA 1925: written notice?; severance by mutual agreement; conditional contract?; course of dealing; if severance, Gary becomes tenant in common in place of Ros; advice to Gary; TOLATA 1996, ss12, 13, 14 and 15; Gary entitled to half share in cottage if he became a tenant in common.

Suggested Solution

Mary and her two daughters have purchased the cottage as co-owners. Until the enactment of the Trusts of Land and Appointment of Trustees Act (TOLATA) 1996, co-ownership of land took effect behind a trust for sale, and if the conveyance to the co-owners did not create an express trust for sale one would be implied by ss34 or 36 Law of Property Act (LPA) 1925 or s36(4) Settled Land Act (SLA) 1925. The choice of section depended on whether the co-owners were joint tenants or tenants in common. In the case of the co-owners being joint tenants, the relevant section was s36 LPA 1925.

TOLATA 1996 took effect on 1 January 1997 and amended the three sections to produce, instead of a trust for sale, a trust of land without a duty to sell the land. The amendment to s36 LPA 1925 was effected by ss4 and 5 of Sch 3 of TOLATA 1996. The amendment was made retrospective by para 4(4) of that Schedule.

In this case, the co-owners are expressed to be beneficial joint tenants. There is no express trust and consequently, although the conveyance was executed in 1996, s36 LPA 1925, as retrospectively amended, is applicable. The result is that the legal estate vests in Mary, Ros and Tina as joint tenants to hold it on a trust of land for themselves as beneficial joint tenants in equity. It should be noted that the legal joint tenancy cannot be severed, eg converted into a legal tenancy in common: s36(2) LPA 1925.

The three co-owners put up the purchase monies in unequal shares. The equitable presumption that such unequal contributions give rise to a tenancy in common is not applicable here, since the conveyance expressly declares them to be beneficial joint tenants: *Goodman* v *Gallant* [1986] 2 WLR 236. Consequently, if severance occurs each co-owner will be entitled to an equal share in the land despite their unequal contributions.

The effect of Mary's expenditure of £1,000 on landscaping must be considered. This appears to be a unilateral act on her part which would increase the value of the property and which all three would share equally.

When Mary died in 1998 she left all her estate to Ros, having obviously made a will to that effect, and this raises the question as to whether the will amounted to an act of severance of her equitable joint tenancy. The answer is clearly in the negative. A will only takes effect on death, and an act of severance must take place during the severor's lifetime, since at the point of death the right of survivorship, which is a characteristic of a joint tenancy, operates immediately to vest the deceased co-owner's share in the surviving joint tenants. When Mary died she was both a legal joint tenant and an equitable joint tenant. On her death her share in the legal joint tenancy vested automatically, by right of survivorship, in the surviving legal joint tenants, Ros and Tina. The same applied to her equitable joint tenancy. The result is that after Mary's death, the legal estate in the cottage was held by Ros and Tina, holding it on a trust of land for themselves as beneficial joint tenants in equity. Ros did not acquire Mary's equitable share in the cottage from Mary's will. Instead, she received half of Mary's share, because of the operation of the doctrine of survivorship.

After moving out of the cottage, Ros wrote to Tina, her fellow joint tenant in equity, offering to sell her interest to her for £100,000 and this raises the question of severance. It must be remembered that only an equitable joint tenancy can be severed. A legal joint tenancy cannot: s36(2) LPA 1925.

There are four methods of severance of an equitable joint tenancy in land. Three of them are contained in *Williams* v *Hensman* (1861) 1 J & H 546. Although that was a case of personalty, the three methods were made applicable to land by s36(2) LPA 1925. The three methods are as follows: an act of any one of the persons interested operating on his own share; mutual agreement; and any course of dealing sufficient to intimate that the interests of all were to be mutually treated as constituting a tenancy in common.

A fourth method was added by s36(2) LPA 1925 where 'any tenant desires to sever the joint tenancy in equity, he shall give to the other joint tenants a notice in writing of such desire'. The words following 'or do such other acts or things as would, in the case of personal estate, have been effectual to sever the tenancy in equity' apply the methods of *Williams* v *Hensman* to land. The four methods must be examined in turn.

An act of one party operating on his share, eg sale or mortgage of that share
Supposing that A, B, C and D are equitable joint tenants and A sells his share to P. This will effect severance in the way described above, but as between themselves B, C and D will remain joint tenants.

In *Hawksley* v *May* [1956] 1 QB 304 Havers J said that this first method 'obviously includes a declaration of intention to sever', but did not indicate whether this had to be in writing or whether an oral declaration of intention would be sufficient. If an oral declaration would have been sufficient this would have rendered s36(2) LPA 1925 (notice in writing) superfluous. In *Burgess* v *Rawnsley* [1975] Ch 429, Pennycuick J clarified the position: 'a mere verbal notice by one party to another clearly cannot operate as a severance'.

Although the wording of this method contemplates a voluntary disposition of the share, it also covers the position where that party is declared bankrupt because his equitable share will then vest in his trustee in bankruptcy. The date when severance occurs in this situation is probably the date of the bankruptcy order.

Mutual agreement
The leading case here is *Burgess* v *Rawnsley* and the student should study it in detail, particularly the judgment of Pennycuick J. In 1967 Mr Honick (H) and Mrs Rawnsley (R) decided to buy a house. They contributed equally to the purchase price, and the house was conveyed to them as legal joint tenants to hold on trust for sale for themselves as equitable joint tenants. Thereafter R and H made an oral agreement that R would sell her share to H for £750. Shortly afterwards, she changed her mind and told H she was not prepared to sell at that price. H then died and his son claimed his share in the house. His argument was that there had been a severance of the equitable joint tenancy which made H a tenant in common. In consequence, on his death, his share did not go to R by right of survivorship, which is the characteristic of a joint tenancy, but to H's estate to which he, the plaintiff son, was entitled.

The trial judge found that there had been an oral agreement for sale and purchase for £750, and this finding was accepted by the Court of Appeal, although not without some reservations.

Did the oral agreement constitute an act of severance? The difficulty was that under s40 LPA 1925 (since repealed) it was unenforceable for want of writing and either party could have withdrawn from it. R contended that because of this it could not constitute severance, citing in support Walton J in *Nielson-Jones* v *Fedden* [1975] Ch 222, who said that conduct cannot amount to severance unless it is irrevocable.

The Court of Appeal *Burgess* v *Rawnsley* held that even though the oral argument was not specifically enforceable, it nevertheless constituted an act of severance because it evinced an intention to sever. To quote Lord Denning: 'it clearly evinced an intention by both parties that the property should henceforth be held in common and not jointly'. Pennycuick J agreed, stating: 'the significance of an agreement is not that it binds the parties, but that it serves as an indication of a common intention to sever'. In the result, therefore, the court held that the plaintiff was entitled to succeed to H's share on the latter's death.

Pennycuick J took the opportunity to clarify the relationship between the second and third methods of *Williams* v *Hensman*. There had always been a doubt as to whether the third method was a subheading of the second, or whether the two were independent of each other. He expressed the view that: 'I do not think that rule three [in *Williams* v *Hensman*] is a mere subheading of rule two. It covers acts of the parties including ... negotiations which although not resulting in agreement, indicate a common intention that the joint tenancy should be regarded as severed.'

In *Burgess* v *Rawnsley* the failure to comply with s40 LPA 1925 did not render the agreement void but merely unenforceable by action. Section 40 LPA 1925 was repealed by the Law of Property (Miscellaneous Provisions) Act 1989, which substituted more stringent requirements that contracts for the sale of land must be made in writing, contain all the contractual terms and be signed by all parties with the consequence that if those requirements were not satisfied the contract was void. Thus, if *Burgess* v *Rawnsley* had been decided today the contract would have been void, not merely unenforceable. Would the result have then been different? It is thought not. The common intention would still have been there, albeit finding expression in a void contract, and there would still have been severance. It must be remembered that *Burgess* v *Rawnsley* [1975] Ch 429 was not a case where enforcement of the contract was sought.

Course of dealing
This is the more difficult of the three methods, particularly in relation to its applicability to any given set of facts. Pennycuick J referred to negotiations falling short of agreement but which had reached a point from which it is possible to infer a common intention to sever. It is not always easy to see if that point has been reached and an illustrative case is to be found in *Gore and Snell* v *Carpenter* (1990) 61 P & CR 456. Blackett-Ord J found that there had been negotiations but pointed out that 'negotiations are not the same thing as a course of dealing'. He felt unable to find a common intention to sever. Each case must be decided on its own facts.

Greenfield v *Greenfield* (1979) 38 P & CR 570 is perhaps a surprising case where there was held to have been no course of dealing to amount to severance, although in that case it was stressed that the onus of proof lay on the party asserting severance. Two brothers were joint tenants of a house. They converted it into two flats and lived in them with their families. One brother died and his widow claimed that there had been severance (the conversion amounting to a course of dealing) and that he therefore died as a tenant in common with the consequence that she was entitled to his share. Her claim failed because the court held that had been no severance.

Section 36: notice in writing

This method was introduced by s36(2) LPA 1925. The section does not specify any particular form which the notice must take, nor is there any requirement that it should be signed. The notice, which must be served on all of the other joint tenants by the party wishing to sever, may take a variety of forms and may come into being without it being realised that it could be construed as a notice of severance, particularly in matrimonial disputes: *Re Draper's Conveyance* [1969] 1 Ch 486 and *Harris v Goddard* [1983] 3 All ER 242.

In *Re Draper's Conveyance* a husband and wife were joint tenants of the matrimonial home. They divorced, and after the decree nisi the wife issued a summons under s17 Married Women's Property Act 1882 seeking an order for sale and distribution of the proceeds. The summons was supported by an affidavit by the wife embodying the application. Both were served on the husband. The husband died and the question arose as to whether the wife had severed. If she had then she was a tenant in common at his death and not entitled to his share. Plowman J held that service of the summons and affidavit constituted an act of severance either under the first method of *Williams v Hensman* or under s36(2) LPA 1925. As regards the first method, it amounted to a written declaration of intention to sever which had been communicated to the other party. It should be noticed that this was so even though the wife could have changed her mind and withdrawn the proceedings.

Harris v Goddard was another matrimonial case and one which was argued in the Court of Appeal. Again husband and wife were joint tenants of the matrimonial home. The wife petitioned for a divorce and in her petition prayed that an order be made 'by way of transfer of property and/or settlement of property and/or variation of settlement as may be just'. The husband later died and again the question was: had there been severance by the wife so as to convert her joint tenancy into a tenancy in common, in which case she was not entitled to the husband's share by right of survivorship? The Court of Appeal decided that there had been no severance. Lawton LJ, in discussing s36(2) LPA 1925, pointed out that a notice served under s36(2) LPA 1925 must take effect forthwith and that it followed that the desire to sever contained in the notice: 'must evince an intention to bring about that wanted result immediately. A notice in writing, which expresses a desire to bring about the wanted result at some time in the future … is not a notice in writing s36(2) … para 3 of the prayer in the petition does no more than invite the court to consider at some future time whether to exercise jurisdiction under s24 [Matrimonial Causes Act 1973] and, if it does so, in one or more of three different ways'. Accordingly, he held, that the prayer and the petition did not amount to a valid s36(2) notice.

He referred also to the consequences set out in s36(2): the notice to be valid must show an intention to bring about the consequences, namely that the net proceeds of the statutory trust for sale: 'shall be held upon the trusts which would have been requisite for giving effect to the beneficial interests if there had been actual severance'. A notice which shows no more than a desire to bring the existing interest to an end is not a good notice.

Could Ros's letter constitute a written notice of intention to sever under s36 LPA 1925 or a written declaration of intention to sever under *Hawksley v May* as clarified by Pennycuick J in *Burgess v Rawnsley*? This is extremely doubtful. It does not evince a firm declaration of intention to sever on Ros's part. It is merely an enquiry of Tina to see if she would be prepared to buy her (Ros's) share. To quote Lawson LJ in *Harris v Goddard* again: 'a desire to sever must evince an intention to bring about the wanted result immediately'. This is clearly not the case here. The same requirement must apply to a written declaration of intention to sever if the law is to be consistent.

The case for arguing that severance has occurred through mutual agreement is stronger, although not conclusive. Tina responded with a conditional acceptance, although we are not told whether she did so in writing or not. This could amount to severance by mutual agreement. If it constitutes a conditional contract it is a contract for the sale and purchase of an interest in land and such contracts must be made in writing: Law of Property (Miscellaneous Provisions) Act (LP(MP)A) 1989, otherwise it is void. We do not know if Tina responded in writing, but even if she did it is unlikely that the provisions of s2 of the statute were complied with since s2(1) requires that all the terms of the contract must be contained in one document unless the contract is made by exchange of contracts. However, it does not inevitably follow that if there is no valid contract between Ros and Tina there is no severance. In *Burgess v Rawnsley* the fact that the parties had demonstrated this intention to sever in an unenforceable contract was irrelevant. The case was not about enforcing the contract, but whether the parties had entered into a mutual agreement to sever, and clearly this agreement that one should buy the other's share constituted an agreement to sever.

The contract in *Burgess v Rawnsley* fell under the provisions of s40 LPA 1925, which enacted that if a contract for the disposition of land was not evidenced in writing it was unenforceable by court action. The 1989 Act repealed s40 and replaced it with the more stringent provision of s2 LP(MP)A 1989. An oral contract for the disposition of land made after the statute is void, not merely unenforceable. It is submitted that if the facts of *Burgess v Rawnsley* occurred now the result would be the same, since, although the contract would be void, the mutual agreement to sever would still be there, albeit embodied in a void contract.

To summarise, if there is a conditional contract between Ros and Tina, this would constitute severance by mutual agreement under the second method in *Williams v Hensman*, even though such a contract was void for want of compliance with s2 LP(MP)A 1989.

Alternatively, it could be argued that severance had occurred under the third method in *Williams* v *Hensman* a course of dealing. In the case of negotiations falling short of mutual agreement it is not always easy to see if the point has been reached where it can be said that the course of dealing is sufficient to intimate that the interests of the parties can be mutually treated as tenancies in common. In this case, it seems likely that Ros and Tina have reached that point, and it can be concluded that severance has been achieved.

It seems likely then that the equitable joint tenancy between the two remaining co-owners, Ros and Tina, was severed. It must be stressed, however, that they both remained joint tenants at law. They would continue to be trustees for themselves by holding the legal estate for themselves as tenants in common in equity.

If that is the case, when Ros died in the car crash, her equitable share in the cottage, being a tenancy in common, would not pass to Tina but would devolve into her estate. Her legal joint tenancy, on the other hand, would automatically pass to Tina by right of survivorship, leaving Tina as sole trustee. Since Ros left her estate to Gary, he would become the owner of her equitable tenancy in common and Tina would hold the cottage on trust of land for herself and Gary as equitable tenants in common.

Gary now claims sale, rent and occupation. He is not a trustee but merely a beneficiary. The powers of dealing with the land are vested in Tina as trustee: s6 TOLATA 1996. She must, however, in exercising the powers conferred upon her under s6, have regard to the rights of the beneficiaries: s6(5).

When exercising any function relating to the land, the trustee must consult the beneficiaries of full age who are beneficially entitled to an interest in possession of the land. Gary is certainly entitled to an interest in possession of the land by virtue of his tenancy in common. We do not know his age and we will assume he is of full age. There is no suggestion on the facts that Tina is proposing to exercise any of her trustee functions under the statute, and if one takes a literal interpretation of the wording of the statute she would not appear to be under any obligation to consult Gary until she is minded to make a positive move. It may be, therefore, that Gary is not entitled to be consulted until that stage is reached.

However, he may apply to the court for an order for sale under s14 TOLATA 1996, and in considering any such application the court must have regard to the matters listed in s15 TOLATA 1996. The most relevant factor would be that contained in s15(1)(b): 'the purposes for which the property subject to the trust is held'. In attempting to predict the court's decision, how much weight should be given to the cases decided under s14's predecessor, s30 LPA 1925, which TOLATA 1996 repealed and replaced with ss14 and 15?

The Law Commission took the view that there was much of value in the cases decided under s30 LPA 1925 and a county court judgment in *TSB Bank plc* v *Marshall* [1998] 39 EG 208 supported that view. However, the Court of Appeal in *Mortgage Corporation* v *Shaire and Others* [2001] Ch 743 took a more cautious view. It noted that in applications for an order for sale under s30, the courts inclined towards ordering sale because such applications were made in the context of a trust for sale, under which the trustees were obliged to sell the land, although they might have a statutory power to postpone sale under s25 LPA 1925. The Court of Appeal decided that the 1996 statute had been drafted with the aim of relaxing the old law so as to enable the courts to have a greater discretion to be exercised in favour of families and against banks and other chargees. This was not to say that the s30 cases were not useful. They were, but should be considered in the light of the new provisions. Thus, it can be said that the inclination of the courts to order sale has diminished, particularly as under s14 TOLATA 1996 applications for an order for sale are now generally made by a party to a trust of land as compared with a trust for sale.

In this case the original parties purchased the cottage with the intention of living in it as a family. Two members of the family are now dead and it can be said that the original purpose has now gone. Bearing in mind s15(1)(b) TOLATA 1996 and the pre-1996 cases in which the courts tended to order sale when the original purpose was no longer existant, eg *Jones* v *Challenger* [1961] 1 QB 176, Gary's application for an order for sale stands a good chance of being successful, even if opposed by Tina.

Gary insists that Tina pays him rent pending sale, since he is not currently in occupation, and this necessitates an examination of ss12 and 13 TOLATA 1996. The effect of these provisions may be stated as follows. Section 12(1) provides that a beneficiary who is entitled to an interest in possession of the land subject to a trust is entitled, by reason of his interest, to occupy the land. Section 12 is subject to the provisions of s13, which covers the situation where two or more beneficiaries are entitled to possession. That is the case here. Under s13, the trustee, in this case Tina, may exclude or restrict that entitlement, although she must not do so in an unreasonable manner: s13(2). If Tina does exclude Gary from occupation she may make that exclusion subject to a condition that the beneficiary who remains in occupation (herself) make payments to the excluded beneficiary (Gary) by way of compensation. This could take the form of rent, which is what Gary is claiming. He can, therefore, claim either occupation under s12 or compensation, eg rent, under s13, but he cannot have both and he must be advised accordingly.

Tina would have to be advised to the same effect. As trustee she would probably exercise her power of exclusion under s12, but would be reluctant to impose upon herself, as a beneficiary in occupation, a condition to pay rent to Gary by way of compensation for his exclusion. If that proved to be the case Gary could make application to the court under s14 that she be ordered to pay compensation. Alternatively, if he opted for occupation instead of compensation and Tina refused, he could apply under s14 for an order to that effect.

If the cottage was sold, since Tina would be selling as a sole trustee, the overreaching provision would not apply and Tina should appoint a second trustee for the purposes of the sale to enable it to take effect.

The final part relates to the division of the proceeds of sale. When Mary died her equitable one third share automatically accrued to her surviving equitable joint tenants: Ros and Tina would share it between them. Mary's will in favour of Ros did not effect severance and Ros would not receive Mary's share in the cottage under the will, as Mary died as an equitable joint tenant. Instead, as stated, she would have received half of Mary's one third share by right of survivorship.

When Ros died, did she die as a joint tenant or a tenant in common? That depends on whether severance had been effected, and this was discussed earlier. If she died as a joint tenant, her equitable share would automatically pass to the surviving joint tenant, Tina, by right of survivorship. Tina would then have become sole owner of the cottage and the trust would have terminated. Gary would have received nothing under Ros's will and would have no rights in the cottage.

If, however, as seems more likely, there had been severance, Ros would have died as a tenant in common and her half share in the cottage would have passed to Gary, making him a tenant in common with Tina, Tina holding a trust of land for them both, each being entitled to a half share.

Chapter 6

Landlord and Tenant

6.1   Introduction

6.2   Key points

6.3   Key cases and statutes

6.4   Questions and suggested solutions

6.1 Introduction

More than any other area of land law this is a topic where the exact knowledge of the syllabus and the style of previous papers will help the student. Some examiners load their land law paper with questions relating to landlord and tenant, others limit the topic to merely one question in the recognition of the width of a pure land law syllabus. In between the two extremes a typical nine question land law paper will probably carry two or three questions directly or indirectly related to landlord and tenant. In particular the areas of landlord and tenant that frequently give rise to examination questions include the following.

a) General principles of landlord and tenant, including:

   i)   perpetually renewable leases: s145 and 15th Schedule LPA 1922;

   ii) s1(1)(b) + s205(1)(xxvii) LPA 1925;

   iii) s149(3) or (6) LPA 1925.

b) Informal/equitable leases.

c) Express covenants.

d) Implied covenants.

e) Legislation conferring security of tenure upon certain leases.

6.2 Key points

Meaning of 'term of years absolute': LPA 1925 s205(1)(xxvii). It is 'absolute' even though it may be determined by notice to quit, operation of law, re-entry or a provision for cesser on redemption. 'Year' includes a term for less than a year.

It is important to appreciate that more than one legal estate can exist concurrently in respect of the same piece of land: s1(5) LPA. For example, A the freehold estate owner of Blackacre grants a legal lease of Blackacre to B for five years.

Unusual leases

a) Lease 'in perpetuity' is void.

b) Perpetually renewable leases allowed pre-1926, but converted by s145 LPA 1922 and 15th Schedule into a 2000-year term. May be created inadvertently.

c) LPA s149(6) – abolished leases for lives by providing that a lease at a rent for life or lives for a term of years determinable on life or lives becomes a 90-year term, determinable after the event by one month's notice expiring on a quarter day.

d) Reversionary leases – s149(3) LPA 1925. Void if it takes effect more than 21 years from the instrument creating it.

Terminology

Privity of contract – binds original parties by a direct contractual relationship (but note the effect of the Landlord and Tenant (Covenants) Act 1995). Privity of estate – binds whoever is presently in the position of landlord and tenant.

Lease/tenancy/term of years.

Lessee is possessed of a term which he may assign.

Lessor leases, or demises, the term and retains a reversion which he may convey (if fee simple) or assign (if a superior lease).

The lessee may sub-demise (underlease) to sub-lessee (underlessee).

Always distinguish the assignment of the whole interest from the sub-lease where a reversion remains.

Nature of terms of years

Lessor must confer upon lessee the right to exclusive possession of land for a period which must be either definite or capable of definition. Consider the three essentials of a lease.

Exclusive possession

See the words of Lord Templeman in *Street v Mountford* [1985] 2 WLR 877: 'Where the only circumstances were that residential accommodation was offered and accepted with exclusive possession for a term at a rent – the result was a tenancy.'

Necessary but not sufficient. Compare 'licence' – see Chapter 9. The general control by owner negatives lease, eg, service occupant.

If exclusive possession is not granted the agreement can only be a licence. The grant of exclusive possession is a factor indicating that a lease has been granted, but it is not a decisive factor as it is possible for a grantee to be given exclusive possession and still not have a lease, eg service occupant. Whether an agreement constitutes a lease or a licence depends on the true intention of the parties.

i.e a money payment

But no need for rent – *Ashburn Anstalt* v *Arnold* [1988] 2 All ER 147 – Fox LJ.

Definite period – certainty of duration

Beginning and end must be capable of being ascertained: LPA s149(3) provides:

a) leasehold term at a rent to take effect more than 21 years from the instrument creating it is void; and

b) a contract to create 'such a term' is also void.

End of term must be capable of being fixed before the lease takes effect:

Note: *Lace* v *Chantler* [1944] 1 All ER 305.

Prudential Assurance Co Ltd v *London Residuary Body* [1992] 3 WLR 279.

Form

Deed: s52 and s54(2) LPA 1925 – term not exceeding three years – oral or written – in possession, at best rent. Section 54(2) is not affected by the Law of Property (Miscellaneous Provisions) Act 1989: see s2(5) of the 1989 Act.

Methods of creation

Compare 'lease' with an 'agreement for a lease' – the latter forms a contract by an intending landlord to grant a lease and by the tenant to take a lease once it has been granted by deed (if required).

Formalities for legal lease

a) Originally a mere contract – even oral would suffice.

b) 1677–1845: Statute of Frauds 1677 required writing, signed by the party or agent authorised in writing, exception for certain leases not exceeding three years.

c) 1845–1925: replaced writing by need for deed – retaining three-year exception – Real Property Act 1845.

d) Now LPA 1925 ss52 and 54 (ss52(2)(d) and 54(2)) – s2 of the Law of Property (Miscellaneous Provisions) Act 1989 does not apply to s54(2): s2(5)(a) of the 1989 Act.

Lease void at law unless by deed. But no deed or writing required for lease taking effect in possession for not more than three years at best rent without a fine (ie premium).

Deed always required for assignment of a legal lease, even if created orally.

The doctrine of frustration may apply to leases, but see *National Carriers Ltd v Panalpina (Northern) Ltd* [1981] AC 675 where the House of Lords concluded that this would not happen very often – 'hardly ever rather than never'.

Formalities for agreement for a lease

a) Final agreement in writing is required. Note that agreement 'subject to contract' is no contract.

b) LPA 1925 s40(1) is repealed and replaced by s2(1) Law of Property (Miscellaneous Provisions) Act 1989 from the 27 September 1989. Section 2(1) provides: 'A contract for the sale or other disposition of an interest in land can only be made in writing and only by incorporating all the terms which the parties have expressly agreed in one document or, where contracts are exchanged, in each.' By s2(3) the contract must be signed by or on behalf of each party to the contract.

c) LPA 1925 s40(2) is also repealed by s2(8) of the 1989 Act. The effect of this repeal is that the rules of part performance for alleged contracts relating to land may not survive s2(1) of the 1989 Act in respect of contracts made after the 27 September 1989. Consideration should now be given to the application of the rules of estoppel to replace the doctrine of part performance in this area of land law. In particular, the Law Commission suggested that estoppel could 'achieve very similar results where appropriate to those of part performance'. (See Law Commission Report on Formalities for Contracts of Sale etc of Land (1987) Law Com No 164.)

Yaxley v Gotts & Gotts [1999] 3 WLR 1217 (CA) endorsed that view. Robert Walker LJ emphasised 'that any general assertion of s2 as a 'no-go' area for estoppel would be unsustainable.

Effect of informal leases

Equity treated an imperfect lease as a contract then ordered specific performance of it. After the Judicature Act 1873 equitable rules prevail: *Walsh v Lonsdale* (1882) 21 Ch D 9. An enforceable agreement for a lease is almost as good as a lease, but:

a) dependent upon specific performance – a discretionary remedy;

b) void against third parties unless registered as an estate contract – land charge Class C(iv), s4(6) LCA 1972;

c) not a 'conveyance' within LPA 1925 s62 and thus does not pass easements and rights;

d) burden of covenant does not run.

LAW - LEGAL ESTATE	EQUITY - EQUITABLE INTEREST
Grants a lease	Agrees to grant a lease
Deed - s52(1) LPA 1925 or oral/writing for term not exceeding three years. S54(2) LPA 1925 [in possession: at best rent]	Agreement - must now satisfy s2(1) of the Law of Property (Miscellaneous Provisions) Act 1989 - contract for disposition of an interest in land can only be made in writing and (by s2(3)) must be signed by each party to the contract.
Requirements of a valid lease: 1) Correct form [ss52/54 LPA 1925] 2) Certainty of duration *Lace* v *Chantler* [1944] 1 All ER 305 3) Exclusive possession *Street* v *Mountford* [1985] 2 WLR 877	Rules of part performance may no longer apply BUT estoppel may become the alternative answer.
'Term of years absolute'. A legal estate within s1(1)(b) LPA 1925	

Consequence of *Walsh* v *Lonsdale* (1882) 21 Ch D 9 – if a conflict between a specifically enforceable agreement for a lease (equity) and a legal periodic tenancy arising from a payment of rent (law) – equity will prevail. But an agreement for a lease is not as good as a lease – because:
1) Discretionary remedies
2) s62 LPA 1925 only applies to a 'conveyance'
3) Third party rights
   a) unregistered land charge Class C(iv) – ss2(4), 4(6) LCA 1972
   b) registered: pre-LRA 2002 – minor interest – notice– s48 LRA 1925 or overriding interest: s70(1)(g) LRA 1925 but not s70(1)(k) LRA 1925 *City Permanent Building Society* v *Miller* [1952] Ch 840
   c) registered: post-LRA 2002 – unilateral notice or agreed notice if there is evidence that owner is agreeable to notice being registered
4) No privity of estate between landlord and assignee of equitable lease
5) 'Usual covenants' only implied in an agreement for a lease

Summary

a) Lease by deed for any period creates a legal estate: LPA s52.

b) Oral or written lease for three years or less may create a legal estate: LPA s54.

c) Lease or agreement *made in writing* for period exceeding three years may confer equitable term: LP(MP)A 1989 s2.

Tenancies

Distinguish between specific tenancies and periodic tenancies.

a) Specific tenancy: a term of certain duration limited to expire at end of term for which granted.

b) Periodic tenancy: granted for definite period, but which continues thereafter until determined. Note: length of notice to quit required: s5 Protection from Eviction Act 1977. Residential property not less than 4 weeks' notice. Any notice to quit must be given to expire at end of period for which it has been granted.

Note also:

c) Tenancy at will: equitable interest for no certain duration to continue during the joint will of both parties. Converted to a legal periodic tenancy once landlord accepts rent from the tenant. For example a tenancy at will would be converted to a tenancy from year to year by payment and acceptance of a yearly rent. Occurs where negotiations for a lease are proceeding – must be consent of landlord.

d) Tenancy at sufferance: tenant remaining in possession after lease expires but without the consent of the landlord.

e) Statutory tenancies – see 'Security of tenure' (below).

f) Licences – see Chapter 9.

Form and assignment of lease

a) Formerly a lease by deed had to be written or printed and be signed, sealed and delivered. Law of Property (Miscellaneous Provisions) Act 1989, s1 abolished the need for a seal in any deed made on or after 31 July 1990. Today an instrument will only be a deed if:

   i) it is made clear on its face that it is intended to be a deed; and

   ii) it is signed by the grantor (or one of them if more than one) in the presence of a witness who attests the signature and it is delivered as a deed by him or by a person authorised to do so on his behalf.

   Note. a grantor may direct someone to sign the deed for him in his presence and in the presence of two witnesses who each attest the signature.

b) Legal lease, however created, transferable inter vivos only by deed: LPA s52. An informal assignment may be effective under *Walsh* v *Lonsdale* (1882) 21 ChD 9 principle.

   Note: distinguish assignment from sub-lease. The former is where the tenant grants to the assignee the whole of the outstanding interest under the lease, whereas the latter is the grant by the tenant of less than his whole interest under the lease.

c) LPA 1925 s62 'general words' clause. A lease of land or land + house passes to the lessee – in the absence of stipulation to the contrary – all fixtures, easements and other things: *Wright* v *Macadam* [1949] 2 KB 744 – renewed lease – existing use of coal shed passed on renewal.

Determination of a lease may be effected as follows

a) Expiry by effluxion of time – specific tenancy ceases when term for which granted comes to an end.

b) Exercise of express power by break clause in lease of commercial premises – often found in association with a rent review clause.

c) Forfeiture – every lease should contain a forfeiture clause which allows the landlord to re-enter on breach of covenant.

   The rules for relief against forfeiture vary – distinguish the rules relating to:

   i) non-payment of rent – from;

   ii) breach of other covenants: s146 LPA 1925 – repair – Leasehold Property (Repairs) Act 1938.

d) Notice to quit – see s5 Protection from Eviction Act 1977.

e) Surrender – to the landlord – the tenant voluntarily yields up the term to the landlord.

f) Merger – to the tenant or a third party. The tenant retains the lease and acquires the reversion or both vest in a third party.

g) Enlargement – s153 LPA 1925 – lease for over 300 years, no rent and still over 200 years to run.

h) Disclaimer – s315 Insolvency Act 1986.

i) Enfranchisement of houses: Leasehold Reform Act 1967, as amended by the Leasehold Reform Housing and Urban Development Act 1993 – must be a house, let under a long lease at a low rent, tenant in occupation for last three years (or three of last ten years). Tenant may acquire reversion or extend term for 50 years (but not if they only qualify under the 1967 Act because of the 1993 Act). Under the 1967 Act the right to enfranchise was restricted to houses having a rateable value limit of up to £1,500 in London and £750 elsewhere. However, the rateable value limits were abolished by the 1993 Act.

j) Enfranchisement of flats: Leasehold Reform Housing and Urban Development Act 1993.

Rights and duties of landlord and tenant

Implied obligations of landlord

a) Covenant for quiet enjoyment – landlord undertakes that the tenant shall be free from disturbance by adverse claims or physical interference with the tenant's enjoyment of the leased premises by the landlord or by persons claiming under him: *Perera v Vandiyar* [1953] 1 WLR 672.

b) Fitness for habitation: Landlord and Tenant Act 1985 s8 – *Quick v Taff-Ely Borough Council* [1985] 3 All ER 321.

c) No derogation from grant – landlord must do nothing to make the property substantially less fit for the purpose for which it was let: *Newman v Real Estate Debenture Corporation Ltd* [1940] 1 All ER 131; *O'Cedar Ltd v Slough Trading Co Ltd* [1927] 2 KB 123.

d) To keep in repair – s32 Housing Act 1961 which has now been consolidated in ss11–16 Landlord and Tenant Act 1985, implies into the leases of dwelling-houses let for less than seven years, granted after 24 October 1961, a covenant by the landlord:

   i) to keep in repair the structure and exterior of the dwelling-house, including drains, pipes and gutters; and

   ii) to keep in repair and proper working order the installations in the house:

   • for the supply of water, gas and electricity and for sanitation (including basins, sinks, baths and sanitary conveniences, but not other fixtures, fittings and appliances for making use of water, gas and electricity); and

   • for space heating or heating water.

Implied obligations and rights of tenant

a) Obligation to repair and also not to commit waste.

b) Obligation to pay rent derived from words such as 'yielding and paying'.

c) Obligation to pay rates and taxes – because the tenant is in occupation.

d) Right to remove fixtures: trade – remove during term; ornamental or domestic – may remove without injury to the property.

'Usual covenants'

Agreement for a lease only: *Chester v Buckingham Travel Ltd* [1981] 1 All ER 386.

Express obligations of tenant

a) Covenant to pay rent.

b) Covenant to repair

   Note meaning of 'fair wear and tear excepted'.

   Regis Property Co Ltd v Dudley [1959] AC 370 relieves tenant from liability for any disrepair which he can show has resulted from the reasonable use of the premises – but there is liability for consequential damage.

i) Normal standard of repair

Such repair as having regard to the age, character and locality of the premises would make them reasonably fit for occupation of a reasonably minded tenant of the class that would be likely to take them: *Proudfoot* v *Hart* (1890) 25 QBD 42.

ii) Covenant construed as at start of the lease: *Anstruther-Gough-Calthorpe* v *McOscar* [1924] 1 KB 716.

iii) Varying obligations – depends on the above standard of repair at the beginning of the lease.

To 'put' into repair. Imposes obligation to reinstate.

'To repair' means to keep in repair.

To 'leave' in repair. Must be in repair at end of lease.

iv) Absolute liability

Repairing covenant imposes an absolute liability.

v) Remedies for non-repair

At common law – action for damages.

Note: measure of damages and Landlord and Tenant Act 1927 s18(1) – the amount by which the value of the reversion is reduced by the breach. Action usually at the end of the lease: *Jones* v *Herxheimer* [1950] 2 KB 106.

If power in lease then lessor may enter and do the repair and charge the lessee.

Probably right of re-entry and forfeiture for breach of covenant reserved in lease, but note:

By statute: LPA 1925 s146(1):

Notice to be served on lessee: specifying the particular breach complained of, requiring remedy if possible and requiring money compensation: *Scala House & District Property Co Ltd* v *Forbes* [1973] 3 All ER 308.

If breach of covenant against assignment/underletting this is incapable of remedy – any notice need not require the breach to be remedied in such a case.

Reasonable time allowed for compliance and lessee must be told of right to serve a counternotice (below).

Landlord and Tenant Act 1927 s18(2):

Right of forfeiture not enforceable unless lessor proves above notice known to lessee or occupier and sufficient time elapsed to enable repairs to be carried out.

Leasehold Property (Repairs) Act 1938:

If lease for seven years or more and at least three years to run, lessee may serve a counternotice and then lessor cannot proceed further without permission of court. Note s1(5) as to the grounds for giving permission:

Immediate remedy to prevent substantial diminution in the value of the reversion.

To give effect to some bye-law.

In the interests of the occupier.

Small expense now compared with greater expense later.

It is just and equitable to give such permision: *SEDAC Investments Ltd* v *Tanner* [1982] 1 WLR 1342; *Hamilton* v *Martell Securities Ltd* [1984] 1 All ER 665.

LPA 1925 s147:

May relieve from liability for internal decorative repair.

LPA 1925 s146(4) – relief for sub-tenants.

c) Covenants to insure against fire: Fires Prevention (Metropolis) Act 1774 – use of insurance money to restore the premises.

d) Covenants against assignment, underletting or parting with possession. Distinguish:

   i) Absolute prohibition.

   ii) Qualified prohibition: s19(1) Landlord and Tenant Act 1927 – such consent is not to be unreasonably withheld. Landlord and Tenant Act 1988 ss1 and 2 now places the burden of proof on the landlord. The onus is on the landlord to reply to any request within a reasonable time and provide adequate reasons for any refusal. The interpretation of 'unreasonably withheld' for the purposes of s19(1) of the 1927 Act is unaltered.

   Section 22 of the Landlord and Tenant (Covenants) Act 1995 amends the 1927 Act by inserting a new s1A into s19. This enables a landlord and tenant to detail in the lease what terms or conditions must be satisfied for the landlord to give his consent to an assignment. If thereafter the terms or conditions are not satisfied and the landlord does not consent to the assignment, his consent will not be regarded as having been unreasonably withheld. Note. this amendment to s19 of the 1927 Act only applies to business premises.

Enforcement of covenants

Distinguish the rules relating to rent from other covenants.

Covenants to pay rent

a) By proceeding for re-entry through forfeiture:

High Court – see ss210–212 Common Law Procedure Act 1852.

County court – *Di Palma* v *Victoria Square Property Co Ltd* [1985] 3 WLR 207.

Section 138 County Courts Act 1984 and s55 Administration of Justice Act 1985.

b) Action on the covenant for arrears.

c) Distress:

   i) essentials;

   ii) what may be distrained;

   iii) how distress levied;

   iv) when distress may be levied;

   v) how much rent can be recovered;

   vi) tenants' remedies for wrongful distress.

Note: waiver of breach: *Central Estates (Belgravia) Ltd* v *Woolgar (No 2)* [1972] 1 WLR 1048 where the landlord shows the tenancy to be continuing, eg, demands and accepts rent either himself or through an agent.

Enforcement for other covenants

a) Action for damages.

b) Injunction.

c) Forfeiture under s146 LPA 1925.

Relief of sub-tenants under s146(4) LPA 1925.

Abbey National Building Society v *Maybeech Ltd* [1984] 3 All ER 262 and *Smith* v *Metropolitan City Properties Ltd* (1986) 277 EG 753 – these two cases give conflicting views on whether there is an inherent equitable jurisdiction to grant relief.

Problem of enforcing covenants

The law in this area underwent significant reform with the coming into force on 1 January 1996 of the Landlord and Tenant (Covenants) Act 1995. This Act applies a new enforcement regime to all new tenancies granted on or after 1 January 1996. Accordingly, the Act is not restrospective and the 'old law' still applies in respect of leases granted before that date.

a) Tenancies granted before 1 January 1996

Can A sue B for breach of covenant, assuming that the lease contains a right of re-entry for breach of the covenant? See diagram below.

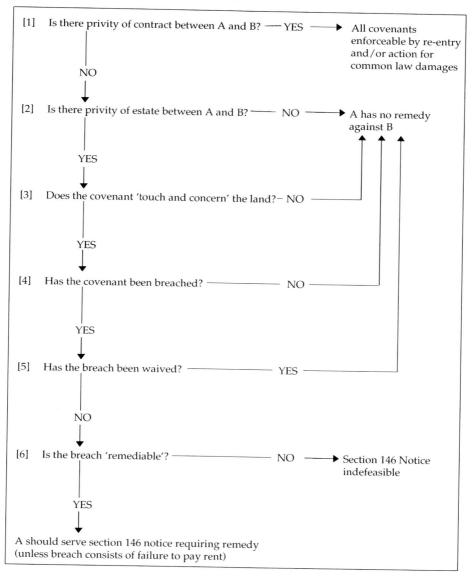

b) Tenancies granted after 31 December 1995

Landlord and Tenant (Covenants) Act 1995.

Applies to all new tenancies (both residential and commercial) granted on or after 1 January 1996.

Makes provision for persons bound by covenants of a tenancy to be released from such covenants on the assignment of the tenancy.

After T assigns he is released from his covenant and ceases to be entitled to the benefit of landlord covenants – unless it is an excluded assignment: s5.

Landlord's right to release: s7. Landlord can obtain release from his covenants when he sells his reversionary interest. Such release is not automatic. To obtain release, a landlord must serve a notice on the tenant as prescribed by s8 either before or within four weeks from completion of the reversionary assignment. If the tenant does not respond to the notice within the prescribed time, the covenants in respect of which the notice is served are released.

BHP Petroleum GB Ltd v *Chesterfield Properties Ltd* [2001] All ER (D) 451 – a covenant can only rank as a landlord covenant for the purpose of the 1995 Act if it had to be complied with on an ongoing basis and was transmissible.

Authorised guarantee agreement: s16.

Security of tenure

a) Agricultural tenancies

Agricultural Holdings Act 1986

Agricultural Tenancies Act 1995

b) Business tenancies

Part II Landlord and Tenant Act 1954

c) Residential tenancies: have been described as a 'status of irremovability'

Rent Act 1977

Housing Act 1980

Rent (Amendment) Act 1985

Landlord and Tenant Act 1985

Housing Act 1985

Housing Act 1988

Housing Act 1996

Summary of residential tenancies currently in existence

Post Housing Act 1996

Assured Shorthold

No notice requirement
Periodic or fixed term
For any period (no minimum)
No security at end of six months
Open market rent to be paid
Increase in rent may be referred to RAC*
Excessive rents may be referred to RAC

Assured

Prior notice required or other exceptions listed in Act
Security of tenure provided by 1988 Act
Open market rental level
Increase in rent to RAC

Tenancies under Housing Act 1988

Assured Shorthold

Prior written notice required
Minimum six month fixed term
No security at end of term
Open market rental level
Excessive rent may be referred to RAC

Assured

No notice required
Periodic or fixed term
Security of tenure (see HA 1988)
Open market rental level
Excessive rent may be referred to RAC

Tenancies under Rent Act 1977 (as amended)

Regulated Tenancies

Can be fixed term or periodic at end of which a statutory tenancy arises
No need for writing
Full security of tenure (see Act)
Only a fair rent may be charged

* RAC = Rent Assessment Committee (see Rent Act 1977 as amended)

d) The effect of security of tenure on the various types of tenancy may be summarised:

   i) Agricultural tenancies: Agricultural Holdings Act 1986, Agricultural Tenancies Act 1995

     Agricultural tenancies created before 1 September 1995 are regulated by the 1986 Act – statutory notice to quit at least 12 months. If tenant issues a counternotice then Agricultural Lands Tribunal must consent to possession.

Agricultural tenancies created on or after 1 September 1995 are regulated by the 1995 Act. Creates new farm business tenancy. It effects a deregulation of the landlord and tenant relationship leaving the parties free to negotiate their own letting arrangements.

ii) Business tenancies: Part II Landlord and Tenant Act 1954

Lease continues automatically. Landlord's notice between 12 and six months from end of tenancy. Parties may negotiate new tenancy.

Note: landlord's grounds for opposing a new tenancy: s30(1).

iii) Long residential tenancies [+ 21 years at low rent]

- Part I Landlord and Tenant Act 1954 – tenant continues in occupation.
- Leasehold Reform Act 1967 and Leasehold Reform Housing and Urban Development Act 1993 – enfranchisement.

iv) Other residential tenancies – see summary of residential tenancies currently in existence ante.

v) Lease/licence debate – *Street v Mountford* [1985] 2 WLR 877.

- Application to commercial property.
- Meaning of exclusive possession in this context.
- The non-exclusive agreement. Joint tenants? No! See House of Lords in *AG Securities v Vaughan; Antoniades v Villiers* [1988] 3 WLR 1205.

6.3 Key cases and statutes

- *AG Securities v Vaughan* [1988] 3 WLR 1205
  Lease/licence distinction – multiple occupancy of a flat – each occupant had exclusive possession of only one room – no collective joint tenancy

- *Antoniades v Villiers* [1988] 3 WLR 1205
  Lease/licence distinction – one bedroom flat granted to co-habiting couple under separate agreements called 'licences' – agreements pretence to avoid Rent Acts and created a joint tenancy not a licence

- *Ashburn Anstalt v Arnold* [1988] 2 All ER 147
  Essentials of a lease. Rent is not a prerequisite for a lease

- *BHP Petroleum GB Ltd v Chesterfield Properties Ltd* [2001] All ER (D) 451
  Landlord and Tenant (Covenants) Act 1995 – meaning of landlord covenant – covenant has to be complied with on an ongoing basis and transmissible

- *Go West Ltd v Spigarolo and Another* [2003] 2 All ER 141
  Valuable guidance as to s1(3) Landlord and Tenant Act 1988 – once a landlord has served written notice of his decision under s1(3)(b) that brought to an end the

reasonable time he was given for deciding whether to grant or withhold consent to the proposed assignment – a landlord could not rely on reasons for withholding consent not specified in his written notice of the decision

- *Lace v Chantler* [1944] KB 368
  A requirement of a legal lease is that both the commencement date and the duration of the term must be certain – lease for the 'duration of the war' was for an uncertain period

- *National Carriers Ltd v Panalpina (Northern) Ltd* [1981] 1 All ER 161
  Lease is capable of being frustrated – however, this was not likely to happen very often

- *Prudential Assurance Co Ltd v London Residuary Body* [1992] 3 WLR 279
  The term or duration of a lease must be certain – this rule applies to periodic tenancies – confirmed principle espoused in *Lace v Chantler*

- *Regis Property Co Ltd v Dudley* [1959] AC 370
  Covenant to repair – meaning of fair wear and tear excepted – tenant not liable for disrepair due to reasonable use of the premises or the weather but was liable for consequential damage

- *Street v Mountford* [1985] 2 WLR 877
  Lease/licence distinction – significance of exclusive possession – label parties attach to an occupancy agreement is not conclusive

- *Walsh v Lonsdale* (1882) 21 Ch D 9
  Equitable leases – an agreement for a lease which was specifically enforceable would be treated in equity as a lease on the same terms as the void legal lease

- *Yaxley v Gotts & Gotts* [1999] 3 WLR 1217
  Law of Property (Miscellaneous Provisions) Act 1989, s2 – proprietary estoppel could operate to give effect to an agreement rendered void by s2

- Landlord and Tenant Act 1927, s19(1)

- Landlord and Tenant Act 1985, s11

- Landlord and Tenant Act 1988

- Landlord and Tenant (Covenants) Act 1995

- Law of Property Act 1925, ss1(1), 1(5), 52, 54(2), 149(3), 149(6)

- Law of Property (Miscellaneous Provisions) Act 1989, s2

6.4 Questions and suggested solutions

Analysis of questions

The questions are wide ranging and cover general principles, the creation of the lease and the agreement for a lease, the covenants which are commonly found in leases (ie express covenants), implied covenants and the rules relating to security of tenure.

Some of the possibilities in this regard are set out below.

a) Informal/equitable leases

  i) Problem question

    Lease to be granted for more than three years. Deed required for lease to be legal. No deed executed.

    Prospective tenant moves into occupation, thereafter property is sold to a third party who tries to get the occupant out. Occupant seeks the assistance of equity.

    Why does equity intervene? 'Equity treats as done that which ought to be done.'

    Requirements for equitable intervention

    • Evidence in writing of the agreement

    • Grant of specific performance

    • 'He who comes to equity must come with clean hands.'

    • *Cornish* v *Brook Green Laundry* [1959] 1 QB 394

    • Occupant ought to register his equitable lease as an estate contract.

    If there is no equitable lease what is the basis of the occupancy and how can it be brought to an end?

  ii) Essay question

    'An agreement for a lease is as good as a legal lease.' Discuss.

    No it is not.

    There are three matters to consider:

    • Remedy – an equitable lease depends upon the grant of specific performance which is a discretionary equitable remedy.

    • Third parties – a contract for a lease only creates an equitable interest. Accordingly, it will not be good against Equity's Darling (the bona fide purchaser of a legal estate for value without notice).

      Protection – unregistered land; registered land.

    • Assignment.

b) Express covenants

  i) Problem question

    Such a question is likely to feature some of the following matters:

- Covenant to pay rent
- Covenant to repair
- Covenant not to assign or sublet

  s19(1) Landlord and Tenant Act 1927

  ss1 and 2 Landlord and Tenant Act 1988

  s22 Landlord and Tenant (Covenants) Act 1995 amending s19 of the 1927 Act

- Enforcement of covenants – the two regimes
  - Tenancies granted before 1 January 1996

    Privity of contract

    Privity of estate
  - Tenancies granted after 31 December 1995

    Landlord and Tenant (Covenants) Act 1995

- Forfeiture clause – different rules as to relief against forfeiture
  - Law Commission Report on Forfeiture of Tenancies 1985 (Law Com No 142)
  - Law Commission Termination of Tenancies Bill 1994 (Law Com No 221)

ii) Essay questions

Identify and evaluate the key provisions of the Landlord and Tenant (Covenants) Act 1995.

Identify the main weaknesses of the current law relating to the forfeiture of leases and consider the proposals of the Law Commission for reform of this area of law.

c) Implied covenants

Questions on this aspect of leases are usually in the form of problems.

The question will usually be structured so as to give the student an opportunity to deal with the main implied obligations of both landlord and tenant (ie implied both by statute and common law). These are as follows:

i) Landlord's implied obligations

Not to derogate from grant

Covenant for quiet enjoyment

Covenant to repair – Landlord and Tenant Act 1985 s11 – applicable in the case of a short lease (lease for less than seven years).

ii) Tenant's implied obligations

To pay rent

Not to commit waste

Invariably there will be a breach of some of these obligations and it will be necessary to consider the appropriate remedy for such a breach.

Frequently the landlord will be in breach of a repairing obligation under s11 of the 1985 Act with the question necessitating a clear statement that such a breach will not entitle the tenant to repudiate the tenancy and requiring an explanation of the tenant's self help remedy (ie carrying out the repairs himself after giving notice and setting off the cost against future rent).

QUESTION ONE

Consider the effect of:

a) a lease of Redacre at a rent to Alf until he marries;

b) a lease of Pinkacre at a rent to Bill for five years which contains a covenant to renew on the same terms;

c) a lease of Greenacre at a yearly rent to Cal until the landlord requires the land for development, Cal goes into possession and pays rent yearly.

University of London LLB Examination
(for External Students) Land Law June 1993 Q4

General Comment

A variation on the usual kind of question dealing with types of leases. The question centres on the relationship between s149(6) Law of Property Act 1925, s145 Law of Property Act 1922 and certainty of duration.

Skeleton Solution

Characteristics of a lease – s149(6) Law of Property Act 1925 – s145 Law of Property Act 1922 – *Parkus* v *Greenwood* – *Marjorie Burnett* v *Barclay* – certainty of duration – periodic leases – *Lace* v *Chantler* – *Prudential Assurance Co Ltd* v *London Residuary Body*.

Suggested Solution

For a valid lease or tenancy to exist four things must be satisfied. First, the premises must be sufficiently defined; second, exclusive possession must have been granted; third, the term or duration must be certain; and, fourth, leases in excess of three years must be granted by deed, whereas periodic tenancies can come into existence without the need for writing at all. Periodic tenancies come into existence through the acts of taking possession and paying rent – the period of the tenancy being determined by the period over which rent is calculated.

a) By virtue of s149(6) Law of Property Act 1925, leases at a rent for life or lives or until the marriage of the lessee (as in Albert's case) are converted into leases for a term of 90 years. Albert therefore has a lease for 90 years which can be determined after his marriage by either party giving one month's written notice to expire on one of the quarter days.

b) A lease for five years with a covenant to renew on the same terms could be a perpetually renewable lease under s145 Law of Property Act 1922. It is a question of construction whether there is a perpetually renewable lease, with the courts tending to lean against such a finding. Basically, if the covenant for renewal is part of a separate obligation then there is no perpetually renewable lease (see *Marjorie Burnett Ltd* v *Barclay* (1980) 258 EG 642), but if the lease is to be renewed on the existing terms 'including the covenant for renewal', then there will be a perpetually renewable lease: *Parkus* v *Greenwood* [1950] Ch 644.

If, on construction, Bill is found to have a perpetually renewable lease, then under s145 of the Act it will be converted into a term of 2,000 years, which can only be determined by the tenant by giving 10 days' notice to expire on the date on which, but for the operation of the statute, the lease would have determined. In other words by Bill giving ten days' notice to expire at the end of the five-year term.

Moreover, if it is found to be perpetually renewable, Bill could, of course assign it provided the assignment is registered with the landlord within six months of it taking place. However, unlike other leases, upon assignment the assignee (Bill) ceases to be liable even in contract for breaches committed after the assignment by the assignor.

c) The problem for Cal here is to establish that there is certainty of duration. In order for a lease for a fixed term to be valid it must have a certain duration: see *Lace* v *Chantler* [1944] KB 368 – where a lease for the duration of the war was void. This principle was reaffirmed in *Prudential Assurance Co Ltd* v *London Residuary Body* [1992] 3 WLR 279, where the House of Lords said that the principle in *Lace* applied to all leases and tenancy agreements, and that a lease 'until the land was required for widening the road' was void because the period was uncertain. Therefore, following *Prudential* Cal could not claim to have a lease for a fixed term, as a lease 'until the land is required for development' is equally uncertain.

However, Cal has gone into possession and pays rent yearly, the combined effect of which is to establish a periodic tenancy in his favour – the period being determined by reference to which the rent is calculated. In Cal's case the rent is assessed yearly and hence there would appear to be a yearly periodic tenancy. Generally speaking yearly leases can be determined by such notice as the parties agree, failing which a half year's notice to expire on one of the normal quarter days is required.

Unfortunately for Cal, the House of Lords also held in *Prudential* that a grant for an uncertain term which takes the form of a yearly tenancy which cannot be determined by the landlord, does not create a lease. In that case although the plaintiffs had gone into possession paying a yearly rent, there could only be a yearly tenancy if the terms of the agreement were such that both the landlord and tenant could give half a year's notice, and that the term preventing the landlord giving notice until the land was required for road widening was inconsistent with a yearly tenancy. On the facts Cal would be in the same position, and his lease would be determinable upon six months' notice.

QUESTION TWO

'The law of forfeiture has become unnecessarily complicated, is no longer coherent and gives rise to injustices.'

With reference to this statement, discuss the principal shortcomings of the law relating to the forfeiture of leases and consider ways in which it should be reformed.

University of London LLB Examination
(for External Students) Land Law June 1995 Q1

General Comment

A particularly challenging essay title. It would not be enough to simply outline the law of forfeiture in relation to leases. An answer must identify the main shortcomings of the current law. Further, a good answer would include coverage of the Law Commission proposals for reform of this area of law.

Skeleton Solution

Determination of leases – forfeiture for non-payment of rent – forfeiture for breach of covenants other than rent – position of lesser interest holders – waiver – main problems with the current law – Law Commission Report on Forfeiture of Tenancies 1985 – Law Commission Termination of Tenancies Bill 1994.

Suggested Solution

There are several ways in which a lease may come to an end, of which forfeiture is one (others include effluxion of time and merger of the reversion and the lease). Forfeiture involves the landlord bringing a lease to a premature end because of serious default on the part of the tenant. A landlord has an implied right to forfeit for breach of a condition. However, he may only forfeit a lease for breach of covenant if there is an express forfeiture clause in the lease (ie he has stipulated for it). Every well-drafted lease will contain an express forfeiture clause. Forfeiture may be effected either by serving a writ for possession, or by peaceable re-entry. However, if the premises are a dwelling house the landlord must secure a court order.

The procedure to be followed to effect a forfeiture differs depending upon whether forfeiture is being sought for (i) non-payment of rent, or (ii) breach of other covenants in the lease. In the ensuing paragraphs an outline of both procedures is given.

In the case of non-payment of rent, the landlord must make a formal demand (ie he or his agent must demand the exact sum due in the demised premises on the day it is due at such convenient hour before sunset as will give time to count out the money) unless excused from doing so. This requirement can be dispensed with if expressly excluded by the lease (which it is in all standard form leases). Further, the need for a formal demand can also be dispensed with if the rent is more than six months in arrears and there are insufficient goods available for distress on the premises to satisfy the arrears: s210 Common Law Procedure Act 1852. The landlord's right to forfeit for non-payment of rent is regarded merely as a security for the sum due. Accordingly, if a landlord brings an action for possession the tenant has the right to have the action discontinued if he pays all arrears and costs at any time before the trial: s212 Common Law Procedure Act 1852. The court can give a tenant relief from forfeiture (ie restore the tenant to his lease) even after judgment. The power to do so was originally equitable but is now regulated by statute: ss210–212 Common Law Procedure Act 1852. The tenant must apply within six months of the judgment and relief will be granted if he pays the rent due and the landlord's costs, and if it is equitable in the circumstances to grant relief. It is important to note that granting relief is a matter for the discretion of the court. If, however, the landlord has re-let the premises relief will not be granted: *Stanhope v Hawarth* (1886) 3 TLR 84. Where the head tenancy is forfeit for non-payment of rent a sub-tenant can seek relief from forfeiture under s146(4) Law of Property Act (LPA) 1925.

If a landlord wishes to forfeit for a breach of some covenant other than rent he must observe a different procedure. He must serve a written notice on the tenant under s146 LPA 1925 and the notice must specify the nature of the breach, demand it to be remedied and, if possible, require the tenant to pay compensation for the breach (unless the landlord chooses to waive this). The landlord must give the tenant a reasonable time to comply with the notice. What is a reasonable time depends on the nature of the breach. Three months is usually considered reasonable. If the breach is irremediable only a short period of time need be given to the tenant (a week or two, to enable the tenant to seek legal advice) before the landlord commences proceedings. A breach of a covenant against assignment or sub-letting would be irremediable: *Scala House & District Property Co Ltd v Forbes* [1974] QB 575. The tenant may apply for relief against forfeiture. Section 146(2) LPA 1925 gives the court a wide discretion to allow the tenant relief on terms that the breach of covenant ceases. In the case of an irremediable breach the court will not allow relief from forfeiture. Nor will relief be allowed if the landlord has already re-entered. Finally, a sub-tenant or mortgagee of the tenant may also apply for relief because if the lease is forfeited any sub-lease or mortgage falls with it.

A landlord may lose his right to forfeit by waiving the breach of covenant. Waiver can be express or implied. An implied waiver will arise if the landlord, knowing of the tenant's breach, does some act which unequivocally shows that he regards the lease as still continuing. The most typical act of waiver is the demand and acceptance of rent. However, it is a question of fact whether or not the landlord has waived the breach of covenant.

The law of forfeiture of leases has a number of shortcomings. The Law Commission has described the current law as 'complex and confused': Law Com No 142. A number of reasons can be advanced in support of such a conclusion. First, the fact that there are separate procedures depending upon whether the landlord is proposing to forfeit for non-payment of rent or for breach of some other covenant is a complication in itself. Second, the present law is both statutory and non-statutory. Originally the court used its inherent equitable jurisdiction to grant relief from forfeiture. Since those early days there have been major statutory incursions into the law of forfeiture, with the result that there is some uncertainty as to the extent to which the inherent equitable jurisdiction has survived these legislative developments: *Abbey National Building Society* v *Maybeech Ltd* [1984] 3 WLR 262 and *Official Custodian for Charities* v *Parway Estates Developments Ltd* [1984] 3 WLR 525. Third, there are different schemes for relief in relation to non-payment of rent between the High Court and county court, which is difficult to justify. Fourth, under the present regime a landlord has to guess accurately whether a given breach is remediable, and also decide how much time to give a tenant to remedy the breach before serving a writ. Finally, waiver is technical and operates irrespective of the merits of the case.

In 1985 the Law Commission published its Report on Forfeiture of Tenancies: Law Com No 142. It recommended that the current law of forfeiture, both statutory and non-statutory, should be abolished and with it the doctrine of re-entry. It was proposed that a landlord should have the right to bring termination order proceedings which would not depend on any clause in the lease (ie no need for a right of re-entry). Such a right could be expressly excluded. Under the new scheme there would be no distinction between termination for non-payment of rent and termination for other reasons. In termination order proceedings the landlord would have to establish a 'termination order event' in order to be successful. These would be: (i) a breach of covenant by the tenant; or (ii) a disguised breach of covenant (broadly a breach by the tenant of an obligation imposed on him otherwise than by covenant); or (iii) the tenant's insolvency. A successful application by a landlord for a termination order would result in either an 'absolute order' (to terminate the tenancy unconditionally on a date specified), or a 'remedial order' (to terminate the tenancy on a date specified unless the tenant has remedied the breach of covenant in conformity with the order of the court by that time). In both cases, the court would have a discretion to grant or refuse to grant an order in accordance with certain guidelines.

In 1994, the Law Commission published a further report which is, in reality, a republication of the 1985 Report with some small changes: Law Com No 221. The latest report includes a draft Termination of Tenancies Bill.

The enactment of the Law Commission's proposals would be advantageous in many respects and would remove much of the current complexity and confusion surrounding this particular area of the law. In particular, bringing to an end the separate procedures for termination for non-payment of rent and termination for other reasons would be a major advance.

QUESTION THREE

'The Landlord and Tenant (Covenants) Act 1995 has remedied important defects in the law relating to the enforceability of leasehold covenants and created a regime for new tenancies that strikes a fair balance between the respective interests of landlords and tenants.'

Discuss.

University of London LLB Examination
(for External Students) Land Law June 1996 Q1

General Comment

A topical question given that the Act came into force on 1 January 1996. A good answer would have succinctly summarised the problems with the pre-Act law, outlined the key provisions of the new legislation and assessed the fairness of the same in the terms requested. The topicality of the question gave students a good opportunity to show evidence of wider reading.

Skeleton Solution

Privity of contract; privity of estate – covenants which touch and concern – Law Commission Report – impact of the 1990s recession – scope of the Act – main provisions of the Act: statutory code for transmission of covenants; release of former tenants; landlords' right to release; amendment to Landlord and Tenant Act 1927; authorised guarantee agreements and overriding leases – striking a balance between the interests of property owners and tenants – future developments.

Suggested Solution

The Landlord and Tenant (Covenants) Act 1995 came into force on 1 January 1996. It reforms the doctrines of privity of contract and privity of estate as far as they relate to the relationship of landlord and tenant. The Act introduces some of the biggest reforms seen in real property law in the last 50 years.

Prior to 1 January 1996, the enforcement of leasehold covenants was governed by the doctrines of privity of contract and privity of estate. As between an original landlord and an original tenant there was privity of contract. This contractual liability subsisted throughout the entire term of the lease. Where there was privity of contract all covenants in the lease were enforceable. Privity of estate existed where the relationship of landlord and tenant existed between the parties. If L granted a lease to T and then T assigned it to A, there was no privity of contract between L and A because there had been no direct transaction between them. There was, however, privity of estate because A had acquired the estate which was created by L. Where there was privity of estate the benefit of the tenant's covenants and the burden of the landlord's covenants ran with the reversion, and the benefit of the landlord's covenants and the burden of the tenant's covenants ran with the lease. However, in each case the doctrine of privity of estate only applied to covenants which 'touched and concerned' the land. A covenant touched and concerned land if it affected the landlord as landlord or the tenant as tenant (ie it was not a personal one). The key point to note about the pre 1 January 1996 law was the 'privity trap' (ie by virtue of the doctrine of privity of contract an original tenant remained liable for future rent and other covenants under a lease notwithstanding that he had parted with all interest in the property).

The need for reform was recognised by the Law Commission in their 1988 Report: Law Com No 174. They concluded that 'it is intrinsically unfair that anyone should bear burdens under a contract in respect of which they derive no benefit and over which they have no control' with the proviso that 'the liability should be preserved where it is necessary but abandoned where it is not'. However, a key catalyst of the legislation was the fact that during the recession of the early 1990s many former tenants were dismayed to discover that they could be required to settle the debts of their insolvent successors long after they had assigned their leases. Further, such tenants often found themselves liable for a higher rent as a result of rent reviews or variations in the lease. As a result, prospective tenants became wary (because of the 'privity trap') about entering into long leasehold commitments from which they could not escape.

The Act applies to all 'new tenancies' (both residential and commercial) granted on or after 1 January 1996. It is not retrospective. Accordingly, the privity of contract/privity of estate regime outlined above still applies to leases created before that date.

The Act introduces a statutory code for the transmission of the benefit and burden of leasehold covenants in respect of new tenancies. Under the Act, the benefit and burden of all covenants pass upon assignment – whether it is the tenant who is assigning the leasehold interest or the landlord assigning the reversion. Accordingly, there is no longer any need to differentiate between covenants that 'touch and concern' the land and those that do not: s3. After a tenant assigns, he is released from his covenants and ceases to be entitled to the benefit of the landlord's covenants: s5. However, s11 expressly excludes the operation of the Act in cases of assignments that are either in breach of a covenant (ie unauthorised assignment) or by operation of law (ie following death or insolvency). In such situations an assigning tenant or landlord cannot be released from the relevant covenants of the lease until there is a subsequent assignment that is lawful. In other words, the Act has brought an end to the 'privity trap' for new tenancies (ie those granted on or after 1 January 1996).

It is not only tenants who can obtain release on assignment. Section 7 provides a new procedure whereby landlords can obtain release from their covenants under a lease when they sell their reversionary interest. However, the release of a landlord is not automatic. To obtain release a landlord must serve a notice (as prescribed by s8) on the tenant either before or within four weeks from completion of the reversionary assignment. The tenant may agree to the release. However, if he does not respond to the notice within the prescribed time the covenants in respect of which the notice is served are released. If the tenant responds in writing objecting to the release, the landlord can seek a declaration from the county court that the release sought is reasonable.

Finally, as to release, s24 somewhat restricts the release provisions by providing that any release under the Act does not affect any liability (of either landlord or tenant) arising from a breach of covenant occurring before the release.

Since the release of a former tenant can weaken a landlord's financial position, the Act amends the Landlord and Tenant Act 1927 to give landlords more control over future assignments. Section 22 of the 1995 Act enables a landlord and tenant to detail in the lease what terms or conditions must be satisfied for the landlord to give his consent to an assignment. If thereafter the terms or conditions are not satisfied, and the landlord does not consent to the assignment, his consent will not be regarded as having been unreasonably withheld. However, this amendment to the 1927 Act only applies to business premises. It does *not* apply to residential premises.

The statutory release of the original tenant from leasehold covenants after an assignment is subject to the possibility of him having to guarantee the performance by the assignee tenant (ie the person to whom he immediately assigns but not subsequent assignees) of the covenants from which he has been released by the assignment under a s16 authorised guarantee agreement.

Accordingly, from 1 January 1996 the only former tenants who can be held liable for debts of a successor are those holding under an 'old lease' (ie one executed before 1 January 1996), or former tenants under a 'new' lease who have entered into a s16 authorised guarantee agreement. In either case, s17 provides that any action for rent can only be brought against a former tenant by a landlord giving him written notice of his liability within six months of the debt becoming due. The aim of this provision is to give a former tenant early notice of his financial liabilities for any subsequent default. However, once a former tenant has discharged his obligations under a s17 notice he has the right to call upon the landlord to grant him an overriding lease under s19. This is a tenancy of the landlord's reversion that puts the former tenant in the position of landlord in relation to the defaulting tenant and in the position of defaulting tenant in relation to the landlord. The overriding lease is a response to the representations made by many original tenants during the 1990s recession who found themselves powerless to control accruing liabilities occasioned by the default of their successors in title. Now, under an overriding lease, an original tenant as immediate landlord of the assignee can exercise all the usual remedies available to a landlord, including the right to forfeit.

Since the Act is not retrospective it creates a two-tier leasehold market with automatic tenant release applying to new tenancies but not to old.

The Act does strike a fair balance between the interests of tenants (to prevent unforeseen claims being made against them) and those of landlords (to enable them to protect the value of their investments). This is demonstrated by the change made by the Act to the Landlord and Tenant Act 1927. It was recognised that any change in the law that took away a landlord's right to sue the original tenant, particularly of commercial property, could adversely affect the value of such property. Hence the ending of privity of contract has been balanced with some controls over assignment without which it is likely that many landlords would simply have prohibited assignment altogether. The fact that a balance between competing interests is achieved by the Act is due in no small part to the fact that a number of major bodies in the property industry (including the British Property Federation and the British Retail Consortium) worked together with the government in order to achieve that end.

Finally, looking to the future it would seem almost inevitable that in due course the removal of privity of contract will be extended to old tenancies too.

QUESTION FOUR

In 1983 Smith granted Jones a lease of Whiteacre for a term of ten years and Jones covenanted to pay £6,000 per annum rent for the duration of the term and to maintain Whiteacre in a good state of decoration and repair. In 1985, Jones requested a licence to assign the lease to Arnold and a deed was made between Smith, Jones, Arnold and Arnold's surety, Paul, in which Smith granted the licence to assign and Arnold covenanted to pay the rent and observe the covenants in the lease. In 1990 Arnold assigned the residue of the term to Tim and Smith assigned his reversion to Robb. Since 1992 no rent has been paid and Whiteacre has fallen into disrepair.

Who has remedies against whom in request of these breaches of covenant?

Would your answer be different if the breaches had occurred after the term had been extended by statute in 1993?

University of London LLB Examination
(for External Students) Land Law June 1994 Q6

General Comment

A question on the enforceability of leasehold covenants covering privity of contract and estate. In the main a well-prepared student should have had no real difficulty in coping with most of the points raised. However, asking for a licence to assign in 1985 (presumably because the lease so required) but not in 1990 was likely to have puzzled many students, as it did the writer.

Skeleton Solution

Privity of contract; privity of estate – covenants which touch and concern – breaches subsequent to assignment of reversion: S no right to sue – benefit passes to R: s141

— 134 —

LPA 1925 – J liable as original covenantor throughout the term – if J has to pay can he recover from A, A's surety or T?: *Moule v Garrett, P & A Swift Investments v Combined English Stores Group* – T liable to R on the basis of privity of estate – statutory extension: *City of London Corporation v Fell*.

Suggested Solution

At the outset it is necessary to explain the concepts of privity of contract, privity of estate and touching and concerning which are central to dealing with this question on leases. As between the original landlord (S) and the original tenant (J) there is privity of contract. This contractual liability subsists throughout the whole term of the lease unless J is excused by the terms of the lease or of the licence to assign. Where there is privity of contract all covenants in the lease are enforceable. Privity of estate exists where the relationship of landlord and tenant exists between the parties. If L grants a lease to T and then T assigns it to A, there is no privity of contract between L and A because there has been no direct transaction between them. There is, however, privity of estate because A has acquired the estate which was created by L. Here there is privity of estate between R and T. Where there is privity of estate the benefit of the tenant's covenants and the burden of the landlord's covenants run with the reversion and the benefit of the landlord's covenants and the burden of the tenant's covenants run with the lease. However, in each case the doctrine of privity of estate only applies to covenants which 'touch and concern' the land. A covenant touches and concerns land if it affects the landlord as landlord or the tenant as tenant (ie it is not a personal one). Here the covenant to pay rent and the covenant to maintain Whiteacre in a good state of decoration and repair both touch and concern the land.

In 1983, S granted J a ten-year lease of Whiteacre. In 1985, J asked for a licence to assign – presumably because the lease so required. What is puzzling is why the parties did not need another licence to assign in 1990 when A assigned to T and if so why S did not follow his earlier precedent and demand a fresh covenant from T. Also in 1990, S assigned his reversion to R. These developments can be represented diagrammatically as follows:

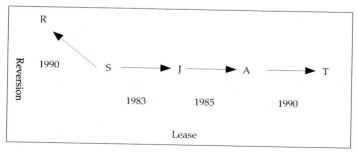

The breaches of covenant date from 1992, ie they did not take place until after S assigned his reversion to R. Accordingly, S has no interest and no right to sue for breach. By s141 Law of Property Act (LPA) 1925 the benefit of all covenants 'having reference to the subject matter'of the lease pass with the reversion to the assignee. Accordingly, the benefit passes to R who is thus the prospective plaintiff.

As previously mentioned, J as original covenantor remains liable on the two covenants throughout the ten-year term unless excused by the terms of the lease or of the licence to assign. Where a legal lease is assigned and thereafter a breach of covenant occurs the landlord can sue either the tenant on the basis of privity of contract or the assignee on the basis of privity of estate. Although in these circumstances the landlord has a choice as to who to sue he cannot obtain a double satisfaction. Here, if J is called upon to pay he would have an indemnity against A by virtue of s77(1)(c) LPA 1925, which provides for a covenant of indemnity to be implied into every assignment for value. Further, J would have an indemnity against A's surety or in quasi-contract against T: see *Moule* v *Garrett* (1872) LR 7 Ex 101.

By entering into express covenants to pay rent and observe the covenants in the lease, A has put himself in the same position as the original covenantor J and he remains liable on the covenants throughout the rest of the term unless excused by the terms of the 1985 licence to assign. By virtue of s77(1)(c) LPA 1925 A has an implied right of indemnity against T. Paul, A's surety, incurs similar liability as original covenantor. This is because of the House of Lords' decision in *P & A Swift Investments* v *Combined English Stores Group* [1988] 2 All ER 885. There their Lordships held that the benefit of a surety covenant could run with the reversion if the surety guaranteed performance of the tenant's covenants, which themselves touched and concerned the land. So long as the surety given here was not expressed to be personal (eg given to S alone) the benefit will pass to R. T is liable to R by virtue of privity of estate.

The aforementioned conclusions would be different if the breaches occurred after the term had been extended by statute in 1993. If there is a statutory extension then, prima facie, the statute extends the tenancy but not the contract. In *City of London Corporation* v *Fell* [1993] 3 WLR 1164 the House of Lords ruled that the liability of an original tenant ceased with the expiry of the contractual term of the lease. Accordingly, here the liabilities of J, A and A's surety would have expired but T would remain liable by virtue of privity of estate.

Finally, it is worth noting that the rule that the original lessor and original lessee remain liable on the covenants throughout the term of the lease, even after respectively assigning the reversion or lease, was a controversial one and was abolished for leases created on or after 1 January 1996 by the Landlord and Tenant (Covenants) Act 1995.

Note: this solution has been revised to take account of the coming into force of the Landlord and Tenant (Covenants) Act 1995.

QUESTION FIVE

Old Mr Grant died in 1990 leaving his Hindley Manor estate to William, his elder son. William (who lived and worked in London) then entered into the following arrangements with members of the family. He executed a deed giving his mother, Alice, the exclusive right to occupy Hindley Manor House for the remainder of her life. He orally agreed to allow his sister, Sarah, to live rent-free in a disused barn on the understanding that she would be responsible for repairing the roof, installing electricity and making the barn generally more habitable. He agreed in writing to let a lodge on the estate to his brother, Ben, at a yearly rent until he (William) obtained planning permission to convert the lodge into a guest house. Recently William has retired from his job and he has written to Alice, Sarah and Ben indicating that he intends to live in the Manor House with his wife and that he wants the barn and the lodge to be vacated for occupation by his children.

Discuss.

University of London LLB Examination
(for External Students) Land Law June 1997 Q5

General Comment

The question concerns a number of issues in respect of leases and licences. The inclusion of a diagrammatical representation of the facts is advisable in order to eliminate the possibility of confusing the various parties and issues in the course of an answer. There does not appear to be any third parties involved in the scenario.

Skeleton Solution

Legal lease – definition of a licence – types of licence – lease for 'life': s149(6) LPA 1925 – trust of land – contractual licence – estoppel licence: *Ramsden* v *Dyson* – Law of Property (Miscellaneous Provisions) Act 1989, s2 – periodic yearly tenancy: *Prudential Assurance Co Ltd* v *London Residuary Body*.

Suggested Solution

It is necessary to consider the various interests which Alice, Sarah and Ben have in Hindley Manor, the barn and the lodge on the Hindley Manor Estate respectively. In particular, it is necessary to decide whether they have a lease or a licence. The facts of the question can be represented diagrammatically (see overleaf).

A lease is one of the two estates capable of existing at law – it gives rise to a proprietary right in land. For a lease to be a legal one it must either be made in accordance with s52 LPA 1925 if it is for more than three years duration *or* by parol if it is to take effect in possession for a term not exceeding three years at the best rent reasonably obtainable: s54 LPA 1925.

A licence is a permission given by the occupier of land which allows the licensee to do some act which would otherwise be a trespass. It does not usually give rise to an interest in property.

There are four main types of licence. First, there is the bare licence (mere personal

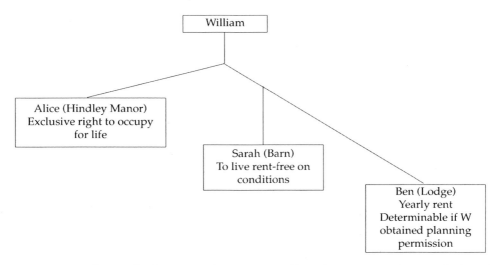

permission to be on the licensor's land). Secondly, a licence may be coupled with the grant of an interest in land, eg a right to enter another man's land to hunt and take away the deer killed. Thirdly, there is the contractual licence (a licence supported by consideration). Finally, there is the estoppel licence. In the context of this question, contractual and estoppel licences are particularly relevant.

William executed a deed giving his mother Alice, the exclusive right of occupation of Hindley Manor House for the rest of her life. It is submitted that Alice may either have a 'lease for life' converted into a 90-year term by s149(6) LPA 1925 or a life interest under a trust of land. Each of these possibilities is considered in turn below.

There are several requirements for a valid lease of which two are relevant on the facts here. First, the lessor must confer upon the lessee the right to exclusive possession of land. Here Alice has exclusive possession of Hindley Manor. Second, there must be certainty of duration (ie the duration of the term must be certain or capable of being ascertained at the outset of the term: s205(1)(xxvii) LPA 1925. Accordingly, Alice would fall foul of this requirement since the Manor House has been granted to her for the rest of her life. However, by virtue of s149(6) LPA 1925 a lease at a rent or in consideration of a fine for life or determinable on life is converted into a term of 90 years, determinable by notice served after the dropping of the life. Under this provision, provided Alice is paying rent or has paid a fine (premium) she would get a 90-year term but William could give notice to terminate after her death. There is no indication as to whether Alice is paying a rent or has paid a fine. Accordingly, it is doubtful whether she can take advantage of s149(6) LPA 1925.

Alternatively, William may be holding Hindley Manor House on a trust of land for Alice for life (presumably with the Manor House reverting back to him on her death). In order to create a trust of land the trust must be evidenced in writing: s53(1)(b) LPA 1925. Here William has executed a deed. Accordingly, the requirement of s53(1)(b) LPA

1925 would be satisfied. The new trust of land regime established by the Trusts of Land and Appointment of Trustees Act 1996 applies to any trust of property which consists of or includes land.

Further, William has orally agreed to allow his sister Sarah to live rent-free in a disused barn subject to conditions. There is no lease since there is no indication as to how long Sarah can stay in the barn (ie there is no certainty of duration – see above). Accordingly, it is necessary to consider whether Sarah has a contractual licence or an estoppel licence. A contractual licence is one granted for valuable consideration (ie Sarah has to show that she has given value for it). On the facts, Sarah could argue that if she has repaired the roof, installed electricity and made the barn generally habitable this could rank as her 'consideration' since her rent free occupancy of the barn was on the understanding that she would so act. The main problem Sarah may have in establishing a contractual licence is that the agreement between her and her brother was oral and s2 of the Law of Property (Miscellaneous Provisions) Act 1989 provides that:

> 'A contract for the sale or other disposition of an interest in land can only be made in writing and only by incorporating all the terms which the persons have expressly agreed in one document or, where contracts are exchanged in each.'

Further, Sarah has to show that there was an intention to create legal relations. Given that William is her brother the agreement would be regarded as a domestic one and with such agreements the presumption is that they are not intended to create legal relations. A presumption can be rebutted and thus the onus would be on Sarah to produce evidence that they intended to create legal relations.

Accordingly, it is submitted that there are quite considerable difficulties in the way of Sarah establishing a contractual licence.

On the facts, Sarah may well have an estoppel licence. Such a licence arises where an owner of land (William) allows another (Sarah) to spend money on that land or otherwise to act to her detriment under an expectation created or encouraged by the landowner (ie a representation or an assurance) that she will be allowed to remain on the land or acquire an interest in the land. In such circumstances, the landowner will not be allowed to defeat that expectation and deny the other's right to remain or to an interest in land: *Ramsden v Dyson* (1866) LR 1 HL 129. In essence the requirements for an estoppel licence are representation, reliance and detriment. The facts are supportive of an estoppel licence. Here William has agreed that Sarah can live rent-free in the barn if she complies with a range of specified conditions (ie there is a representation). Sarah repairing the roof, installing electricity and making the barn generally habitable could be seen as detriment and evidence that she had acted consistently with William's representation.

If, as seems likely, an estoppel licence arises in favour of Sarah, the task for the court will be to decide how best to satisfy it and the court will do the minimum necessary to do justice to the estoppel: *Crabb v Arun District Council* [1976] Ch 179. The courts have shown great flexibility in this regard. Remedies used include transfer of fee simple to licensee (*Pascoe* v *Turner* [1979] 1 WLR 431), life interest for licensee (*Inwards* v *Baker* [1965] 2 QB 29) and reimbursement of licensee's expenses/outgoings: *Dodsworth* v *Dodsworth* (1973) 228 EG 1115. However, this in turn has produced uncertainty because it is difficult for practitioners to anticipate how the equity will be satisfied in a given case. It seems that the remedy granted in cases of estoppel licence is largely dependent on the representation made (ie the applicant gets what she has been promised). Here there is no indication as to what assurances, if any, William gave Sarah as to how long she could stay in the barn. It is submitted that any such assurance would greatly influence the court in deciding what remedy to grant in order to satisfy the equity. If there was no representation/assurance given by William as to duration, Sarah could expect to be given reasonable notice to vacate the barn and to be reimbursed the costs she incurred in repairing the roof, installing electricity and making the barn generally habitable.

Finally, William agreed in writing to let a lodge on the estate to his brother Ben at a yearly rent until William obtained planning permission to convert the lodge into a guest house. As previously noted, one of the requirements for a valid lease is certainty of duration (ie the duration of the lease must be certain or capable of being ascertained at the outset of the term: s205(1)(xxvii)). In *Lace* v *Chantler* [1944] KB 368 a lease granted during the course of the 1939–45 war for the duration of the war was void. This principle was reaffirmed in *Prudential Assurance Co Ltd* v *London Residuary Body* [1992] 2 AC 386 where the House of Lords said that the principle in *Lace* applies to all leases and tenancy agreements. Here Ben can occupy a lodge on the estate until William obtains 'planning permission to convert the lodge into a guest house'. Such a determinable clause is similar to the one in *Prudential Assurance Co Ltd* v *London Residuary Body*. There the tenancy was to continue until the land was wanted for road widening. The House of Lords concluded that a yearly tenancy arose by virtue of the tenant's possession and paying a yearly rent. Here Ben is in possession (William recently wrote asking him to vacate the barn) and is paying a yearly rent. Accordingly, on the strength of the *Prudential Assurance Case* it is submitted that Ben has a periodic yearly tenancy and that William could get him out by giving six months notice to quit.

QUESTION SIX

'In the absence of special circumstances negativing the grant of a tenancy, a tenancy will arise where exclusive possession of land is granted for a term at a rent.'

Discuss.

University of London LLB Examination
(for External Students) Land Law June 2000 Q3

General Comment

The quotation is from *Street* v *Mountford*, an important House of Lords' decision, and candidates are required to examine the circumstances in which, despite the presence of the three elements of exclusive possession for a term at a rent, there will not be a tenancy. Candidates should focus their answers on those circumstances, and it would not appear necessary from the wording of the question to discuss whether or not exclusive possession is present. This could lead to a time-consuming discussion on cases involving shared occupation and artificial arrangements with the intention to avoid conferring exclusive possession on an occupant. The question assumes the existence of exclusive possession.

Skeleton Solution

Statement of the law by Lord Templeman – importance of exclusive possession – exclusive possession distinguished from exclusive occupation – three situations where, despite exclusive possession, there will be no tenancy: no intention to create a legal relationship; exclusive possession referable to a relationship other than that of landlord and tenant; where a grantor has no power to grant a lease.

Suggested Solution

The question embodies a statement of principle enunciated in *Street* v *Mountford* [1985] 2 WLR 877 by Lord Templeman. That case was an important one in the lease/licence debate. It clarified the law considerably and went a long way to clear up the confusion which had developed since *Errington* v *Errington and Woods* [1952] 1 KB 290. Lord Templeman said: 'if the agreement satisfied all the requirements of a tenancy then the agreement produced a tenancy and the parties cannot alter the effect of the agreement by insisting they only created a licence' and 'the only intention which is relevant is the intention demonstrated by the agreement to grant exclusive possession for a term at a rent'.

Of the factors mentioned by Lord Templeman, two are nearly always present: a term, whether it be fixed or periodic, and rent. The exclusive possession factor merits more discussion. He emphasised that exclusive possession is of first importance in considering whether an occupier is a tenant but, as he pointed out, it is not decisive because an occupier who enjoys exclusive possession is not necessarily a tenant. Without exclusive possession, however, there can be no lease. It is therefore necessary to enquire in the first place whether the occupant has exclusive possession. He acknowledged that sometimes it might be difficult to discover whether, on the true construction of an agreement, exclusive possession has been conferred. In *Hadjiloucas* v *Crean* [1987] 3 All ER 1008 Mustill LJ observed that *Street* v *Mountford* gave little guidance as to how the intention of the parties (that the occupant should enjoy exclusive possession) was to be ascertained, the reason being that it was not disputed in that case that the occupant had exclusive possession. Nor did it deal with the problem associated with shared occupation, since there was only one occupant in the case.

The notion of exclusive possession must be understood and distinguished from exclusive occupation. A person with exclusive possession is entitled to exclude the whole world, which in the case of a lease includes the landlord. If the landlord exercises control over the whole premises, then, even though the occupant is exclusively entitled to occupy his part of the premises, he will not have exclusive possession of that part: *Luganda* v *Service Hotels Ltd* [1969] 2 Ch 209.

Given that exclusive possession is present, Lord Templeman indicated that despite its presence, there were three situations where there would be no relationship of landlord and tenant.

Firstly, where the parties did not intend to enter into a legal relationship. Although the arrangement could constitute a tenancy at will it is more likely that it will create a licence: *Cobb* v *Lane* [1952] ITLR 1037. Generally these arrangements are to be found in the context of the family or arising out of friendship. In *Cobb* v *Lane* an owner allowed his brother to occupy a house rent-free. The Court of Appeal held there was no intention to create a legal relationship, nor was there a tenancy at will, but there was a licence. In *Booker* v *Palmer* [1942] 2 All ER 674 an evacuee was allowed to live in a house rent-free for the duration of the war. Lord Greene MR explained that the law does not impute an intention to enter into a legal relationship where the circumstances and conduct of the parties negatives an intention of that kind. In *Errington* v *Errington and Woods* Denning LJ observed: 'although a person who is let into exclusive possession is prima facie to be considered a tenant, nevertheless he will not be held to be so if the circumstances negate any intention to create a tenancy'. If, however, a family member is let into exclusive possession and pays rent, this may give rise to a tenancy: *Nunn* v *Dalrymple* (1989) 21 HLR 569. It is not impossible, therefore, for a tenancy to exist in the context of a family relationship.

Circumstances outside a family relationship can negative any intention to create legal relations. A case in point was *Burrows* v *Brent London Borough Council* [1996] 1 WLR 1448. In that case, a local authority was a council tenant's landlord. The tenant defaulted on the rent and the local authority obtained a possession order against him. It then decided to allow the tenant to remain on condition that he paid the arrears and future rent when due, and undertook not to enforce the possession order providing the tenant complied with those conditions. The House of Lords held that the parties did not intend that the arrangement should constitute a legal relationship and in consequence there was no tenancy. Lord Browne-Wilkinson described the occupant as 'a tolerated trespasser'.

In *OGWR BC* v *Dykes* [1989] 1 WLR 295 the local authority was under a statutory duty to provide accommodation for the homeless. It provided an occupant with exclusive possession of accommodation but the Court of Appeal decided that, since the accommodation was being provided by the local authority in accordance with its statutory obligations, this negated any intention to create a tenancy.

Secondly, it may be that possession is referable to a relationship other than that of landlord and tenant. Lord Templeman gave as examples 'occupancy under a contract of sale of the land, occupancy pursuant to a contract of employment, or occupancy referable to the holding of an office'. Although Lord Templeman uses the word 'occupation', it may be taken that he is referring to exclusive possession.

In *Gray v Taylor* [1998] 1 WLR 1093, the occupant had exclusive possession of an almshouse, but the Court of Appeal held that she was in possession as a beneficiary under a charitable trust and not as a tenant.

A purchaser of land, once contracts have been exchanged, holds an equitable fee simple in the land, and if the vendor allows him into possession after exchange but before completion, since his occupation arises from that equitable interest, he is not a tenant although he may have exclusive occupation: *Essex Plan Ltd* v *Broadminster* (1988) 56 P & CR 353.

In some instances an employee is required to occupy premises as part of his contract of employment. In such a case his possession is referable to the relationship of an employer and an employee and not that of landlord and tenant. There will therefore be no tenancy: *Dover v Prosser* [1904] 1 KB 84.

Lord Templeman explained that a servant occupier is a servant who occupies his master's premises in order to perform his duties as a servant. In those circumstances the possession and occupation of the servant is treated as the possession and occupation of the master, and the relationship of landlord and tenant is not created. However, the occupation of the servant must be necessary for the performance of his duties, and the occupier must be required to reside on the premises in order to perform those duties: *Smith v Seghill Overseers* (1875) LR 10 QB 422. A fee simple owner has exclusive possession as does a squatter, although clearly in those situations there is no relationship of landlord and tenant.

Thirdly, although someone may purport to grant a lease it seems obvious that there will be no effective grant of a lease if they had no power to grant one in the first instance: *Camden London Borough Council* v *Shortlife Community Housing Ltd* (1992) 90 LGR 358. However, this does not always follow, as evidenced in *Bruton v Quadrant Housing Trust* [1999] 3 WLR 150. In that case the local authority gave a licence of a block of flats to a housing trust to enable it to provide short term accommodation for the homeless. The trust then gave an occupant a licence to occupy one of the flats. Sometime later the housing trust acquired the lease of the block of flats. The occupant wished to establish that he was a tenant in order to claim the benefit of statutory repairing obligations, which were only available to tenants. The House of Lords held that the occupant had been granted exclusive possession for a term at a rent, and when the trust acquired the lease of the block, he became a tenant by estoppel.

We may state the law as follows: where an occupant has been granted exclusive possession for a term at a rent, then prima facie he is a tenant under a lease, despite any label to the contrary which the parties have attached to it. This could not be more clearly demonstrated by *Street v Mountford* and by the later case of *Antoniades v Villiers* [1988] 3 WLR 1205. However, even when the parties have intended to create an arrangement with these three elements present, it does not automatically follow that the parties have entered into a landlord and tenant relationship, as Lord Templeman explained in *Street v Mountford*.

QUESTION SEVEN

Kenneth owned two farms, Blackacre and Whiteacre. In 1996 he leased Blackacre to Alf and Whiteacre to Bill. The leases were for 15-year terms and contained covenants to pay rent, to maintain the buildings in good repair and not to erect any buildings without Kenneth's consent. In 1999 Alf sublet Blackacre to Susan for eight years and Bill assigned his lease to Tanya. The buildings on Blackacre are in disrepair and no rent has been paid on Whiteacre since 1997. Moreover, in 1997, Ray, a neighbouring farmer, enclosed a small field on Blackacre where he is currently building a storage shed.

Against whom can Kenneth enforce the covenants?

University of London LLB Examination
(for External Students) Land Law June 2001 Q4

General Comment

This is a question on the application of the Landlord and Tenant (Covenants) Act (LT(C)A) 1995. Candidates should always note the date of the commencement of leases in leasehold questions, since the Act, subject to two important retrospective provisions, only applies to leases created on or after 1 January 1996. Conversely, if a lease was created before that date, the retrospective provisions should not be overlooked. Both leases in the problem were created during 1996. The question simply requires a straightforward application of the Act to the facts given. The provisions of s3(5) LT(C)A 1995 should be noted, as they are relevant to Susan and Ray, while s24(1) LT(C)A 1995 is relevant to Bill's arrears of rent.

Candidates should beware of including material which examiners do not require. They are asked against whom Kenneth can enforce the covenants. A discussion of remedies is not being asked for, nor should candidates succumb to the temptation to discuss adverse possession because of Ray's activities. He has only occupied the land for four years and is simply a trespasser.

Skeleton Solution

LT(C)A 1995: effective from 1 January 1996 – Alf: remains tenant despite sublease; Kenneth may proceed against him – Bill: automatic release from covenants on assignment (s5 LT(C)A 1995); remains liable for accumulated rental arrears (s28 LT(C)A 1995); not applicable to subleases (s5 LT(C)A 1995) – Tanya: on assignment of the lease, all covenants pass (s3 LT(C)A 1995); burden of rental covenant passes to Tanya – Susan: Kenneth may proceed against her under s3(5) LT(C)A 1995 – Ray: Kenneth may proceed against him under s3(5) LT(C)A 1995.

Suggested Solution

Both leases were granted in 1996 and are therefore governed by the Landlord and Tenant (Covenants) Act (LT(C)A) 1995, which applies to all leases granted after 1

January 1996. The parties against whom Kenneth may bring an action for the breaches of covenants described in the question will be considered in turn.

Alf

There are two covenants in the lease of Blackacre which have been broken: the repairing covenant and the one prohibiting the erection of buildings on the demised premises without Kenneth's consent. Although Alf has sublet to Susan, he has not parted with the estate conferred on him by the lease to him of Blackacre. He remains the tenant and remains liable to Kenneth for the performance of the covenants in the lease, even after he parted with possession to his subtenant, Susan. This is so even if it is Susan who has allowed the buildings on Blackacre to fall into disrepair. Likewise, although it is Ray who is erecting a storage shed on Blackacre, Alf remains liable to Kenneth for breach of the covenant not to erect buildings on Blackacre without Kenneth's consent. The fact that third parties have occasioned the breaches of covenant in Alf's lease affords him no defence to the remedies available to Kenneth for breach of covenant.

Bill

Bill took a lease of Whiteacre in 1996 and in 1999 he assigned it to Tanya. He has paid no rent to Kenneth since 1997, so that when he assigned the lease to Tanya in 1999 there was a substantial accumulation of rental arrears at that date. However, when he assigned the lease to Tanya, by virtue of s5 LT(C)A 1995, he obtained automatic release from his further obligations under the lease, eg he ceased to be liable for future rental payments. However, the release afforded by s5 does not apply to any tenant's liabilities which have accrued before that date (s24(1) LT(C)A 1995). Kenneth may therefore sue Bill for breach of the rental covenant in respect of the accrued arrears.

Tanya

The lease of Whiteacre was assigned to Tanya in 1999. Under s3 of the 1995 statute, the benefits and burdens of all landlord and tenant covenants are annexed to the lease and the reversion, and automatically pass when either is assigned. Formerly, only benefits and burdens of covenants which touched and concerned the land passed on assignment of the lease and the reversion. This restriction has been removed by s3. Thus obligations imposed by the rental covenant automatically passed to Tanya at the date of the 1999 assignment, and at that date she became the new tenant of Whiteacre. It appears she has paid no rent either, and Kenneth may pursue her for such arrears as have accumulated from the date she became the assignee.

Susan

Blackacre is now in the exclusive possession of Susan, who occupies it as Alf's subtenant. Can Kenneth enforce the covenants in respect of repairs and the erection of new buildings against her? Under the old law, it would not have been possible for Kenneth to have done so under leasehold law because there was no privity of estate between Kenneth and Susan. Privity of estate can only exist between parties to a legal lease, because only a tenant of a legal lease can hold an estate in land. A tenant holding under an equitable lease only has an equitable interest in land: s1(1)(3) Law of Property Act 1925. The concept of privity of estate has now no application as far as the statute is concerned, since it defines a tenancy as including an agreement for a lease, eg an equitable lease: s28(1) LT(C)A 1995. However, it was possible for a landlord to obtain an injunction against a subtenant for breach of a restrictive covenant in the head lease under the principle enunciated in *Tulk* v *Moxhay* (1848) 2 Ph 774.

Now, under s3(5) LT(C)A 1995, any landlord or tenant covenant which is restrictive of the user of land 'shall ... be capable of being enforced against any other person who is the owner or occupier of any demised premises to which the covenant relates'. Kenneth may, therefore, enforce the covenant forbidding the erection of buildings against Susan. Since Ray is a trespasser she would have no difficulty in complying with the injunction by evicting Ray from the land and demolishing the shed. Section 3(5) only applies to covenants restrictive of the user of the land, and Kenneth could not avail himself of that provision in respect of the repairing covenant.

Ray
Kenneth could proceed against Ray under s3(5) LT(C)A 1995, since although a trespasser, he is in occupation and Kenneth could obtain an injunction against him.

Chapter 7

Covenants Relating to Freehold Land

7.1   **Introduction**

7.2   **Key points**

7.3   **Key cases and statutes**

7.4   **Questions and suggested solutions**

7.1 Introduction

This chapter concerns covenants affecting land held in fee simple (ie freehold covenants). In this area two important preliminary points must be established. The first is to establish the nature of the covenant, whether it is positive or negative. Then, secondly, to consider the different rules which apply to the running of the benefit and burden of those covenants.

As an aid to revision this may be expressed in the form shown overleaf.

First: Consider the nature of the covenant: whether positive or negative.

Then: Apply the following rules as to running of the benefit and burden observing the sequence of arrows from (1) to (4).

(1) COMMON LAW - BENEFIT - YES	(2) BURDEN - NO
1. Must touch and concern the land 2. Intention to run 3. Covenantee has legal estate: now 4. S78(1) LPA 1925: 'successors in title' 5. S56 LPA 'successors in title': may take even though not named expressly. [But: must satisfy benefit rules] *Smith and Snipes Hall Farm v River Douglas Catchment Board* [1949] 2 KB 500	*Austerberry v Oldham Corporation* (1885) 29 Ch D 750; *Rhone v Stephens* [1994] 2 All ER 65 Methods of circumvention 1. Positive easement - *Crow v Wood* [1971] 1 QB 77 2. Estate rentcharge - s2 Rentcharges Act 1977 3. Enlarge long lease - s153 LPA 1925 4. Chain of indemnity covenants 5. Planning obligations - s12 Planning and Compensation Act 1991 6. Right of re-entry 7. Benefit - burden rule: *Halsall v Brizell* [1957] Ch 169
(4) EQUITY - BENEFIT - YES	**(3) BURDEN - YES**
Annexation - express/statutory - s78(1) LPA *Federated Homes v Mill Lodge Properties* [1980] 1 All ER 371 *Roake v Chadha* [1983] 3 All ER 503 Assignment Scheme of development - building scheme *Elliston v Reacher* [1908] 2 Ch 374 *Reid v Bickerstaff* [1909] 2 Ch 305 *Baxter v Four Oaks Properties Ltd* [1965] Ch 816 *Re Dolphin's Conveyance* [1970] Ch 654	*Tulk v Moxhay* (1848) 2 Ph 774 1. Restrictive/negative covenant only 2. Dominant land retained: *Formby v Barker* [1903] 2 Ch 539 3. Must touch and concern the dominant land 4. Must show intention to annex the burden to servient land - s79 LPA 1925 5. Must show benefit intended to run in equity

Covenants created before 1926   –   Protected by doctrine of notice

Covenants created after 1925   –   Unregistered land: land charge Class D(ii), s2 LCA 1972

Registered land:

a) Pre-LRA 2002

    Minor interest protected by notice on charges register

b) Post-LRA 2002

    i)   If covenant created on a transfer of part of the land – covenant recorded in the actual deed of transfer of part of the land. When tranferee applies to get land registered with his own title to the transferred land, the Registry will note the restrictive covenant on both the new title and the title of the land from which the new title was transferred (ie noted on both the servient and dominant land)

ii) If covenant created in any other way owner of dominant land would apply for note to be made on his land using Form AP1. At same time he would protect his interest with restriction on the servient land either by an agreed notice or a unilateral notice

7.2 Key points

Covenants affecting FEE SIMPLE

Note s56 LPA 1925: 'A person may take an immediate or other interest in land or other property, or the benefit of any ... covenant ... although he may not be named as a party ...' Section 56 is *not* concerned with the rules for passing the benefit but the giving of the benefit to other persons not named in the deed: *Smith and Snipes Hall Farm* v *River Douglas Catchment Board* [1949] 2 KB 500.

Do benefit and burden of covenants affecting fee simple bind successive owners?

a) Original parties.

b) Third parties or successors: see s56 LPA 1925.

Running of covenants at common law

a) Benefit – note conditions: must touch and concern land of covenantee and covenantee has legal estate.

b) Burden, not at common law – *Austerberry* v *Oldham Corporation* (1885) 29 Ch D 750. See also *Rhone* v *Stephens* [1994] 2 All ER 65.

c) Consider methods of circumvention.

These are indirect methods for facilitating the running of the burden of positive covenants.

i) Positive easement – *Crow* v *Wood* [1971] 1 QB 77;

ii) Estate rentcharge – s2 Rentcharges Act 1977;

iii) Chain of indemnity covenants;

iv) Planning obligations under s12 Planning and Compensation Act 1991;

v) Long lease which is then enlarged into the fee simple under s153 LPA 1925;

vi) The benefit/burden rule in *Halsall* v *Brizell* [1957] Ch 169 by which anyone who enjoys the benefit of an obligation must also observe the corresponding burdens. See also *Tito* v *Waddell (No 2)* [1977] Ch 106.

Intervention of equity

a) Burden of a restrictive covenant runs with the land in equity:

Tulk v *Moxhay* (1848) 2 Ph 774 – originally based on notice.

b) Characteristics and enforceability of restrictive covenants:

i) Must be negative in nature – substance not form;

ii) Must be dominant land retained by the covenantee: *Formby* v *Barker* [1903] 2 Ch 539;

iii) Successor to dominant land must prove benefit has passed to him.

Methods of acquiring benefit:

- Annexation express or by statute – s78 LPA 1925 – *Federated Homes Ltd* v *Mill Lodge Properties Ltd* [1980] 1 All ER 371; *Roake* v *Chadha* [1983] 3 All ER 503.

- Express assignment.

- Scheme of development – building scheme – *Elliston* v *Reacher* [1908] 2 Ch 374.

   Originally five requirements had to be satisfied for a building scheme to create 'local law'. They were as follows:

   – common vendor;

   – estate laid out in lots consistent with a scheme of development;

   – restrictions benefit all the lots;

   – the parties purchased on that basis;

   – the area must be clearly defined: *Reid* v *Bickerstaff* [1909] 2 Ch 305.

   At present it seems only two requirements are essential. They are as follows:

   – the area of the scheme must be defined;

   – those who purchase from the creator of the scheme do so on the footing that all purchasers shall be mutually bound by and mutually entitled to enforce a defined set of restrictions.

See *Baxter* v *Four Oaks Properties Ltd* [1965] Ch 816 and *Re Dolphin's Conveyance* [1970] Ch 654.

Enforceability

Persons against whom restrictive covenant enforceable:

a) before 1926 – doctrine of notice applies;

b) after 1925 – unregistered land – land charge Class D(ii), ss2 and 4 LCA 1972.

c) Registered land:

   i) Pre-LRA 2002 – minor interest protected by notice on charges register.

   ii) Post-LRA 2002

   - If covenant created on a transfer of part of the land – covenant recorded in the actual deed of transfer of part of the land. When tranferee applies to get land registered with his own title to the transferred land, the Registry will note the restrictive covenant on both the new title and the title of the land from which the new title was transferred (ie noted on both the servient and dominant land).

   - If covenant created in any other way owner of dominant land would apply for note to be made on his land using Form AP1. At same time he would protect his interest with restriction on the servient land either by an agreed notice or a unilateral notice.

Discharge of restrictive covenants

a) In equity: *Chatsworth Estates Co* v *Fewell* [1931] 1 Ch 224. Covenants may be lost by showing that because of a change in the character of the neighbourhood no value is left in the covenant or that this change has arisen by acts or omissions of the covenantee which give rise to the belief that covenants would no longer be enforced.

b) By statute:

   i) LPA s84(1), (1A), (1B), (1C) – *Gilbert* v *Spoor* [1983] Ch 27 and *Re Martin's Application* (1989) 57 P & CR 119.

   Lands Tribunal on four grounds:

   - obsolete;

   - obstructs reasonable use and no substantial benefit or contrary to public interest;

   - parties agree;

- no injury.

Appeal from the Lands Tribunal is to the Court of Appeal on a point of law by case stated.

i) LPA s84(2) – declaration by court whether or not land is affected by a covenant and its nature and extent – *J Sainsbury plc* v *Enfield London BC* [1989] 2 All ER 817.

ii) Housing Act 1985 s610. County court may allow conversion to two or more tenements within one house.

c) Unity of seisin: where a person becomes entitled to *both* the dominant and servient land to which the covenant relates. See *Re Tiltwood, Sussex, Barrett* v *Bond* [1978] Ch 269; *Texaco Antilles Ltd* v *Kernochan* [1973] AC 609 – but not if in a building scheme.

d) Insure against the risk of enforcement.

Relationship between restrictive covenants and the law of town and country planning

Both private and public codes must be satisfied – but planning permission may show that the covenant is no longer in the public interest for the purposes of an application to the Lands Tribunal under s84(1) LPA 1925: *Gilbert* v *Spoor* [1983] Ch 27. Otherwise the law of restrictive covenants is quite distinct from the law of town and country planning – a person wishing to develop land must be able to do so under both private and public branches of the law – a grant of planning permission does not itself entitle a person to breach a restrictive covenant: *Re Martin's Application* (1989) 57 P & CR 119.

7.3 Key cases and statutes

- *Austerberry* v *Corporation of Oldham* (1885) 29 Ch D 750
  The burden of a covenant, whether positive or negative, made between a vendor and purchaser does not run with the fee simple at common law

- *Ballard's Conveyance, Re* [1937] Ch 473
  Express annexation – the annexation of the benefit of a covenant was not effective if the land to which the covenant was annexed was of too great an area for it all to benefit from the covenant

- *Elliston* v *Reacher* [1908] 2 Ch 665
  Benefit of a restrictive covenant could pass in equity under a building scheme – requirements of such a scheme – but see also *Baxter* v *Four Oaks Properties Ltd* [1965] 1 All ER 906 and *Re Dolphin's Conveyance* [1970] 2 All ER 664

- *Federated Homes Ltd* v *Mill Lodge Properties Ltd* [1980] 1 WLR 594
  Annexation – effect of s78(1) LPA 1925 was to automatically annex the covenant to the land so long as it was intended to benefit the land in question

- *Haywood* v *Brunswick Permanent Benefit Building Society* (1881) 8 QBD 403
  In equity only the burden of a restrictive covenant could run with freehold land

- *Martin's Application, Re* [1989] 5 EG 85
  The grant of planning permission did not entitle a person to ignore a restrictive covenant – rather such a grant was one matter that the Lands Tribunal should take into account in exercising its jurisdiction under s84 LPA 1925

- *Rhone* v *Stephens* [1994] 2 All ER 65
  Rule in *Austerberry* v *Corporation of Oldham* affirmed by House of Lords – burden of a positive covenant could not run directly with freehold land at law or in equity.

- *Roake* v *Chadha* [1984] 1 WLR 40
  Statutory annexation – restricted principle of *Federated Homes* – s78(1) LPA 1925 could not be used to annex the benefit of a covenant where the express wording of the covenant precluded annexation – covenant to pass had to be expressly assigned

- *Rogers* v *Hosegood* [1900] 2 Ch 388
  Effect of express annexation was to confer the benefit of the covenant upon the land and not an individual – wording used sufficient to annex benefit of the covenant to the land – test for whether a freehold covenant 'touches and concerns' the land was the same as for leasehold covenants

- *Tulk* v *Moxhay* (1848) 2 Ph 774
  The burden of a covenant could run with freehold land in equity

- Land Charges Act 1972, ss2 and 4

- Law of Property Act 1925, ss56, 78, 79, 84 and 153

- Rentcharges Act 1977, s2

While the decision in *Federated Homes* was good news for conveyancers (s78 could come to the rescue if the express annexation formula used by them turned out to be deficient), the reasoning of the Court of Appeal on that occasion is not beyond criticism: see (1981) 97 LQR 32; (1982) 98 LQR 202 and [1982] JPL 295 (G H Newsom QC).

It may be useful to appreciate the facts and decision in the following form:

FEDERATED HOMES LTD v *MILL LODGE PROPERTIES LTD* [1980] 1 All ER 371

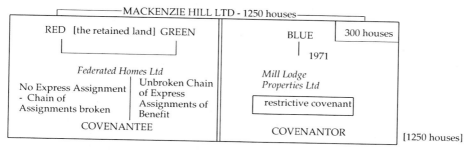

1970 – M Ltd – outline planning permission to develop whole site – set maximum number.

1971 – Conveyance of blue land contained [restrictive covenant] 'not to build at a greater density than a total of 300 dwellings' [so as not to reduce the number of units which the vendor (M Ltd) might eventually build on the retained land [red and green].

1977 – Planning permission to F to develop red and green land. Defendants had also obtained planning permission to develop blue land at higher density than covenant. Action by F to restrain defendants from breaking the restrictive covenant.

Question: Had benefit passed to F in respect of red land?

Court of Appeal held: If restrictive covenant touched and concerned covenantee's land then s78(1) LPA 1925 annexed the benefit of the covenant to that land. The restrictive covenant was for the benefit of the retained land and that was sufficiently described in the 1971 conveyance for the purposes of annexation.

Section 78(1) annexed the benefit to the retained land for the benefit of M Ltd and their successors in title and persons deriving title under them. Thus s78(1) caused the benefit to run with every part of the retained land including the red land. F could enforce for both red and green land.

But will not apply if contrary intention is shown – by stipulation that benefit will only pass by express assignment: *Roake v Chadha* [1983] 3 All ER 503.

7.4 Questions and suggested solutions

Analysis of questions

Questions on freehold covenants tend to be problem ones. The problem will definitely contain a restrictive covenant and probably a positive one. It is crucial to determine at the outset whether the covenants you are dealing with are positive or negative ones. The heart of the problem will be considering whether the benefit and burden of the covenants run with the land. In this regard, the equity rules will be more important than the common law ones. In relation to positive covenants, indirect devices to enable the burden of a positive covenant to run with the land (eg chain of indemnity covenants, doctrine of *Halsall v Brizell* [1957] Ch 169) may have to be considered. As to the running of the benefit of a restrictive covenant in equity, students should be particularly familiar with the impact on annexation and assignment of the decision of the Court of Appeal in *Federated Homes v Mill Lodge Properties* [1980] 1 All ER 371, and with the current requirements of a building scheme. Finally, it is important to note that some examiners are prepared to draft a question which covers both restrictive covenants and easements.

QUESTION ONE

Why do different principles govern the running of positive and restrictive covenants affecting freehold land? Are the differences justified?

University of London LLB Examination
(for External Students) Land Law June 1987 Q2

General Comment

The candidate is given the opportunity to think in the terms of a Law Commissioner considering how to introduce a working paper or a report on the potential for reform in the law of covenants affecting freehold land. Those students who had taken the opportunity to read the Law Commission Report No 127 – 'Transfer of Land: The Law of Positive and Restrictive Covenants' – would have been at an advantage in attempting this question.

Skeleton Solution

a) Why?: Question of history – need to construe with care any obligation to spend money – equity introduced reforms but nature of equity jurisdiction ensured these reforms must be limited – consequence – different principles for the running of positive and restrictive covenants – briefly consider the respective rules: (i) positive – and methods of circumvention; (ii) restrictive – *Tulk* v *Moxhay*.

b) Justification?: None – problems: they create eg Megarry and Wade – solutions: land obligations to cover both forms of covenant – report of Law Commission No 127, 'Transfer of Land: The Law of Positive and Restrictive Covenants'.

c) Conclusion: recommendations of Law Commission – in brief – see Part V for full details of the Land Obligation – the report also contains a draft Bill to implement the recommendations – commonhold proposals.

Suggested Solution

The fact that different principles do apply for the running of positive and restrictive covenants affecting freehold land is a question of history. In the case of covenants generally, both positive and negative, the benefit of a covenant will run. Cheshire states:

> 'The rule at law for several centuries has been that the benefit of covenants, whether positive or negative, which are made with a covenantee, having an interest in the land to which they relate, passes to his successors in title: *The Prior's Case* (1368) YB 42 Ed 3 Hil, pl 14.'

This benefit will pass on four conditions being satisfied:

a) the covenant touches and concerns the land of the covenantee;

b) there is an intention that the benefit should run with the land then owned by the covenantee;

c) the covenantee, at that time, has the legal estate in the land to be benefited;

d) the assignee seeking to enforce the covenant has that same legal estate in the land. This rule has now been extended by s78 LPA 1925 in that for covenants made after 1925 it is sufficient to show that the person seeking to enforce the covenant is a 'successor in title' of the covenantee.

On the other hand, when the question relates to the burden of covenants it is clear that the burden of a positive covenant does not run at common law: *Austerberry* v *Oldham Corporation* (1885) 29 Ch D 750. The reasoning in this case is not entirely satisfactory, but the statement of the law by Lindley LJ is quite clear:

'... in the absence of authority it appears to me that we shall be perfectly warranted in saying that the burden of this covenant does not run with the land ... If the parties had intended to charge this land for ever, into whosesoever hands it came, with the burden of repairing the road, there are ways and means known to conveyancers by which it could be done with comparative ease: all that would have been necessary would have been to create a rentcharge and charge it on the tolls, and the thing would have been done. They have not done anything of the sort, and, therefore, it seems to me to show that they did not intend to have a covenant which should run with the land. That disposes of the part of the case which is perhaps the most difficult.'

During that statement Lindley LJ did point to one of the methods of circumvention of the rule which have become necessary – to use a rentcharge rather than a covenant, and this method remains available today by way of the estate rentcharge under s2 of the Rentcharges Act 1977. Other methods of enforcing the burden of positive obligations which have been suggested include:

a) using a lease rather than a conveyance of the fee simple;

b) chains of indemnity covenants;

c) use of positive easements rather than covenants – *Crow* v *Wood* [1971] 1 QB 77;

d) imposing covenants in a long lease then converting this long lease into the freehold under s153 LPA 1925;

e) the so-called benefit/burden rule established in *Halsall* v *Brizell* [1957] Ch 169, which obliges a person who wishes to take advantage of a facility such as roads or drainage to observe any corresponding obligation to contribute to the cost of providing or maintaining it.

Throughout these exceptions the problems of enforcing positive obligations appear to hinge on the financial issue of supervision where the spending of money is concerned. The law takes great care where the consequence of a direction will require the spending of money. No such problem arises in the case of negative or restrictive covenants. As a result, the burden of a restrictive covenant will run in equity based on the principle established in *Tulk* v *Moxhay* (1848) 2 Ph 774. In order for the burden of the restrictive covenant to run the following conditions must be satisfied:

a) the covenant is negative in substance;

b) the covenantee must continue to own land capable of being protected by the covenant;

c) the covenant must touch and concern the dominant land; and

d) it must be the common intention of the parties that the burden of the covenant shall run with the land of the covenantor.

Thus the different rules depend on the nature of the covenant and appear to arise out of the attitude adopted by the courts as to their ability to supervise negative obligations and the difficulties that arise in enforcing and supervising positive obligations.

Are the differences justified? The fact that they exist indicates there must be justification in the eyes of the court. The question today is whether the continuation of the differences can be justified. The fact that the burden of a positive covenant cannot run directly with freehold land gives rise to obvious practical problems. Megarry and Wade put the matter thus:

> 'The rule that the burden of positive covenants does not run with freehold land is in sharp contrast to the position in relation to leasehold property where such covenants are enforceable if, in the case of leases granted before 1996, they touch and concern the land and there is privity of estate, or, in leases granted after 1995, the covenants are not expressed to be personal. The 'ill-consequences' of the rule have often been noted. Two of the most obvious are as follows.
> (i) Two neighbours cannot enter into agreements for such everyday matters as the maintenance of a wall or the pruning of trees in such a way that the burden will run with the land.
> (ii) Flying freeholds cannot in practice be granted because of the difficulties of ensuring rights of support for the upper floors and for the maintenance of the roof. Flats are therefore granted by means of a lease so that the necessary covenants can be both imposed and enforced.
> Although there have been a number of proposals for reform (of which the most recent are considered below), to date "nothing has been done".'

Thus the short answer to the question as posed is, no! The differences are no longer justified.

In January 1984 the Law Commission published report No 127 – 'Transfer of Land: The Law of Positive and Restrictive Covenants'. The report gives a comprehensive review of the present law and provides suggested solutions to the problems posed in this question. The report states at paragraph 4.16: '... there can be no doubt that the law of positive covenants is in urgent need of radical reform, and we are committed to a project designed to achieve this. The real question, therefore, is whether the law of restrictive covenants can stay as it is in the context of that project.' In the following paragraph 4.17 the Law Commission identify the real difficulty of reform in this area of land law. It is not enough merely to bring both covenants into line by using the present rules for restrictive covenants for the enforcement of positive covenants. They say:

'The real objection is that the existing law of restrictive covenants is not suitable for positive covenants in any case. Two of the main reasons for this are as follows:
(a) ... a restrictive covenant requires people merely to refrain from doing something. But positive covenants require them actually to do something, and that something may be a burdensome and expensive thing ... Liability to perform a positive covenant ... cannot rest on all those interested in the burdened land.
(b) The burden of a restrictive covenant runs only in equity, so that equitable remedies alone are available for its enforcement. This may not greatly matter in the case of a restrictive covenant because ... the remedy most often sought will be the equitable remedy of injunction, or damages in lieu. But legal remedies must be available for positive covenants. The idea of enforcing a simple covenant to pay money by means of equitable remedies is wholly artificial. And the normal remedy for breach of a covenant to carry out works must be legal damages (including, if appropriate, damages for consequential loss). This point goes to the heart of the conceptual nature of the covenant: legal remedies cannot be available unless the burden runs at law and it cannot do that unless it amounts to a legal – not an equitable – interest in land. The law for restrictive covenants is therefore fundamentally unsuitable ...'

The Law Commission concluded at paragraph 4.18:

'We hope that we have said enough to show that the law of restrictive covenants could not be retained and simply expanded so as to embrace positive covenants. Positive covenants demand a legal regime which is different in fundamental respects.'

And at paragraph 4.20 stated:

'This requires a totally new "legal regime" and this is, in the opinion of the Law Commission, provided by the Land Obligation. This would be achieved by extending the process of law reform to include both positive and restrictive covenants and welding the two into a system which is both unified and more satisfactory.'

The Land Obligation would be a new interest in land 'whereby in appropriate circumstances obligations (whether positive or negative) may be imposed on one piece of land for the benefit of other land, and be enforceable by or on behalf of the owners for the time being of the one piece of land against the owners for the time being of the other': paragraph 4.21.

The new interest would be more like the easement and similar rules to easements would apply. Basically the new Land Obligation would be registerable, there would be limits on the persons who are liable for breach of the obligation, remedies should be made appropriate to the nature of the obligation and the provisions of s84 LPA 1925 should apply to enable the Land Obligations to be modified or discharged.

The Land Obligation is seen as a multi-faceted form of obligation suitable to all forms of land development. The major objective, however, is to do away with the problems raised in this question and provide 'for the first time, a means whereby the burden of positive covenants may be made to run with the servient land under English law'.

Part V of the Law Commission Report No 127 explains the Land Obligation in detail and the report contains the draft of a proposed Bill to implement the recommendations of the Law Commission.

In recent years there has been an emphasis upon introducing a new form of land ownership – commonhold – to alleviate the problems in this area of law and in particular to facilitate the freehold ownership of flats. Commonhold is a 'new kind of freehold ownership with special statutory attributes'. The Commonhold and Leasehold Reform Act 2002 received Royal Assent in May 2002 but it is still to come into force. It constitutes a radical reform of property ownership.

Not surprisingly, the Act draws upon the established schemes in other parts of the common law world.

Under the commonhold regime, each unit in a multi-unit structure will be held on commonhold (in essence a freehold estate in the unit) with the common parts and facilities being run by a management company limited by guarantee, whose membership will be limited to the unit holders (for the time being) of the development in question. The company will be a private one which will have the standard set of Memorandum and Articles of Association prescribed by regulations. Further, there will be a Commonhold Community Statement setting out the rules and regulations of the commonhold. These documents will set out the voting rights of the unit holders, the necessary majorities, dispute-handling procedures and the machinery for determining and collecting commonhold costs etc.

Accordingly, there will be no landlord. Rather, each unit holder will have two interests (ownership of his unit and an interest in the management company). The new regime will apply to both residential and non-residential multi-unit structures. However, the government has decided against a compulsory system of commonhold. It will be possible for an existing multi-unit structure held on a leasehold basis to be converted to commonhold.

In a commonhold no one will have rights in the property superior to the unit holders. Further, the owner's interest in the property will not run out over time as it does in the case of a leasehold interest. Given that most people lay out considerable sums of money in acquiring a long lease of a flat, but have little control over the funding of the building in which it is located (the landlord usually has a monopoly over the supply of services with the tenant having to pay the cost), this will mean that the 'non-wasting asset' nature of a commonhold unit will be very attractive.

Note: this solution has been revised to take account of the Commonhold provisions.

QUESTION TWO

Alex divided up his land (unregistered land) into four equal sized plots (Plots A, B, C and D) and built a substantial house on each of them. He decided to live on Plot A himself and he sold Plots B, C and D to Barry, Carol and Diana in that order. When they purchased their plots, Barry, Carol and Diana entered into identical covenants 'with Alex and his successors-in-title', covenanting (i) to use the house as a single dwelling-house, (ii) to use the house for residential purposes only, (iii) to maintain the house in a good state of repair. All four plots have since been sold: Plot A to Paul, Plot B to Quentin, Plot C to Rachel and Plot D to Stella. The house on Plot B has fallen into disrepair and Quentin proposes to divide the house into flats which he will sell. Rachel has started a massage business on Plot C. Paul and Stella want to enforce the covenants against Quentin and Rachel.

Advise them.

University of London LLB Examination
(for External Students) Land Law June 1994 Q4

General Comment

This is a question concerning the enforcement of freehold covenants against successors in title of the original parties. The biggest problem with the question concerns Stella. As with most problem questions on this topic the inclusion of a diagrammatical representation of the facts is advisable, not least because it should eliminate the possibility of a student confusing the various parties in the course of an answer.

Skeleton Solution

Definition of a covenant – distinguishing between positive and restrictive covenants – running of the burden to successors in title of the original covenantor: equity rules – running of the benefit to successors in title of the original covenantee: equity rules; express annexation; *Rogers* v *Hosegood*, statutory annexation; *Federated Homes Ltd* v *Mill Lodge Properties Ltd* and scheme of development – registration.

Suggested Solution

A covenant, in the context of real property law, is an agreement by deed whereby one party (the covenantor) promises with another party (the covenantee) that he will or will not engage in some stated activity in relation to a specified piece of land. The land owned by the covenantee will have the benefit of the covenant and that owned by the covenantor will have the burden. On the facts Alex, who owns Plot A, is the original covenantee and Barry, Carol and Diana who respectively bought Plots B, C and D are the original covenantors.

There are two kinds of freehold covenant – positive and negative. A positive covenant is one which obliges the owner to do something on his land (a work covenant, eg a covenant to fence) or to contribute money towards work to be done or services to be provided for the benefit of his land (a money covenant, eg a covenant to contribute towards the construction or maintenance of a private road). A restrictive covenant is one which restrains a landowner in some respect from the uninhibited use of his property, eg a covenant which prevents the covenantor from using his land for the purpose of conducting trade or business. On the facts, covenant (i) to use the house as a single dwelling-house is a restrictive one, covenant (ii) to use the house for residential purposes only is also a restrictive one and covenant (iii) to maintain the house in a good state of repair is a positive one.

On the facts, Alex has sold Plot A to Paul (assignee of original covenantee) and the three original covenantors Barry, Carol and Diana have sold their respective plots to Quentin, Rachel and Stella. These developments can be represented diagrammatically as follows:

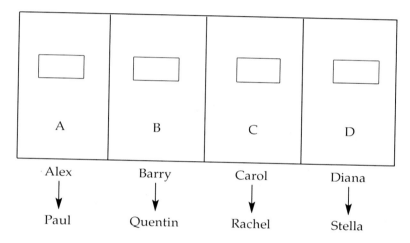

On the facts, Plot B is in disrepair (breach of covenant (iii)), Quentin is proposing to divide the house on Plot B into flats (breach of covenant (i)) and Rachel has started a massage business on Plot C (breach of covenants (i) and (ii)).

Paul and Stella want to enforce the three covenants against Quentin and Rachel. To do so they have to establish that the burden of the covenants has passed to Quentin and Rachel and that the benefit of the covenants has passed to them under either the common law or equity rules.

Turning first to the running of the burden of the covenants, the position at common law is that the burden of a covenant, whether positive or negative, made between a vendor and purchaser cannot run directly with freehold land. This was laid down in *Austerberry v Oldham Corporation* (1885) 29 Ch D 750. Accordingly, it is necessary to consider whether the burden of the three covenants can run in equity. The burden of a covenant will only run in equity if three conditions are satisfied. First, the covenant must be a negative one. This was laid down in *Haywood v Brunswick Permanent Benefit Building Society* (1881) 8 QBD 403. It is enough if the covenant is negative in nature. Covenants (i) and (ii), as previously mentioned, are negative ones. Covenant (i) is negative in nature though worded positively. Since covenant (iii) is a positive one – it involves the spending of money – the burden cannot run either at law or in equity. Accordingly, Paul and Stella cannot enforce covenant (iii) against Quentin. Secondly, the covenant must have been made for the protection of land retained by the covenantee (Alex). The authority for this is *London County Council v Allen* [1914] 3 KB 642. Both covenants (i) and (ii) would satisfy this requirement. Thirdly, the burden of the covenant must have been intended to run with the covenantor's land. By virtue of s79 LPA 1925 covenants relating to the covenantor's land which are made after 1925 are deemed to have been made by the covenantor on behalf of himself, his successors in title and the persons deriving title under him or them, unless a contrary intention appears. Assuming that the covenants were entered into after 1925 (the question is silent on the matter), this third requirement would be satisfied. Accordingly, it seems that the burden of covenants (i) and (ii) have passed to Quentin and Rachel.

There is one final matter to consider in relation to the burden of the covenants – registration. Where, as here, the land is unregistered the restrictive covenants must, if entered into after 1925, be registered as Class D(ii) land charges under the Land Charges Act 1972. Failure to register would render covenants (i) and (ii) void against a purchaser for value of a legal estate in the land: s4(6) Land Charges Act 1972.

Having shown that the burden of covenants (i) and (ii) can pass to Quentin and Rachel in equity it is now necessary for Paul and Stella to show that the benefit of these two covenants has passed to them. At common law the benefit of a covenant can run with freehold land if certain conditions are satisfied. However, since the burden of a covenant cannot run with freehold land directly at common law there is no real point in establishing if the benefit of covenants (i) and (ii) has passed to Paul and Stella at common law. Rather, it is crucial to consider whether the benefit has passed to them in equity.

For the benefit of a restrictive covenant to pass in equity to a successor in title of the covenantee (Paul) the covenant must 'touch and concern' or 'benefit' some land of the covenantee and the benefit must be transmitted in one or more of the ways prescribed by equity (annexation, assignment or scheme of development). Here covenants (i) and (ii) touch and concern Plot A. The key issue is whether the benefit has passed to Paul and Stella in one or more of the ways recognised by equity.

In relation to Paul, it is necessary to consider annexation. Express annexation confers the benefit of the covenant upon the land and not individuals. Whether the benefit is so annexed to the land depends upon the wording of the covenants. In particular it must be possible to identify the land to be benefited from such wording. In *Rogers v Hosegood* [1900] 2 Ch 388 the covenant was deemed to be annexed since it referred to the dominant land. However, in *Renals v Cowlishaw* (1879) 11 Ch D 866 the covenant was not annexed because it only referred to 'the vendors, their heirs, executors, administrators and assigns' (ie no reference was made to any land). Here the covenants were made 'with Alex and his successors in title'. This would not be enough for express annexation because there is no real identification of the benefited land.

However, statutory annexation is likely to be of help to Paul. In *Federated Homes Ltd* v *Mill Lodge Properties Ltd* [1980] 1 WLR 594 the Court of Appeal held that where a restrictive covenant touches and concerns the covenantee's land, s78(1) LPA 1925 annexes the benefit of the covenant to the covenantee's land and the covenant is enforceable at the suit of the covenantee and his successors in title. On the strength of *Federated Homes* it would seem that Paul could show that the benefit of covenants (i) and (ii) have passed to him. However, it is important to note that while the decision in Federated Homes was good news for conveyancers (s78 could come to the rescue if the express annexation formula used by them turned out to be deficient) the reasoning used by the Court of Appeal on that occasion is not beyond criticism. Accordingly, provided Paul can show statutory annexation (which seems likely) he will be able to enforce covenant (i) against Quentin and covenants (i) and (ii) against Rachel.

For Stella to be able to enforce covenants (i) and (ii) against Quentin and Rachel she would have to show that the land is subject to a scheme of development – not an impossible task given that Alex divided up the land into four equal-sized plots. The requirements for a scheme of development were first laid down in *Elliston* v *Reacher* [1908] 2 Ch 374. Today it seems that for such a scheme to exist two requirements have to be satisfied. First, the area of the scheme must be defined. Secondly, those who purchase from the creator of the scheme do so on the footing that all purchasers should be mutually bound by and mutually entitled to enforce a defined set of restrictions. Clearly, if a scheme of development can be established it could be pleaded by Paul, together with statutory annexation.

Assuming that Paul and Stella can show that the benefit of covenants (i) and (ii) has passed to them in equity and that the burden has passed to Quentin and Rachel in equity, the remedy that they would seek to stop Quentin dividing the house on Plot B into flats and to stop Rachel's massage business on Plot C would be an injunction.

QUESTION THREE

Alfred was the owner of a piece of undeveloped land (unregistered land) and in 1980 he decided to divide it into three plots, each of them fronting on to the highway, and to build a substantial house on each plot. He decided to live in the house built on the central plot, plot B. He sold plot A in fee simple to Vince, who covenanted with Alfred and his successors-in-title to use the house for residential purposes only and to maintain the garden and the dividing wall in good condition. Alfred for his part covenanted with Vince and his successors-in-title to use his house for residential purposes only and to maintain the garden on plot B in good condition. A year later Alfred leased plot C to Larry for a term of 99 years, Larry covenanting to use the house for residential purposes only and to maintain the garden and the dividing wall in good condition.

Mary, who purchased plot B in 1983, would like to know whether she can enforce the covenants against Pete, who has recently purchased plot A from Vince and against Quentin, who has recently taken an assignment of Larry's lease.

Advise.

University of London LLB Examination
(for External Students) Land Law June 1995 Q5

General Comment

This question is primarily concerned with the enforcement of freehold covenants against successors-in-title of the original parties. In addition, some coverage of the enforcement of leasehold covenants is required (such a question structure was doubtless designed to test whether students were aware of the different enforcement regimes between the two types of covenant). As with most problem questions on this topic, the inclusion of a diagrammatical representation of the facts is advisable, not least because it should eliminate the possibility of a student confusing the various parties in the course of an answer.

Skeleton Solution

Freehold covenants

Definition of a covenant – distinguishing between positive and restrictive covenants – indirect devices for enforcement of positive covenants – running of the burden of a restrictive covenant in equity – running of the benefit of a restrictive covenant in equity: express annexation, statutory annexation (*Federated Homes Ltd* v *Mill Lodge Properties Ltd*) and schemes of development – registration.

Leasehold covenants

Formalities for creation of a legal lease – assignment of a lease – privity of estate.

Suggested Solution

Freehold covenants

A covenant in the context of real property law is an agreement by deed whereby one party (the covenantor) promises with another party (the covenantee) that he will or will not engage in some stated activity in relation to a specified piece of land. The land owned by the covenantee will have the benefit of the covenant and that owned by the covenantor will have the burden. Here, on the sale of Plot A to Vince there are two sets of covenants. First, Vince (original covenator) entered into covenants for the benefit of Alfred (original covenantee) and his successors. Second, Alfred (original covenantor) entered into covenants for the benefit of Vince (original covenantee) and his successors.

There are two kinds of freehold covenant – positive and restrictive. A positive covenant is one which obliges the owner to do something on his land (a work covenant, eg a covenant to fence) or to contribute money towards work to be done or services to be provided for the benefit of his land (a money covenant, eg a covenant to contribute towards the construction or maintenance of a private road). A restrictive covenant is one which restrains a landowner in some respect from the uninhibited use of his property, eg a covenant which prevents the covenantor from using his land for the purpose of conducting trade and business. Here, Vince's covenant to maintain the garden of Plot A and the dividing wall in good condition, and Alfred's covenant to maintain the garden on Plot B in good condition are positive ones, while the covenants to use the houses on Plots A and B for residential purposes only are restrictive ones.

The factual developments recounted in the question can be represented diagrammatically as follows:

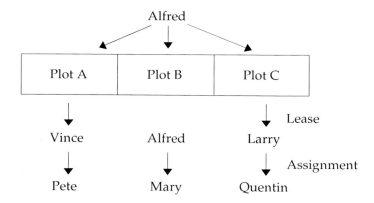

Mary, Alfred's successor-in-title in respect of Plot B, wishes to know whether she can enforce the covenants originally entered into by Vince on purchasing Plot A from Alfred against Pete, and whether she can enforce the covenants originally entered into by Larry on the leasing of Plot C against Quentin. The issues in respect of Plot A will be dealt with first and those in respect of Plot C second.

For Mary to be able to enforce the covenant to use the house on Plot A for residential purposes only and the covenant to maintain the garden and dividing wall in good condition against Pete she has to show that the burden of these covenants has passed to him, and that the benefit of them has passed to her under either the common law or equity rules.

Dealing first with the positive covenant (to maintain the garden and dividing wall in good condition), the burden of such a covenant cannot run directly with freehold land either at law or in equity: *Austerberry* v *Oldham Corporation* (1885) 29 Ch D 750. However, certain indirect devices (none of which are fool-proof) are resorted to by conveyancers to try to circumvent the latter rule. In the circumstances, the indirect device which could be of assistance is the chain of indemnity covenants. For this device to be available it would have been necessary for Vince to have taken a covenant of indemnity from Pete when he sold Plot A to him. Vince should have so acted because as an original covenantor he remains liable on the covenant on the basis of privity of contract even after he has parted with the land. (If there was such a covenant, once Vince was sued he would then sue Pete on the indemnity covenant – in practice both actions would be consolidated.) It is only through such an indirect device that the positive covenant will be enforceable against Pete. However, there is nothing in the question to indicate that Vince took an indemnity covenant from Pete. Accordingly, it would seem that Mary would be unable to enforce the positive covenant against Pete.

As to the negative covenant (to use the house on Plot A for residential purposes only), it is necessary to consider the equity rules. The common law rules are of little use once, as here, the original covenantor and covenantee have parted with the land, because although the benefit of a covenant can run at law the burden cannot. Mary has got to establish that the burden of the negative covenant has passed to Pete in equity. To do this, three conditions have to be satisfied. First, the covenant must be a negative one. This was laid down in *Haywood* v *Brunswick Permanent Benefit Building Society* (1881) 8 QBD 403. It is enough if the covenant is negative in nature. Here, the covenant is negative in nature, though worded positively (the house cannot be used for any purposes other than residential ones). Second, the covenant must have been made for the protection of land retained by the covenantee: *London County Council* v *Allen* [1914] 3 KB 642. Here, it would seem that the covenant was made for the protection of Plot B, retained by Alfred. Third, the burden of the covenant must have been intended to run with the covenantor's (Vince's) land. By virtue of s79 Law of Property Act (LPA) 1925, covenants relating to the covenantor's land which are made after 1925 are deemed to have been made by the covenantor on behalf of himself, his successors-in-title and the persons deriving title under him or them unless a contrary intention appears. Since here the covenant was entered into after 1925, and there is no such contrary intention, this third requirement would be satisfied. Accordingly, it seems that the burden of the restrictive covenant has passed to Pete.

There is one final matter to consider in relation to the burden of the restrictive covenant – registration. Where, as here, the land is *unregistered* the restrictive covenant must be registered as a Class D(ii) land charge under the Land Charges Act (LCA) 1972 since it was entered into after 1925. Failure to so register the covenant would render it void against a purchaser for value of a legal estate in the land: s4(6) LCA 1972. For the purposes of this question it is assumed that this registration requirement has been satisfied.

Having shown that the burden of the restrictive covenant can pass to Pete in equity it is now necessary for Mary to show that the benefit of the covenant has passed to her in equity. For the benefit of a restrictive covenant to pass in equity to a successor-in-title of a covenantee the covenant must 'touch and concern' or 'benefit' some land of the covenantee, and the benefit must be transmitted in one or more of the ways prescribed by equity (annexation, assignment or scheme of development). Here the covenant to use the house (on Plot A) for residential purposes only clearly touches and concerns Plot B. The key issue is whether the benefit has passed to Mary in one or more of the ways recognised by equity.

In this regard it is necessary to consider annexation. Express annexation confers the benefit of the covenant upon the land, not individuals. Whether the benefit is so annexed to the land depends upon the wording of the covenants. In particular, it must be possible to identify the land to be benefited from such wording. In *Rogers* v *Hosegood* [1900] 2 Ch 388 the covenant was deemed to be annexed since it referred to the dominant land. However, in *Renals* v *Cowlishaw* (1879) 11 Ch D 866 the covenant was not annexed because it only referred to 'the vendors, their heirs, executors, administrators and assigns' (ie no reference was made to any land). Here the covenant was made 'with Alfred and his successors-in-title'. This may not be enough for express annexation because there is no real identification of the benefited land.

However, statutory annexation is likely to be of help to Mary. In *Federated Homes Ltd* v *Mill Lodge Properties Ltd* [1980] 1 WLR 594 the Court of Appeal held that where a restrictive covenant touches and concerns the covenantee's land, s78(1) LPA 1925 annexes the benefit of the covenant to the covenantee's land and the covenant is enforceable at the suit of the covenantee and his successors-in-title. On the strength of *Federated Homes* it would seem that Mary could show that the benefit of the covenant has passed to her. However, it is important to note that while the decision in *Federated Homes* was good news for conveyancers (s78 could come to the rescue if the express annexation formula used by them turned out to be deficient), the reasoning of the Court of Appeal on that occasion is not beyond criticism. Accordingly, provided Mary can show statutory annexation (which seems likely) she will be able to enforce the restrictive covenant against Pete.

Further, it may also be possible for Mary to show that the land is subject to a scheme of development, given that in 1980 Alfred divided a piece of undeveloped land into three plots. The requirements for a scheme of development were first laid down in *Elliston* v *Reacher* [1908] 2 Ch 374. Today, it seems that for such a scheme to exist two requirements have to be satisfied. First, the area of the scheme must be defined. Second, those who purchase from the creator of the scheme do so on the footing that all purchasers should be mutually bound by and mutually entitled to enforce a defined set of restrictions. Clearly, if a scheme of development can be established it could be pleaded by Mary, together with statutory annexation.

Leasehold covenants

Finally, can Mary enforce against Quentin the covenants originally entered into by Larry when he took the 99-year lease of Plot C from Alfred? Given that it is for more than three years it is crucial that the lease was made by deed in order to create a legal estate: s52(1) LPA 1925. Further, a legal lease, once created, can only be transferred inter vivos by deed: s52 LPA 1925. For the purposes of this answer it is assumed that the relevant formalities have been complied with, both in respect of the creation of the lease between Alfred and Larry and its assignment by Larry to Quentin. The reason why it is crucial to ascertain if we are dealing with a legal lease here is because if we are then privity of estate exists. The enforcement of a leasehold covenant between assignees either of the lease (ie Quentin) or of the reversion, depends upon whether there is privity of estate between plaintiff and defendant, and whether the covenant in question touches and concerns the land: *Spencer's Case* (1583) 5 Co Rep 16a. Here the covenants to use the house on Plot C for residential purposes only and to maintain the garden and dividing wall in good condition clearly touch and concern the land. If privity of estate can be established then all covenants, whether positive or negative, are enforceable. If Mary can show that there is privity of estate between herself and Quentin then she would be able to enforce the covenants against him. Mary could show that there is privity of estate between herself and Quentin by establishing that she acquired the freehold reversion of Plot C from Alfred. However, there is no suggestion in the question that she has so acted. Accordingly, it would seem that Mary cannot enforce the covenants against Quentin.

Note: since the lease was entered into prior to 1 January 1996 the Landlord and Tenant (Covenants) Act 1995 has no application to the question.

QUESTION FOUR

In 1985 Jack sold a plot of land which formed part of his Alban Estate to Priscilla who covenanted with Jack and his successors-in-title to use the land for residential purposes and to maintain the house in a good state of repair. Consider the extent to which these covenants are enforceable (a) by a lessee of the Alban Estate against Priscilla, (b) by Jack against a lessee of Priscilla's land, and (c) by a purchaser of the Alban Estate against a person who inherited Priscilla's land.

University of London LLB Examination
(for External Students) Land Law June 1997 Q8

General Comment

The question is concerned with rights against third parties in respect of freehold covenants. A somewhat untypical and challenging question which gives a student well versed in the relevant law a good opportunity to demonstrate his knowledge and understanding. Important that each of the three scenarios is given broadly equal coverage in an answer.

Skeleton Solution

Definition of a covenant – distinguishing between positive and negative covenants.

a) Running of the benefit at law, in equity and under s56 LPA 1925.

b) Burden of positive covenant cannot run at law or in equity – indirect devices for enforcement of positive covenants: *Halsall v Brizell*.

c) Running of benefit and burden at law and in equity – registration requirements for post-1925 covenants – position of non-purchaser

Suggested Solution

A covenant, in the context of real property law, is an agreement by deed whereby one party (the covenantor) promises another party (the covenantee), that he will or will not engage in some stated activity in relation to a specified piece of land. The land owned by the covenantee has the benefit of the covenant and that owned by the covenantor has the burden. On the facts, Jack who owns the Alban Estate is the original covenantee and Priscilla who bought the plot, formerly part of that estate, is the original covenantor. Accordingly, the Alban Estate is the dominant (ie benefited) land and the plot sold off is the servient (ie burdened) land.

There are two kinds of freehold covenant – positive and restrictive. A positive covenant is one which obliges the owner to do something on his land (a work covenant, eg a covenant to fence) or to contribute money towards work to be done or services to be provided for the benefit of his land (a money covenant, eg a covenant to contribute towards the construction or maintenance of a private road). A restrictive covenant is one which restrains a landowner in some respect from the uninhibited use of his property, eg a covenant which prevents the covenantor from using his land for the purpose of conducting trade and business. Here the covenant to use the land for residential purposes is a restrictive one while the covenant to maintain the house in a good state of repair is a positive one (it basically requires Priscilla not to allow the house to fall into disrepair).

a) The scenario under consideration here can be represented diagrammatically as follows:

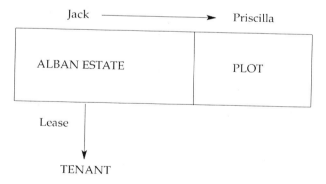

For the lessee of the Alban Estate to be able to enforce the covenants against Priscilla he must show that the benefit of them has passed to him. There are three possibilities in this regard. First, he could seek to claim the benefit under s56 LPA 1925 which provides that: 'A person may take ... the benefit of any covenant [ie positive or restrictive] over or respecting land ... although he may not be named as a party to the conveyance ...' In order to qualify under s56 of the 1925 Act a person who was not a party to the original deed must show that the contract purported to be made with him, not just for his benefit (ie the provision can only benefit a person who is in existence and identifiable when the covenants were made). Accordingly, the tenant of the Alban Estate can only claim the benefit of the covenants under s56 LPA 1925 if he was a tenant at the time they were created.

Secondly, he could claim that the benefit of the covenants passed to him at law. The benefit of a covenant (both positive or restrictive) can run with the land of the covenantee at common law if certain conditions are satisfied including, in particular, that the covenant touches and concerns the land of the covenantee. Here both covenants do touch and concern the Alban Estate. However, if the tenant utilises this option his remedy would be in damages. Thirdly, the benefit could be claimed in equity if the covenant is restrictive and touches and concerns the land. Accordingly, the tenant could claim the benefit of the use covenant in this way. Given that the landlord, Jack, is the original covenantee it would not be necessary for the tenant to show that the benefit had passed to him by annexation or assignment.

In conclusion, a lessee of the Alban Estate could either enforce both covenants at common law (claiming damages) or enforce the user covenant in equity by seeking an injunction.

b) The scenario under consideration here can be represented diagrammatically as follows:

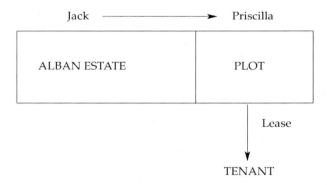

Jack as the original covenantee can enforce the covenants against a lessee of Priscilla's land if the burden of the covenants has passed to the lessee.

Dealing first with the positive covenant (to maintain the house in a good state of repair) the burden of such a covenant cannot run directly with freehold land either at law or in equity: *Austerberry v Oldham Corporation* (1885) 29 Ch D 750. However, certain indirect devices (none of which are foolproof) are used to try to circumvent the latter rule. For example, there is the doctrine of *Halsall v Brizell* [1957] Ch 169 – a person who takes the benefit under a deed/agreement must also bear the burden (ie perform any obligation of a reciprocal nature). The lessee of Priscilla's land cannot be liable for any breach of the positive covenant unless the aforementioned doctrine applies which on the facts it does not (there is no reciprocal benefit).

Dealing second with the restrictive covenant, the burden of such a covenant cannot pass at law but can pass in equity. For the burden to run in equity three conditions have to be satisfied. First, the covenant must be a negative one. This was laid down in *Haywood v Brunswick Permanent Benefit Building Society* (1881) 8 QBD 403. It is enough if the covenant is negative in nature, though worded positively (the house cannot be used for any purposes other than residential ones). Secondly, the covenant must have been made for the protection of land retained by the covenantee: *London County Council v Allen* [1914] 3 KB 642. Here, it would seem that the covenant was made for the protection of the Alban Estate retained by Jack. Thirdly, the burden of the covenant must have been intended to run with the covenantor's (Priscilla's) land. By virtue of s79 LPA 1925, covenants relating to the covenantor's land which are made after 1925 are deemed to have been made by the covenantor on behalf of himself, his successors in title and the persons deriving title under him or them unless a contrary intention appears. Since here the covenant was entered into after 1925 and there is no such contrary intention this third requirement would be satisfied.

In conclusion, it seems that Jack can enforce the restrictive covenant against Priscilla's tenant.

c)   The scenario under consideration here can be represented diagrammatically as follows:

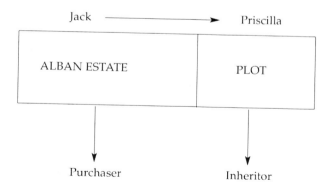

The issue here is whether the purchaser of the Alban Estate (the benefited land) can enforce the covenants against the person who has inherited Priscilla's land (the burdened land). To do so the purchaser has to show that the benefit of the covenants has passed to him and that the burden of the covenants has passed to the person who inherited the servient land. Since the covenants were entered into by Priscilla 'with Jack and his successors-in-title' the benefit has passed to the purchaser of the Alban Estate. As to the burden, it is submitted that the burden of the restrictive covenant has passed to the person who inherited the plot formerly owned by Priscilla: see (b) above.

However, since the restrictive covenant was created after 1925 it must be protected by registration for the burden to run with the servient land and bind a subsequent purchaser of the same. If the land is unregistered the restrictive covenant must be registered as a Class D(ii) land charge under the Land Charges Act 1972. If the land is registered the restrictive covenant must be protected by the entry of a notice under the Land Registration Act 1925. Such registration of the restrictive covenant constitutes actual notice in each situation. However, if the restrictive covenant is not so registered it will be void and unenforceable against a subsequent purchaser for money or money's worth of a legal estate even though he purchases with notice of it. Since on the facts the servient land is inherited, the person who becomes so entitled to the land is not a purchaser. Hence even if the restrictive covenant is not registered it is submitted that it will be enforceable against the person who inherited the servient land.

QUESTION FIVE

Arthur owned two plots of land (plots A and B). He built a large detached house on each plot. He retained plot A for his own occupation and he sold plot B to Bertram who covenanted 'with Arthur and his successors in title' to use the house for residential purposes only and to maintain the wall that divided the two plots. Recently, Arthur died leaving plot A to his widow, Paula. Bertram sold plot B to Rachel. Rachel has opened a massage-parlour in her house and the wall has collapsed in various places.

Advise Paula.

University of London LLB Examination
(for External Students) Land Law June 1999 Q6

General Comment

A generally straightforward question, but candidates should be aware of the problems arising in connection with the passing of the benefit of the residential covenant in equity. Although the covenant is intended to benefit Arthur's successors in title, it contains no express reference to the land to be benefited by the covenant, and this will prevent annexation. It is then necessary to consider transmission by express assignment of the benefit, but although this possibility should be mentioned there is not enough material for discussion. Candidates should not assume that the covenant has been registered as a Class D(ii) land charge and should deal with both possibilities.

Skeleton Solution

Paula must prove that the benefit of the covenants have passed to her and the burdens have passed to Rachel – positive burdens cannot run – burden passing under *Tulk* v *Moxhay* – benefits may pass in equity – annexation – express assignment – easement regarding wall – injunction.

Suggested Solution

Paula wishes to be advised as to whether she can enforce the covenants originally made between Arthur and Bertram against Rachel.

Neither Paula nor Rachel were parties to the covenants and it will therefore be necessary for Paula to prove that the benefits of the covenants have passed to her and that the burdens have passed to Rachel.

While the benefit of a covenant may pass at common law, its burden cannot: *Austerberry* v *Oldham Corporation* (1885) 29 Ch D 750. It may, however, pass in equity according to the principles developed in *Tulk* v *Moxhay* (1848) 2 Ph 774 and subsequent cases. It must be noted that if Paula is to invoke equity to ensure the passing of the burden to Rachel, she cannot then use the common law rules to make the benefit of the covenant pass. She must instead use the equitable rules: *Re Union of London and Smith's Bank Ltd's Conveyance, Miles* v *Easter* [1933] Ch 611. Bearing this in mind, the equitable rules governing the transmission of burdens will be examined first followed by the equitable rules relating to the transmission of benefits.

The equitable rules governing the transmission of burdens are as follows.

a) The covenant must be negative in substance. Whether the wording is positive or negative is immaterial. It is the substance that matters. The wording of the covenant in *Tulk* v *Moxhay* was positive, but was clearly negative in substance. A covenant not to allow a fence to fall into disrepair, although negative in wording, is positive because it imposes on the servient owner a positive obligation to repair the fence: see *Haywood* v *Brunswick Permanent Benefit Building Society* (1881) 8 QBD 403.

b) At the time the covenant was made, the covenantee must have owned land which was capable of being benefited by the covenant, and for the benefit of which the covenant was taken: *London County Council* v *Allen* [1914] 3 KB 642, following *Formby* v *Barker* [1903] 2 Ch 539; *Re Nisbet and Pott's Contract* [1906] 1 Ch 386.

A landlord holding the reversion of a lease will satisfy the requirement (*Hall* v *Ewin* (1887) 37 Ch D 74), with the result that a landlord may sue a sub-tenant under the doctrine of *Tulk* v *Moxhay*, whereas he would normally be precluded from doing so because of the absence of privity of estate between him and the sub-tenant.

This requirement is indicative that equity is enforcing the covenant to protect land rather than its owner. It follows therefore that although the original covenantee may always sue the original covenantor (under their contractual relationship) once the covenantee has parted with the land he cannot sue a successor in title to the original covenantor. Equity will not assist the original covenantee because he no longer owns the land to be protected: see *Formby* v *Barker*.

It further follows that a successor in title to the original covenantee can only enforce the covenant while he holds the land. Once he has parted with it he loses his right to sue.

c) At the time the covenant was made, the original parties must have intended that the burden of the covenant should run with servient land. The wording of the covenant must be examined to see if such an intention has been expressed. If the covenantor covenants on behalf of himself, his heirs and assigns, this will be indicative of that intention. In the absence of wording to that effect then s79 LPA 1925 may be applicable. Covenants relating to the land of the covenantor, if made after 1925, are deemed to be made on behalf of himself and his successors in title unless a contrary intention is expressed. Section 79(2) enacts that in the case of restrictive covenants the phrase 'successors in title' includes owners and occupiers for the time being.

d) The covenant must 'touch and concern' the dominant land. In the words of Farwell J in *Rogers* v *Hosegood* [1900] 2 Ch 388 'the covenant must either affect the land as regards mode of occupation, or it must be such as per se and not merely from collateral circumstances, affect the value of the land.' This is a further indication that the basis of equitable intervention is to protect land rather than the owner personally.

e) Restrictive covenants made on or after 1 January 1926 are registrable as a land charge, Class D(ii): s2(5) Land Charges Act (LCA) 1972. If not registered then it is void against a purchaser of the legal estate in the land for money or money's worth: s4(6) LCA 1972. If the covenant was made before that date, then it is subject to the doctrine of notice. In the case of registered land, being a minor interest, it should be protected by an entry, notice or caution, on the register of title of the servient land. The entry should be made in the charges register.

Applying those principles here the first question is whether the two covenants are negative in substance. Although the wording of the covenant relating to residence purposes is positive the substance of the covenant is negative and it will satisfy requirement (a). The covenant to maintain the wall is clearly positive and does not satisfy requirement (a). It does not therefore merit further consideration under these rules.

Requirement (b) is probably satisfied. The covenantee (Arthur) owed the dominant land which was adjacent to the servient land of the covenantor (Bertram). It is a question of fact whether the dominant land was capable of benefiting from the covenant and whether the covenant was taken to achieve that objective.

As regards requirement (c) it is clear that the covenantor intends to benefit the successors in title to the covenantee (Arthur) but there is no wording in the covenant to bind the successors in title of the covenantor (Bertram). Section 79 LPA 1925 will therefore apply unless a contrary intention has been expressed in the conveyance, and there is nothing on the facts to suggest that the applicability of s79 has been excluded. Requirement (c), therefore, is satisfied.

The covenant certainly touches and concerns the dominant land, and so requirement (d) is also satisfied.

The last requirement relates to regulation as a land charge under the LCA 1972, this being unregistered land. We do not know if the covenant was registered before the sale of the servient land (Plot B) to Rachel. If it was she will take subject to it. If it was not she will take free of it as she was a purchaser of the legal estate in the servient land for money or money's worth. We cannot say for certain whether requirement (e) has been met as we do not know whether registration has been effected or not. Subject to the registration point we may conclude that the burden of the residential covenant has passed to Rachel.

We must now consider whether the benefit of the covenant has passed to Paula. The benefit may pass in equity in three ways:

a) annexation of the benefit to the dominant land; or

b) express assignment of the benefit; or

c) a building scheme.

We shall take annexation first. Did the original parties to the covenant annex the benefit to the dominant land? This is a matter of intention as expressed in the wording of the covenant, but the covenant must refer to the land to be benefited. In *Reid* v *Bickerstaff* [1909] 2 Ch 305 the covenant was made with 'the vendors, their heirs and assignees'. This was held to be ineffective to annex the benefit to the dominant land because there was no reference to the land. A similar result was reached in *Renals* v *Cowlishaw* (1879) 11 Ch D 866. By contrast, in *Rogers* v *Hosegood* the covenant was made 'with the intent that they might enure to the benefit of the vendors, their heirs and assigns and others claiming under them to all or any of their lands adjoining'. This wording was held to be effective to annex the benefit to the dominant land.

If there is no wording expressing the original parties' intention then s78 LPA 1925, as construed by the Court of Appeal in *Federated Homes Ltd* v *Mill Lodge Properties Ltd* [1980] 1 WLR 594, will be applicable. That case decided that s78 was no mere word saving section but actually of itself annexed the benefit of a covenantor's covenant to the dominant land and to each and every part thereof. However, it is thought that s78 can only apply if the covenant identifies the land to be benefited. The section contains no provision that it may be excluded, but in *Roake* v *Chadha* [1983] 3 All ER 503 it was held that its application could be excluded by the parties.

Because of the construction put on s78 by the Court of Appeal decision, the second method of transmission – assignment – has considerably diminished in importance, since in most cases the benefit will have been annexed to the dominant land thus obviating the necessity for it to be expressly assigned. When the dominant land is transferred the annexed benefit will automatically pass with it.

The difficulty with annexation in this case arises from the absence of any express reference in the covenant's wording to the land to be benefited, with the result that Paula will not be able to rely on this method. The second method of transmission must therefore be considered: *Newton Abbot Co-operative Society* v *Williamson and Treadgold Ltd* [1952] Ch 286.

The conditions required by equity for an express assignment were discussed by Romer LJ in *Re Union of London and Smith's Bank Ltd's Conveyance, Miles* v *Easter*.

When Arthur died his estate including Plot A would have passed to his executors, who would in turn then have conveyed the plot to Paula. There is no evidence of any assignment by them to Paula of the covenant's benefit and the matter cannot be taken further, but the possibility of that occurrence must be noted.

We may now return to the wall. As has been explained, the burden cannot run even in equity because of its positive nature. It is, however, possible to ensure that an obligation to maintain a wall can run with servient land by the creation of an easement to that effect: *Crow* v *Wood* [1971] 1 QB 77. This is an exception to the general rule that an easement must not impose a positive obligation on the servient owner. However, the obligation imposed must be worded as an easement and not as a covenant. It is clear that Arthur and Bertram entered into a covenant and not an easement and Paula will not be able to compel Rachel to maintain the wall.

If Paul were able to establish that she had acquired the benefit of the residential covenant she could apply to the court for an injunction restraining Rachel from opening a massage parlour.

QUESTION SIX

'The decision of the Court of Appeal in *Federated Homes Ltd* v *Mill Lodge Properties Ltd* (1980) did much to simplify the law relating to the transmission of the benefit of restrictive covenants.'

Discuss.

University of London LLB Examination
(for External Students) Land Law June 2001 Q8

General Comment

Candidates should avoid the temptation to write a general description of the law relating to restrictive covenants and instead address their minds precisely to the question which the examiner has asked. To assess the impact of the decision in *Federated Homes Ltd* v *Mill Lodge Properties Ltd* it is necessary to examine the previous state of the law, and having done that, to consider the impact of the decision on the earlier law and the consequences for the future.

Skeleton Solution

Burden will only pass in equity: in that case benefit can only pass in equity; three methods – annexation: intention of the parties; covenant must refer to the benefited land; problem where dominant land too large in extent to benefit from the covenant; s78 Law of Property Act (LPA) 1925; reasoning of Brightman LJ in *Federated Homes*; wide wording of s78 in contrast to s58 Conveyancing Act 1881; effect of s78 LPA 1925: automatic annexation of benefit to whole and each and every part unless a contrary intention expressed; *Roake v Chadha*: s78 LPA 1925 may be excluded; *Federated Homes* followed in subsequent cases despite criticism; s78 LPA 1925 does not apply to pre-1926 restrictive covenants; effect of decision is to diminish importance of assignment of benefit.

Suggested Solution

The benefit of a restrictive covenant relating to freehold land may pass at common law but the burden cannot: *Austerberry v Oldham Corporation* (1885) 29 Ch D 750; *Rhone v Stephens* [1994] 2 All ER 65. The burden may, however, pass in equity under the rule in *Tulk v Moxhay* (1848) 2 Ph 774 as developed by subsequent cases. Where both dominant and servient tenements have changed hands, if a successor in title to the original covenantee wishes to enforce a restrictive covenant against the successor in title to the original covenantor, he must establish that the burden has passed to the latter and that he has acquired the benefit. To prove that the burden has passed he must necessarily invoke equity. It is now settled that in those circumstances he cannot use the common law rules to show that the benefit has passed: he must instead rely on equity; *Re Union of London and Smith's Bank Ltd's Conveyance, Miles v Easter* [1933] Ch 611.

In order to answer the question it is necessary to examine equity's approach to the transmission of the benefit of restrictive covenants relating to freehold land before the enactment of s78 Law of Property Act (LPA) 1925. The section only applies to covenants made on or after 1 January 1926: s78(2).

Before that date there were three methods by which the benefit could pass in equity: annexation, express assignment and a building scheme. We are only concerned here with the first of the three.

Whether the benefit of the restrictive covenant had been annexed to the dominant land was a question of intention of the original parties, to be deduced first of all from the wording of the covenant. A form of words commonly used to express that intention was 'with intent that the covenant may enure to the benefit of the vendors, their successors and assigns and others claiming under them to all or any of their lands adjoining'. The use of the words was held in *Rogers v Hosegood* [1990] 2 Ch 388 to be effective to annex the benefit of the covenant to the dominant land. They show an intention to confer the benefit, not just on the covenantee personally, but also on his successors in title. Put another way, the intention was to annex the benefit to the land.

It is important to note that the covenant must refer to the land to be benefited. If it does not, there will be no annexation. In *Reid v Bickerstaff* [1909] 2 Ch 305 the covenant was made with 'the vendors, their heirs and assignees'. There was no mention of land and the court held that the words were ineffective to annex the benefit. A similar result was reached in the earlier case of *Renals v Cowlishaw* (1879) 11 Ch D 866.

Problems arose in this connection when the dominant land covered a large area. An illustration is provided by *Re Ballard's Conveyance* [1937] Ch 473. In that case the restrictive covenant was expressed to be made for the benefit of the 'owners for the time being of the Childwickbury Estate'. The estate comprised about 1,700 acres of land. The court held that although the land had been sufficiently identified, the extent of its area was too great for it to derive benefit from the covenant. Clauson J observed that while a breach of the covenant might affect part of the dominant land, the greater part could not possibly be affected by it. He also pointed out that he could find no authority, nor was any cited to him, which would justify severing the covenant and confining its application to that portion of the land which could benefit from the covenant. If the covenant had been expressed to be for the benefit of the whole or any part or parts of the land, then the problem would not have arisen. For example, see *Zetland v Driver* [1939] Ch 1.

So far we have been dealing with wording which expressly annexes the benefit to the dominant land. Is implied annexation possible? In *Marten v Flight Refuelling Ltd* [1962] Ch 115 Wilberforce J acknowledged that possibility. Having examined the pre-1926 law we may now turn to the construction placed on s78 LPA 1925 by the Court of Appeal in *Federated Homes Ltd v Mill Lodge Properties Ltd* [1980] 1 WLR 594.

The section reads as follows:

'(1) A covenant relating to any land of the covenantee shall be deemed to be made with the covenantee and his successors in title and the persons deriving title under him or them, and shall have effect as if such successors and other persons were expressed. For the purposes of this subsection in connexion with covenants restrictive of the user of land "successors in title" shall be deemed to include the owners and occupiers for the time being of the land of the covenantee intended to be benefited.

(2) This section applies to covenants made after the commencement of this Act, but the repeal of s58 of the Conveyancing Act 1881 does not affect the operation of covenants to which that section applied.'

In the *Federated Homes* case the covenantor covenanted with the vendor (eg the covenantee) that it would not build on the purchased land at a greater density that a total of 300 dwellings, so as not to reduce the number of units which the vendor might eventually erect on any adjoining or adjacent land retained. The plaintiff later acquired the covenantee's land and then discovered that the covenantor had obtained planning permission to develop the land to a higher density than 300 units. It therefore sought to restrain the covenantor from building in breach of covenant. In order to succeed it had to show that it had acquired the benefit of the covenant. At first instance the judge expressly stated that s78 LPA 1925 'does not have the effect of annexing the benefit of the covenant to anything' and he described s78 as being 'simply a statutory shorthand', eg a word-saving section. He held that the benefit of the covenant had passed to the plaintiff under s62 LPA 1925.

The Court of Appeal rejected that view and held that s78 effected a statutory annexation of the covenant's benefit to the dominant land. The reasoning is to be found in the judgment of Brightman LJ. He made the comparison between s78 and its predecessor, s58(1) Conveyancing Act (CA) 1881. By s78(1) LPA 1925 a covenant relating to any land of the covenantee is deemed to be made with the covenantee and his successors in title and the persons deriving title under him or them. Further, that subsection provides that, for the purposes of the subsection, in the case of restrictive covenants, 'successors in title' shall be deemed to include the owners and occupiers for the time being of the land intended to be benefited. By contrast, s58(1) CA 1881 was limited to the covenantee, his heirs and assigns and did not include successors in title, persons deriving title under him or them, and owners and occupiers for the time being. In Brightman LJ's view, because s78 conferred the right to enforce the covenant on such a wide class of persons, in contrast to s58: 'it must … follow that the covenant runs with the land' given that it touches and concerns that land. He was fortified in his view by the decision in two earlier cases to the same effect: *Smith and Snipes Hall Farm Ltd v River Douglas Catchment Board* [1949] 2 KB 500 and *Williams v Unit Construction Co Ltd* (1955) 19 Conv 262.

Reference has been made to *Re Ballard's Conveyance* [1937] Ch 473 when Clawson J held that the dominant land was so large in extent that the covenant could not possibly have conferred a benefit on it. He also referred to consider severance. A different result was reached in *Zetland v Driver* because the covenant there had been expressed to be for the benefit of the whole or any part or parts thereof.

Brightman LJ considered that s78 annexed the benefit of the covenant not only to the whole of the dominant land, but to each and every part of it: 'I would have thought, if a benefit of a covenant is on a proper construction of a document annexed to the land, prima facie, it is annexed to every part thereof, unless a contrary intention appears'.

In this result, whereas before annexation of the benefit of the covenant to the dominant land depended on the intention of the covenanting parties as expressed in the covenant's wording, annexation is now automatically effected by the operation of the statute, regardless of those intentions, and moreover that annexation is to each and every part of the land.

This raises the question as to whether or not the operation of the section can be excluded by the parties, particularly as s78, unlike s79, makes no provision for the expression of a contrary intention. The point was considered in *Roake v Chadha* [1983] 3 All ER 503 when Judge Baker decided that the parties could exclude the application of s78 if they wished. He referred to the words of Brightman LJ, quoted above, which clearly envisage that s78 may be excluded by an expression of a contrary intention. He considered that, had the legislature intended to prohibit the parties from excluding s78, it would have expressly said so, quoting by way of example the language the legislation had adopted in s146 LPA 1925. In *Roake v Chadha* itself, the parties had excluded s78 by providing that the benefit could only pass by express assignment.

It is clear that the necessity for the covenant to identify the land to be benefited remains, although Brightman LJ seemed to consider it an open question as to whether the covenant itself had to identify the benefit land or whether its identity could be deduced from the surrounding circumstances.

The construction placed on s78 by the Court of Appeal in the *Federated Homes* case has certainly simplified the law relating to the transmission of the benefit of restrictive covenants. The decision, however, has not been free from criticism. One commentator, G H Newson QC, wrote that 'it really seems impossible that the view of Brightman LJ can be correct'. Nevertheless the decision has been followed in subsequent cases: eg *Jalarne Ltd v Ridewood* (1989) 61 P & CR 143 and *Robins v Berkeley Homes (Kent) Ltd* [1996] EGCS 75.

However, it should be remembered that s78 only applies to covenants created on or after 1 January 1926. It does not apply to covenants made before that date. Such covenants fall under s58 Conveyancing Act 1881. In *J Sainsbury plc v Enfield London Borough Council* [1989] 1 WLR 590 he covenant was made before 1926 and the court held that the wording of s58 was such that it did not annex the benefit to the dominant land in the absence of an expression of intention by the parties that it should pass with the dominant land.

A large number of restrictive covenants made before 1926 still exist and they will not enjoy the benefit of the decision in *Federated Homes Ltd v Mill Lodge Properties Ltd*.

Because s78 will now automatically annex the benefit to the dominant land unless a contrary intention is expressed, the second method of transmission has diminished in importance, since recourse to this method is only necessary where there has been no annexation.

Chapter 8

Easements and Profits à Prendre

8.1   Introduction

8.2   Key points

8.3   Key cases and statutes

8.4   Questions and suggested solutions

8.1 Introduction

Although they are often seen in the context of easements the specific rules relating to profits à prendre should not be overlooked and it is important to know where the rules differ as to these respective rights in alieno solo. The easement is said to be a privilege without a profit because it allows either the use of another person's land or controls the use of that land by the owner, but in neither case does it allow the taking of anything from that land. On the other hand the profit à prendre is a clear right to take something from the land of another person.

The flow chart on the following page illustrates the approach to be adopted once it has been established that the problem relates to a potential easement.

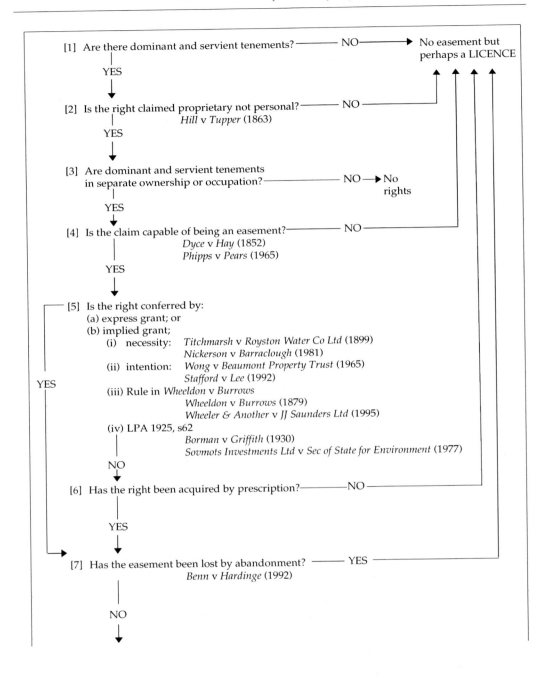

[8] Is the easement registered or otherwise protected?
    Unregistered land
    - LCA 1972 class D(iii)
    Registered land
    i) Pre 2002
        LRA 1925 s70(1)(a) *Celsteel Ltd v Alton House Holdings Ltd* (1985)
    ii) Post LRA 2002
        - If easement created on a transfer of part of the land – easement recorded in transfer of part. When transferee applies to get land registered with its own title the Registry will note the easement on the title of the land transferred out of and also on the new title.
        - If easement created in any other way owner of dominant land would apply for note to be made on his land using Form AP1. At same time he would protect his interest with restriction on the servient land either by an agreed notice or a unilateral notice.

    YES
    ↓

[9] What is the extent of the easement?
        Rosling v *Pinnegar* (1986)
        BRB v *Glass* (1965)
        London & Suburban Land & Building Co (Holdings) Ltd v *Carey* (1992)
        Groves v *Minor* (1997)

8.2 Key points

Easements

If legal is a legal interest – s1(2)(a) LPA 1925 – requires a deed or prescription to permanently bind the servient land.

Essentials of an easement: Re Ellenborough Park *[1956] Ch 131*

a) There must be a dominant and servient tenement.

b) Easement must accommodate the dominant tenement: see *Hill v Tupper* (1863) 2 H & C 121.

c) Dominant and servient tenements must be owned or occupied by different persons.

d) The right must be against other land. It is not a right to possession of other land: *Copeland v Greenhalf* [1952] Ch 488.

e) Easement must be capable of forming the subject matter of a grant. New types of easement may be created: *Crow v Wood* [1971] 1 QB 77; see also *Dyce v Lady Hay* (1852) 1 Macq 305 – the category of servitudes and easements must alter and expand with the changes that take place in the circumstances of mankind.

Easements distinguished from other rights

a) Examples of easements – way, light, problems vis-à-vis right of storage – *Copeland* v *Greenhalf* [1952] Ch 488 and *Grigsby* v *Melville* [1974] 1 WLR 80 but see *Wright* v *Macadam* [1949] 2 KB 744 and *Attorney-General of Southern Nigeria* v *John Holt & Co (Liverpool) Ltd* [1915] AC 599.

b) Compare easements with:

    i) licences – cannot exist as a legal interest – more flexible, revoke unilaterally;

    ii) quasi-easements – rights over own land;

    iii) other natural rights, eg support of land;

    iv) restrictive covenants – wider eg right to view – but only *burden* runs and must be *negative*;

    v) customary rights – exercised by everyone within the custom.

Creation of easements

a) Statute – private local Acts.

b) Express grant – deed.

c) Implied grant – easements of necessity (*Nickerson* v *Barraclough* [1981] Ch 426) and intended easements – *Wong* v *Beaumont Property Trust* [1965] 1 QB 173; *Stafford* v *Lee* (1992) 65 P & CR 172.

    i) Rule in *Wheeldon* v *Burrows* (quasi easements)

    On the grant of *part* of a tenement there will pass to the grantee as easements all quasi easements which are continuous and apparent or are necessary for the reasonable enjoyment of the land granted and were used by the grantor for the benefit of the part granted.

    Continuous – permanent without the need for constant use.

    Apparent – capable of discovery by careful inspection of the land.

    Wheeler & Another v *J J Saunders Ltd and Others* [1995] 3 WLR 466.

    The facts of *Wheeldon* v *Burrows* (1879) 12 Ch D 31 may be demonstrated by the following diagram:

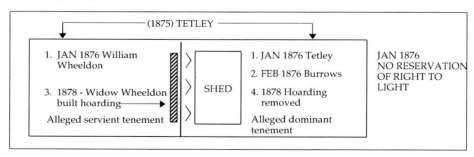

JAN 1876: sale of alleged servient tenement to William Wheeldon.

FEB 1876: sale of alleged dominant tenement to Burrows.

1878: widow Wheeldon erected hoarding to exclude light to shed.

Burrows knocked this down – successful action by widow in trespass because no right of access of light to shed windows had been reserved by Tetley in Jan 1876.

Thesiger LJ put the matter thus:

> '... on the grant by the owner of a tenement of part of that tenement as it is then used and enjoyed there will pass to the grantee all those continuous and apparent easements (by which I mean quasi-easements) or [in other words] all those easements which are necessary to the reasonable enjoyment of the property granted, and which have been and are at the time of the grant used by the owners of the entirety for the benefit of the part granted.' Quote in Cheshire.

Thesiger LJ then mentioned the exception of 'cases of what are called ways of necessity' and concluded:

> 'In the case of a grant you may imply a grant of such continuous and apparent easements or such easements as are necessary to the reasonable enjoyment of the property conveyed, and have in fact been enjoyed during the unity of ownership, but that, with the exception ... of easements of necessity you cannot imply a similar reservation in favour of the grantor of the land.'

ii) Section 62 LPA 1925.

Contains 'general words' which, unless excluded in express terms, imply into any conveyance of a legal estate in land a number of rights (including easements) thenceforth to be enjoyed by the grantee of that estate.

There must be a conveyance: *Borman* v *Griffith* [1930] 1 Ch 493; and there must have been some diversity of ownership or occupation of the two tenements prior to the conveyance: *Sovmots Investments Ltd* v *Secretary of State for the Environment* [1977] 2 WLR 951.

d) Presumed grant – prescription – long usage based on presumption that grant by deed was made at some time. Requirements for prescription at common law are:

i) Enjoyed as of right – nec vi, nec clam, nec precario.

ii) Continuous – enjoyed as and when required.

iii) Used by a fee simple owner against a fee simple owner.

iv) Must lie in grant.

v) Common law prescription. A grant would be presumed if continuous user as of right could be shown to have continued from 'time immemorial' (1189). This presumption can be rebutted by showing that the right must have arisen since 1189.

vi) Lost modern grant. The doctrine is a legal fiction. If there is an obstacle to establishing an easement under common law prescription but user as of right for a sufficient period can be established (usually 20 years), the court *may* presume that there was an actual grant of the easement subsequent to 1189 but prior to the commencement of the period of user relied on and that the deed making the grant has subsequently been lost. Uncertainty is the major weakness with this device – the court has a discretion – *Tehidy Minerals Ltd* v *Norman* [1971] 2 QB 528.

vii) Prescription Act 1832 ss1–4. The effect of the 1832 Act is that if a right has been enjoyed for a certain period of time before the action is brought the claim to the right shall NOT be defeated merely by proving the enjoyment began since 1189.

viii) Easements other than light – s2.

ix) Profits – s1.

x) Easement of light – s3 – *Colls* v *Home and Colonial Stores Ltd* [1904] AC 179; *Allen* v *Greenwood* [1979] 2 WLR 187; and *Carr-Saunders* v *Dick McNeil Associates Ltd* [1986] 1 WLR 922.

xi) Note 'interruption': s4. Interruption to have effect must be submitted to or acquiesced in for one year after the party interrupted shall have notice thereof (and of the person making or authorising the same to be made) – *Davies* v *Du Paver* [1953] 1 QB 184.

Extinguishment of easements

a) Release – deed

   i) Express

   ii) Implied

   Release may be implied if there is evidence of an intention on the part of the dominant owner to abandon the easement. The question is always whether an intention to abandon can properly be inferred from all the circumstances of the given case. See *Benn* v *Hardinge* (1992) 66 P & CR 246.

b) Unity of seisin

   Must have the fee simple in *both* properties – if only a leasehold interest the easement is suspended.

Alterations to the respective tenements

a) Alteration to the servient tenement – must *not* deprive of access as in *Celsteel Ltd* v *Alton House Holdings Ltd* [1985] 1 WLR 204.

b) Alteration to dominant tenement – may *not* destroy the easement by enlarging the dominant tenement from a flat to the whole house: *Graham v Philcox* [1984] 3 WLR 150. Remedy – *injunction* – as to the terms of the injunction: see *Rosling v Pinnegar* (1987) 54 P & CR 124.

Extent of easement

a) Right of way

    i) Express – matter of construction against grantor. Normally only a means of access to dominant tenement – common form: 'At all times and for all purposes' – and not confined to purpose for which land is used at time of grant. House to hotel – easement allowed in *White v Grand Hotel Eastbourne Ltd* [1913] 1 Ch 113: see *Groves & Another v Minor* (1997) The Times 20 November and *Batchelor v Marlow* (2001) 92 P & CR 36; *London & Suburban Land & Building Co (Holdings) Ltd v Carey* (1993) 62 P & CR 481.

    ii) Implied – necessity. Limited to necessity at time right arose (*London Corporation v Riggs* (1880) 13 Ch D 798). Other cases – right measured by extent of enjoyment overall: if no major change in dominant tenement user is not limited by reference to numbers and a right of way to a little used caravan site may still be used when site holds more caravans (*British Railways Board v Glass* [1965] Ch 538), or a right of way for business purposes may expand as the business expands: *Woodhouse & Co Ltd v Kirkland (Derby) Ltd* [1970] 1 WLR 1185. If the character of the user remains constant – there is no objection to an increase in its intensity even if the dominant tenement is enlarged from a flat to the user for the whole house: *Graham v Philcox* [1984] 3 WLR 150. *British Railways Board v Glass* (above), Harman LJ: 'A right to use a way for this purpose or that has never been … limited to a right to use the way so many times a day or for such a number of vehicles so long as the dominant tenement does not change its identity.'

b) Right of light – amount of light. Megarry & Wade:

'The right … to have access of light for all ordinary purposes to which the room may be put.' The ordinary purposes for which the premises might reasonably be expected to be used: *Carr-Saunders v Dick McNeil Associates Ltd* [1986] 1 WLR 922.

c) Rights of water – includes right to take water from a river or pond and may draw extra water if for same purpose: *Cargill v Gotts* [1981] 1 All ER 682. Metered supply of water paid for by servient owner no easement: *Rance v Elvin* (1985) 50 P & CR 9. Further, the drainage of natural water from higher land onto separately owned lower land cannot exist as an easement because such drainage is an essential incident of land ownership: *Palmer & Another v Bowman and Another* [2001] 1 All ER 22.

d) Right of support – may extend to providing buttresses and even weather proofing a party wall (*Bradburn v Lindsay* [1983] 2 All ER 408), but general rule is that an easement should not involve expenditure: *Phipps v Pears* [1965] 1 QB 76; cf *Crow v Wood* [1971] 1 QB 77.

Miscellaneous matters

It is now clear that a right to park can amount to an easement provided it is not a right to park in a defined place: *London and Blenheim Estates Ltd v Ladbroke Retail Parks Ltd* [1993] 1 All ER 307. In each case it is a question of degree whether the dominant rights are so extensive as to destroy the very nature of an easement. In *Batchelor v Marlow* (2000) The Times 7 June the Chancery Division held that a right to park cars could be acquired by prescription. The Court of Appeal in *Batchelor v Marlow* (2001) 92 P & CR 36 emphasised that a key factor in seeking to establish an easement of car parking was that the right granted/claimed had to leave the servient owner with reasonable use of his land. There the court decided that an exclusive right to park six cars for nine-and-a-half hours for each working day of the week rendered the servient owner without any reasonable use of his land. However, in *Saeed v Plustrade Ltd* [2001] EWCA Civ 2011 the Court of Appeal somewhat suprisingly, in view of the aforementioned case-law, 'left open' the question whether a right to park could amount to an easement.

The Access to Neighbouring Land Act 1992 deals with the situation of a person who needs to gain access to neighbouring land in order to carry out works on his own land, eg to enter a neighbour's land in order to erect a new fence.

Profits à prendre

Nature – may exist in gross

Distinguish from easements – different prescriptive periods under the Prescription Act 1832. Owner of the profit does have possessory rights over the land.

Classification

a) As to ownership:

 i) several – enjoyed by one person;

 ii) profits in common – enjoyed along with others.

b) In relation to land:

 i) profit appurtenant – annexed to nearby dominant land;

 ii) profit appendant – annexed to land by operation of law;

 iii) profit pur cause de vicinage – two adjacent commons;

 iv) profit in gross – may be enjoyed severally or in common but no land owned.

c) By subject matter:

 i) pasture – see Commons Registration Act 1965;

ii) turbary – to cut peat or turf for fuel;

iii) estovers – to cut wood for fuel or repairs;

iv) piscary – to take fish;

v) profit in the soil – to take gravel.

Acquisition and extinguishment

Thirty or sixty years under s1 of the Prescription Act 1832.

Public rights similar to profits

a) Public rights – eg to fish in sea or tidal waters – enjoyed by all members of the public.

b) Rights of fluctuating bodies of persons – at common law not a legal person to whom a grant could be made. The common law rules could be avoided by showing long enjoyment *and* right derives from the Crown *and* the beneficiaries act like a corporation: *Goodman v Mayor of Saltash* (1882) 7 App Cas 633.

   i) Presumed charter of incorporation.

   ii) Presumed charitable trust.

8.3 Key cases and statutes

- *B & Q plc v Liverpool & Lancashire Properties Ltd* (2000) The Times 6 September
  Established the test for actionable interference with an easement

- *Batchelor v Marlow* [2003] 1 WLR 764
  For a right to park to exist as an easement the right granted/claimed must leave the servient owner with reasonable use of his land

- *Benn v Hardinge* (1992) 66 P & CR 246
  Extinguishment of an easement – intention to abandon is usually *presumed* after 20 years non-user of the easement – however, this presumption may be set aside if the non-user is explicable on some other basis

- *Borman v Griffith* [1930] 1 Ch 493
  Acquisition by implied grant – an agreement for a lease was not a conveyance for the purposes of s62 LPA 1925 – however, the rule in *Wheeldon v Burrows* applied to such an agreement

- *Carr-Saunders v Dick McNeil Associates Ltd* [1986] 1 WLR 922
  Easement of light – amount of light had to be sufficient to enable the premises to be adequately lit for the ordinary purposes for which they might reasonably be expected to be used – only access to light to a building can be acquired as an easement

- *Central Midlands Estates* v *Leicester Dyers* (2003) The Times 18 February
  A right to park an unlimited number of cars could not amount to an easement

- *Copeland* v *Greenhalf* [1952] Ch 488
  Characteristics of an easement – for a right to be an easement it must be a right against other (ie servient) land and not a right to possession of the servient land

- *Crabb* v *Arun District Council* [1975] 3 All ER 865
  Acquisition by estoppel – even where no formal grant was made an easement could be acquired by virtue of the conduct of the parties

- *Ellenborough Park, Re* [1955] 3 All ER 667
  Leading authority on characteristics of an easement – Court of Appeal approved the classification made by Cheshire

- *Hill* v *Tupper* (1863) 2 H & C 121
  Characteristics of an easement – a right to be an easement had to accommodate the dominant tenement – conferring a personal benefit on its owner would not suffice

- *London & Blenheim Estates Ltd* v *Ladbroke Retail Parks Ltd* [1993] 4 All ER 157
  A right to park could exist as an easement – however, such a right must not leave the servient owner without any reasonable use of his land

- *Long* v *Gowlett* [1923] 2 Ch 177
  Acquisition by implied grant – to acquire an easement under s62 LPA 1925 diversity of ownership/occupation of the dominant and servient tenements prior to the relevant conveyance was required

- *Mobil Oil Co Ltd* v *Birmingham City Council* [2002] 2 P & CR 14
  Courts attach importance to commercial efficacy when construing legal documents in respect of commercial land transactions

- *Saeed* v *Plustrade Ltd* [2001] EWCA Civ 2011
  The question whether a right to park cars could amount to an easement was surprisingly 'left open'

- *Wheeldon* v *Burrows* (1879) 12 Ch D 31
  Leading authority on acquisition by implied grant – established how on a grant of part of a tenement certain quasi easements could pass to the grantee as easements

- *Wright* v *Macadam* [1949] 2 KB 744
  Established, somewhat controversially, that a right to store goods on another's land could exist as an easement

- Access to Neighbouring Land Act 1992

- Commons Registration Act 1965

- Law of Property Act 1925, ss1(2)(a) and 62

- Prescription Act 1832, ss2, 3 and 4

8.4 Questions and suggested solutions

Analysis of questions

Problem questions on easements can frequently be approached as follows: (i) identify the rights being claimed and consider whether they are capable of existing as easements – need to consider the characteristics of an easement as confirmed in *Re Ellenborough Park* [1956] Ch 131; (ii) consider whether the rights capable of existing as easements have been acquired in one or more of the ways which the law recognises – this will usually be the heart of the question and acquisition by implied grant and/or prescription is regularly favoured by examiners; and (iii) consider whether the easement properly acquired is a legal or equitable one and relate to whether the land is registered or unregistered. Finally, a brief resumé of the appropriate remedies for infringement of an easement may be required. As to essay questions on easements, an old favourite involves contrasting the doctrine of *Wheeldon* v *Burrows* with LPA s62.

QUESTION ONE

In 1970 Bob, a builder, asked his friend and neighbour, Frank, a farmer, whether he could store his building materials somewhere on Frank's land. Frank agreed, 'Of course. You can use that old shed adjoining your land. It is virtually empty and I have no immediate use for it.' Bob has used the shed for his materials ever since and on two occasions, in 1976 and in 1986, he reroofed the shed to keep it waterproof. In 1977 Frank sold his farm to Gus. Gus never objected to Bob's use of the shed and he never used the shed for his own purposes, though he thought that the shed might be useful in the future if he started a market garden on his land. In 1994 Gus sold his land to Spike. Spike has now refused to allow Bob to enter the shed.

Discuss.

University of London LLB Examination
(for External Students) Land Law June 1995 Q3

General Comment

The question is primarily concerned with a number of issues relevant to the law of easements. Further, some comment upon estoppel licences would also be appropriate. The question provides students well-versed in these areas of law with a fairly straightforward opportunity to display their knowledge and understanding.

Skeleton Solution

Characteristics of an easement – easement of storage – acquisition of an easement: express grant, prescription, doctrine of proprietary estoppel – registration requirements – estoppel licences – remedies to give effect to an estoppel licence.

Suggested Solution

An easement is a right in or over the land of another. In order to be an easement the right in question must satisfy the following five characteristics (see *Re Ellenborough Park* [1956] Ch 131): (i) there must be a dominant and servient tenement; (ii) the easement must accommodate the dominant tenement; (iii) the dominant and servient tenements must not be both owned and occupied by the same person; (iv) a right over land cannot amount to an easement unless it is capable of forming the subject matter of a grant; and (v) the right must be against other land (ie it is not a right to possession of other land).

Here, Bob is storing building materials in Frank's old shed. The first four characteristics of an easement listed above would appear to be satisfied. For example, there is a dominant tenement (Bob's adjoining land) and a servient tenement (Frank's land). However, there might be a problem with the final characteristic – an easement cannot be a right to possession of other land (ie the right claimed must not amount to joint use of the servient tenement by the dominant owner). In essence the issue is: can there be an easement of storage? Case law on this point is somewhat conflicting. In *Copeland v Greenhalf* [1952] Ch 488 a claim to stand an unlimited number of vehicles on another's land was held not to be capable of being an easement because it was held to amount to a claim to joint possession of the land (orthodox line taken). However, in *Wright v Macadam* [1949] 2 KB 744 the Court of Appeal upheld the right of a tenant to store her coal in a shed on the landlord's land. Further, in *Attorney-General of Southern Nigeria v John Holt & Co (Liverpool) Ltd* [1915] AC 599 the courts recognised as an easement the right to store casks and trade-produce on land. The decision in *Wright v Macadam*, in particular, has been the subject of much comment and criticism. Accordingly, given the current state of authority there must be some doubt as to whether the right being claimed by Bob can exist as an easement. However, for the purposes of this question let us assume that it can.

In order for a right to be an easement, not only must it satisfy the characteristics of an easement, it must be properly acquired as an easement. There are a variety of ways in which an easement can be acquired. In the context of this question three methods of acquisition deserve comment – express grant, prescription under the Prescription Act 1832 and estoppel.

Here, Frank, in response to Bob's request to store building materials on Frank's land, said: 'Of course. You can use that old shed adjoining your land.' An express grant of an easement is usually made by the use of express words in the conveyance of the legal estate of the dominant tenement, and provided it is granted for a period of time equivalent to a freehold or leasehold estate, and the conveyance itself complies with the formal requirements (ie it is made by deed), the easement will be legal. Here, there is an oral grant. It has been held that an oral grant can succeed as an equitable easement when supported by an act of part-performance: *McManus v Cooke* (1887) 35 Ch D 681 and *May v Belville* [1905] 2 Ch 605. Bob's use of the shed would rank as an act of part-performance. Accordingly, it is submitted that Bob could have acquired the easement by express grant. However, both the aforementioned decisions pre-dated the coming into force of s2 Law of Property (Miscellaneous Provisions) Act 1989, in consequence of which this method of acquisition (oral grant supported by an act of part performance) may no longer be available.

The basis of holding that an easement is acquired by prescription is that if long user as of right is proved the courts will presume that the use began lawfully, ie as a result of a grant. Since Bob's user commenced 25 years ago, in 1970, it is necessary to consider the possibility of him having acquired an easement by prescription. One of the prerequisites of prescription is user as of right, ie the use must have been exercised without force, without secrecy and, most significantly for the purposes of this question, without permission. Of the three methods of acquiring an easement by prescription the one which may be of most assistance to Bob is the Prescription Act 1832. In order to establish a claim under the Act to an easement other than light, Bob must show user as of right, user without interruption and user for one of the statutory periods (shorter period is 20 years, longer period is 40 years). Under the Act, user as of right has the same meaning as above, except that there are specific rules relating to the effect of permission. Such rules are particularly relevant here since Frank gave Bob oral permission to store material in the old shed. Under the 1832 Act, an oral consent given at the outset of user (and extending throughout) defeats a claim under the shorter period but not the longer period. Here, since user commenced in 1970, it is not feasible to utilise the longer period. As to the shorter period, since Frank gave Bob oral permission at the outset this would seem to preclude any possibility of successfully establishing a claim under the 20-year period of the Act: *Healey* v *Hawkins* [1968] 1 WLR 1967. Further, to acquire an easement under the Act it is necessary to litigate because s4 provides that both the 20- and 40-year periods must be 'next before action', ie both periods are measured backwards from the action in which the right is questioned.

Finally, in relation to acquisition of an easement it may be possible for Bob to argue that he has acquired an easement by operation of the doctrine of proprietary estoppel. This method of acquisition covers a situation where no formal grant of an easement is made but an easement arises in consequence of the conduct of the parties. For example, in *Crabb* v *Arun District Council* [1976] Ch 179 Crabb owned two plots of land only one of which (Plot A) had an exit to the highway. The local authority led Crabb to believe that he would be allowed a right of way across their land onto the highway from Plot B if he sold Plot A. In reliance upon this assurance, Crabb sold Plot A without reserving a right of way across it from Plot B to the exit. There was no formal grant of an easement by the local authority. Shortly afterwards the local authority fenced off the exit point from Plot B which they had installed. Crabb sought an injunction. The Court of Appeal concluded that the local authority were estopped from going back on their assurance and they granted Crabb a right of way across the council's land, free of charge. Here, if Bob can show that Frank or Gus gave him an assurance as to his use of the shed prior to the reroofing, then the reroofing could be used as detrimental reliance upon the assurance and thus establish the estoppel. An easement created by estoppel can only be equitable.

Accordingly, as to acquisition, it is submitted that Bob may have acquired an easement either by an oral express grant or by estoppel. In either case, the easement would rank as an equitable one (for an easement to be legal it must be created by deed and be granted for a period of time equivalent to a freehold or leasehold estate). The enforcement of an equitable easement against a purchaser of the servient land (ie Spike) turns on several factors, including whether the land is registered or unregistered. In the case of unregistered land an equitable easement must be registered as a Class D(iii) land charge to bind a purchaser for value. Accordingly, if so registered, Spike would be bound by it. However, if not registered as a land charge Spike might still be bound if he knew about Bob's use of the shed: *ER Ives Investments Ltd* v *High* [1967] 2 QB 379. In the case of registered land the equitable easement is an overriding interest by virtue of *Celsteel Ltd* v *Alton House Holdings Ltd* [1985] 1 WLR 204, and thus binding on Spike.

Given that there is some uncertainty as to whether the right Bob is claiming is capable of existing as an easement, it is worth considering whether any possibilities other than easements are open to him.

In the circumstances it may be possible for Bob to argue that he has an estoppel licence. It has long been accepted that a licensor is estopped from revoking a licence where he has acquiesced to or encouraged the use of land. Bob might be able to show that Frank or Gus have so acted – Gus never objected to Bob's use of the shed. Further, and very importantly here, given that Gus has sold the land on which the shed is located to Spike, an estoppel licence can bind a third party. Whether in practice Spike would be bound turns on a number of factors. If the land is unregistered, Spike would be bound if he has notice of Bob's right because a licence by estoppel is not registerable as a land charge under the Land Charges Act 1972: *ER Ives Investments Ltd* v *High*. If the land is registered Spike would be bound if the estoppel licence has been protected by the entry of a notice or caution on the register, unless it is an overriding interest under s70(1)(g) LRA 1925, which in this case it is not.

Finally, if the court found that Bob had an estoppel licence what remedy would they grant to give effect to it (ie satisfy the equity)? In this regard the courts have shown great flexibility (ranging from a transfer of the fee simple to the licensee to reasonable notice to quit). Such flexibility has produced uncertainty because it is difficult for practitioners to anticipate how the estoppel will be applied in a given situation. Here it is submitted that Bob would get reasonable notice to quit the shed and reimbursement of any monies spent by him in reroofing it.

QUESTION TWO

Peter owned two adjacent shops which fronted directly on to a busy street. In one shop he sold arts and crafts and in the other he ran a café. On the outside wall of the café he affixed a notice advertising his arts and crafts shop. Behind the two shops there was a large yard belonging to Peter which backed on to a road. Deliveries for the shops were usually made to the yard and Peter parked his car there. In 1991, wishing to concentrate on his arts and crafts business, Peter leased the café to James for ten years. Initially Peter did not object to James using the yard for deliveries to the café or parking his van there, but early in 1994 differences arose between Peter and James, and Peter told James to stop using the yard. James retaliated by removing the advertising notice from the wall of the café.

Discuss.

Would your answer be different if Peter had conveyed the freehold reversion in the café to James in 1993?

University of London LLB Examination
(for External Students) Land Law June 1994 Q7

General Comment

A somewhat deceptive question. At first sight it seems to be a fairly straightforward question on easements but the more you get into it the more issues that emerge. A thorough understanding of the relevant methods of acquiring an easement is essential in order to tackle this question.

Skeleton Solution

Characteristics of an easement – implied grant: common intention; *Pwllbach Colliery Co Ltd* v *Woodman* – easement of car parking: *London & Blenheim Estates Ltd* v *Ladbroke Retail Parks Ltd* – bare licence – voluntary waste – implied grant: s62 LPA 1925 – easement to have a sign on neighbouring property: *Moody* v *Steggles* – reservation.

Suggested Solution

An easement is a right in or over the land of another. In order to be an easement the right in question must satisfy the following characteristics (see *Re Ellenborough Park* [1956] Ch 131): (i) there must be a dominant and servient tenement; (ii) the easement must accommodate the dominant tenement; (iii) the dominant and servient tenements must not be both owned and occupied by the same person; (iv) a right over land cannot amount to an easement unless it is capable of forming the subject matter of a grant; and (v) the right must be against other land (ie it is not a right to possession of other land). James' claim to use the yard behind the two shops for deliveries is a claim to a right of way which will satisfy the aforementioned characteristics of an easement.

In order for a right to be an easement, not only must it satisfy the characteristics of an easement, it must also be properly acquired as an easement. There are a variety of ways in which an easement can be acquired. On the facts, assuming the 1991 lease of the café by Peter to James is silent on the matter, the issue is whether there is an implied grant to James of a right to use the yard for deliveries. There are a variety of ways in which a grant of an easement may be implied in favour of a purchaser/lessee of land.

The first is necessity where the implied grant is necessary to prevent land-locking. In

Titchmarsh v *Royston Water Co Ltd* (1899) 81 LT 673 it was held that the availability of an alternative route enjoyable as of right was destructive of any claim of necessity, even though the alternative route was inconvenient. Here there is no easement of necessity because it is possible to make deliveries to the café via the busy road onto which it fronts.

The second is s62 Law of Property Act (LPA) 1925, by virtue of which unless a contrary intention appears every conveyance of land passes with it all easements 'appertaining or reputed to appertain to the land … or at the time of the conveyance occupied or enjoyed with the land …' However, for s62 to be available there must have been some diversity of ownership or occupation of the quasi-dominant and quasi-servient tenements prior to the conveyance: see *Sovmots Investments Ltd* v *Secretary of State for the Environment* [1977] 2 WLR 951. Given that prior to the 1991 lease the arts and crafts shop and the café were in Peter's sole ownership and occupation, s62 is not available because of no diversity of ownership or occupation.

The third is the doctrine of *Wheeldon* v *Burrows* (1879) 12 Ch D 31. Under this doctrine, on the grant of part of a tenement there passes to the grantee, as easements, all quasi-easements which were continuous and apparent and were used by the grantor for the benefit of the part granted. 'Apparent' means capable of discovery by careful inspection of the land. On the facts the doctrine would not be available as the right being claimed by James is unlikely to be apparent. Finally, in relation to implied grant there are intended easements. These are easements necessary to carry out the clear common intention of the parties: see *Pwllbach Colliery Co Ltd* v *Woodman* [1915] AC 634. It may be that an easement of way could be inferred on the basis of the common intention of Peter and James.

As to James' claim to park his van in the yard at the back of the shops, it is now clear that there can be an easement to park provided that exclusive occupation of the servient land is not given: see *London & Blenheim Estates Ltd* v *Ladbroke Retail Parks Ltd* [1992] 1 All ER 307. However, there seems to be no basis for implying the grant of a right to park a van here. Accordingly, it seems that on the facts James parks by virtue of a bare licence which can be revoked by the licensor at any time provided he gives the licensee reasonable notice. Further, there is nothing on the facts to raise an estoppel as in *ER Ives Investments Ltd* v *High* [1967] 2 QB 379.

Peter telling James to stop using the yard constitutes an infringement of James' right to enjoy what seems to be an established easement. However, such infringement does not entitle James to take retaliatory action by way of removing the advertising notice from the wall of the café. On the facts James' removal of the shop-sign is an act of voluntary waste (a positive act which damages the land) by a tenant for which he may, subject to the terms of the lease, be held liable.

A conveyance of the freehold reversion in the café to James in 1993 would affect the above conclusions in several respects. Subject to any relevant provisions in the conveyance, James could claim an implied right to use the yard for deliveries as before.

However, the parking of his van hitherto by way of licence would now be by an easement by virtue of s62 LPA 1925 provided the extent of the right claimed does not amount to a claim to possession of part of the servient land.

Finally, if James was the freehold owner of the café he could remove the notice advertising the arts and crafts shop unless prevented by some counter-right in Peter. It is questionable whether Peter could establish any such right. In *Moody* v *Steggles* (1879) 12 Ch D 261 it was held that a right to fix a sign board on a neighbouring house could be an easement. However, on the facts it is necessary to ask whether this right accommodates Peter's land or merely his business: see *Hill* v *Tupper* (1863) 2 H & C 121. In any event was any such right ever granted? If it was it would have to be by way of an express reservation in the 1993 conveyance as there is no necessity and insufficient evidence of common intention.

QUESTION THREE

Alf was the owner of the Bleakacre Estate (the title to which is unregistered) where he lived and reared sheep. In 1965 he built a house on one of his fields (Swallowfield) and leased the field to Bert for five years. Alf built a fence dividing his land from the field, which Bert intended to use to establish as a market garden. Alf agreed to allow Bert to use an empty outbuilding on Bleakacre for storage purposes until Bert had time to erect a shed on Swallowfield. In 1970 Alf sold Swallowfield to Bert. Bert's market garden was very successful and, although he never erected a shed, in 1975 he built a swimming-pool which he allowed Alf and his family to use whenever they wanted. Recently Alf died and his executors sold Bleakacre to Ray. Ray now insists on Bert removing his property from the outbuilding. Bert refuses to allow Ray to use the swimming-pool and he complains that, owing to the poor state of the fence on Bleakacre, Ray's sheep have been straying on to Swallowfield and damaging his garden.

Discuss.

University of London LLB Examination
(for External Students) Land Law June 1996 Q3

General Comment

This is a question on easements. It is essential for students to identify at the outset the rights being claimed and to realise that the question contains an issue that does not usually feature in examination questions on easements – the 'quasi easement' of fencing. As with most problem questions on this topic, the inclusion of a diagrammatical representation of the facts is advisable, not least because it should eliminate the possibility of a student confusing the various parties and issues in the course of the answer.

Skeleton Solution

Characteristics of an easement: *Re Ellenborough Park* – easement of storage: *Wright* v *Macadam*; *Copeland* v *Greenhalf* – acquisition of an easement under Prescription Act 1832, by s62 LPA 1925 – whether a right of mere recreation can be an easement: *Re Ellenborough Park* – easement of fencing: *Jones* v *Price*; obligation on servient owner to repair required; acquisition.

Suggested Solution

An easement is a right in or over the land of another. In order to be an easement the right in question must satisfy the following five characteristics (see *Re Ellenborough Park* [1956] Ch 131):

a) there must be a dominant and servient tenement;

b) the easement must accommodate the dominant tenement;

c) the dominant and servient tenements must not be both owned and occupied by the same person;

d) a right over land cannot amount to an easement unless it is capable of forming the subject matter of a grant; and

e) the right must be against other land (ie it is not a right to possession of other land).

There are three main issues in the question. First, whether Bert has acquired an easement of storage in respect of the outbuilding on Bleakacre. Second, whether Ray has an easement to use the swimming-pool on Swallowfield. Third, whether Bert has acquired an easement that his neighbour Ray is required to fence the boundary between the Bleakacre Estate and Swallowfield. The factual developments recounted in the question can be represented diagrammatically as follows:

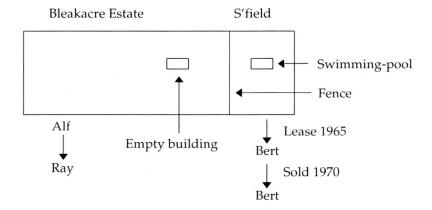

Bert has used an empty outbuilding on Bleakacre for storage purposes. Has he acquired an easement of storage in respect of that outbuilding? There are two matters to consider. First, whether there can be an easement of storage. Second, assuming that there can be such an easement, has Bert acquired it in one of the ways recognised by law?

The first four characteristics of an easement listed above would appear to be satisfied. For example, there is a dominant tenement (Swallowfield) and a servient tenement (Bleakacre). However, there might be a problem with the final characteristic – an easement cannot be a right to possession of other land (ie the right claimed must not amount to joint use of the servient tenement by the dominant owner). In essence the issue is: can there be an easement of storage? Case law on this point is somewhat conflicting. In *Copeland* v *Greenhalf* [1952] Ch 488 a claim to stand an unlimited number of vehicles on another's land was held not to be capable of being an easement because it was held to amount to a claim to joint possession of the land (orthodox line taken). However, in *Wright* v *Macadam* [1949] 2 KB 744 the Court of Appeal upheld the right of a tenant to store her coal in a shed on the landlord's land. Further, in *Attorney-General of Southern Nigeria* v *John Holt & Co (Liverpool) Ltd* [1915] AC 599 the courts recognised as an easement the right to store casks and trade produce on land. The decision in *Wright* v *Macadam*, in particular, has been the subject of much comment and criticism. Accordingly, given the current state of authority, there must be some doubt as to whether the right being claimed by Bert can exist as an easement. However, for the purposes of the question let us assume that it can.

In order for a right to be an easement, not only must it satisfy the characteristics of an easement, it must be properly acquired as an easement. There are a variety of ways in which an easement can be acquired. In the context of Bert using the outbuilding on Bleakacre for storage purposes two methods of acquisition deserve comment – prescription under the Prescription Act 1832 and implied grant under s62 Law of Property Act (LPA) 1925.

The basis of holding that an easement is acquired by prescription is that if long user as of right is proved the courts will presume that the use began lawfully, ie as a result of a grant. Since Bert's user seemingly commenced 31 years ago, in 1965, it is necessary to consider the possibility of him having acquired an easement by prescription. One of the prerequisites of prescription is user as of right, ie the use must have been exercised without force, without secrecy and, most significantly for this part of the question, without permission. Of the three methods of acquiring an easement by prescription the one which may be of most assistance to Bert is the Prescription Act 1832. In order to establish a claim under the Act to an easement other than light (as here), Bert must show user as of right, user without interruption and user for one of the statutory periods (shorter period is 20 years, longer period is 40 years). Under the Act, user as of right has the same meaning as above, except that there are specific rules relating to the effect of permission. Such rules are particularly relevant here since Alf 'agreed to allow Bert to use an empty outbuilding on Bleakacre for storage purposes until Bert had time to erect a shed on Swallowfield'. Under the 1832 Act, an oral consent given at the outset of user (and extending throughout) defeats a claim under the shorter period but not the longer period. Here, since user commenced in 1965, it is not feasible to utilise the longer period. As to the shorter period, since Alf seemingly gave Bert oral permission at the outset this would seem to preclude any possibility of successfully establishing a claim under the 20-year period of the Act: *Healey v Hawkins* [1968] 1 WLR 1967.

A better prospect for Bert to argue is that he has acquired the easement of storage by implied grant under s62 LPA 1925, which provides that every conveyance of land passes with it all easements 'appertaining or reputed to appertain to the land ... or at the time of conveyance occupied or enjoyed with the land'. Here Bert leased Swallowfield in 1965 and then bought it in 1970. For s62 to be available three requirements must be satisfied:

a) There must be a conveyance (the sale of Swallowfield in 1970).

b) There must be no contrary intention in the conveyance (no evidence to suggest there is).

c) There must have been some diversity of ownership or occupation of the tenements prior to the conveyance: *Sovmots Investments Ltd v Secretary of State for the Environment* [1979] AC 144. Given that prior to the conveyance in 1970 the dominant tenement (Swallowfield) was occupied by Bert and the servient tenement (Bleakacre) was owned by Alf, this final requirement is clearly satisfied. Accordingly, assuming that you can have an easement of storage it seems that Bert may well have acquired it under s62 LPA 1925.

Finally, in this regard if Bert's claim to an easement of storage failed he would have a temporary licence with permission given what Alf said to him at the outset of his usage of the empty outbuilding.

Has Ray an easement to use the swimming-pool on Swallowfield? Two matters have to be considered in this regard. First, can using a swimming-pool on a neighbour's land amount to an easement? It seems not. In *Re Ellenborough Park* the Court of Appeal stated that a right of mere recreation and amusement could not rank as an easement. The use of the swimming-pool on Swallowfield would seem to be caught by this proposition (for which there is some support in *Mounsey v Ismay* (1865) 3 H & L 486). Second, even if Ray can convince the court that a right to use the swimming-pool could exist as an easement, it is doubtful whether he has acquired it in one of the ways recognised by the law. Given that the swimming-pool was built in 1975 (it is assumed that Alf and his family started to use it that year), acquisition by prescription requires comment. However, one of the prerequisites of prescription, as already noted, is user as of right, ie the use must have been exercised without force, without secrecy and most significantly for this part of the question, *without permission*. Given that Bert *allowed* Alf and his family to use the pool whenever they wanted, there would seem to be no realistic prospect of Ray successfully arguing acquisition by prescription.

Has Bert acquired an easement that Ray is required to fence the boundary between the Bleakacre Estate and Swallowfield? The right to require a neighbouring landowner to repair his fence has been described as a 'quasi easement' (see *Jones* v *Price* [1965] 2 QB 618) because it necessitates positive action by the servient owner, whereas the hallmark of an orthodox easement is that only sufferance is required on the part of the servient owner. Nevertheless in practice it is treated by the courts as being an easement.

In order to establish the easement the owner of the dominant land must show that the owner of the servient land repaired the fence as a matter of obligation (ie at the demand or on notice from the owner of the dominant land), not just to keep his animals in. Mere proof that the owner of the servient land has repaired the fence at his own cost is not sufficient. There is nothing in the question to conclusively show that Alf/Ray (the servient owners) repaired the fence as a matter of obligation. Indeed, if the requisite element of obligation did exist, Bert could demand that Ray repair the fence – not just complain about the poor state of repair of it. If evidence supportive of the element of compulsion could be found it is necessary for Bert to show that he has acquired the right in one of the ways recognised by law. The easement of fencing lies in grant and it can be acquired by prescription or under s62 LPA 1925. Given that the fence was erected before the sale of Swallowfield to Bert in 1970, it seems that the right could be acquired by implied grant under s62 since all the requirements of that provision would appear to be satisfied (see above).

Finally, it follows from the preceding analysis that establishing an easement in this scenario is not without some difficulty. The best prospect is that Bert will be able to establish an easement of storage in respect of the empty building. This is because there is clear case authority for an easement of storage (albeit somewhat controversial) and it seems that he has acquired the right under s62 LPA 1925.

QUESTION FOUR

Farmer George and Farmer John were friends and neighbours. In 1973 George asked John if he could use a track across John's land for the purposes of carrying timber to the local timber yard. John agreed subject to George paying him a token yearly sum. For the first couple of years George paid the sum, but thereafter he stopped paying it and John never mentioned it. In 1982 George started storing his timber in the corner of one of John's fields. At first he just stacked it in the open, but in 1985 he built a shelter for it. In 1990 George established a market garden on his land and began using the shed for storing vegetables and the track for transporting them to market. In 1995 John sold his farm to Paul. Paul has recently written to George forbidding him to use the track and requiring him to remove the shelter from his land.

Discuss.

University of London LLB Examination
(for External Students) Land Law June 1997 Q6

General Comment

A not untypical problem question on easements. It is essential for students to identify at the outset the rights being claimed and the methods of acquisition of easements relevant to the facts. The question contains several issues (eg change of use) which require more than a basic knowledge of the subject matter in order to be dealt with effectively.

Skeleton Solution

Characteristics of an easement: *Re Ellenborough Park* – right of way – easement of storage: *Wright* v *Macadam* – acquisition of an easement by prescription, effect of oral permission under the 1832 Act: *Healey* v *Hawkins* – acquisition of an easement by s62 LPA 1925 and estoppel – change of use – building on servient land: trespass to land – Limitation Act 1980, s15 – legal or equitable easements.

Suggested Solution

An easement is a right in or over the land of another. In order to be an easement the right in question must satisfy the following five characteristics: (i) there must be a dominant and servient tenement; (ii) the easement must accommodate the dominant tenement; (iii) the dominant and servient tenements must not be both owned and occupied by the same person; (iv) a right over land cannot amount to an easement unless it is capable of forming the subject matter of a grant (see *Re Ellenborough Park* [1956] Ch 131 as to (i) to (iv)); and (v) the right must be against other land (ie it is not a right to possession of other land).

On the facts it is submitted that George will be claiming an easement of way in respect of the track across John's land and an easement of storage in respect of one of John's fields. The methods of acquisition of easements relevant include prescription and possibly estoppel and s62 LPA 1925. Further it is necessary to consider whether George was entitled to build a shelter on John's land and whether his claims to the aforementioned easements are in any way affected by his change of use of the track (from carrying timber to the local timber yard to transporting vegetables to market) and the storage facility (from storing timber to storing vegetables from his market garden).

A right of way is capable of being an easement and on the facts the five characteristics of an easement listed above would appear to be satisfied in respect of the track that George is using across John's land. Turning to the right of storage being claimed, the first four characteristics of an easement mentioned above would seem to be satisfied. For example, there is a dominant tenement (George's land) and a servient tenement (John's land). However, there might be a problem with the final characteristic – an easement cannot be a right to possession of other land (ie the right claimed must not amount to joint use of the servient tenement by the dominant owner). In essence the issue is: Can there be an easement of storage? Case law on the point is somewhat conflicting. In *Copeland* v *Greenhalf* [1952] Ch 488 a claim to stand an unlimited number of vehicles on another's land was held not to be capable of being an easement because it was held to amount to a claim to joint possession of the land (orthodox line taken). However, in *Wright v Macadam* [1949] 2 KB 744 the Court of Appeal upheld the right of a tenant to store her coal in a shed on the landlord's land. Further, in *Attorney-General of Southern Nigeria v John Holt & Co (Liverpool) Ltd* [1915] AC 599 the court recognised as an easement the right to store casks and trade produce on land. The decision in *Wright v Macadam*, in particular, has been the subject of much comment and criticism. Accordingly, given the current state of authority, there must be some doubt as to whether there can be an easement of storage. However, for the purposes of the question it is assumed that George's claim to a right to store timber/vegetables in the corner of one of John's fields meets the characteristics of an easement.

In order for a right to be an easement, not only must it satisfy the characteristics of an easement, it must be properly acquired as an easement. There are a variety of ways in which an easement can be acquired. In relation to the right of way across the track, it is necessary to consider whether George has acquired this right by prescription under the Prescription Act 1832. Further, in relation to the right of storage, acquisition of an easement under s62 LPA 1925 and possibly estoppel need to be considered. In the ensuing paragraphs these three methods of acquisition are considered in turn.

The basis of holding that an easement is acquired by prescription is that if long user as of right is proved the courts will presume that the use began lawfully, ie as a result of a grant. Since George's use of the track across John's land commenced in 1973, ie 24 years ago, it is necessary to consider the possibility of him having acquired an easement by prescription. One of the prerequisites of prescription is user as of right, ie the use must have been exercised without force, without secrecy and, most significantly for the purposes of this question, without permission. Of the three methods of acquiring an easement by prescription the one which may be of most assistance to George is the Prescription Act 1832. In order to establish a claim under the Act to an easement other than light, George must show user as of right, user without interruption and user for one of the statutory periods (shorter period is 20 years, longer period is 40 years). Under the Act, user as of right has the same meaning as above, except that there are specific rules relating to the effect of permission. Such rules are particularly relevant here since John seemingly gave George oral permission to use the track across his land subject to George paying 'a token yearly sum'. Under the 1832 Act, an oral consent given at the outset of user and extending throughout defeats a claim under the shorter period (*Healey v Hawkins* [1968] 1 WLR 1967) but not the longer period. Here since user commenced in 1973, it is not feasible to utilise the longer period but it may be possible to utilise the shorter period. To do so it is necessary to show that John's permission did not extend throughout the 20-year period. Here George paid the 'token yearly sum' for a couple of years but then stopped with John never mentioning the non-payment. Accordingly, it could be argued on these facts that John's oral permission did not extend throughout but rather ran out a couple of years after 1973 – say in 1975 and thus over 20 years ago.

Further, to acquire an easement under the 1832 Act it is necessary to litigate because s4 of the Act provides that both the 20- and 40-year periods must be 'next before action', ie both periods are measured backwards from the action in which the right is questioned. Accordingly, George should immediately seek (not least because Paul the new owner of the alleged servient land has written to him forbidding him from using the track) a declaration from the court that he has acquired a right of way over the track across Paul's land by prescription under the 1832 Act.

As to the easement of storage in respect of one of Paul's fields, prescription is not available as a possible method of acquisition since George only started storing timber in 1982. Section 62 LPA 1925 provides that every conveyance of land passes with it all easements 'appertaining or reputed to appertain to the land ... or at the time of conveyance occupied or enjoyed with the land'. For s62 to be available three requirements must be satisfied: (i) there must be a conveyance; (ii) there must be no contrary intention in the conveyance; and (iii) there must have been diversity of ownership or occupation of the tenements prior to the conveyance: *Sovmots Investments Ltd* v *Secretary of State for the Environment* [1979] AC 144. Although there is a conveyance here (the sale in 1995 by John of his farm to Paul) s62 only applies in favour of the grantee of the conveyance. Here Paul is the grantee of the conveyance but he has acquired the servient land whereas it is George who is claiming the easement and he is *not* a grantee. Accordingly, in such circumstances, the 1995 conveyance will not facilitate the acquisition of an easement of storage under s62 LPA 1925.

Further where no formal grant is made an easement may be created arising from the conduct of the parties. In *Crabb* v *Arun District Council* [1976] Ch 179 the claimant was encouraged to believe that he had an easement and it was held to be unreasonable to deny him that right. Given that in 1985 George built a shelter in the corner of one of John's fields this might be suggestive of an estoppel easement (for such an easement to be established there has to be a representation by John which George relied upon to his detriment), ie that George built the shelter following encouragement from John. However, there is no clear evidence of this.

Accordingly, in the light of the above there must be a question-mark over whether George has acquired an easement of storage in one of the ways recognised by law.

If George can acquire an easement of way over the track by prescription it is necessary to consider whether his claim to an easement would be affected in any way by the fact that initially he used the track to carry timber to the local timber yard but from 1990 he has used it to transport vegetables to market. This requires consideration of the extent of any easement acquired. In the case of an easement acquired by prescription extent is defined by mode of user in fact enjoyed during the relevant period. User for purposes *radically different* in character is not permissible. For example, a right of way acquired by prescription for, say, farming purposes cannot be used for industrial purposes: *Bradburn* v *Morris* (1876) 3 Ch D 812. Here it is submitted that any right of way acquired by George has been acquired for business purposes – it is assumed that he conveyed the timber to the timber yard for reasons of business and that business considerations again motivate his transportation of vegetables to market. It is also submitted that transporting vegetables across the track is not radically different from transporting timber. Further, apart from any radical change in the dominant tenement a user of way is not restricted by reference to frequency during the prescriptive period (although there is no suggestion that the change of products being conveyed has resulted in an increased user of the track) so that user of a right of way acquired for business purposes can expand with the expansion of the business. Accordingly, it is submitted that the change from timber to vegetables being conveyed by George should not jeopardise his claim to an easement.

Nor should the fact that George now stores vegetables rather than timber in the shelter jeopardise his claim to an easement of storage. It is a mere alteration to the mode of enjoyment.

Reverting to the right of storage claimed by George, it is clear from *Copeland* v *Greenhalf* that if the right claimed is so extensive as to amount to exclusive or joint user of the servient tenement it cannot exist as an easement. This is a question of degree. Further, if there is nothing to suggest that John allowed George to build the shelter he cannot claim a licence. George could rank as a trespasser vis-à-vis the shelter. However, given that he built it in 1985 he may be able to claim title to the shelter by adverse possession under s15(1) of the Limitation Act 1980 (which sets a 12-year period for the recovery of land). To establish a right by adverse possession George must bring proceedings under the 1980 Act and have had an intention to exclude the owner as well as other people (there is no conclusive evidence in the question that George had such an intention).

Finally, if George is able to establish an easement of way by prescription over the track it will rank as a legal one and would thus be binding on Paul, whereas if he is able to establish an estoppel easement in respect of the storage any such easement would be equitable and would require to be registered in order to bind Paul.

QUESTION FIVE

Liza owned a property (registered land) which consisted of a large house which had behind it a long garden, at the end of which there was a cottage. The house fronted on to the main highway and the cottage fronted on to a minor road. A drive ran along the side of the property joining the highway and the minor road. In 1991 Liza granted a five-year lease of the cottage to her friend, Jim. She allowed him to store things in her garage and she invited him to use the swimming pool in the garden whenever he wished. Jim often used the drive when he wanted a short-cut to the highway. In 1996 Liza sold the cottage to Jim and in 1997 she sold the rest of the property (comprising the house, garden and drive) to Ben. Ben has now written to Jim informing him that he has no right to use the garage or the pool or the drive.

Discuss.

University of London LLB Examination
(for External Students) Land Law June 1999 Q8

General Comment

A straightforward question on the nature and acquisition easements. The claim to use the swimming pool would fail as an easement, since the law does not recognise easements of recreation. Section 62 LPA 1925 must be applied as regards the garage and the drive. Ben will take subject to the easements created by s62 because of s70(1)(a) LRA 1925.

Skeleton Solution

Licences to use the garage and swimming pool – acquisition of easements under s62 LPA 1925 – rights claimed under s62 must be capable of being easements – right of storage – right to use the swimming pool: a recreational facility – conditions for the application of s62: conveyance; diversity of ownership or occupation – right of storage converted into an easement under s62 – binding on Ben under s70(1)(a) LRA 1925 – the drive: an implied licence – converted into an easement under s62 – binding on Ben under s70(1)(a) LRA 1925.

Suggested Solution

When Ben purchased Liza's property in 1997 did he take subject to, or free from, any rights in the property that Jim might have previously acquired? It is necessary to consider first what rights, if any, Jim acquired in Liza's land in respect of the garage, the pool and the drive.

When Jim was Liza's tenant between 1991 and 1996 she gave him permission to store things in her garage and to use her swimming pool. In doing this, she was conferring on Jim no more than bare licences to do specific things on her land, revocable whenever she wished. Such licences were purely personal to Jim and did not confer on him any interests in her land which would be binding on a purchaser in the event of her selling the land. However, in 1996 Liza sold the cottage to Jim and it is possible that the licences were then converted into easements by virtue of s62 LPA 1925.

Section 62, which is a word saving section, enacts that a conveyance of land is deemed to include all the advantages apertaining to the land at the time of the conveyance, unless a contrary intention is expressed in the conveyance. Its application in this case will be discussed later.

Before passing to the application of s62 it is necessary to discuss whether a right of storage, and the use of a swimming pool, can exist as easements. A right can only be successfully claimed as an easement if it enjoys the four characteristics as set out in *Re Ellenborough Park* [1956] Ch 131. Particularly relevant to this case are the second and fourth characteristics: the easement must accommodate the dominant tenement (Jim's cottage) and the right must be capable of forming the subject matter of a grant. In discussing the second characteristic, Evershed MR observed that it is not enough that the right increases the value of the property. It must also be shown that it is connected with the normal enjoyment of that property, which is a question of fact depending on the nature of the dominant tenement and the nature of the right itself. The fourth characteristic requires that the right being claimed as an easement must not be expressed in terms that are too wide or too vague.

To take the right of storage first, this could satisfy the second characteristic, and it is now well settled that a right of storage can exist as an easement (*Wright v Macadam* [1949] 2 KB 744) subject to the proviso that it must not be so wide as to amount to a claim to possession, or grant possession of the servient tenement: *Copeland v Greenhalf* [1952] Ch 488. It is a matter of degree and each case must be decided on its own facts: *Grigsby v Melville* [1974] 1 WLR 80; *London & Blenheim Estates Ltd v Ladbroke Retail Parks Ltd* [1993] 1 All ER 307. The amount of space that was claimed in *Wright v Macadam* to store coal in a garden shed is not disclosed in the report, but clearly it was within reason since the claim succeeded. We do not know in this case how much storage space is being claimed in the garage, but providing it does not amount to a claim to possession or joint possession of the garage then the right to store may be claimed as an easement.

The right to use the swimming pool would satisfy the fourth characteristic because it is sufficiently definite. However, the use of the pool is in the nature of a recreational facility and this may preclude a successful claim to its being an easement. In *Aldred's Case* (1610) 9 Co Rep 576, 586 Wray CJ laid down the proposition that the law would not protect 'things of delight', and in *Mounsey v Ismay* (1865) 3 H & L 486 it was said: 'to bring the right within the term "easement" … it must be a right of utility and benefit, and not one of mere recreation and amusement': per Martin B. In *Re Ellenborough Park* it was, however, successfully argued that a right to use the park could rank as an easement: this would appear to say that a recreational use can be an easement, but that would be to misunderstand the Court of Appeal's reasoning. The reason why the right to use the park was upheld in that case was because the right to use the park was an 'attribute to the ordinary enjoyment of the residence'. That cannot be said of the right to use a swimming pool, and this case may be distinguished from the facts of *Re Ellenborough Park*. The fact is that the use of a swimming pool is a purely recreational facility and therefore cannot be classified as an easement. It is not therefore eligible for conversion by s62 to the status of an easement.

By contrast, the right of storage is eligible, as has been seen, and we must now turn to the question of the application of s62 LPA 1925 when Liza sold the cottage to Jim in 1996. For s62 to be applicable, two conditions must be satisfied: there must be a 'conveyance' as defined by s205(1)(ii) LPA 1925. The constituents of a conveyance are that there must be an 'instrument', that is to say a document (*Rye v Rye* [1962] AC 496) and that document must effect 'an assurance of property or interest therein', ie it must create or convey a legal estate in the land granted. That condition was satisfied here when Liza sold the cottage to Jim in 1996.

The second condition is that there must be diversity of ownership or occupation at the time of the conveyance: *Long v Gowlett* [1923] 2 Ch 177 which was a decision on s62's predecessor, s6 of the Conveyancing Act 1881. This means that at the time of the conveyance, or immediately prior thereto, the dominant and servient tenements must have been owned or occupied by different persons. The decision received affirmation by the House of Lords in *Sovmots Investments Ltd* v *Secretary of State for the Environment* [1979] AC 144. That condition too is satisfied. In 1996 at the time of the conveyance, Liza owned and occupied the servient tenement, the site of the garage, and John occupied the dominant tenement under the lease granted to him by Liza in 1991. As a result the conveyance to John incorporated the licence to use the garage and converted it into a legal easement to endure in perpetuity.

It may well be that Liza did not appreciate that her generosity would have that unexpected result, but that is the effect of s62 and was the result under s6 of the Conveyancing Act 1881: *International Tea Stores* v *Hobbs* [1903] 2 Ch 165. Not only has Jim's cottage acquired the benefit of that easement, but the corresponding result is that its burden has been imposed on Liza's land. The next step is to consider whether Ben took subject to it when he purchased Liza's land in 1997, and the answer to that is in the affirmative. This being registered land Ben took subject to all overriding interests listed in s70(1) Land Registration Act 1925. The legal easement falls within s70(1)(a); Ben is therefore obliged to allow Jim to continue to use the garage for storage purposes, but he is entitled to forbid Jim the continued use of the swimming pool because it did not pass under s62.

The final point for consideration is Jim's use of the drive. We are not told if he had Liza's express permission to use the drive, but since there is no suggestion that she objected to his use we may conclude that he had an implied licence to do so. That right is certainly capable of being an easement, and it would be included in the conveyance to Jim under s62, the two conditions being satisfied, with the same result that Ben would take subject to it as a legal easement under s70(1)(a) LRA 1925.

QUESTION SIX

George and Fred were friends and neighbours. George owned Cedar Farm and Fred owned Windmill Farm. Both farms were registered land. For many years Fred used a path across Cedar Farm to walk to the village pub and George never objected. In 1995 George orally agreed to allow Fred to store his timber in an empty barn on Cedar Farm for an annual payment of £20 and in 1996 George executed a deed granting Fred the right to pasture his sheep on a field on Cedar Farm for 30 years. George has recently died and Cedar Farm has been sold to Stephen. Stephen has written to Fred informing him that Fred has no right to use the path or the barn or the field.

Advise Fred.

University of London LLB Examination
(for External Students) Land Law June 2000 Q4

General Comment

Candidates should notice that this question is set in the context of registered land and should bear in mind that s70(1)(a) Land Registration Act (LRA) 1925 is relevant. The issue of the path clearly necessitates discussion of a presumed grant, because of the phrase in the question, 'for many years Fred used a path across Cedar Farm'. This type of phraseology is always indicative that the examiner has prescription in mind. Candidates, when discussing the case of the barn, may be tempted to discuss easements of storage, but this must be revisited as there is no easement arising from the agreement between George and Fred. Because that agreement may give rise to a contractual licence candidates must point out that it will not bind Stephen unless there is a constructive trust, and that there is nothing on the facts to justify one. Candidates should not forget that the examiner may include profits à prendre in this type of question, as is the case here.

Skeleton Solution

The path: long user; presumed grant; presumed grants based on acquiescence; Prescription Act 1832; the 20-year period; user as of a right; acquiescence distinguished from precario (consent): easements acquired by prescription; legal; s70(1)(a) LRA 1925 – the barn: contractual licence; not binding on third parties; legal yearly lease; s70(1)(k) LRA 1925; termination of a yearly lease; six months' notice – pasture: profits à prendre; legal; s70(1)(a) LRA 1925; automatically binding on third parties.

Suggested Solution

Has Fred acquired any rights over Cedar Farm which will bind Stephen when he purchased it? Fred may have acquired three possible rights and each will be examined in turn.

Firstly, in using a path over Cedar Farm for many years, has Fred acquired an easement over the farm which accommodates Windmill Farm? It is unnecessary to discuss whether the user can constitute an easement, since a right of way is one of the most well known of easements. The question is whether Fred has acquired an easement from his long user, and the provisions of the Prescription Act 1832 must be considered. Two preliminary observations must be made. A claim to an easement by presumed grant, ie prescription, except in the case of easements of light claimed under the Prescription Act 1832, must be made on behalf of the fee simple estate in the dominant land against the fee simple estate in the servient land: *Bright* v *Walker* (1834) 1 Cr M & R 211.

The second observation is derived from *Dalton* v *Angus & Co* (1881) 6 App Cas 740 where Fry J explained that the law of prescription is based on the acquiescence of the servient owner to the user of his land. There will be acquiescence by the servient owner if he has: knowledge of the acts done on his land; powers to stop those acts; and abstinence on his part from the exercise of that power – knowledge of the acts done includes constructive knowledge: *Diment* v *NH Foot Ltd* [1974] 1 WLR 1427.

We may assume that if Fred makes a claim under the statute he is doing so on behalf of his fee simple estate and Windmill Farm and that he is asserting to claim against the fee simple in Cedar Farm. Whether George has acquiesced in Fred's activity will be discussed later when the requirement of 'user as of right' is examined.

Attention must now turn to the Prescription Act 1832, the main purpose of which was to shorten the period of legal memory, as Lord MacNaghten observed in *Gardner* v *Hodgson's Kingston Brewery Co Ltd* [1903] AC 229. The statute provides for two periods of user in respect of easements other than easements of light: 20 years and 40 years (s2). The provisions for the shorter period of 20 years may be stated as follows where:

1. there has been user for 20 years; and

2. that user has been enjoyed for the 20 years immediately preceding the action; and

3. that user has been enjoyed 'as of right'; and

4. there has been no 'interruption' as defined by s4.

Then the servient owner cannot defeat the claim by showing that the user commenced after 1189. The significance of (2) 'next before action' must be understood. For the section to apply, there must be a court action, the subject matter of which is the existence, or non-existence, of the easement. The 20-year period of user is the preceding 20 years before that action was commenced.

The user during that period must be enjoyed 'as of right'. This is a technical phrase and comprises three elements: the user must not be enjoyed as a result of force being used against the servient owner (nec vi); it must not be exercised in secret (nec claim); and it must not be enjoyed with the permission of the servient owner (nec precario). In other words it must have been enjoyed openly and in a manner that a person rightfully entitled would have used it: *Bright* v *Walker*.

Finally, the user must be exercised without interruption. An interruption is defined by the statute. There will only be an interruption if there has been some overt act on the part of the servient owner which hinders or obstructs the user: *Carr* v *Foster* (1842) 3 QB 581, and it must be a positive act of a hostile nature: *Davies* v *Williams* (1851) 16 QB 546. The act must be known to the dominant owner and he must acquiesce in it for one year. Only after one year's acquiescence on his part will there be an interruption recognised by the statute.

We are not informed how long Fred used the path, only that it was for many years. To claim the benefit of the statute Fred must show at least 20 years user and, in addition, to fix the period, he must bring a court action as described above. This element must not be overlooked, since without a court action the statute cannot be applied. He may seek a declaration from the court to the effect that he is entitled to the easement. Alternatively, the court action may arise by George bringing an action against him for trespass.

Attention must now be focused on George's failure to object. There is no suggestion that Fred has employed force against George in order to facilitate his user, nor is it suggested that the user was exercised secretly. It is highly likely that George knew of the user, and since he did not object we may deduce that he acquiesced in it. That being the case, the essential requirement of acquiescence by the servient owner as explained by Fry J in *Dalton v Angus & Co* is present. Can, however, the failure to object be construed as permission (precario)? If that is the case, then the user cannot be said to have been enjoyed as of right. A distinction must be drawn between acquiescence by the servient owner and passive consent on his part, and the application of that distinction is not always easy. Basically, it is an issue of fact. It would seem from *Mills v Silver* [1991] 2 WLR 324 that if it would appear to a reasonable person that a dominant owner is asserting a right over the servient owner's land and the latter does nothing to prevent it, then this would be more likely to be construed as acquiescence rather than permission.

On the facts the matter cannot be taken further, and we cannot come to a conclusion as to whether George was acquiescing in the user or permitting it. If the latter case applies then that would be fatal to Fred's claim. There is nothing in the facts to indicate an interruption as defined by the statute.

Providing Fred can establish the requirements of the 20-year period then he can successfully claim an easement over George's land (if we ignore the potential problem over the acquiescence/consent issue).

Assuming he has acquired an easement under the 20-year period, would that easement bind Stephen when he purchased Cedar Farm? Easements acquired under the Prescription Act 1832 fall within the definition of a legal easement contained in s1(2)(a) Law of Property Act (LPA) 1925. However, both farms were registered land and the provisions of the Land Registration Act (LRA) 1925 must be considered. A legal easement is an overriding interest under s70(1)(a) LRA 1925 and as such would automatically bind Stephen when he purchased Cedar Farm.

The next matter to be examined concerns the storage of timber in the barn at Cedar Farm at an annual payment of £20. What is the right that Fred has thereby acquired, and is it binding on Stephen? The agreement was an oral one. No question of a legal easement can arise, since the right conferred on Fred was not made by deed. Nor can the agreement made between George and Fred amount to an equitable easement. It was at one time possible to create an equitable easement orally, provided it was for value and supported by part performance, but the Law of Property (Miscellaneous Provisions) Act 1989 effectively abolished the doctrine of part performance concerning agreements which relate to land. It is necessary, therefore, to discuss easements of storage. The agreement made could either be a contractual licence or a yearly tenancy. The question does not require a discussion about how that issue is determined. Instead both alternatives will be examined. If the agreement constitutes a contractual licence, it is unlikely that Stephen will be bound by it because of the doctrine of privity of contract. It is true that contractual licences may in some circumstances bind third parties through the medium of a constructive trust: *Ashburn Anstalt v Arnold* [1989] Ch 1, but the facts do not justify a discussion of that possibility. A contractual licence of this nature does not confer upon the licensee an interest in land which will bind third parties: *King* v *David Allen & Sons Billposting Ltd* [1916] 2 AC 54. Nor does a contractual licence, for that reason, fall within the ambit of s70(1)(g) LRA 1925, since s70(1) provides that the rights within its ambit must subsist 'in reference to' the land.

If Fred has only a contractual licence to store timber in George's barn, it will not bind Stephen and Fred must relinquish his use of the barn when Stephen lawfully revokes the licence. Stephen's rights of revocation are governed by the terms of the contract, either express or implied.

The alternative is that George has granted a yearly tenancy to Fred. The barn was empty and so we may assume that Fred was given exclusive possession of it. Because the rent was expressed to be payable by reference to a year, a yearly tenancy may have been created instead of a licence. Will that tenancy bind Stephen? Normally, a legal tenancy must be created by deed: s52 LPA 1925. However, s54 provides a dispensation from this rule. A legal tenancy may be created without any formalities if, inter alia, it is not to exceed three years. A yearly tenancy falls within that provision and, providing the other requirements of the section are satisfied, then Fred will have a legal yearly tenancy. Such a tenancy constitutes an overriding interest under s70(1)(k) LRA 1925 and accordingly Stephen will be bound by it when he purchases Cedar Farm. He cannot simply tell Fred that he can no longer use the barn. A yearly tenancy is only terminable upon the giving of six months' notice, and that is what Stephen must do if he wishes to bring Fred's tenancy to an end.

In executing a deed conferring upon Fred the right to pasture his sheep on Cedar Farm for 30 years, George granted Fred a profit à prendre. Having been created by deed for a fixed period, it is a legal interest in land as it falls within s1(2)(a) LPA 1925. As such it is also an overriding interest under s70(1)(a) LRA 1925 and Stephen, as the purchaser of Cedar Farm, will be bound by it.

Chapter 9

Licences

9.1   **Introduction**

9.2   **Key points**

9.3   **Key cases and statutes**

9.4   **Questions and suggested solutions**

9.1 Introduction

This subject comprises the following two distinct areas of study.

a) The licence as a substitute for the lease. This has occupied the courts for some time with two important decisions of the House of Lords, in 1985 (*Street* v *Mountford* [1985] 2 WLR 877) and 1988 (*AG Securities* v *Vaughan; Antoniades* v *Villiers* [1988] 3 All ER 1058). The importance of this has diminished with the coming into force of the Housing Act 1988 which allowed landlords to create asssured tenancies at a full rent without the problem of security of tenure under the Rent Act 1977.

b) The licence also operates as a right on its own, a new right in alieno solo is the suggested description. This is the extreme effect but there are gradations of licence beneath that from the bare licence which, in its simplest form is a mere permission to enter the land' to the licence by estoppel which deserves the description of a 'new right in alieno solo'.

From an examination perspective the latter area is very topical because it seems that a new right in alieno solo is emerging with the expansion of the licence by estoppel. The decision in *Street* v *Mountford* is a landmark one (it is to licences what *Donoghue* v *Stevenson* [1932] AC 562 is to the tort of negligence) and merits particular attention.

9.2 Key points

Licences must be considered in two parts:

a) Lease substitute – often identified by questions incorporating a document headed: 'This licence'.

b) A permission to use the land of another – which emerges in some cases as an equitable right through the rules of proprietary estoppel.

Lease substitute

Residential occupation – begin with words of Lord Templeman in *Street* v *Mountford* '…
relevant … intention demonstrated by the agreement to grant exclusive possession for
a term at a rent'. The test is whether the residential occupier is a 'lodger or a tenant'
unless there are exceptional circumstances, as applied in *Royal Philanthropic Society* v
County (1985) 276 EG 1068 and *AG Securities* v *Vaughan* [1988] 3 WLR 1025 (see below).
Problems in application:

a) Does it apply to occupiers of commercial premises?

   Yes – *London & Associated Investment Trust plc* v *Calow* (1986) 280 EG 1252.

   No – *Dresden Estates Ltd* v *Collinson* (1987) 281 EG 1321.

   May become restricted to residential occupation.

b) Is rent necessary for a tenancy?

   Section 205(1)(xxvii) LPA 1925 defines 'term of years absolute' as '… a term of years
   (taking effect either in possession or in reversion *whether or not at a rent*)' and Fox
   LJ in *Ashburn Anstalt* v *Arnold* [1988] 2 All ER 147 made it clear that rent is not a
   pre-requisite for a lease.

c) What is exclusive possession? The non-exclusive agreement.

   If occupier is not a lodger (no attendance/services) it does not necessarily mean
   there is exclusive possession and a tenancy. Lodging is just one way of not granting
   exclusive possession but not the only way: *Hadjiloucas* v *Crean* [1987] 3 All ER 1008.
   The Court of Appeal gave several conclusions:

   i)   Lord Templeman may be too wide in non-exclusive licences;

   ii) may not be relevant to multiple occupations;

   iii) then consider any agreement against factual background (factual matrix):

   • each occupier is a licensee if he cannot exclude others; or

   • parallel leases – if right to exclude; but

   • a joint agreement will not produce a joint tenancy.

d) This joint tenancy approach had been accepted by the Court of Appeal but was
   rejected by the House of Lords in *AG Securities* v *Vaughan*; *Antoniades* v *Villiers*
   [1988] 3 WLR 1205. Lord Bridge: 'I do not understand by what legal alchemy they
   could ever become joint.'

e) Other continuing exceptions: no intention to create legal relations and statute itself:
   ss7–9 Rent Act 1977, s1 Housing Act 1988.

f) In addition to *Street* v *Mountford* [1985] 2 WLR 877, see *AG Securities* v *Vaughan*;

Antoniades v *Villiers*. See also *Mikeover Ltd* v *Brady* [1989] 3 All ER 618 in which *Antoniades* was distinguished.

AG Securities v *Vaughan*

Facts

The appellants owned a block of flats, one of which contained six living rooms in addition to a kitchen and bathroom. They furnished four living rooms as bedrooms, a fifth as a lounge and the sixth as a sitting room and entered into short-term agreements with four individuals referred to in the relevant agreement as 'licensee'.

The agreements were made at different times and on different terms and were normally for six months' duration. Each agreement provided that the licensee had 'the right to use [the flat] in common with others who have or may from time to time be granted the like right ... but without the right to exclusive possession of any part of the ... flat'. When a licensee left, a new occupant was mutually agreed by the appellants and the remaining licensees.

Held

The occupants were licensees.

Antoniades v *Villiers*

Facts

The attic of the respondent's house was converted into furnished residential accommodation. Wishing to live together there, the appellants signed identical agreements called 'licences' which were executed at the same time and stressed that they were not to have exclusive possession. In particular, the agreements provided that 'the licensor shall be entitled at any time to use the rooms together with the licensee and permit other persons to use all of the rooms together with the licensee.' No attempt was made by the respondent to use the rooms or to have them used by others. Stressing, too, that the real intention of the parties was to create a licence not coming under the Rent Acts, the agreements provided for a monthly payment of £87 and that they were determinable by one month's notice by either party.

Held

The agreements created a joint tenancy.

Lord Templeman:

'My Lords, in *Street* v *Mountford* this House stipulated with reiterated emphasis that an express statement of intention is not decisive and that the court must pay attention to the facts and surrounding circumstances and to what people do as well as to what people say...

... My Lords, in the second appeal now under consideration, there was, in my opinion, the grant of a joint tenancy for the following reasons. (1) The applicants for the flat applied to rent the flat jointly and to enjoy exclusive occupation. (2) The landlord allowed the applicants jointly to enjoy exclusive occupation and accepted rent. A tenancy was created. (3) The power reserved to the landlord to deprive the applicants of exclusive occupation was inconsistent with the provisions of the Rent Acts. (4) Moreover, in all the circumstances the power which the landlord insisted on to deprive the applicants of exclusive occupation was a pretence only intended to deprive the applicants of the protection of the Rent Acts.'

Licence as a right in alieno solo

Definition: a permission given by the occupier of land which allows the licensee to do some act thereon which otherwise would be a trespass.

Types of licence

a) Bare licence

   A gratuitous permission which saves the action of the licensee from being a trespass. Revocable at will.

b) Licence coupled with an interest or grant

   Licensee given some interest in the land or in something on the land and licence necessary to exploit that interest, eg a right to enter another man's land to hunt and take away the deer killed.

c) Contractual licence

   An ordinary contract subject to the usual rules of contract.

d) Licence by estoppel

   If an owner permits another person to spend money or alter his position to his detriment in the expectation that he will enjoy some privilege or interest in the land, the owner will be prevented from acting inconsistently with that expectation.

Enforceability of licence between licensor and licensee

a) Bare licence – revoke at any time.

b) Licence coupled with an interst or grant – not revocable.

c) Contractual licence: *Hounslow London Borough Council v Twickenham Garden Developments Ltd* [1970] 3 All ER 326 – depends on the terms of the contract.

d) Licence by estoppel – not revocable during period for which created – but depends on facts – *Dillwyn v Llewellyn* (1862) 4 De GF & J 517 (fee simple): *Pascoe v Turner* [1979] 2 All ER 945 (fee simple): *Inwards v Baker* [1965] 2 QB 29 (life interest).

Enforceability of licence against third parties – does the burden run?

a) Bare licence – not binding on third parties.

b) Licence coupled with an interest or grant – probably is binding on third parties.

c) Contractual licence – *Clore* v *Theatrical Properties Ltd* [1936] 3 All ER 483 not binding on third parties – *Ashburn Anstalt* v *Arnold* [1988] 2 All ER 147 – Court of Appeal stated obiter that a contractual licence did not create an interest in land capable of binding third parties.

d) Licence by estoppel – the law on this point is still in the process of development, but it seems that a new right in alieno solo is emerging (Cheshire). This is increasingly binding on third parties. Rules of notice apply. *Ives (E R) Investments Ltd* v *High* [1967] 2 QB 379.

Assignability of benefit of licence by licensee – does the benefit run?

a) Bare licence – no, personal to licensee.

b) Licence coupled with interest or grant – yes, with the grant.

c) Contractual licence – yes, unless excluded by contract.

d) Licence by estoppel – undecided – *Inwards* v *Baker* [1965] 2 QB 29. But see Cumming-Bruce LJ in *Pascoe* v *Turner* [1979] 2 All ER 945 – can be relied upon as a sword not merely as a shield.

These answers to the above paragraphs may be illustrated in diagrammatic form (see following page).

Deserted spouse's rights to the matrimonial home:

Matrimonial Homes Act 1983 s2(8), now Family Law Act 1996 s31(10)(b) which reproduces s2(8) – not an overriding interest for the purposes of s70(1)(g) LRA because the provision says so and requires a notice to be entered on the register instead.

PARAGRAPH	BARE LICENCE	LICENCE COUPLED WITH AN INTEREST	CONTRACTUAL LICENCE	LICENCE BY ESTOPPEL
REVOCABLE	YES Any time. Reasonable notice	NO Must not derogate from grant	DEPENDS ON TERMS May be express/ implied term against revocation. Injunction *Hounslow LBC v Twickenham Garden Developments* [1970] 3 All ER 326	HOW TO SATISFY The conveyance of legal estate *Pascoe v Turner* [1979] 2 All ER 945 As long as licensee wishes/life interest *Inwards v Baker* [1965] 2 QB 29
BURDEN RUNS?	NO	YES If the interest/ grant is an interest in land	NO Not binding on third parties. *King v David Allen* [1916] 2 AC 54 *Ashburn Anstalt v Arnold* [1988] 2 All ER 147 Problem case *Binions v Evans* [1972] Ch 359	YES Will depend on the rules of notice *Ives (ER) Investments v High* [1967] 2 QB 379 'A new right in alieno solo is emerging' Cheshire
BENEFIT RUNS?	NO Personal to licensee	YES May pass with sale of the interest	YES As with benefit of any other contract	DOUBTS - DEPENDS ON THE FACTS NO - *Inwards v Baker* [1965] 2 QB 29 YES - *Ives v High* [1967] 2 QB 379 Both a sword and a shield *Pascoe v Turner* [1979] 2 All ER 945 Cumming-Bruce LJ

9.3 Key cases and statutes

- *AG Securities v Vaughan* [1988] 3 WLR 1205
  Lease/licence distinction – multiple occupancy of flat – each occupant had exclusive possession of only *one* room, rest of accommodation shared

- *Antoniades v Villiers* [1988] 3 WLR 1205
  Lease/licence distinction – occupancy of one bedroom flat granted to co-habiting

couple under separate agreements called 'licences' – agreements a sham to avoid the Rent Acts – joint tenancy created

- *Ashburn Anstalt* v *Arnold* [1988] 2 All ER 147
  Contractual licence did not create an interest in land capable of binding third parties

- *Clore* v *Theatrical Properties Ltd* [1936] 3 All ER 483
  Contractual licence could not bind a successor in title of licensor even if that successor had notice of the licence

- *Dillwyn* v *Llewellyn* (1862) 4 De GF & J 517
  Proprietary estoppel – licensee given possession of land with consent of licensor spent money building a house thereon – licensor left licensee life interest by will – licensee successfully claimed full fee simple

- *Errington* v *Errington & Woods* [1952] 1 KB 290
  Contractual licence for the occupancy of a house – such a licence gave rise to an equitable interest binding on allcomers except a purchaser of the legal estate without notice of the interest – but see *Ashburn Anstalt* v *Arnold*

- *Inwards* v *Baker* [1965] 2 QB 29
  Proprietary estoppel – an estoppel licence bound a third party whether he was a volunteer or a purchaser

- *Ives (ER) Investments Ltd* v *High* [1967] 2 QB 379
  Proprietary estoppel – an equitable right based on estoppel not registerable under the Land Charges Act but was protected by the doctrine of notice

- *Pascoe* v *Turner* [1979] 2 All ER 945
  Proprietary estoppel acted as both a sword and a shield – transfer of fee simple ordered to give effect to the equity becaues of the nature of the assurances given

- *Street* v *Mountford* [1985] 2 WLR 877
  Lease/licence distinction – exclusive possession led to presumption of a licence which had to be rebutted by the landlord – situations where exclusive possession would not give rise to a lease – label parties attached to an occupancy agreement not conclusive of the matter

- *Wood* v *Leadbitter* (1845) 13 M & W 838
  Contractual licence revocable at common law even when granted for consideration because it did not confer any interest in the land

- *Yaxley* v *Gotts & Gotts* [1999] 3 WLR 1217
  Proprietary estoppel could operate to give effect to an agreement rendered void by s2 Law of Property (Miscellaneous Provisions) Act 1989

- Housing Act 1988

- Housing Act 1996

- Rent Act 1977

9.4 Questions and suggested solutions

Analysis of questions

There are a number of possibilities in this regard. Five in particular are worth noting. First, an essay question on the extent to which a licence may now be recognised as a right in alieno solo is not uncommon. Secondly, there is the possibility of an essay question on the lease/licence distinction and the contemporary importance of that distinction. Thirdly, there is the 'pure' licences problem. This usually involves one or more informal occupational arrangements inviting candidates to discuss, inter alia, the requirements of contractual and estoppel licences, whether such licences can be enforced against third parties and the remedy the court may grant if an estoppel licence is established. Fourthly, licences can arise in a 'mixed' question touching on several other areas of land law eg matrimonial property, leases and aspects of registration. Finally, questions concerning a licence being used as a substitute for a lease used to be common. However, the popularity of such questions with examiners has probably diminished since the coming into force of the Housing Act 1988.

QUESTION ONE

'A disposition or licence properly passeth no interest nor alters or transfers property in anything ...'

(Vaughan CJ)

'The doctrine of the licence ... is no more than a mechanism by which the law sanctions the informal creation of proprietary rights in land.' (Moriarty)

Does either of these statements accurately reflect the current status of licences in property law?

University of London LLB Examination
(for External Students) Land Law June 1987 Q6

General Comment

A question to be welcomed in an area which any land law student should be able to consider at length. The form of the question may well give the examiner the opportunity to study the examination techniques of the candidates. There are many ways of attempting such an answer and it could well be that technique alone will raise the marks awarded to those candidates who are able to assemble their answers in a logical and progressive form outside the stricter discipline of a problem-style question.

Skeleton Solution

Briefly outline the four types of licence.

a) Bare licence;

b) Licence coupled with an interest;

c) Contractual licence – *Hounslow LBC* v *Twickenham Garden Developments Ltd*;

d) Licence by estoppel – Lord Kingsdown – *Ramsden* v *Dyson*; *Inwards* v *Baker*.

Quote 1: 'A disposition or licence properly passeth no interest nor alters or transfers property in anything.'

a) True;

b) Not true;

c) True – *Clore* v *Theatrical Properties Ltd* – confirmed by *Ashburn Anstalt* v *Arnold*, but note exception: *Binions* v *Evans*;

d) A state of change from true to not true: *Ives (E R) Investments Ltd* v *High*.

Quote 2: 'The doctrine of the licence... is no more than a mechanism by which the law sanctions the informal creation of proprietary rights in land.'

a) Mainly true;

b) Mainly true;

c) True – *but* see the exceptions above;

d) More to the licence by estoppel than this: *Pascoe* v *Turner*.

Cheshire: 'it seems that a new right in alieno solo has emerged ...'.

Conclusion: Can the word 'licence' continue to describe such diverse interests?

Suggested Solution

There are four main types of licence:

a) bare licence;

b) licence coupled with an interest;

c) contractual licence;

d) licence by estoppel or proprietary estoppel.

In relating the current status of licences in property law to the given statements of Vaughan CJ and Moriarty it is necessary to briefly analyse each of these four types of licence and then to apply the respective quotations to each in turn. In this way we should establish whether either statement does accurately reflect the current status of the various forms of licence in property law.

a) Bare licence. This is a gratuitous permission which protects the licensed activity from becoming a trespass. The licence is revocable at any time and is not enforceable against subsequent holders of the land.

b) Licence coupled with an interest. The licensee receives some proprietary interest in the land and the licence is necessary to enter in order to exploit that interest. The licence and the interest tend to become inter-connected and each survives with the other.

c) Contractual licence. This is basically an ordinary contract which creates a licence supported by consideration. It creates a contractual right to do things on land which would otherwise be a trespass. The contract itself, however, is construed as any ordinary contract: *Winter Garden Theatre (London) Ltd* v *Millennium Productions Ltd* [1948] AC 173.

The courts will not recognise any wrongful repudiation of the contract: *Hurst* v *Picture Theatres Ltd* [1915] 1 KB 1. The law relating to contractual licences is summarised by Megarry J in *Hounslow London Borough Council* v *Twickenham Garden Developments Ltd* [1971] Ch 233:

'I find it difficult to see how a contractual licensee can be treated as a trespasser so long as his contract entitled him to be on the land... I do not think that the licence can be detached from the contract and separately revoked.'

This is emphasised by Megarry and Wade:

'The judicial consensus is now to the effect that a licensor has no right to eject a licensee in breach of contract, even where equity will not assist the licensee, and that if he does so forcibly the licensee can sue for assault.'

d) Licence by estoppel. Now recognised as a separate form of licence following earlier links with both contractual licences and the constructive trust. If an owner permits another person to spend money or alter his position in any way to his detriment in the expectation that he will enjoy some interest in the land that owner will be prevented from acting inconsistently with the expectations raised. The licence emerges from the words of Lord Kingsdown in a dissenting speech in *Ramsden* v *Dyson* (1866) LR 1 HL 129:

'If a man, under a verbal agreement, with a landlord for a certain interest in land, or, what amounts to the same thing under an expectation, created or encouraged by the landlord, that he shall have a certain interest, takes possession of such land with the consent of the landlord and upon the faith of such promise or expectation, with the knowledge of the landlord, and without objection by him, lays out money upon the land, a Court of Equity will compel the landlord to give effect to such promise or expectation.'

The proprietary estoppel will be enforced as an equitable proprietary interest. It is this area of licences which has seen most expansion over recent years. The estoppel is created by either expenditure on the land or encouragement or acquiescence by the land owner. The essence of the licence was described by Lord Denning MR in *Inwards* v *Baker* [1965] 2 QB 29:

'If the owner of land requests another, or indeed allows another, to expend money on the land under an expectation created or encouraged by the owner of the land that he will be able to remain there, that raises an equity in the licensee such as to entitle him to stay.'

The Master of the Rolls went on to say:

'All that is necessary is that the licensee should, at the request or with the encouragement of the owner of the land, have spent money in the expectation of being allowed to stay there. If so, the court will not allow that expectation to be defeated where it would be inequitable so to do.'

The licence by estoppel is protected in equity but in the case of unregistered land it is not capable of being registered as a land charge for the purposes of the Land Charges Act 1972. As a consequence it relies for protection against third parties on the equitable doctrine of notice: *Ives (E R) Investments Ltd* v *High* [1967] 2 QB 379.

Most of the discussion today on the exact nature of the licence is related to this expansion in the licence by estoppel.

Each quotation will now be considered in relation to these four forms of licence.

'A disposition or licence properly passeth no interest nor alters or transfers property in anything': Vaughan CJ.

a) Bare licence. True, it creates no interest in the land and is not enforceable against subsequent holders of the land.

b) Licence coupled with an interest. If the subject matter of the grant is an interest in land and the legal interest has passed the licence does become a 'property' which will be binding on third parties.

c) Contractual licence. Generally does not create any interest which would be enforceable against third parties: *Clore* v *Theatrical Properties Ltd* [1936] 3 All ER 483. This view was confirmed by the Court of Appeal in *Ashburn Anstalt* v *Arnold* [1988] 2 All ER 147 where Fox LJ confirmed that *Errington* v *Errington* [1952] 1 KB 290 was wrongly decided.

However there is one case which goes against this statement and which prevents a clear cut answer on this point.

In *Binions* v *Evans* [1972] Ch 359 the widow who occupied a cottage after the death of her husband was held to be protected against purchasers of the cottage who knew of her occupation and even paid a reduced price because of it. The problem with this decision is that, although the Court of Appeal were unanimous in protecting the widow, their unanimity did not extend to the reasons. The majority decided that Mrs Evans was a tenant for life under the SLA 1925, whereas Lord Denning held that she was a contractual licensee and that the licence created a constructive trust which bound the plaintiffs to permit Mrs Evans to live in the cottage during her life or for as long as she wished. Whatever the reason Mrs Evans could remain, the problems created by these conflicting views are still with us.

d) Licence by estoppel. There is an increasing willingness to recognise an interest which is enforceable against third parties. This is seen in *Ives (E R) Investments Ltd v High* (above), where the Court of Appeal held that High had a right of estoppel which was not capable of registration as a land charge, but it was binding on the plaintiffs who had purchased the legal estate with actual notice.

'The doctrine of the licence ... is no more than a mechanism by which the law sanctions the informal creation of proprietary rights in land': Moriarty.

a) Bare licence. Mainly true, it is worthy of an over-statement where the bare licence is concerned because there is no attempt to create any proprietary right in the land, merely a provision to use the land for a limited time.

b) Licence coupled with an interest. Again there is more to this licence and a formal right may exist to which the licence is ancillary.

c) Contractual licence. The exceptional case of *Binions v Evans* mentioned above does create problems in relation to this statement. The statement is probably true in certain very exceptional circumstances as indicated by Megarry and Wade:

> 'The law for so long set its face firmly against the notion that a contractual licence could be binding on the licensor's successor in title, on the principle that licences were personal transactions which created no proprietary interests in land. A purchaser of the licensor's land therefore had no concern with any mere licence, even when he bought with express notice of it.'

Megarry and Wade conclude:

> 'All the indications now are that contractual licences are capable of binding successors in title as equitable interests ... In this development the useful mechanism of the constructive trust is clearly destined to play a part ... The courts appear to be well on their way to creating a new and highly versatile interest in land which will rescue many informal and unbusinesslike transactions, particularly within families, from the penalties of disregarding legal forms. Old restraints are giving way to the demands of justice.'

But this must now be read in the light of the words of Fox LJ in *Ashburn Anstalt v Arnold* where the two exceptional cases were reduced to only *Binions v Evans*. The future may well be with the constructive trust: *Grant v Edwards* [1986] Ch 638.

d) Licence by estoppel. It is here where the development of new interests is most clear. The estoppel interests do bind third parties and the debate is now as to the extent, if any, of this as a proprietary right in land. The general view is that it is an interest in land. Gray and Symes in *Real Property and Real People* said:

> 'This result adds to the category of unregisterable, non-overreachable equitable interests in land, with consequent insecurity and uncertainty for both the licensee and the purchaser.'

The extent of this licence by estoppel is best seen in *Pascoe v Turner* [1979] 1 WLR 431 where the right enabled a successful claim for the conveyance of the fee simple to be made. The second quotation is, therefore, probably most apt in describing the licence by estoppel. The licence has, however, gone further by the recognition which has been given to those 'proprietary rights in land'. Cheshire probably provides the most apposite conclusion:

> 'The law on this point is still in the process of development but it seems that a new right *in alieno solo* has emerged in this century as did one in the previous century under the doctrine of *Tulk* v *Moxhay*.'

The time is now here when the word 'licence' is too broad to cover the various rights which now shelter beneath its umbrella. The above analysis shows that generalised phrases which may refer to the bare licence are quite inappropriate when the more sophisticated relationships arising out of the licence by estoppel have to be considered and construed.

QUESTION TWO

'Since *Street* v *Mountford* the lease/licence distinction has ceased to cause problems for the courts.'

Discuss.

University of London LLB Examination
(for External Students) Land Law June 1998 Q8

General Comment

This question concerns the developments after *Street* v *Mountford* but it does require some knowledge of the previous law in order to explain its significance. Candidates need to be familiar with Lord Templeman's judgment, but the emphasis of the answer must be on subsequent cases as these reveal the limits of the decision and the problems it left unresolved.

Skeleton Solution

Reasons for the importance of the distinction between leases and licences; statutory provisions and third parties – the development of the law regarding the distinction – *Lynes* v *Snaith* – *Errington* v *Errington* – *Street* v *Mountford* – although *Street* v *Mountford* clarified the law, it left unanswered questions; it did not deal with shared occupancies (*Hadjiloucas* v *Crean*) – *AG Securities* v *Vaughan* showed Lord Templeman's test (a tenant or a lodger?) to be inadequate – *Antoniades* v *Villiers* – conclusion: the statement in the question is not accurate.

Suggested Solution

The distinction between a lease and a licence has been of fundamental importance for a number of years principally for two reasons:

a) legislative provisions confer on tenants various important rights not enjoyed by licensees; and

b) the different effects of leases and licences on third parties.

Taking the legislative provisions first, the Rent Acts conferred on domestic tenants considerable security of tenure and the benefits of controlled rents: see the Rent Act 1977. These measures were, of course, unpopular with landlords, who sought to evade them by granting licences to occupants instead, which did not come within the ambit of the Acts. The Housing Acts of 1988 and 1996 went a long way to alleviating landlords' problems in this respect by allowing them to grant assured tenancies, which did not give the tenants anywhere near the same degree of security of tenure. Moreover, the control of rents was considerably reduced. Under these statutes, therefore, landlords were able to grant tenancies (as opposed to licences) without the considerable disadvantages which attached to tenancies created under the earlier Rent Acts.

As far as domestic tenancies are concerned, then, the importance of the distinction between leases and licences has considerably diminished and landlords need no longer fear the consequences of granting tenancies under the Housing Acts referred to.

Legislation also conferred rights on business and agricultural tenants, which landlords considered detrimental to their interests (see the Landlord and Tenant Act 1954 and the Agricultural Holdings Act 1986), although the Agricultural Tenancies Act of 1995 has reduced the degree of security of tenure conferred upon business tenancies.

In 1967 the Leasehold Reform Act gave tenants holding a long lease of a house the right to purchase the freehold. The Leasehold Reform, Housing and Urban Development Act 1993 extended this right to tenants of flats.

The efforts of landlords to create licences, instead of tenancies, so as to avoid the effects of the legislative provisions embracing the latter has led to much litigation between landlords and occupants, in which the landlords have sought to argue that the occupant was a contractual licensee while the occupant has argued that he was a tenant. This litigation will be examined later.

The distinction between a lease and a licence is also important as regards third parties. If a lease is legal, it will automatically bind a third party (a purchaser of the reversion). In the case of registered land, it will either be an overriding interest under s70(1)(k) LRA 1925 or registered with its own substantive title. If equitable, in the case of unregistered land, it will bind a purchaser if registered under the LCA 1972 as a land charge, class C(iv). In the case of registered land, it should be protected as a minor interest by entry of a notice on the landlord's register of title. Failing that protection it may bind a purchaser if it falls within s70(1)(g) LRA 1925.

If, on the other hand, the occupant only enjoys a contractual licence, none of the foregoing applies. The traditional view is that licences, being personal, do not bind purchasers: *King v David Allen & Sons Billposting Ltd* [1916] 2 AC 54. In rare instances, contractual licences have been held to bind third parties through the medium of a constructive trust (see *Binions* v *Evans* [1972] Ch 359), although there are limits to this as pointed out in *Ashburn Anstalt* v *Arnold* [1989] Ch 1.

The evolution of the law dealing with the distinction between leases and licenses will now be examined in stages.

In 1899 the distinction was clear: if the occupant enjoyed exclusive possession he was a tenant; if not, he was a licensee: *Lynes* v *Snaith* [1899] 1 QB 486. However, the straightforward distinction became blurred in *Errington* v *Errington and Woods* [1952] 1 KB 290 when Denning LJ held that a licensee could also enjoy exclusive possession and as a result the volume of litigation on the issue increased. Attention then focused on the question: What did the parties intend: a lease or a licence? If the intention was not clear, it had to be deduced from the surrounding circumstances of the case. The description applied to the arrangement was a factor to be taken into account but it was not conclusive.

In the 1970s life became more difficult for landlords, with the further extension of protection to tenants. Furnished tenancies came within the ambit of protection along with occupants enjoying exclusive occupation under a contractual licence. Lawyers advising landlords began to develop agreements which did not confer exclusive possession on occupants. It will be appreciated than an essential characteristic of a lease is exclusive possession. Without it there can be no lease.

If an arrangement could be established where there were two occupants, neither of whom had exclusive possession, then such an arrangement could not be a lease and this idea was ingeniously developed in *Somma* v *Hazelhurst* [1978] 1 WLR 1014, which was upheld by the Court of Appeal, despite the artificiality of the arrangement.

The next stage was reached by the House of Lords in *Street* v *Mountford* [1985] 2 WLR 877 which was a case of a domestic tenancy. This case clarified the law considerably and went a long way to clear up the confusion which had developed since *Errington* v *Errington and Woods*.

It is clear that the parties in *Street* v *Mountford* intended to create a licence. The document they signed leaves no doubt about it, but Lord Templeman was not impressed. Acknowledging the parties' freedom to contract, he went on to point out that:

> '... the consequences in law of the agreement ... can only be determined by consideration of the effect of the agreement. If the agreement satisfied all the requirements of a tenancy, then the agreement produced a tenancy and the parties cannot alter the effect of the agreement by insisting that they only created a licence.'

He summarised the position in these words: 'the only intention which is relevant is the intention demonstrated by the agreement to grant exclusive possession for a term at a rent.' That intention was obviously present and accordingly there was a lease, not a licence.

He agreed that it is not always easy to find whether exclusive possession had been conferred or not, and that if it had been it was possible that it might be that the right to exclusive possession was referable to a legal relationship other than a tenancy, eg where exclusive possession was given to a purchaser under a contract of sale of land, or where it was enjoyed pursuant to a contract of employment. It may be, he noted, that the parties did not intend to enter into a legal relationship. In that case there would be no lease.

Thus, exclusive possession, although necessary for the existence of a tenancy, does not inevitably result in one. He refers to rent, but strictly speaking this is not a necessary ingredient for a tenancy because of the wording of the definition of a term of years absolute in s205(1)(xxvii) LPA 1925, ie 'a term of years (taking effect either in possession or in reversion whether or not at a rent)'. As Fox LJ pointed out in *Ashburn Anstalt v Arnold* Lord Templeman was not saying you cannot have a tenancy without rent. What he was saying was that where you had exclusive possession for a term at a rent, this was a tenancy unless there was no intention to create legal relations or the exclusive possession was referable to some other relationship between the parties.

The decision in *Street v Mountford* unquestionably meant that thereafter it would be much more difficult for landlords to assert that they had only conferred upon their occupants a licence. Of the three ingredients listed by Lord Templeman, two are inevitably present: a term and rent. If exclusive possession is also present then, in the absence of a legal relationship other than landlord and tenant, there will be a tenancy assuming there is an intention to create a legal relationship.

However, although *Street and Mountford* provided much needed clarification on this area of law, it did not provide for every situation. Three points should be noted:

a) exclusive occupation was not disputed in that case;

b) there was only one occupant (Mrs Mountford); and

c) it did not deal with commercial occupancies. It was a case concerned with a residential occupancy.

Also, it did not deal with cases of shared occupancy. Those cases are much more complex than cases of sole occupation as Mustill LJ pointed out in the later case of *Hadjiloucas v Crean* [1987] 3 All ER 1008. In such cases:

> 'The choice is not simply between licence and tenancy, but rather a three-fold choice between a licence and two different kinds of tenancy. One kind will involve a pair of parallel tenancies, each between the landlord and one tenant, in relation to an identifiable separate portion of the premises; the other will consist of a single tenancy for the whole of the premises with the two occupiers as joint tenants of the whole.'

Moreover, he noted, *Street v Mountford* gave no indication as to the manner in which the intention to create exclusive possession should be ascertained, since the landlord in that case conceded that Mrs Mountford, the occupant, enjoyed exclusive possession. He observed that:

'Sometimes the task is straightforward and sometimes it will be difficult … sometimes a meticulous perusal of the document will be required … on other occasions it will not. The surrounding circumstances will always be material on this point as well as on the questions of sham and the intention to create legal relations. *Street* v *Mountford* does not itself explain how the exercise is to be performed.'

Two important cases of 1988, both concerned with shared occupation, must now be examined: *AG Securities* v *Vaughan* [1988] 3 WLR 1205 and *Antoniades* v *Villiers* [1988] 3 WLR 1205. Both were decided by the House of Lords.

In *AG Securities* v *Vaughan* the appellants owned a block of flats, one of which contained six rooms in addition to a kitchen and bathroom. They furnished four rooms as bedrooms, a fifth as a lounge and the sixth as a sitting-room, and entered into short-term agreements with four individuals, each referred to in the relevant agreement as a 'licensee'.

The agreements were made at different times and on different terms and were normally for six months' duration. Each agreement provided that the licensee had 'the right to use [the flat] in common with others who have or may from time to time be granted the like right … but without the right to exclusive possession of any part of the … flat.' When a licensee left, a new occupant was mutually agreed by the appellants and the remaining licensees.

In *Vaughan* there was no question that the agreements were in any way sham agreements. They reflected the true bargains between the parties. The question was: were the occupants licensees or did the agreements collectively create a joint tenancy between the occupants with joint exclusive possession? Lord Templeman had said in *Street* v *Mountford* that 'An occupier of residential accommodation for rent is either a lodger or a tenant.' He went on to say that 'the courts which deal with these problems will, save in exceptional circumstances, only be concerned to enquire whether as a result of the agreement relating to residential accommodation, the occupier is a lodger or a tenant.'

AG Securities v *Vaughan* shows that this is not an exhaustive test. The occupants were not lodgers and if Lord Templeman's test was to be applied they were, therefore, joint tenants with exclusive possession. That could not be the case here. A joint tenancy requires the four unities of time, title, interest and possession. The agreements were made at different times and on different terms. Lord Oliver found that none of these factors were present and it was 'impossible to say that the argreements entered into … created either individually or collectively, a single tenancy either of the entire flat or of any part of it.' In the result, despite Lord Templeman's dicta, the occupants were held to be licensees.

In *Antoniades* v *Villiers* the attic of the respondent's house was converted into furnished residential accommodation. Wishing to live together there, the applicants signed identical agreements called 'licences' which were executed at the same time and each stressed that they were not to have exclusive possession. In particular, the agreements provided that 'the licensor shall be entitled at any time to use the rooms together with the licensee and permit other persons to use all of the rooms together with the licensee.' No attempt was made by the respondent to use the rooms or to have them used by others. Stressing, too, that the real intention of the parties was to create a licence not coming under the Rent Acts, the agreements provided for a monthly payment of £87 and that they were determinable by one month's notice by either party.

The landlords argued that the occupants were licensees while the occupants maintained they were joint tenants with joint exclusive possession.

The premises were clearly not suitable for occupation by more than one couple. Lord Oliver said that there was an air of total unreality about the two licence documents signed by the occupants because the occupants were seeking a flat as a quasi matrimonial home. Nor, he opined, could the clauses entitling the landlord to occupy the premises personally, or introduce a third party into them, have been seriously intended to have any practical operation.

Looking at the substance of the transaction, rather than its face value, the occupants were joint tenants of the premises with joint exclusive possession and not licensees.

It is clear that although *Street* v *Mountford* brought the law into sharper focus, making it much more difficult for landlords to create licences as opposed to tenancies, the decision was limited by the facts of the case. It did not deal with shared occupancies, although Lord Templeman did say that the shared occupancy case of *Somma* v *Hazelhurst* was wrongly decided because the agreement was a sham, and warned courts in the future to be aware of sham devices. Nor did it offer guidance as to how exclusive possession was to be ascertained. Serious problems remain in cases of shared occupancies which did not arise in *Street* v *Mountford*.

The simple test of whether the occupant is a lodger or a tenant is not sufficient for all cases, as *AG Securities* v *Vaughan* demonstrated. And this test is clearly inapplicable to commercial occupancies. The extent to which *Street* v *Mountford* will apply to them needs further clarification.

Thus, the statement that since *Street* v *Mountford* the lease/licence distinction has ceased to cause problems for the courts cannot be considered to be accurate.

QUESTION THREE

Jack Bird had one son, Paul, who had emigrated to Australia, and two nieces, Frances and Grace. When, in 1988, Frances told him about her plans to raise poultry, Jack offered her the use of an unoccupied cottage he owned in the country. 'You are welcome to use it,' he said, 'it needs quite a lot doing to it to make it habitable, but you don't need to pay me any rent.' Frances and her boyfriend moved into the cottage, made it habitable and embarked on their poultry business. In 1989 Grace lost her job and Jack suggested that she should go and live with him in his London house and assist him as unpaid housekeeper and secretary. In 1992, at a time when Jack was ill, he told Grace not to worry about the future as he was leaving her the London house in his will. In 1994 Jack retired, sold the house and bought a bungalow by the sea. Jack and Grace lived in the bungalow for two months until his death later the same year. In his will Jack left his whole estate to his son, Paul, who now seeks possession of both the cottage and the bungalow.

Advise Frances and Grace.

University of London LLB Examination
(for External Students) Land Law June 1995 Q2

General Comment

An interesting question on licences which gives students a good opportunity to display their knowledge of this area of law. However, the facts of the question are such that the possibility of there being a constructive trust in respect of the bungalow ought to be considered.

Skeleton Solution

Definition of a licence – types of licences – contractual licence – estoppel licence – *Greasley* v *Cooke* – enforcement of contractual and estoppel licences against third parties – *Ashburn Anstalt* v *Arnold* – constructive trusts: no formalities for creation required: *Binions* v *Evans*.

Suggested Solution

This question is primarily concerned with licences. A licence is a permission given by the occupier of land which allows the licensee to do some act which would otherwise be a trespass. There are four main types of licence. First, there is the bare licence (mere personal permission to be on the licensor's land). Second, a licence may be coupled with the grant of an interest in land, for example a right to enter another man's land to hunt and take away the deer killed. Third, there is the contractual licence (a licence supported by consideration). Finally, there is the estoppel licence. In the context of this question, contractual and estoppel licences are particularly relevant.

In 1988, Jack allows his niece Frances to use his country cottage in the following terms: 'it needs quite a lot doing to it to make it habitable, but you don't need to pay me any rent'. Clearly, Frances does not have a lease. The fact that she is not paying rent does not preclude her from having a lease: *Ashburn Anstalt* v *Arnold & Another* [1988] 2 All ER 147. The reason she does not have a lease is because her occupancy is for an indefinite period of time, and it is a requirement of a valid lease that it must be of certain duration in the sense that its ultimate date of expiry must be ascertainable at or before the commencement of the term: *Lace* v *Chantler* [1944] KB 368.

The issue here is what type of licence Frances has. She has more than a bare licence, as by making the cottage habitable and embarking on a poultry business (presumably at the cottage) this implies work and probably expenditure on the cottage by Frances

—— 231 ——

and her boyfriend. Accordingly, it would seem that Frances and her boyfriend have got either a contractual licence or an estoppel licence.

A contractual licence is one granted for valuable consideration (ie Frances has to show that she has given value for it). On the facts it is submitted that the case for a contractual licence is a bit thin. It is necessary to show that Frances has provided value, and she is not paying rent. All she has got to rely upon in this regard is the work done to make the cottage habitable. Even if she could establish a contractual licence it may not avail her much against Paul as the consensus view now is that a contractual licence is not binding on a successor-in-title of the licensor.

On the facts, Frances may have a stronger claim to an estoppel licence. Such a licence arises where A, the owner of land, allows B to spend money on that land or otherwise to act to his detriment under an expectation created or encouraged by A that he will be allowed to remain on the land or acquire an interest in the land. In such circumstances A will not be allowed to defeat that expectation and deny B's right to remain or to an interest in the land: *Ramsden v Dyson* (1865) LR 1 HL 129. In essence the requirements for an estoppel licence are representation, reliance and detriment. In this case, Frances told Jack about the plan to raise poultry. He in turn offered her the use of his country cottage and indicated that quite a lot needed to be done to render it habitable. Frances and her boyfriend moved into the cottage, made it habitable and set up a poultry business. For an estoppel licence, the prospective licensee must have acted to his detriment (the expenditure of money is the usual evidence of detriment relied upon). Here, Frances and her boyfriend have clearly acted to their detriment by rendering the cottage habitable and establishing the poultry business. It is not unreasonable in the circumstances to infer that Jack knew that they were so acting, and that in the light of his advance knowledge of Frances' plans he had encouraged them to so act. Accordingly, it is submitted that Frances may have an estoppel licence in respect of the cottage (the position of a third party vis-à-vis such a licence is considered below).

Turning to Grace, in 1989 she lost her job and Jack suggested that she should go to live with him in his London home and help him as an unpaid housekeeper and secretary. Such facts are supportive of a contractual licence. A contractual licence is basically an ordinary contract which creates a licence supported by consideration. It creates a contractual right to do things on land which would otherwise be a trespass. Here it could be argued that the contract is that Grace can live in Jack's London house in return for working unpaid as his housekeeper and secretary (ie she is providing consideration).

Further, Grace may be able to establish an estoppel licence if she can prove that Jack allowed her to spend money or alter her position in any way to her detriment in the expectation that she would enjoy some interest in the land. If that is the case, then Jack will be prevented from acting inconsistently with the expectation as raised. Two issues merit consideration in this regard. First, has Jack given Grace an assurance appropriate for an estoppel licence? Second, can Grace show that she has acted to her detriment?

The question is not conclusive as to whether, between 1989 and 1992, Jack gave Grace an appropriate assurance. However, in 1992 when he was ill, he told her not to worry about the future since he was going to leave his London house to her in his will. At least since 1992, Grace could show an assurance appropriate for an estoppel licence. There must be detriment for an estoppel licence. However, the fact that Grace has not spent money does not prevent her showing detrimental reliance upon Jack's assurance. In *Greasley v Cooke* [1980] 1 WLR 1306 it was held that the expenditure of money was not a necessary element of detriment. It was sufficient that the party to whom the assurance was given acted on the faith of it in circumstances in which it would be unjust and inequitable for the party making the assurance to go back on it. Accordingly, it is submitted that Grace may have an estoppel licence in respect of the house.

In 1994, Jack died leaving his entire estate to his son Paul. Two issues now have to be addressed. First, can Paul obtain possession of the country cottage from Frances? Second, can he obtain possession of the bungalow from Grace?

As to the country cottage, if, as previously suggested, Frances has an estoppel licence then it is capable of binding a third party (ie Paul). Whether, in practice, Paul would be bound turns on a number of factors. If the land is unregistered, Paul would be bound if he has notice of Frances' interest, because a licence by estoppel is not registerable as a land charge under the Land Charges Act (LCA) 1972: *ER Ives Investments Ltd v High* [1967] 2 QB 379. If the land is registered Paul will be bound if the estoppel licence has been protected by the entry of a notice or caution on the register, unless it is an overriding interest under s70(1)(g) Land Registration Act (LRA) 1925, in which case he is bound because it *is* an overriding interest (given that Frances is in actual occupation of the cottage she may be able to establish an overriding interest under s70(1)(g)). If Frances has an estoppel licence what remedy will the court grant her to give effect to it? In this regard the courts have shown great flexibility. In *Pascoe v Turner* [1979] 1 WLR 431 the Court of Appeal held that the licensee's equitable rights arising under the estoppel could only be satisfied by granting to her the fee simple of the house in question. In *Inwards v Baker* [1965] 2 QB 29 the licensee was granted a life interest. However, in *Dodsworth v Dodsworth* (1973) 228 EG 1115 the licensees were only allowed to remain in the property until their expenditure was reimbursed. Unfortunately, such flexibility has produced uncertainty because it is difficult for practitioners to anticipate how the estoppel will be satisfied in a given case. Accordingly, it is a matter of speculation as to what relief Frances would be granted here. What is likely to be crucial to the remedy that Frances is granted is the nature of the assurance given to her by Jack. For example, where there is an assurance that the licensee can remain in the property for as long as he or she wishes, then the court usually so orders. Accordingly, it is crucial for Frances to produce as much relevant evidence as possible as to any assurances given to her by Jack.

Finally, what is the position of Grace in relation to the bungalow? It was suggested above that Grace might have had a contractual licence, or an estoppel licence, in respect of Jack's London house. However, in 1994 Jack sold that house and bought the bungalow and moved to it with Grace who has presumably remained there since his death. It is submitted that these property dealings of Jack before his death will not jeopardise Grace's position because in *Re Basham* [1986] 1 WLR 1498 it was said that the belief/assurance encouraged in the licensee by the licensor did not have to relate to a particular property. If Grace is deemed to have a contractual licence the current view is that such a licence is not binding on a third party: *Ashburn Anstalt* v *Arnold*. However, as previously noted, an estoppel licence can bind a third party.

Given the clear assurance made by Jack to Grace the court may well find a constructive trust (ie that Paul is holding the legal title to the bungalow on a constructive trust for Grace). A constructive trust arises by operation of law when the court is of the view that it is in the interests of justice that such a trust should be imposed. The courts have frequently protected a licence (both contractual and estoppel) by way of imposing a constructive trust on a purchaser or successor-in-title of the licensor with notice of the licence. Here, it is submitted that Paul is likely to have notice of Grace's licence. Such a use for the constructive trust was first developed by Lord Denning MR in his dissenting judgment in *Binions* v *Evans* [1972] Ch 359. Currently, the use of the constructive trust is much favoured by the courts: see Fox LJ in *Ashburn Anstalt* v *Arnold*. The use of the constructive trust in this regard is facilitated by s53(2) Law of Property Act (LPA) 1925 which exempts it from the requirements of s53(1) LPA 1925 (for example, a declaration of trust respecting land must be evidenced by writing signed by some person able to declare the trust or by his will), ie it can arise from a mere oral declaration – like that of Jack to Grace. Accordingly, it is submitted that Grace would have a good case in resisting Paul's claim to possession of the bungalow.

QUESTION FOUR

When Tim married Janet, Barbara, Tim's mother, bought a house for the couple to live in. Barbara paid the whole of the purchase price and the house was registered in her sole name. The couple agreed to be responsible for repairs and other outgoings and they insisted, against Barbara's wishes, on paying her a token monthly 'rent'. A few years later the marriage broke down and Tim moved out of the house. Janet continued living in the house, doing the repairs and paying the rent. Finding herself short of cash, Barbara decided to sell the house and, while Janet was away on holiday, she sold it to a local building company. As the new registered proprietor, the company seeks possession of the house with a view to redeveloping the site.

Advise Janet.

University of London LLB Examination
(for External Students) Land Law June 1995 Q7

General Comment

A mixed question which touches upon several areas of land law including matrimonial property, licences, leases and aspects of registration. It provides students well-versed in the relevant areas with a fairly straightforward opportunity to display their knowledge and understanding. Not a question for students who had only revised some of, but not all, the areas covered.

Skeleton Solution

Legal estate in one party – acquisition of a beneficial interest: indirect contributions, constructive trusts – overriding interest under s70(1)(g) LRA 1925 – periodic tenancy – contractual licence: *Errington* v *Errington* – estoppel licence.

Suggested Solution

In view of the fact that Barbara provided all the purchase money for the house, and had it registered in her sole name, it is necessary to see if Janet can establish an interest in the property which will be binding on the building company to whom Barbara subsequently sold the house. Having regard to the facts of the question, it would seem appropriate to consider whether Janet has acquired a beneficial interest, a periodic tenancy or a licence.

A person not on the legal title can acquire a beneficial interest in a variety of ways including by way of resulting or constructive trust. For example, a direct contribution to acquisition of the property (contribution to purchase price or mortgage instalments, paying legal costs, etc) will give rise to a resulting trust with the size of the shares being proportionate to the parties' contributions. Here, since Barbara paid the whole of the purchase price, this rules out any form of direct financial contribution by Janet to the acquisition of the house. While a direct contribution to acquisition is clearly sufficient to acquire a beneficial interest, the position as to indirect contributions is much more difficult. In essence Janet is relying upon indirect contributions, ie 'repairs and other outgoings'. Formerly the courts sometimes took a liberal approach to indirect contributions: *Hazell* v *Hazell* [1972] 1 WLR 301. However, that approach has now been rejected. For example, in *Burns* v *Burns* [1984] Ch 317 a woman whose contribution amounted to paying for the housekeeping and some bills, as well as buying some electrical appliances and furniture, was held not to have a beneficial interest. In *Lloyds Bank plc* v *Rosset* [1990] 2 WLR 867 the House of Lords laid down guidelines concerning indirect contributions and constructive trusts (which traditionally has been the mechanism used to give effect to a beneficial interest arising by indirect contributions). Where there is an express oral declaration or agreement between the legal title owner and the other party (which does not meet the requirements of s53 Law of Property Act (LPA) 1925) then for a constructive trust to be imposed the other party has to have relied on the agreement to his/her detriment (ie there has to be common intention and detrimental reliance). Detrimental reliance is shown by significant contributions in money or money's worth which need not be direct: *Grant* v *Edwards* [1986] Ch 638. In *Lloyds Bank* v *Rosset* the claim of Mrs Rosset to a beneficial interest based on her interior decorating and supervision of builders carrying out renovation work was unsuccessful. Lord Bridge said that what Mrs Rosset was relying upon as a contribution, when set against the cost of the property which exceeded £70,000, was 'so trifling as to be almost de minimis'. Here it is submitted that Janet will be unlikely to be able to establish a beneficial interest in the house – the facts are not supportive of any common intention between Barbara, Tim and Janet to share the beneficial interest, nor are contributions to repairs and other outgoings likely to be regarded as significant contributions in money or money's worth for purposes of detrimental reliance.

Since this is registered land, if Janet could establish an equitable interest in the house she might be able to claim an overriding interest under s70(1)(g) Land Registration Act (LRA) 1925. Overriding interests bind a purchaser without appearing on the register and even though he has no knowledge of them. There are three aspects to establishing an overriding interest under s70(1)(g). First, the claimant must have a proprietary interest in the property (eg an equitable interest). Second, the claimant must be in actual occupation of the land prior to completion of the transaction: *Abbey National Building Society v Cann* [1990] 2 WLR 832. Whether a person is in actual occupation is a question of fact and degree. There must be some degree of permanence and continuation, not a mere fleeting presence. It is submitted that Janet could show a degree of permanence and continuity as to her occupation, and this would not be destroyed just because she was temporarily absent on holiday at the time Barbara sold the house to the building company. Third, if an enquiry is made by a prospective purchaser and the right is not disclosed (because of active concealment on the part of the person claiming an overriding interest under para (g)), then the purchaser will take free of that right. Here Janet's main problem with claiming an overriding interest under s70(1)(g) LRA 1925, which would be binding on the new registered proprietor, is that, as previously mentioned, she is unlikely to be able to show that she has an equitable interest in the house.

Next, it is necessary to see if Janet has a lease as she is paying a token monthly rent and after the marriage breaks down she continues to do so. A periodic tenancy (from week to week or month to month) can be created, either by express agreement or by inference – such as that arising from the payment and acceptance of rent measured by reference to the period in question (week or month, etc). In this case there is obviously no express agreement as the payments are against Barbara's wishes. Nevertheless, if Barbara accepted these payments from Janet, then it is submitted that Janet could have a monthly periodic tenancy by inference. However, a monthly periodic tenancy is not very advantageous to Janet vis-à-vis the new registered proprietor, since such a tenancy can be brought to an end by the tenant being given a month's notice to quit (subject to any contrary agreement between the parties).

Finally, it is necessary to consider whether Janet has a licence which would be binding on the building company.

A contractual licence is one granted for valuable consideration (ie Janet has to show that she has given value for it. Clearly, Janet could show she has given value because she is paying rent and is responsible for repairs and other outgoings. If Janet has a contractual licence would it bind the building company? Originally, contractual licences were seen as personal transactions between the parties and not creating any interest which would be enforceable against a third party: *Clore* v *Theatrical Properties Ltd* [1936] 3 All ER 483. However, in *Errington* v *Errington and Woods* [1952] 1 KB 290 the Court of Appeal held that a contractual licence was binding on a third party except a purchaser for value without notice. Thereafter there was much uncertainty as to whether a contractual licence could bind a third party or not, with cases going either way. The position was substantially clarified in *Ashburn Anstalt* v *Arnold* [1988] 2 All ER 147 when the Court of Appeal (albeit obiter) held that a contractual licence did not bind a third party and that *Errington* v *Errington and Woods* had been wrongly decided on this point. Accordingly, establishing that Janet has a contractual licence will not avail her much since it is not likely to be binding on the building company.

The other possibility for Janet in respect of licences is to try to show that she has an estoppel licence. Such a licence arises as follows. If a landowner (Barbara) allows another person (Janet) to spend money or alter his position to his detriment in the expectation that he will enjoy some privilege or interest in the land, then the owner will be prevented (ie estopped) from acting inconsistently with that expectation. In essence the requirements of an estoppel licence are representation, reliance and detriment. The main attraction for Janet in establishing an estoppel licence is that such a licence is capable of binding a third party (ie the building company). The possible problem for Janet in this regard is showing that Barbara made an appropriate representation, or created an expectation in Janet vis-à-vis the house, since the facts given are not really conclusive of this matter. Janet can certainly show expenditure of money on the house, and the expenditure of money is the usual evidence of detriment relied upon in such cases. Further, since this is registered land, for a third party to be bound by the estoppel licence it has to be protected by the entry of a notice or caution on the register, unless it is an overriding interest under s70(1)(g) LRA 1925, in which case he is bound because it *is* an overriding interest. Here, as discussed previously, it is unlikely that Janet will be able to establish a para (g) overriding interest, and therefore it seems that if there is an estoppel licence the question whether it is binding on the building company will turn on whether or not it has been entered as a notice or caution on the register. Finally, if Janet has an estoppel licence there is no certainty as to what relief will be granted by the court to satisfy the equity (ie what remedy she will get). In this regard, the courts have shown great flexibility (remedies used include transfer of fee simple to licensee; life interest for licensee; and reimbursement of licensee's expenses). However, this in turn has produced uncertainty because it is difficult for practitioners to anticipate how the equity will be satisfied in a given case.

In conclusion, it seems that Janet's best hope for resisting the building company's attempt to gain possession of the house would be to try to establish an estoppel licence. However, it is by no means certain that such a licence can be found here.

QUESTION FIVE

John had an empty cottage on his estate (registered land) and, when he heard that his old friend, Charlie, was desperately looking for somewhere to live, he offered to let him live there. They entered into a written agreement that Charlie could occupy it for a small monthly payment for as long as he wished provided that he maintained the cottage and garden in good order.

The agreement expressly denied Charlie exclusive possession of the cottage. John retained a set of keys to the cottage and reserved the right to enter it whenever he wished. Charlie went into occupation of the cottage and observed the terms of the agreement. A few years later John sold his estate (including the cottage) to Paul expressly 'subject to Charlie's rights, if any'. Paul now seeks possession of the cottage.

Advise Charlie.

> University of London LLB Examination
> (for External Students) Land Law June 1996 Q6

General Comment

The question straddles both the lease/licence distinction and licences. It gives students a good opportunity to demonstrate their understanding of the relevant legal principles and case law. In terms of licences, the crux of the question is what type of licence has been created and whether it is enforceable against the third party.

Skeleton Solution

Define lease and licence – essential requirements of a lease – exclusive possession: *Street* v *Mountford* – periodic tenancies – contractual licences – estoppel licences – enforcement of a contractual licence against a third party: *Ashburn Anstalt* v *Arnold*.

Suggested Solution

A lease gives rise to an estate in land – it is proprietary in nature. A licence, on the other hand, is generally merely a personal right giving rise to no interest in land. The distinction between a lease and a licence is of fundamental importance in relation to the occupancy of residential premises because of the differing degrees of protection afforded to lessees and licencees. In short, lessees enjoy security of tenure whereas licencees do not. Accordingly, it is going to be better for Charlie if he can show that he has a lease rather than a licence.

For there to be a valid lease four requirements must be satisfied. First, the premises must be sufficiently defined. Second, the tenant must have been granted exclusive possession of the property, ie the tenant can exclude everyone including the landlord from the property for the duration of the term. Third, both the commencement date and the duration of the term must be certain or capable of being ascertained at the outset of the term: see s205(1)(xxvii) Law of Property Act (LPA) 1925. Fourth, any relevant formalities must be complied with. A lease can be created by parol if it takes effect in possession for a term not exceeding three years at the best rent reasonably obtainable: s54 LPA 1925. However, a lease in excess of three years must be granted by deed: s52(1) LPA 1925.

In deciding whether Charlie has a lease or not, the second and third requirements mentioned above need in particular to be considered in the light of the facts given.

As to the second requirement, if there is no grant of exclusive possession there is no lease. However, it is possible to have exclusive possession and yet still have a licence. In *Street v Mountford* [1985] AC 809 the House of Lords laid down that exclusive possession for a term (including a periodic arrangement) at a rent gave rise to a lease save in exceptional circumstances. Generally it seems that the right to exclusive possession is to be inferred from the fact of exclusive occupation, and in deciding whether the occupation is exclusive it is necessary to look at the reality of the situation in question and not just at the terms of the agreement. Here the fact that the agreement expressly denied Charlie exclusive possession of the cottage is not conclusive of the matter.

The fact that John has reserved to himself the right to enter the cottage whenever he wants raises the spectre of a 'sham'. Over the years, landowners have used numerous devices to try to prevent a lease being created with its consequential protection for the tenant. One such device was for the landowner to reserve to himself the right to move in with the occupant (ie the aim was to show that the occupant did not enjoy exclusive possession and therefore did not have a lease). In *Antoniades v Villiers* [1988] 3 WLR 1205, the owner granted a 'licence' to an unmarried couple to occupy a two-roomed flat and purported to reserve the right to go into occupation with the couple or introduce another occupier, but the House of Lords said that there had been a grant of exclusive possession as this term was never intended to be acted upon and was a sham. The case for a sham here is not as strong as in *Antoniades*. Charlie is living on his own and a cottage suggests more space than a two-roomed flat. Nevertheless, the court will consider the status of the term and may conclude that Charlie has exclusive possession despite the reservation of entry to John. It is submitted that the question whether Charlie has exclusive possession or not is a finely balanced one. If exclusive possession has not been granted there can be no lease. However, as already mentioned, it is possible for a person to be given exclusive possession and still not have a lease.

The court will look at the circumstances in which John and Charlie reached their agreement in deciding whether there is a lease or a licence. Charlie, who is an old friend of John, is desperately looking for somewhere to live and John allows him to occupy his cottage on 'favourable terms'. This could be seen as an act of friendship or generosity on John's part. Such an act may negative any intention to create a lease: *Facchini v Bryson* [1952] 1 TLR 1386. However, it should also be noted that occupation granted in circumstances of friendship or generosity does not inevitably lead to a licence: *Sopwith v Stutchbury* (1983) 17 HLR 50.

Also relevant in deciding whether Charlie has a lease or a licence is the third requirement for a valid lease mentioned above. In order for a lease for a fixed term to be valid it must have a certain duration. In *Lace v Chantler* [1944] KB 368, a lease granted during the course of the 1939–45 war for the duration of the war was void. This principle was re-affirmed in *Prudential Assurance Co Ltd v London Residuary Body* [1992] 2 AC 386 where the House of Lords said that the principle in *Lace* applied to all leases and tenancy agreements. Here Charlie could occupy the cottage 'for as long as he wished'. As such there is no certainty of duration (ie it would seem that Charlie does not have a lease). However, Charlie has gone into occupation of the cottage and, if the small monthly payments and maintenance work could be regarded as rent (there is nothing to prevent rent being reserved in kind or in services, eg cleaning a church), the combined effect of this could be to establish a periodic tenancy in his favour (assuming he has exclusive possession). In *Javad v Mohammed Aqil* [1991] 1 WLR 1007 Nicholls LJ expressed the view that, where the tenant moves into possession on payment of a weekly or monthly rent

> 'failing more the inference sensibly and reasonably to be drawn is that the parties intended that there should be a weekly or monthly tenancy'.

Here it would be a monthly periodic tenancy and if this is the court's analysis of the situation then Charlie would have to be advised that Paul could recover possession of the cottage by giving him one month's notice.

If Charlie does not have a lease he will have a licence. What sort of licence would it be? There are four main types of licence. First, there is the bare licence (mere personal permission to be on the licensor's land). Second, a licence may be coupled with the grant of an interest in land, for example a right to enter another man's land to hunt and take away the deer killed. Third, there is the contractual licence (a licence supported by consideration). Finally, there is the estoppel licence. Here Charlie has more than a mere licence and the second type of licence is not relevant. Accordingly, contractual and estoppel licences merit consideration.

A contractual licence is one granted for valuable consideration (ie Charlie has to show that he has given value for it). On the facts it is submitted that the case for a contractual licence is a strong one. John and Charlie entered into a written agreement whereby in return for being able to occupy the cottage, Charlie was to make a small monthly payment and maintain the cottage and garden in good order (ie it is submitted that he can show that he has provided value). However, even if Charlie could establish a contractual licence it may not avail him much against Paul, the third party, as the consensus view now is that a contractual licence is not binding on a successor-in-title of the licensor: *Ashburn Anstalt v Arnold* [1989] Ch 1.

An estoppel licence arises where A, the owner of land, allows B to spend money on that land or otherwise to act to his detriment under an expectation created or encouraged by A (ie a representation or an assurance) that he will be allowed to remain on the land or acquire an interest in the land. In such circumstances A will not be allowed to defeat that expectation and deny B's right to remain or to an interest in land: *Ramsden* v *Dyson* (1866) LR 1 HL 129. In essence the requirements for an estoppel licence are representation, reliance and detriment. However, the facts of the question do not seem to support an estoppel licence. For example, there is nothing to suggest that John has given Charlie an appropriate assurance for an estoppel licence. This is unfortunate from Charlie's point of view because an estoppel licence is capable of binding a third party.

In conclusion, Charlie should be advised that if he has a periodic tenancy Paul could bring it to an end by giving him a month's notice and that if he has a contractual licence it is probably not binding on Paul.

QUESTION SIX

Lance owned a two-bedroom flat. He entered into two separate but identical agreements with Tom and Tom's girlfriend, Mary, under which he gave each of them a 'licence' to use the flat on a shared basis in consideration of a monthly payment of £200. The arrangement could be terminated by a month's notice on either side. Lance retained a set of keys to the flat and reserved the right to occupy the flat whenever he wished. Tom and Mary went into occupation of the flat. After four months their relationship broke down and Mary moved out. Rick, a school friend of Tom's, entered into a 'licence' agreement with Lance and moved in. After an argument with Lance, Tom wants to know whether he and Rick are licensees or tenants.

Advise Tom.

University of London LLB Examination
(for External Students) Land Law June 2001 Q5

General Comment

The problem calls for an application of the decision on *Street* v *Mountford* and subsequent cases, with considerable emphasis on the issue of exclusive possession. Providing a candidate is familiar with the material, its application to the facts should occasion no particular difficulty.

Skeleton Solution

Pre-*Street* v *Mountford* position – *Street* v *Mountford* clarified the law – importance of exclusive possession: Lance's reservation to occupy; courts now treat such clauses with scepticism – *Antoniades* v *Villiers* – rent obligation: joint or several?; Tom and Mary probably joint lessees – Tom and Rick: do they have joint exclusive possession?; are the four unities present? – *A G Securities* v *Vaughan* – no joint exclusive possession: Tom and Rick licensees.

Suggested Solution

In deciding whether Tom and Rick have a lease or a licence, the starting point of the enquiry is the decision of the House of Lords in *Street v Mountford* [1985] 2 WLR 877, which clarified a number of issues which had given rise to difficulties in this area of the law before 1985. One of the difficulties had arisen from the decision of Denning LJ in *Errington v Errington and Woods* [1952] 1 KB 290, that a licensee could enjoy exclusive possession, which meant that the presence of exclusive possession under an occupation arrangement was no longer conclusive: the occupant could be either a tenant or a licensee. The distinction was an important one from the points of view of both the property owner and the occupant. It was in the interest of the former to argue for a licence in order that the impact of the Rent Acts could be avoided, and it was in the interest of the occupant to argue that he had a tenancy, since he would then enjoy the protection of the Rent Acts.

Property owners went to considerable lengths to draft occupancy documentation to ensure that the occupant was given only a licence, and some of those documents had a distinct air of artificiality about them. See, for example, *Somma v Hazelhurst* [1978] 1 WLR 1014; *Aslan v Murphy* [1989] 3 All ER 130 and *Crancour Ltd v Da Silvaesa* [1986] 1 EGLR 80.

In *Street v Mountford* itself, the property owner drafted a 'licence agreement' which was signed by the occupant, Mountford, and it was clear that the parties intended to create a licence. The document they signed leaves no doubt about it, but Lord Templeman was not impressed. Acknowledging the parties' freedom to contract, he went on to point out that:

> '... the consequences in law of the agreement ... can only be determined by consideration of the effect of the agreement. If the agreement satisfied all the requirements of a tenancy, then the agreement produced a tenancy and the parties cannot alter the effect of the agreement by insisting that they only created a licence.'

He summarised the position in these words: 'the only intention which is relevant is the intention demonstrated by the agreement to grant exclusive possession for a term at a rent'. That intention was obviously present and accordingly there was a lease, not a licence.

The decision in *Street v Mountford* unquestionably meant that thereafter it would be much more difficult for landlords to assert that they had only conferred upon their occupants a licence. Of the three ingredients listed by Lord Templeman, two are inevitably present: a term and rent. If exclusive possession is also present then, in the absence of a legal relationship other than landlord and tenant, there will be a tenancy assuming there is an intention to create a legal relationship.

With these observations in mind we may now turn to the facts of the problem, beginning with the original agreement between Lance on the one hand and Tom and Mary on the other. It is clear what Lance had in mind: he intended that Tom and Mary should each have a licence and that they should not enjoy exclusive possession of the premises. If there is no exclusive possession, no question of a tenancy arises. A key clause in the agreement was directed to negating exclusive possession, namely Lance's reservation that he could occupy the flat whenever he wished. Taken on its face value, this is completely inconsistent with the occupants' entitlement to exclusive possession. If occupants enjoy exclusive possession, they are entitled to exclude from the premises the whole world, including the landlord.

The courts now, however, view such reservations by the property owner with considerable scepticism. In *Somma* v *Hazelhurst* the Court of Appeal took the reservation clause at its face value and held that the occupants were licensees. In his judgment in *Street* v *Mountford* Lord Templeman disapproved of the Court of Appeal's decision. He described the agreement as a 'sham' and went on to say that 'the court should be astute to detect and frustrate sham devices and artificial transactions whose only object is to disguise the grant of a tenancy and to evade the Rent Acts.'

In *Antoniades* v *Villiers* [1988] 3 WLR 1205 the House of Lords did just that. There the attic of the respondent's house was converted into furnished residential accommodation. Wishing to live together there, the applicants signed identical agreements called 'licences', which were executed at the same time and each stressed that they were not to have exclusive possession. In particular, the agreements provided that 'the licensor shall be entitled at any time to use the rooms together with the licensee and permit other persons to use all of the rooms together with the licensee'. No attempt was made by the respondent to use the rooms or to have them used by others. Stressing, too, that the real intention of the parties was to create a licence not coming under the Rent Acts, the agreements provided for a monthly payment of £87 and that they were determinable by one month's notice by either party. The landlords argued that the occupants were licensees, while the occupants maintained they were joint tenants with joint exclusive possession.

The premises were clearly not suitable for occupation by more than one couple. Lord Oliver said that there was an air of total unreality about the two licence documents signed by the occupants, because the occupants were seeking a flat as a quasi-matrimonial home. Nor, he opined, could the clauses entitling the landlord to occupy the premises personally, or introduce a third party into them, have been seriously intended to have any practical operation. Looking at the substance of the transaction, rather than its face value, the occupants were joint tenants of the premises with joint exclusive possession, and not licensees.

It is submitted that the court would come to the same conclusion in the case of Tom and Mary. Retention of the keys would not of itself negative exclusive possession, since a property owner might well need them to enter the premises in an emergency, but Lance's retention of the keys is linked to his reservation to occupy and the courts are highly unlikely to conclude that either he or the occupants seriously intended that the right would be exercised. A further point that is relevant to the issue of exclusive possession is the agreement relating to rent. Was it a joint liability or a several one?

In *Mikeover* v *Brady* [1989] 3 All ER 618 the defendants, an unmarried couple, occupied a flat for which each signed a separate licence agreement. Each agreement gave the owner the right to put in another licensee. Each paid separate deposits and made separate monthly payments. The woman moved out and the owner sought possession of the flat from the man. He pleaded he was a tenant, but the court rejected his claim. It held that there were two genuinely separate agreements, and that the two occupants were severally liable for the rent and not jointly liable. There was, therefore, no joint exclusive possession and accordingly no tenancy. The key point is that the court decided that the arrangement was a genuine one, and that the occupants intended that they should be separately liable for the rent.

The case is easily distinguishable from *Antoniades v Villiers*, in which the House of Lords confirmed the finding of the judge at first instance that the occupants were joint tenants with exclusive possession on the footing that the two agreements were to be construed together, and that in consequence they were jointly and severally responsible for the whole rent.

We do not have much information from the problem about the agreement to pay rent. We do not know if it was a joint responsibility or a several responsibility, as in *Mikeover v Brady*. We cannot take the matter any further.

However, if Lance's reservation to occupy the premises whenever he wished is not genuine, and is not believed to be genuine by any of the parties, then we must return to Lord Templeman's statement: 'the only intention which is relevant is the intention demonstrated by the agreement to grant exclusive possession for a term at a rent'. If that intention is present, then regardless of how the parties describe the arrangement, a lease has been created. In this case, assuming there is exclusive possession and there is joint liability for the rent, then Tom and Mary will be tenants under a legal monthly tenancy.

Four months later the picture changed. Mary moved out and Rick moved in, having signed a 'licence' agreement with Lance. The question then became: are Tom and Rick joint tenants of the premises with joint exclusive possession, in which case they are tenants under a lease, or are they both licencees with neither having exclusive possession? To be joint tenants holding under a lease the four unities have to be present. Firstly, their rights would have to derive from the same document and originate at the same time. That clearly has not happened here. Both derive their rights from different documents, each being signed at different times. They cannot have joint exclusive possession and consequently cannot be tenants under a lease.

A case from which this reasoning is derived is *AG Securities v Vaughan* [1988] 3 WLR 1205. In that case the appellants owned a block of flats, one of which contained six rooms in addition to a kitchen and bathroom. They furnished four rooms as bedrooms, a fifth as a lounge and the sixth as a sitting-room and entered into short-term agreements with four individuals, each referred to in the relevant agreement as a 'licensee'.

The agreements were made at different times and on different terms and were normally for six months' duration. Each agreement provided that the licensee had 'the right to use [the flat] in common with others who have or may from time to time be granted the like right ... but without the right to exclusive possession of any part of the ... flat'. When a licensee left, a new occupant was mutually agreed by the appellants and the remaining licensees.

In *Vaughan* there was no question that the agreements were in any way sham agreements. They reflected the true bargains between the parties. The question was: were the occupants licensees or did the agreements collectively create a joint tenancy between the occupants with joint exclusive possession? Lord Templeman had said in *Street* v *Mountford* that: 'an occupier of residential accommodation for rent is either a lodger or a tenant'. He went on to say that: 'the courts which deal with these problems will, save in exceptional circumstances, only be concerned to enquire whether as a result of the agreement relating to residential accommodation, the occupier is a lodger or a tenant'.

AG Securities v *Vaughan* shows that this is not an exhaustive test. The occupants were not lodgers and if Lord Templeman's test was to be applied they were, therefore, joint tenants with exclusive possession. That could not be the case here. A joint tenancy requires the four unities of time, title, interest and possession. The agreements were made at different times and on different terms. Lord Oliver found that none of these factors were present and it was: 'impossible to say that the agreements entered into ... created either individually or collectively, a single tenancy either of the entire flat or of any part of it'. In the result, despite Lord Templeman's dicta, the occupants were held to be licensees.

The answer to Tom's question, therefore, must be that he and Rick are licensees and not tenants.

Chapter 10

Mortgages

10.1 Introduction

Most land law examinations will contain a question on mortgages. Key areas for revision include the following: the form of the mortgage; the rights of the mortgagor (particularly the right to redeem); the remedies of the mortgagee (particularly the right to take possession and the power of sale); the application of s36 of the Administration of Justice Act 1970 as amended; and whether the mortgage is to be regarded as a commercial or a consumer one. Further, students should be aware that in recent years one of the most dynamic areas of land law has concerned the question of husbands who use undue influence over their wives in order to procure their agreement to a mortgage transaction for the benefit of the husband's business. Accordingly, 'undue influence' is currently a topical examination issue. Finally, any question within the general theme of 'once a mortgage always a mortgage' will usually provide an opportunity to display knowledge of the extensive case law on this theme.

10.2 Key points

a) Nature of mortgage – a conveyance of land in order to secure a loan. It is only a security for a loan.

b) Form of a legal mortgage of freehold land: s85 LPA 1925

   i)   Pre-1926 – conveyance of fee simple or long lease.

   ii) Post-1925:

   - demise for a term of years absolute subject to a proviso for cesser on redemption;

   - charge by deed expressed to be by way of legal mortgage – s87 LPA 1925 – now the most popular method of creating legal mortgages;

- under the LRA 2002 mortgages of registered land can no longer be created by demise or sub-demise: s23(1) LRA 2002. Rather, the charge will be the only method of creating a mortgage over registered land.

iii) Second and subsequent mortgages – possible as either legal or equitable mortgages today.

c) Form of a legal mortgage of leasehold land

   i) Pre-1926 – assignment or sub-lease.

   ii) Post-1926:

   - mortgage by sub-demise – usually less last 10 days;

   - charge by deed expressed to be by way of legal mortgage.

   iii) Second and subsequent mortgages – plus one day on the earlier mortgage.

d) Equitable mortgages

   i) Mortgage of an equitable interest – eg tenant for life's own interest under a strict settlement. However, since the coming into force of the Trusts of Land and Appointment of Trustees Act 1996 generally speaking no new strict settlement can now be created under the Settled Land Acts.

   ii) Agreement to create a mortgage – mortgage of a legal estate not made by deed. If the agreement is made after 26 September 1989 it must satisfy the requirements of s2 Law of Property (Miscellaneous Provisions) Act 1989.

   iii) Formerly an equitable mortgage could be created by deposit of title deeds. The effect of s2 Law of Property (Miscellaneous Provisions) Act 1989 has been to bring this centuries old practice to an end: *United Bank of Kuwait plc v Sahib* [1996] 3 All ER 215.

   iv) Contrasted with an equitable charge – although there are similarities between an equitable charge and an equitable mortgage (chargee like mortgagee has the right to apply to the court for an order of sale or for the appointment of a receiver to protect his security), there are important differences between the two. In particular, an equitable charge, unlike an equitable mortgage, does not give the chargee any interest in the land and thus no right of possession. See *Bland* v *Ingram's Estates Ltd* (2001) The Times 18 January.

e) Rights of mortgagor

   i) Rights of redemption.

   ii) Once a mortgage always a mortgage: Lord Eldon in *Seton v Slade* (1802) 7 Ves 265.

   iii) The right to redeem must not be excluded.

   A term in a mortgage which gives the mortgagee an option to purchase the mortgaged property is void even if it is not oppressive: *Samuel* v *Jarrah Timber and Wood Paving Corporation* [1904] AC 323. However, once the mortgage has been made, equity will not interfere if the mortgagor then gives the mortgagee such an option: *Reeve* v *Lisle* [1902] AC 461.

iv) The right to redeem may be postponed.

However, equity will not allow the right of redemption to be postponed to such an extent that the right would be rendered nominal.

Fairclough v *Swan Brewery Co Ltd* [1912] AC 565 – 20 years less last 6 weeks of a lease – period of postponement rendered right to redeem worthless; cf *Knightsbridge Estates Trust Ltd* v *Byrne* [1939] Ch 441 – fee simple – 40-year period of postponement not such as to render right to redeem illusory. Differences with *Fairclough* – freehold not leasehold property; borrower a company (with perpetual existence) whereas in *Fairclough* a private individual.

v) Consumer Credit Act 1974, ss137–139.

The court may re-open a credit agreement which is 'extortionate', ie one which requires payments which are 'grossly exhorbitant' or which 'grossly contravene ordinary principles of fair dealing'. These provisions apply to all mortgages (including building society mortgages) entered into by private individuals.

A Ketley Ltd v *Scott* [1981] ICR 241

vi) The equity of redemption must not be clogged.

Noakes & Co Ltd v *Rice* [1902] AC 24 – buy beer from mortgagee brewer for full period of lease – 26 years whether mortgage repaid or not; cf *Biggs* v *Hoddinott* [1898] 2 Ch 307 – 5 years – for as long as money due on the mortgage

vii) Collateral advantages to the mortgagee.

Today there is no rule of equity which prevents a lender from stipulating for a collateral advantage. Rather, equity endeavours to 'hold the ring' so far as collateral advantages are concerned. The current law can be summarised in the following two propositions

- a collateral advantage which exists until redemption can be valid but will be void if it is oppressive or unconscionable;

- a collateral advantage which exists beyond redemption is void (but see *Kreglinger* v *New Patagonia Meat and Cold Storage Co Ltd* [1914] AC 25.

viii) Who may exercise the right to redeem? – mortgagor and any assignee of equity of redemption.

ix) Notice of intention to redeem – borrower may redeem on legal date for redemption without giving notice of his intention to do so. Thereafter when seeking to redeem under the equitable right to redeem he must either give the lender reasonable notice of his intention to redeem (usually 6 months) or else pay six months' interest in lieu of notice.

x) Price of redemption – must pay principal + interest + costs.

xi) Loss of the right of redemption – release of equity of redemption to mortgagee, sale by mortgagee, foreclosure.

xii) Discharge of the mortgage: s115 LPA 1925 – statutory receipt signed by mortgagee, naming person who pays.

xiii) Mortgagor's right to a sale – s91 LPA 1925.

xiv) Mortgagor's right to compel transfer instead of himself redeeming – s95 LPA 1925.

xv) Mortgagor's right to bring actions – because he is in possession.

xvi) Mortgagor's right to lease: s99 LPA 1925 – agricultural/occupation 50 years – building 999 years – best rent – possession within 12 months – condition for re-entry if rent in arrears for 30 days.

xvii) Mortgagor's right to accept surrender of lease: s100 LPA 1925.

xviii) Mortgagor's right to cut timber.

xix) Mortgagor's right to inspect the title deeds.

xx) Upon redemption mortgagee must deliver title deeds to person next entitled: s96(2) LPA 1925. Registration not enough, mortgagee must have *actual notice* of later mortgages.

f) Consolidation of mortgages: s93 LPA 1925

The right of a person who holds two or more mortgages (ie mortgagee) granted by the same mortgagor on different properties to refuse in certain circumstances to be redeemed as to one unless he is also redeemed as to the other. Consolidation is part of the price paid by the mortgagor for the court's assistance to recover his property.

i) Definition

ii) Four conditions:

- rights reserved in one mortgage deed;
- both mortgages created by same mortgagor;
- legal date for redemption passed on all mortgages;
- at one time all mortgages vested in one person and all equities in another.

Theme of consolidation is he who seeks equity must do equity.

g) Rights and remedies of the mortgagee

Remedies

i) Right to take possession: *Four-Maids Ltd* v *Dudley Marshall (Properties) Ltd* [1957] Ch 317 – before ink is dry on the mortgage – *White* v *City of London Brewery Co* (1889) 42 Ch D 237, s36 Administration of Justice Act 1970 *and* s8 AJA 1973 – *Quennel* v *Maltby* [1979] 1 WLR 318 – remedies only available if used bona fide to enforce the security and *not* for some ulterior motive such as avoiding the Rent Acts.

ii) Right to sue the mortgagor personally.

iii) Power of foreclosure.

iv) Power of sale: s101 LPA 1925.

   Tse Kwong Lam v *Wong Chit Sen* [1983] 3 All ER 54.

   Distinguish when the power of sale *arises* from when it becomes *exercisable*.

v) Power to appoint a receiver: s101 LPA 1925, s37 Supreme Court Act 1981.

Rights

vi) Power to insure the property

vii) Undue influence.

   • The effect of seeking to avoid the practical consequences of *Williams & Glyn's Bank Ltd* v *Boland* [1980] 3 WLR 138 To avoid the consequences of an overriding interest under s70(1)(g) LRA 1925 many lenders require occupiers to sign a form consenting to the mortgage and postponing the interests of the occupier to the mortgagee.

   • Problems of such method of avoidance – has undue influence been used in obtaining the signature of the occupier?

   • Solution of the courts – *National Westminster Bank plc* v *Morgan* [1985] AC 686 – House of Lords said that before a transaction could be set aside on the grounds of undue influence must show it constituted a manifest disadvantage to the person seeking to avoid it. Not so here, because the loan saved the home from possession by original mortgagee.

   Kingsnorth Trust Ltd v *Bell* [1986] 1 All ER 423 – Court of Appeal – undue influence exerted by husband in obtaining wife's signature to a second mortgage. Court emphasised importance of independent legal advice. Conclusion: any document postponing rights of an occupier in favour of mortgagee should only be signed in the presence of a solicitor. *Morgan* case applied in:

   Barclays Bank plc v *O'Brien* [1993] 3 WLR 786 (HL) – wife agreed, following a misrepresentation by her husband, that the family home could be used as security for her husband's debts. Wife able to have the legal charge set aside because the bank was fixed with constructive notice of husband's misrepresentation. Why? (1) Transaction on its face not to the wife's financial advantage; (2) substantial risk in such transactions that in getting the wife to act as surety the husband will have committed a legal or equitable wrong that would entitle the wife to set the transaction aside. To avoid constructive notice, it was necessary for the bank to have taken steps (in husband's absence) to bring home to the wife the risk she was running as surety and advise her to take independent advice.

For post-*O'Brien* developements see:

Massey v *Midland Bank plc* [1995] 1 All ER 929;

TSB Bank plc v *Camfield* [1995] 1 All ER 951;

Credit Lyonnais Bank Nederland NV v *Burch* (1996) The Times 1 July;

Barclays Bank plc v *Caplan* (1997) The Times 12 December;

Barclays Bank plc v *Boulter and Another* [1999] 1 WLR 1919;

Barclays Bank plc v *Coleman* [2000] 1 All ER 385;

Royal Bank of Scotland plc v *Etridge (No 2) and Other Appeals* [2001] 4 All ER 449;

Bank of Scotland v *Bennett* [1999] 1 FLR 1115;

National Westminster Bank plc v *Amin* [2002] 1 FLR 735.

10.3 Key cases and statutes

- *Adamson* v *Halifax plc* [2003] 1 WLR 60
  When a mortgagee sells a mortgaged property at an undervalue and in breach of its duty to take reasonable care to obtain the best price reasonably obtainable, the measure of damages to be paid to the mortgagor was the reduction in the value of the equity of redemption, ie the real loss

- *Barclays Bank plc* v *O'Brien* [1993] 3 WLR 786
  Wife who, following misrepresentation by husband, agreed that family home could be used as security for husband's debts was able to have legal charge set aside when husband defaulted because bank had constructive notice of misrepresentation – circumstances in which lender could avoid such notice identified

- *Biggs* v *Hoddinott* [1898] 2 Ch 307
  A collateral advantage which was not unconscionable and not in restraint of trade was valid during the currency of the mortgage

- *CIBC Mortgages plc v Pitt* [1993] 3 WLR 802
  The *Barclays Bank v O'Brien* principle only applied to a situation where the wife acted as surety for her husband's debt – it did not apply to an advance by a lender to a husband and wife jointly seemingly for their joint benefit despite undue influence on the husband's part

- *Cityland & Property (Holdings) Ltd v Dabrah* [1967] 2 All ER 639
  A collateral advantage which was unconscionable or oppressive was not permissible – the status of a mortgage (whether a consumer or commercial one) could have a bearing on how the courts assess the validity of its terms

- *Corbett v Halifax plc* [2003] 4 All ER 180
  A sale by a mortgagee would not be set aside just because it was at an undervalue. For a sale to be set aside the 'sale had to be tainted by some kind of impropriety or an element of bad faith on the part of the mortgagee in the exercise of the power of sale'

- *Cuckmere Brick Co Ltd v Mutual Finance Ltd* [1971] 2 WLR 1207
  Mortgagee when exercising its statutory power of sale was under a duty (a) to act in good faith, and (b) to take reasonable care to get the best price for the mortgaged property at the date on which it decided to sell

- *Fairclough v Swan Brewery Co Ltd* [1912] AC 565
  Mortgagor's right to redeem could be postponed provided the period of postponement would not render the right worthless

- *Freeguard v Royal Bank of Scotland plc* (2002) The Times 25 April
  Mortgagee owed a duty of care to the legal owner of land even if the owner was not the mortgagor

- *Knightsbridge Estates Trust Ltd v Byrne and Others* [1940] AC 613
  Forty-year period of postponement of mortgagor's right to redeem did not render right worthless where the mortgagor was a company and the property was freehold

- *Kreglinger (G & C) v New Patagonia Meat and Cold Storage Co Ltd* [1914] AC 25
  Exceptionally a collateral advantage survived redemption because the mortgage was a commercial one, the parties were of equal bargaining strength and the clauses dealing with the collateral advantage were seen as a separate agreement

- *Multiservice Bookbinding Ltd v Marden* [1978] 2 All ER 489
  Companies of equal bargaining strength agreed that payments of capital and interest were to be index linked to the value of the Swiss franc – such index linking not contrary to public policy even though repayments rose substantially owing to a sharp fall in value of pound sterling as against the Swiss franc

- *Newport Farms Ltd v Damesh Holdings Ltd & Others* (2003) 147 SJLB 1117
  Property sold to company in which mortgagee interested – in such a sale, the mortgagee and the company had to show that the sale was in good faith and that the

mortgagee had taken reasonable precautions to obtain the best price reasonably obtainable at the time. In relation to reasonable precautions the mortgagee did not have to observe a set of inflexible rules

- *Noakes* v *Rice* [1902] AC 24
  Collateral advantage would not usually survive after mortgage redeemed even if borrower accepted a term that it should continue after redemption

- *Paragon Finance plc* v *Nash & Another; Paragon Finance plc* v *Staunton & Another* (2001) The Times 25 October
  Lender's discretion to vary interest rates subject to an implied term to vary rates fairly

- *Reeve* v *Lisle* [1902] AC 461
  Once a mortgage had been made, equity would not interfere if the mortgagor then gave the mortgagee an option to purchase the mortgaged property

- *Ropaigealach* v *Barclays Bank plc* [1999] 3 WLR 17
  The protection provided to a borrower by s36 AJA 1970 only applied where the lender had brought an action for possession

- *Royal Bank of Scotland* v *Etridge (No 2)* [2001] 4 All ER 449
  Redefined the duties owed by lenders in *O'Brien*-type cases and reduced the role of a solicitor advising a wife in such cases to in essence ensuring that she understood the nature and effect of the transaction

- *Samuel* v *Jarrah Timber and Wood Paving Corporation Ltd* [1904] AC 323
  A term in a mortgage which gave the mortgagee an option to purchase the mortgaged property was void even if it was not oppressive

- *United Bank of Kuwait plc* v *Sahib & Others* [1996] 3 All ER 215
  The centuries old practice of creating an equitable mortgage by deposit of title deeds was ended by s2 Law of Property (Miscellaneous Provisions) Act 1989

- Administration of Justice Act 1970, s36

- Administration of Justice Act 1973, s8

- Consumer Credit Act 1974, ss137–139

- Land Registration Act 2002, s23(1)

- Law of Property Act 1925, ss1(2)(c), 85, 91, 93, 94, 101 and 105

- Law of Property (Miscellaneous Provisions) Act 1989, s2

10.4 Questions and suggested solutions

Analysis of questions

The areas of the subject favoured by examiners include the general area of 'once a mortgage always a mortgage', the remedies of the lender, the rights of the borrower (particularly whether the court is likely to exercise its discretion under s36 Administration of Justice Act 1970), the rules of priority and undue influence. A not untypical problem question could comprise a series of hypothetical clauses (involving eg postponement of the right to redeem collateral advantages etc) with the student being required to consider their validity, consideration as to whether the mortgage is a consumer or commercial one, the remedies open to the lender and the rights of the borrower. Further, the registered land aspect is important and the significance of the decision in *Williams & Glyn's Bank Ltd* v *Boland* [1980] 3 WLR 138 should not be understated, not least because of the steps taken by institutional lenders to avoid the practical consequences of the decision.

Essay titles on mortgages are not uncommon in examinations and this reality is reflected in the following questions.

QUESTION ONE

'In recent times the courts have so elevated the standard of conduct expected of the selling mortgagee that the mortgagee's duty to his mortgagor has become analogous to a fiduciary duty.'

Discuss.

University of London LLB Examination
(for External Students) Land Law June 1994 Q5

General Comment

A somewhat challenging essay title because of its specific focus, which would give a student well versed in the relevant law a good opportunity to exhibit his knowledge and understanding. Not a question to be undertaken by a student with only an outline understanding of the relevant law.

Skeleton Solution

Definition of a mortgage – power of sale: arising – power of sale: exercisable – mortgagee not a trustee of the power of sale – duty to mortgagor to take reasonable care: *Cuckmere Brick Co Ltd* v *Mutual Finance – Parker-Tweedale* v *Dunbar Bank plc (No 1)* – sale by mortgagee to himself: *Tse Kwong Lam* v *Wong Chit Sen* – s13 Building Societies Act 1986 – s105 LPA 1925.

Suggested Solution

A mortgage is essentially a transaction whereby an interest in property, be it land, house or business, is transferred to a mortgagee (lender) as security for the loan, subject to a right of redemption vested in the mortgagor (borrower).

The most important rights enabling the mortgagee to recover the capital sum and/or interest are taking possession, sale, foreclosure and appointing a receiver. The question concerns the power of sale which is the remedy most commonly used as it enables a mortgagee to recover his capital speedily. It is usually combined with an action to obtain vacant possession to allow the best price to be obtained.

The power of sale arises when the mortgage has been made by deed and the legal date of redemption has passed and there is no contrary intention expressed in the mortgage deed: s101 Law of Property Act (LPA) 1925. Once the power of sale has *arisen* it becomes *exercisable* when one or more of the following conditions have been fulfilled: (i) default for three months after notice; or (ii) interest two months in arrear; or (iii) breach of some other term of the mortgage: s103 LPA 1925. The statutory power of sale is exercisable without a court order.

Over the last 25 years the responsibilities of a mortgagee to a mortgagor when selling mortgaged property have been considered by the courts on a number of occasions. In the first place it is important to note that a mortgagee has an absolute discretion as to the mode and time of sale. It can choose to sell by way of private treaty or by way of auction and it is not required to wait until the market improves. Further, the mortgagee's motive for selling – spite against the mortgagor – has been held immaterial: see *Nash v Eads* (1880) 25 SJ 95.

However, once the mortgagee decides to sell it is subject to certain duties. First and foremost, it was laid down in *Cuckmere Brick Co Ltd v Mutual Finance Ltd* [1971] Ch 949 that a mortgagee is not a trustee for the mortgagor in respect of the power of sale because the power is given to the mortgagee for his own benefit to enable him the better to realise his security.

However, the mortgagor is the person interested in the proceeds of sale in so far as they exceed the mortgage debt, and his interests must not be sacrificed. Accordingly, a mortgagee is under some duty to the mortgagor with regard to the sale. Originally the duty was considered to be no more than a duty to act in good faith: see *Kennedy v De Trafford* [1897] AC 180. However, since the early 1970s it has been recognised that more than good faith is required. In the landmark case of *Cuckmere Brick Co Ltd v Mutual Finance Ltd* it was held that the mortgagee owes the mortgagor a duty to take reasonable care. There the mortgagee advertised the property for sale by auction but omitted to mention a valuable planning permission. Salmon LJ stated that the mortgagee was under a duty to take reasonable precautions to obtain the true market value of the mortgaged property at the date when the mortgagee decides to sell. In *Standard Chartered Bank v Walker* [1982] 1 WLR 144 the Court of Appeal held that this duty was owed not only to the mortgagor but also to any guarantor of the mortgagor's debt. Any breach of this duty of care will render the mortgagee liable to the mortgagor for the difference between the price obtained and the price that he could have obtained. Where the mortgagee is a building society s13(7) and Sch 4 para 1(1)(a) of the Building Societies Act 1986 requires the selling building society to achieve 'the best price that can reasonably be obtained'.

In *Parker-Tweedale* v *Dunbar Bank plc (No 1)* [1990] 3 WLR 767 the Court of Appeal further considered the duty of care owed by a mortgagee to a mortgagor. The court stated that the duty arose in equity and not in negligence. Accordingly, it did not give rise to liability against third parties. There the duty of care did not extend to the beneficiary under a trust of which the mortgagor was a trustee.

A sale by the mortgagee to himself either directly or through a third party may be set aside. In *Tse Kwong Lam* v *Wong Chit Sen* [1983] 3 All ER 54 the matter was considered by the Privy Council. There it was held that there was no inflexible rule that a mortgagee exercising his power of sale under a mortgage could not sell to a company in which he had an interest. However, the mortgagee and the company had to show that the sale was made in good faith and that the mortgagee had taken reasonable precautions to obtain the best price reasonably obtainable at the time.

After paying off all prior mortgages, the money received from the purchase is held by the mortgagee on trust. This money must be used by the mortgagee, in the following order, to: (i) pay all expenses incidental to the sale; (ii) pay himself the principal, interest and costs due under the mortgage; and (iii) pay the surplus, if any, to the next mortgagee, or if none, to the mortgagor: see s105 LPA 1925. If there is a subsequent mortgagee he will hold the balance on trust to discharge the money owing to him and to pay the balance to the person next entitled.

The question of the mortgagee's responsibilities on sale to the mortgagor is an area of land law which has seen considerable development over the last 25 years. It is now clear that more than good faith is entailed. Rather, it is now clearly established that the mortgagee owes to the mortgagor a duty to take reasonable care. Given the view of the Court of Appeal in *Parker-Tweedale* v *Dunbar Bank plc (No 1)* that the mortgagee's duty arises in equity and not in negligence it is true to say that the duty is now analogous to a fiduciary one.

QUESTION TWO

'There is now no rule in equity which precludes a mortgagee ... from stipulating for any collateral advantage.' (Per Lord Parker of Waddington).

Explain this statement and consider the circumstances in which the courts will still be prepared to strike down collateral advantages.

University of London LLB Examination
(for External Students) Land Law June 1995 Q4

General Comment

A fairly straightforward essay title on a mainstream area of mortgages which would give students well-versed in the relevant law a good opportunity to exhibit their knowledge and understanding. Essential to have a good grasp of the relevant case law.

Skeleton Solution

Definition of a mortgage – no clogs or fetters on the equity of redemption – definition of a collateral advantage – initial attitude of the courts – role of equity – three classes of collateral advantage: those that are: (1) unconscionable and oppressive (*Cityland & Property (Holdings) Ltd* v *Dabrah*); (2) enforceable for the duration of the mortgage (*Biggs* v *Hoddinott*); and (3) capable of surviving redemption of the mortgage (*Kreglinger* v *New Patagonia Meat and Cold Storage Co Ltd*).

Suggested Solution

A mortgage is essentially a transaction whereby an interest in property, be it land, house or business, is transferred to a mortgagee (lender) as security for the loan subject to a right of redemption vested in the mortgagor (borrower).

Once a mortgage is entered into the equity of redemption comes into existence – this is the borrower's right of ownership of the property subject to the mortgage. Equity protects the borrower's equity of redemption through the maxim 'once a mortgage always a mortgage'. One of the ways in which this maxim is applied is that there must be no clog or fetter on the equity of redemption. This means that the borrower cannot be stopped from (a) ultimately redeeming his property, and (b) redeeming it free from any condition in the mortgage.

The basic purpose of a mortgage is to provide security for the repayment of the money lent by the mortgagee. However, in the case of commercial properties the lender may succeed in negotiating for some additional advantage (collateral advantages are not usually encountered in mortgages of domestic properties). For example, a brewery will often advance money on mortgage to the licensee of a public house, provided the borrower agrees to buy all his beer from the lending brewery. Comparable arrangements are often made between petrol companies and garage owners.

The original view of the courts was that all collateral advantages taken by a lender were void. This was because they were regarded as a disguised form of interest, contravening the old usury laws: *Jennings* v *Ward* (1705) 2 Vern 520. In 1854 the last of the statutes dealing with usury was repealed and thereafter the attitude of the courts to collateral advantages began to change.

The quotation given in the question comes from the judgment of Lord Parker in *Kreglinger* v *New Patagonia Meat and Cold Storage Co Ltd* [1914] AC 25. It is true to say that today there is no rule of equity which prevents a lender from stipulating for a collateral advantage. Rather, equity endeavours to 'hold the ring' so far as collateral advantages are concerned.

Equity divides collateral advantages into three classes. First, the collateral advantage may be held to be unconscionable and oppressive if it was imposed in a morally reprehensible way. In such a case the collateral advantage is void and therefore unenforceable even during the currency of the mortgage. In *Cityland & Property*

(Holdings) Ltd v *Dabrah* [1968] Ch 166 a term in the mortgage which imposed an extremely high premium, rather than requiring payment of interest, was held to be unenforceable as being oppressive and unreasonable because the whole balance of the premium and loan became immediately repayable on default. The mortgage was rewritten by the court.

Second, the collateral advantage may be regarded as fair and enforceable for the duration of the mortgage (many solus ties come within this second class). In *Biggs* v *Hoddinott* [1898] 2 Ch 307 a mortgage of a public house was granted by a brewer to a publican. The mortgage required the borrower to take all his beer from the mortgagee during the currency of the mortgage (ie a solus agreement).

The Court of Appeal upheld the collateral advantage as valid. Chitty LJ put the matter thus:

> 'The present appears to me to be a reasonable trade bargain between two businessmen who enter into it with their eyes open and it would be a fanciful doctrine of equity that would set it aside.'

So far as solus agreements are concerned, they come within the category of agreements in restraint of trade and must therefore be justified on the ground of reasonableness: *Esso Petroleum Co Ltd* v *Harper's Garage (Stourport) Ltd* [1968] AC 269. Accordingly, in such cases, the test is unreasonableness not unconscionability. Equity will intervene if the solus agreement is unreasonable, ie an excessive restraint of trade.

Third, the collateral advantage may survive redemption of the mortgage. Normally a collateral advantage will not survive redemption of the mortgage (even if the mortgagor has agreed to a term that the collateral advantage shall continue beyond redemption), for otherwise the borrower would get back an estate encumbered in a way that the estate he mortgaged was not. Nevertheless, in the case of commercial mortgages entered into by parties bargaining on equal terms, the courts may be prepared to enforce a collateral advantage even after redemption by treating it as if it was a separate agreement, part of the consideration for entering the mortgage. The lead case in this regard is *Kreglinger* v *New Patagonia Meat and Cold Storage Co Ltd*. There, a meat company mortgaged its property to a wool-broker. It was a term of the mortgage that the mortgagor would for five years offer its sheepskins to the mortgagee for purchase. Although the mortgage was redeemed after two years the House of Lords held that the option was valid even though it continued for three years after redemption. The option was regarded as being reasonable – it was for a short period of time and the mortgagee had to pay the best price for the sheepskins. The collateral advantage here was seen as forming part of a bigger commercial deal done between the two parties well capable of looking after their own interests (ie it was a separate agreement, not really part of the mortgage).

Finally, it is true that there is now no rule of equity which prevents a mortgagee from stipulating for a collateral advantage. However, in certain circumstances, the courts will still be prepared to strike down a collateral advantage. The present position can be summarised as follows: a collateral advantage which exists until redemption can be valid, but will be struck down if it is oppressive or unconscionable; a collateral advantage which exists beyond redemption will be struck down unless it exists as an independent transaction.

QUESTION THREE

Bill owned a baker's shop and an adjoining sandwich-bar, and he mortgaged the shop to Gus, the local grocer. The mortgage deed provided that the mortgage should be paid off only in 40 half-yearly instalments, that Bill should not sell biscuits or chocolates in the baker's shop so long as he owned it, that he should not sell biscuits or chocolates in the sandwich-bar so long as he owned it, and that he would never sell either of his properties without giving Gus the chance of buying it for the best price that anyone else offered.

To what extent is Bill bound by these provisions?

University of London LLB Examination
(for External Students) Land Law June 1996 Q8

General Comment

The question raises a number of fairly standard examination issues in respect of commercial mortgages. It is crucial for students to spot that the question deals solely with a commercial mortgage. A good answer would be well supported by reference to relevant case law.

Skeleton Solution

Definition of a mortgage – domestic and commercial mortgages – no clog or fetter on the equity of redemption – postponement of the right to redeem: *Knightsbridge Estates Trust Ltd* v *Byrne* – collateral advantages: surviving redemption: *Noakes* v *Rice*; *Kreglinger* v *New Patagonia Meat and Cold Storage Co Ltd* – option to purchase mortgaged property given to mortgagee: *Samuel* v *Jarrah Timber and Wood Paving Corp; Reeve* v *Lisle*.

Suggested Solution

A mortgage is essentially a transaction whereby an interest in property be it land, house or business, is transferred to a mortgagee (lender) as security for the loan, subject to a right of redemption vested in the mortgagor (borrower).

Once a mortgage is entered into the equity of redemption comes into existence – this is the borrower's right of ownership of the property subject to the mortgage. Equity protects the borrower's equity of redemption through the maxim 'once a mortgage always a mortgage'. One of the ways in which this maxim is applied is that there must be no clog or fetter on the equity of redemption. This means that the borrower cannot be stopped from (a) ultimately redeeming his property, and (b) redeeming it free from any condition in the mortgage.

The basic purpose of a mortgage is to provide security for the repayment of the money lent by the mortgagee.

Here we are dealing with a commercial mortgage. Bill the owner of a bakery shop mortgages it to Gus, the local grocer. This is an important fact to note because the attitude of the courts to the terms of a mortgage seems to differ depending on whether they are dealing with a consumer/domestic mortgage or a business/commercial mortgage. The courts are more likely to intervene to prevent a lender taking advantage of a borrower in the former category of mortgage than in the case of the latter (see, eg, *Cityland and Property (Holdings) Ltd v Dabrah* [1968] Ch 166 and *Multiservice Bookbinding Ltd v Marden* [1978] 2 WLR 535). This is because there is usually great disparity of bargaining power between the parties to a domestic mortgage than between the parties to a commercial mortgage.

The mortgage deed provides that the mortgage is only to be paid off in 40 half-yearly instalments (ie, it is an attempt to postpone the right to redeem for 20 years). Equity allows the equitable right to redeem to be postponed provided the period of postponement is not so long as to render the right illusory (*Fairclough v Swan Brewery Co Ltd* [1912] AC 565), and that the mortgage as a whole is not so unconscionable that equity would not enforce it. In *Knightsbridge Estates Trust Ltd v Byrne* [1940] AC 613, a 40-year period of postponement was upheld. There both the borrower and the lender were large companies, they had entered into a commercial mortgage and the court refused to allow the borrower's claim for early redemption (they wanted to take advantage of a fall in interest rates and borrow money more cheaply elsewhere), and concluded that the agreement was 'a commercial agreement between two important companies experienced in such matters, and had none of the features of an oppressive bargain where the borrower [was] at the mercy of an unscrupulous lender'. Further, the right of redemption was in no way illusory because the borrower was a company and the mortgaged property was freehold (ie, the postponement would not have rendered the property worthless when redeemed).

Would the 20-year period of postponement here be acceptable? This turns on whether the court concludes that the period of postponement renders Bill's right to redeem illusory (ie, would it render the shop worthless when the mortgage is redeemed?). For example, in *Fairclough v Swan Brewery Co Ltd* a 20-year lease of a public house was mortgaged and one of the terms of the mortgage was that it was not to be redeemed until six weeks before the end of the leasehold term. Not surprisingly the court concluded that in the circumstances of the case such a period of postponement rendered the right to redeem illusory and the mortgagor was allowed to redeem after three years. However, the facts given here bear a number of similarities with *Knightsbridge Estates Trust Ltd v Byrne* (where as previously noted a 40-year period of postponement was upheld). In particular, it is a commercial mortgage affecting freehold property and the parties seem to be of equal bargaining strength. Accordingly, there is much in favour of the period of postponement being upheld (the courts generally do not interfere with a bargain made between two parties of equal bargaining strength). There is, however, at least one important difference between the facts given and the *Knightsbridge* case. There the mortgagor was a large company, but here the mortgagor is a private individual and 20 years is a long period of time for an individual borrower. Accordingly, predicting the outcome of any challenge to the term is not without some difficulty. Further, even if the court is minded to conclude that the period of postponement does not render the right to redeem illusory the term will only stand if the mortgage as a *whole* is not so unconscionable that equity would not enforce it. The likely attitude of the court to the mortgage as a whole is considered below.

As to the restrictions imposed by the mortgage on what Bill can sell in the baker's shop and the sandwich bar, they rank as collateral advantages. Although the basic purpose of a mortgage is to provide security for the repayment of the money lent by the mortgagee, in the case of commercial properties the lender may succeed in negotiating for some additional (collateral) advantage. For example, a brewery will often advance money on mortgage to the licensee of a public house, provided the borrower agrees to buy all his beer from the lending brewery. The orginal view of the courts was that all collateral advantages taken by a lender were void. This was because they were regarded as a disguised form of interest contravening the old usury laws: *Jennings* v *Ward* (1705) 2 Vern 520. In 1854, the last of the statutes dealing with usury was repealed and thereafter the attitude of the courts to collateral advantages began to change.

Today there is no rule of equity which prevents a lender from stipulating for a collateral advantage. Rather, equity endeavours to 'hold the ring' so far as collateral advantages are concerned. The current law on collateral advantages can be summarised in the following two propositions. First, a collateral advantage which exists until redemption can be valid (*Biggs* v *Hoddinott* [1898] 2 Ch 307), but will be void if it is oppressive or unconscionable: *Cityland and Property Holdings Ltd* v *Dabrah*. Second, a collateral advantage which exists beyond redemption is void (*Noakes* v *Rice* [1902] AC 24) unless it exists as an independent transaction: *Kreglinger* v *New Patagonia Meat and Cold Storage Co Ltd* [1914] AC 25.

Here Bill is required not to sell biscuits or chocolates in the baker's shop (the mortgaged property) 'so long as he owned it'. A collateral advantage which is limited in duration to the time of redemption is not inconsistent with the right to redeem and is therefore usually enforceable. However, here the collateral advantage is not so restricted because it is to apply so long as Bill owns the shop. Such a collateral advantage is void unless it exists as an *independent transaction*. A leading authority on this point is *Kreglinger* v *New Patagonia Meat and Cold Storage Co Ltd*. There a meat company mortgaged its property to a firm of woolbrokers. The mortgage was for a period of five years, though the mortgagors were free to repay it within the five years if they wanted. It was a term of the mortgage that the mortgagors would for a five-year period (irrespective of whether the mortgage ended within that time) offer their sheep's skins (a by-product of its meat business) to the mortgagees for purchase, who would offer the market price. The mortgagors redeemed after two years and they claimed to be able to offer their sheep's skins to persons other than the mortgagee. The House of Lords held that the mortgagors were still bound by the agreement as to the sheep's skins because the granting of the collateral advantage was a *separate contract* independent of the mortgage contract. The agreement was regarded as being reasonable in its terms (it was only to last for five years from the making of the mortgage). Accordingly, in *Kreglinger* the entire transaction was something more than a mere mortgage. The '*Kreglinger* principle' reflects the reality that today a mortgagor is not necessarily the traditional oppressed figure of the nineteenth century.

Whether in a given case a collateral advantage is the product of a separate transaction despite being concluded at the same time as the mortgage is a question of construction. Here it is submitted that the collateral advantage would not rank as an independent transaction – not least because it is to last so long as Bill owns the shop, whereas in *Kreglinger* it was only to last for five years from the making of the mortgage. Further, the collateral advantage may also fail on the additional ground that it is an unreasonable restraint of trade: *Esso Petroleum* v *Harper's Garage (Stourport) Ltd* [1968] AC 269.

Further, Bill is required not to sell biscuits or chocolates in the sandwich bar 'so long as he owned it'. A point of distinction between this collateral advantage and the former one is that the sandwich bar is not subject to the mortgage. Such an agreement which restricts Bill's freedom in the way he carries on his trade is likely to be declared void on the basis that it is not reasonably necessary to protect the mortgagee's interest.

These conclusions in respect of the collateral advantages are also pertinent to the postponement of the right to redeem. This is because if a postponement is coupled with a 'tie' between mortgagor and mortgagee which is void as being in restraint of trade then the postponement will also be void.

Finally, the mortgage in requiring Bill not to sell either property without giving Gus 'the chance of buying it for the best price that anyone else offered' is giving the mortgagee an option to buy both the mortgaged property and the non-mortgaged property. Equity will not allow a term which has the effect of preventing or limiting redemption. In *Samuel* v *Jarrah Timber and Wood Paving Corp* [1904] AC 323 the court held that a term in a mortgage which gives the mortgagee an option to purchase the mortgaged property was void even if it was not oppressive. However, once the mortgage has been made, equity will not interfere if subsequently the mortgagor gives the mortgagee such an option. In *Reeve* v *Lisle* [1902] AC 461 an option to buy granted to the mortgagee 12 days after the mortgage was entered into was upheld. The reason for the difference in approach is that in the first scenario the mortgagor is in the defenceless position of seeking a loan and equity will protect him, whereas in the second scenario equity's protection – after he has obtained the loan – is not required. Accordingly, on the authority of *Samuel* v *Jarrah Timber & Wood Paving Co* Gus's option in respect of the mortgaged property is clearly void and is not saved by the fact that Gus has to give 'the best price that anyone else offered'. The result of the exercise of the option would be that the mortgagee becomes the owner of the land, a result that is inconsistent with the right to redeem.

As to Gus's option to buy the sandwich bar (the non-mortgaged property) the position is not so clear cut. If, as seems to be the case, Gus and Bill are of equal bargaining strength, and if this option is deemed to be a separate agreement, it may be upheld. If on the other hand it is not so regarded then it would be void.

In conclusion, it is submitted that Bill would not be bound by the collateral advantages or the option to purchase the baker's shop (the mortgaged property) granted to the mortgagee and that he could redeem the mortgage earlier than provided for in the mortgage deed. However, in practice, before advising Bill to disregard these terms of the mortgage at the very least counsel's opinion on their validity should be sought.

QUESTION FOUR

Explain the ways in which legal and equitable mortgages of land may be created today, indicating any reforms you consider to be necessary.

University of London LLB Examination
(for External Students) Land Law June 1997 Q7

General Comment

A somewhat untypical essay question on mortgages which deals with a single aspect of the subject. It is essential to be fully conversant with the law on the creation of legal and equitable mortgages and to be able to identify its shortcomings. A good answer would include coverage of the Law Commission Report on Land Mortgages.

Skeleton Solution

Definition of a mortgage – *Samuel* v *Jarrah Timber & Wood Paving Corporation Ltd* – legal mortgage created by deed – two ways of creating a legal mortgage: by demise or by way of legal charge – methods of creating an equitable mortgage of a legal estate – mortgage of an equitable interest – process of creation cumbersome – consequences of recognising legal and equitable mortgages: plethora of legal and equitable interests exisiting in same piece of land, two different schemes of protection, complex rules for determining priorities of mortgages – Law Commission Report on Land Mortgages.

Suggested Solution

A mortgage is essentially a transaction whereby an interest in property, be it land, housing or business, is transferred to a mortgagee (lender) as security for the loan, subject to a right of redemption vested in the mortgagor (borrower). However, unlike the definition, the practicalities of mortgages are rather complex. In *Samuel* v *Jarrah Timber and Wood Paving Corporation Ltd* [1904] AC 323 Lord MacNaghten noted that 'no-one ever understood an English mortgage of real estate'.

A legal mortgage can only be created by deed in one of two ways and can only be created in respect of a legal estate: s85 LPA 1925. First, a legal mortgage can be created by demise for a term of years absolute. The mortgage is made in the form of a lease of the mortgagor's property with a proviso (known as the proviso for cesser on redemption) that the lease should be determined when the mortgage is redeemed, that is, when all the capital and interest are paid off. If the mortgage is of a freehold the term of the lease is usually 3,000 years, if of a leasehold then the mortgage is a sublease for about ten days less than the mortgagor's unexpired term. Subsequent mortgages are created by granting a lease (or sublease in the case of mortgages of leaseholds) for at lease one day longer than the previous mortgage. Secondly, a legal mortgage can be created by charge by deed expressed to be by way of legal mortgage: s87 LPA 1925. It is the more popular method of creation and is usually called a 'legal charge'. It is a simpler document than the mortgage by demise, but it imposes exactly the same rights on both mortgagor and mortgagee. Its main advantage is that freeholds and leaseholds can be mortgaged together in one document, which is not possible when the mortgage is by demise. A legal charge is a legal interest within s1(2)(c) LPA 1925. However, under the Land Registration Act 2002 mortgages of registered land can no longer be created by demise or sub-demise: s23(1) LRA 2002. Rather, the charge will be the only method of creating a mortgage over registered land.

English law does recognise the creation of equitable mortgages. An equitable mortgage may be of either the *legal estate* or an *equitable interest*. There are several ways of creating an equitable mortgage of the legal estate. An equitable mortgage arises where there is an agreement to create a mortgage. If the agreement is entered into after 26 September 1989 then it must be in writing and signed by the parties in order to meet the requirements of s2 of the Law of Property (Miscellaneous Provisions) Act 1989 (ie equitable mortgages do not have to be made by deed).

Formerly a deposit of title deeds with the intention that they were to be retained as a security for a loan created an equitable mortgage: *Russel v Russel* (1783) 1 Bro CC 269. The deposit of title deeds was treated as being an act of part performance (under s40 LPA 1925 no action could be brought upon any contract for the sale or other disposition of land or any interest therein unless it was in writing or evidenced by a memorandum in writing or a sufficient act of part performance). In this way an oral argeement coupled with a deposition of title deeds could give rise to an equitable mortgage. With the repeal of s40 LPA 1925 by s2 of the Law of Property (Miscellaneous Provisions) Act 1989 the law in this regard has now changed. No longer can a contract merely be evidenced in writing, it must be made in writing. Further, s2 of the 1989 Act has abolished the doctrine of part performance so far as it relates to land law. The repeal of s40 LPA 1925 by s2 of the 1989 Act has had the effect of bringing the centuries-old practice of creating an equitable mortgage by oral agreement coupled with deposit of title deeds to an end. In *United Bank of Kuwait plc v Sahib and Others* [1996] 3 All ER 215 the Court of Appeal held that the deposit of title deeds (or land certificate in the case of registered land) took effect as a contract to mortgage and fell within s2 of the 1989 Act. Since there was no written document here the mere deposit of the land certificate by way of security could not create a mortgage or charge. To create a valid equitable charge by a deposit of title deeds or the land certificate there had to be a written mortgage agreement meeting the requirements of s2 of the 1989 Act. Where a charge of a legal estate is not made by deed expressed to be by way of legal mortgage it can be equitable if it is made in writing and signed by the charger. To create such a charge it suffices if an intention to use the property as a security for the discharge of some debt or other obligation is expressed in writing.

As to the mortgage of an equitable interest, if the borrower only has an equitable interest (eg a life interest) then clearly he can only give an equitable mortgage.

The method of creating mortgages was simplified by the 1925 legislation. However, the whole process is still cumbersome. Legal mortgages no longer involve a conveyance of the fee simple but instead, as noted above, are created either by a demise for a term of years or by a legal charge. However, the fact that English law still recognises the creation of equitable mortgages means that the law of mortgages suffers from the same defects which were apparent in land law prior to the 1925 legislation, namely a plethora of interests both legal and equitable which can exist in the same piece of land.

Other consequences of recognising legal and equitable mortgages are: (i) two different schemes of protection; and (ii) complex rules for determining priorities of mortgages. Legal mortgagees either protect themselves by taking title deeds, registering legal charges or puisne mortgagees (C(i) land charge), whereas equitable mortgagees have to register general equitable charges (C(iii)). Where recognition is required for protection the normal rules apply making a mortgage void against a subsequent purchaser for want of registration. In consequence of the different types of mortgage, complex rules have evolved governing the determination of priorities between competing mortgages. Generally speaking, legal mortgages prevail over equitable, and the first in time has priority. Equitable mortgages are governed by the rule in *Dearle* v *Hall* (1828) 3 Russ 1 (as amended by ss138, 139 LPA 1925) which provides that priority depends upon the order in which notice of the mortgages is received by the owner of the legal estate.

The aforementioned criticisms of the law of mortgages led the Law Commission in its Working Paper (Land Mortgages Working Paper No 99) published in 1986 and in its 1991 Report (Law Com No 204) to recommend that all the existing methods of creating mortgages be abolished and replaced by a Formal Land Mortgage created by statute. Implementing the Commission's recommendation would have at least three main benefits. First, it would remedy the plethora of interests both legal and equitable which can exist at present in relation to the same piece of land. Secondly, the adoption of a single form of statutory mortgage would render the differing forms and methods of protection unnecessary. Thirdly, the adoption of a single statutory mortgage which must be registered would eradicate a lot of the problems which currently arise as to priorities between competing mortgages.

Note: this solution has been revised to take account of the coming into force of the Land Registration Act 2002.

QUESTION FIVE

'A mortgagee will be restrained from getting possession except where it is sought bona fide and reasonably for the purpose of enforcing the security and then only subject to such conditions as the court thinks fit to impose.'

To what extent is this an accurate statement of the present law?

University of London LLB Examination
(for External Students) Land Law June 1999 Q2

General Comment

A straightforward question which should present no difficulty to a candidate familiar with the subject matter. *Quennel* v *Maltby,* from which the quotation in the question is derived, must be discussed, as must *Ropaigealach* v *Barclays Bank plc* which is a decision adverse to mortgagors because it enables mortgagees to deprive mortgagors of their statutory protection.

Skeleton Solution

Two methods of creating a legal mortgage – mortgagee's right to possession – equity holds mortgagees in possession arguably to account – mortgagee's application to the court for possession: must not be made for an improper motive – statutory relief available to mortgagors: Consumer Credit Act 1974; AJAs 1970, 1973 – relief only available to mortgagors under AJAs where mortgagee seeks a possession order through the courts.

Suggested Solution

Section 85 of the Law of Property Act 1925 enacted that henceforth a mortgage of an estate shall only be capable of being effected at law either by a demise for a term of years absolute subject to a provision for cesser on redemption, or by a charge by deed expressed to be by way of a legal mortgage. Section 87 provided that where a legal mortgage of land is created by a charge by deed expressed to be by way of legal mortgage, the mortgagee shall have the same protection, powers and remedies as if the mortgage had been created by a demise for a term of years.

In the first instance the relationship of landlord and tenant is created between the mortgagor and the mortgagee with the latter being the tenant. In the second instance, although the relationship of landlord and tenant is not created between the parties, the mortgagee's rights are nevertheless the same.

It follows therefore that the mortgagee is entitled to possession of the mortgaged property, and this was acknowledged by Harman J in *Four-Maids Ltd* v *Dudley Marshall (Properties) Ltd* [1957] Ch 317:

'The right of the mortgagee to possession in the absence of some contract has nothing to do with default on the part of the mortgagor. The mortgagee may go into possession before the ink is dry on the mortgage unless there is something in the contract, express or by implication whereby he has contracted himself out of that right. He has the right because he has a legal term of years in the property or its statutory equivalent.'

Although this is a correct statement of the mortgagee's position, mortgagees are not interested in exercising that right, since the purpose of the mortgage is to provide the mortgagee with security for the loan and, as Harman J pointed out, there may be an express or implied contract where the mortgagee has contracted himself out of that right.

Apart from the fact that mortgagees, in the absence of default on the mortgagor's part, are not interested in taking possession, equity imposes rigorous obligations on those who do, as illustrated by *White* v *City of London Brewery Co* (1889) 42 Ch D 237. In that case the tenant of a lease of a public house mortgaged the lease to the brewery to provide security for a loan from the brewers. When the tenant defaulted on the repayments, the mortgagee exercised its right to take possession. It then leased the public house to another tenant and extracted from him a covenant that he would purchase all his liquors exclusively from the brewers. The onerous nature of this covenant was reflected in the rent, which was lower than it would otherwise have been had the lease not contained the covenant. As a result there was less money available to the mortgagees to discharge the mortgage debt. The mortgagor sued the brewery in respect of the difference between the rent actually recovered and that which it could have obtained by omitting the covenant, and the Court of Appeal upheld his claim in deciding that the mortgagees were accountable for the difference. In practice therefore mortgagees are generally only interested in taking possession of the property with a view to selling it with vacant possession to enforce their security as a result of the mortgagor's default.

If a mortgagee seeks possession through the courts, he will find that his application is scrutinised to ensure that he is genuinely seeking possession with a view to enforcing his security, and that he is also acting in good faith. The court's attitude and approach can be seen in *Quennel* v *Maltby* [1979] 1 WLR 318 which demonstrates the court's willingness to exercise its equitable jurisdiction to give relief to a mortgagor where it considers that to be appropriate.

In that case Quennel (Q) had mortgaged his house to the bank. He eventually let the house to a tenant (Maltby) who had statutory security of tenure under the Rent Acts. Q could not obtain possession against the tenant, but since the protected tenancy was not binding on the bank Q asked it to bring possession proceedings against the tenant. The object of this was to enable Q to sell the house with vacant possession. The bank, however, refused to co-operate with Q. Q then pursuaded his wife to pay the mortgage monies to the bank in return for its transfer to her of the mortgage, so that she became the mortgagee in place of the bank. As a mortgagee she too was not bound by the protected tenancy, and she sought possession against Maltby. Although she succeeded at first instance, the Court of Appeal allowed Maltby's appeal. Lord Denning pointed out that the object of the manoeuvre was not to enforce her security but to overcome the protection which Maltby enjoyed under the Rent Acts. Explaining the position he said 'a mortgagee will be restrained from getting possession except where it is sought bona fide and reasonably for the purpose of enforcing the security and then only subject to such conditions as the court thinks fit to impose', although he pointed out that this would not apply where the mortgagor was in default. He went on: 'but so long as the interest is paid and there is nothing outstanding, equity has ample power to restrain any unjust use of the right to possession'. In addition to equitable protection, statutory relief is also available to the mortgagor.

Firstly, where the mortgage falls within the provisions of the Consumer Credit Act 1974 the court is empowered to suspend a possession order (s135), and in addition allow the mortgagor to discharge the arrears by reasonable payments, taking into account his financial circumstances: s129.

Where the mortgaged property is a dwelling house, relief is available to the mortgagor under the Administration of Justice Act (AJA) 1970. Under that statute, where a mortgagee brings an action for possession, the mortgagor may ask the court to adjourn the application, suspend any possession order it may make or postpone its execution: s36 AJA 1970. However, the court's powers are limited to the situation where it appears that 'the mortgagor is likely to be able within a reasonable period to pay any sums due under the mortgage': s36.

Reference must be made to s8(1) Administration of Justice Act 1973. Some mortgages contain a provision that in the event of arrears of mortgage instalments, the whole mortgage debt shall become due and payable. Section 36 did not really apply to that situation, because it is only applicable where 'the mortgagor is likely to be able within a reasonable period to pay any sums due under the mortgage' and clearly a mortgagor who had become liable to pay the whole mortgage debt could not fall within that wording. To provide for that situation s8(1) AJA 1973 enacted that the phrase 'sums due' should be construed as referring to the actual instalments in arrears and not the whole mortgage debt.

The phrase 'reasonable period' confers upon the court a flexibility of approach, but the court must consider the interests of both parties: *Cheltenham & Gloucester Building Society v Norgan* [1996] 1 WLR 343. It is possible for a reasonable period to be construed as the whole mortgage term: *First Middlesborough Trading v Mortgage Co Ltd* (1973) 28 P & CR 69. Each case will be considered on its merits, and the courts have declined to lay down firms guidelines as to how it will exercise its powers: *Cheltenham & Gloucester Building Society v Grant* (1994) 26 HLR 703. It is not necessary (for the application of s36) for the mortgagor to be in default: *Western Bank Ltd v Schindler* [1977] Ch 1.

Section 36 only affords the statutory relief to a mortgagor where the mortgagee seeks possession by means of a court order: *Ropaigealach v Barclays Bank plc* [2000] 1 QB 263. This case enables a mortgagee to deprive a mortgagor of the statutory protection afforded by the Administration of Justice Acts.

In that case the mortgagee did not obtain a court order for possession before sale and the mortgagor argued that under s36 he was obliged to so. Had he done so the mortgagor would have sought the statutory relief provided by that section. In the event he was deprived of that opportunity. The Court of Appeal held that a mortgagee was under no obligation to seek a court order entitling him to possession. In this case, the mortgagee entered by peaceful possession and he was entitled to do so. There was nothing in the section compelling him to seek a court order first. In the result the mortgagor's submission failed.

This decision is a serious set-back for mortgagors, because it enables mortgagees to deprive mortgagors of the relieving provision of s36. Henry LJ expressed the need for reform but it remains to be seen if the legislature will respond.

Subject to the decision in that case the quotation in the question may be said to be a reasonably accurate statement of the present law, as embodied in *Quennel v Maltby* (from which it is derived) and of the statutory provisions and their application, as illustrated above.

QUESTION SIX

In 1990 Ken, a poultry farmer, needed to raise £100,000 to invest in his business. He found it difficult to borrow such a large sum, but in the end Bob, the owner of a local farm-supply business, agreed to lend him that amount secured by a mortgage of the farm containing the following terms: (i) repayment was to be made by half-yearly instalments of £5,000 over 20 years, (ii) Bob was granted an option to purchase Ken's farm at market value, (iii) Ken was to purchase all his farm equipment from or through Bob. Recently Ken has discovered that he can raise money on much more attractive terms and he wants to redeem the mortgage.

To what extent is Ken bound by its terms?

University of London LLB Examination
(for External Students) Land Law June 2000 Q8

General Comment

A classic problem on mortgages which should occasion no difficulty to a candidate reasonably familiar with the relevant material. Although the problem is concerned mainly with the application of equitable principles, the common law point on restraint of trade should not be overlooked.

Skeleton Solution

Postponement of redemption – the rate of interest: premium – the Consumer Credit Act 1974: extortionate credit bargains – option to purchase: 'once a mortgage, always a mortgage' – covenant to purchase equipment: collateral advantages; collateral advantages extending beyond redemption date; can be an independent transaction extending beyond redemption date; covenants in restraint of trade contrary to common law.

Suggested Solution

Is Ken bound by the terms of the mortgage which he has entered into with Bob? Each term will be examined in turn.

i) The loan of £100,000 is to be repaid by half-yearly instalments of £5,000 spread over 20 years, making a total repayment of £200,000. The rate of interest is not expressed.

    This term raises several issues. First, consider the repayment period of 20 years. The effect of this is that Ken cannot redeem the mortgage before 20 years has elapsed. Should he wish to redeem before the expiry of the 20-year period, can he ask equity to relieve him of the obligation imposed by the term? Equity's approach to this question is revealed in *Knightsbridge Estates Trust Ltd v Byrne* [1939] Ch 441. Greene MR, giving judgment in the Court of Appeal, emphasised that the test to be applied was not to ask if the term was reasonable, but whether there had been any unconscionable or oppressive behaviour on the part of the mortgagee resulting in the inclusion of the term in the mortgage. In that case the repayment period extended over a 40-year period. The Court declined to interfere because the mortgage was a commercial transaction made between commercial men of equal bargaining power, and there was no unconscionable or oppressive conduct by the mortgagee.

    Has the mortgagee, in this case Bob, conducted himself in that manner? There is no evidence that he has, and in the absence of any such conduct Ken cannot obtain relief from equity. There is nothing on the facts to suggest that the parties did not enjoy equal bargaining power. It has to be remembered that Ken freely entered into the contract with Bob, and equity will not allow him to resile from his bargain simply because he considers, at a later date, that he made an unreasonable bargain.

    It can be said, therefore, that although equity has developed the maxim that it will not suffer any clogs or fetters of the equity of redemption, this does not mean it will not allow postponement of redemption. It will only interfere if the mortgagee has been guilty of some morally reprehensible behaviour inducing the postponement clause.

    The second aspect of this term which must be considered is the total amount Ken has committed himself to repaying. The loan itself was for £100,000 but he has agreed to pay double that amount, namely £200,000, which seems excessive.

    There are two cases on the point which can be usefully examined. In *Multiservice Bookbinding Ltd v Marden* [1978] 2 WLR 535 the plaintiff mortgagor mortgaged its property to the defendant mortgagee for a loan of £36,000, which was to be repaid at the end of a 10-year period. In order to protect himself from inflation the mortgagee stipulated, and the mortgagor agreed, that capital and interest should be index-linked to the Swiss franc. During the 10-year period the pound's value against the Swiss franc fell heavily, with the result that at the end of the period the mortgagor owed the mortgagee a total of £133,000. The mortgagor contended before Browne-Wilkinson J that the term was unreasonable and should be declared void. Browne-Wilkinson J agreed that the mortgagee had made a hard bargain and that the term was unreasonable but, as he pointed out, the test for the term's validity in 'the eyes of equity' was not one of reasonableness. The true test was to ask if there had been any oppressive or morally reprehensible behaviour by the mortgagee, and he found that there had been none. The mortgagor company was operated by businessmen who had entered into the bargain with their eyes open and with the benefit of independent advice. Accordingly, he rejected the mortgagor's contention.

The facts of *Multiservice Bookbinding Ltd* v *Marden* differ markedly from those of *Cityland and Property (Holdings) Ltd* v *Dabrah* [1968] Ch 166, while the repayment terms in *Cityland* have a similarity with the instant case. Dabrah mortgaged his house to the plaintiff mortgagee for £2,900. The interest rate was not expressed but the repayment term provided that the total sum to be paid by the mortgagor was £4,553, payable by monthly instalments spread over six years. This was £1,653 higher than the loan, and Dabrah argued that this was an unlawful premium of 57 per cent which was unconscionable and oppressive. The court agreed, because the unequal bargaining powers between the parties was in marked contrast to the position of the parties in the *Multiservice* case. The court held that the mortgagee was only entitled to interest at the rate of seven per cent on £2,900.

Although the final sum payable by Ken was not expressed it is easily calculated at being £200,000, which provides a point of comparison with *Cityland*. Obviously there is the other similarity that there is a formidable premium. Can Ken hope for the same result as was reached in *Cityland*? It would appear not, since there is no evidence of unconscionable behaviour by Bob and nothing to suggest there was unequal bargaining power between Ken and Bob.

There is a further avenue which Ken can explore. The Consumer Credit Act 1974 provides that a mortgagor may apply to the court to be relieved from an 'extortionate credit bargain', which is defined by s138 of the statute as one which requires a debtor or his relative to make payments which are grossly exorbitant, or otherwise grossly contravene ordinary principles of fair dealing. If Ken made an application under the statute it would be for the creditor, Bob, to prove that the payment was not exorbitant: s171(2). The court would take into account the matters referred to in s138.

There are not enough facts available in the question to predict the outcome of an application by Ken, and further investigation of the matters referred to in s138 would be necessary before advising Ken further on this point.

ii) Ken granted to Bob an option to purchase the farm, which is the mortgaged property, at market value.

In *Samuel* v *Jarrah Timber and Wood Paving Corporation Ltd* [1904] AC 323 the mortgagor mortgaged debenture stock to the mortgagee to secure a loan of £5,000.

A term in the mortgage gave the mortgagee the option to purchase all or any of the stock within 12 months. The House of Lords held that the option was void, being in breach of the maxim 'once a mortgage, always a mortgage'. This means, as Lord Lindley explained: 'that no contract made between the mortgagor and mortgagee ... as part of the mortgage transaction ... can be valid if it prevents the mortgagor from getting back his property on paying off what is due on his security'. The mortgagor's right to redeem is an essential characteristic of a mortgage, and any term which is inconsistent with that characteristic is void. Another way of understanding the maxim is to appreciate that equity will not allow the mortgage transaction to be converted into something else, eg a contract for sale and purchase.

Applying this authority here, the option to purchase would be void and Bob could not enforce it against Ken. It should be noticed that this is so even in the absence of oppressive or unconscionable conduct by the mortgagee.

iii) The last term for consideration is Ken's undertaking to purchase all his farm equipment from or through Bob. This is what is known as a collateral advantage, eg one which gives a benefit to a mortgagee in addition to the interest on the loan. Since the repeal of the usury laws in 1854, equity has permitted mortgagees to stipulate for collateral advantages as part of the mortgage transaction. Equity's approach was summarised by Lord Parker in *Kreglinger* v *New Patagonia Meat and Cold Storage Co Ltd* [1914] AC 25: a collateral advantage will be invalid if it is unconscionable or if it clogs the equitable right to redeem. It must be noticed that the term which Ken and Bob have agreed is not limited to the duration of the mortgage, but is for an indefinite period. This means that Ken will remain liable under the term even after the mortgage has been redeemed. In order to escape liability from this indefinite obligation, Ken should seek to rely on *Noakes & Co Ltd* v *Rice* [1902] AC 24. In that case Rice, the mortgagor, mortgaged his lease to Noakes & Co, the mortgagee, to secure a loan and undertook to purchase his liquor exclusively from Noakes, who was a brewer, both during the mortgage term and thereafter until the lease expired in 1923. The House of Lords held that the obligation ceased to bind the mortgagor once the mortgage had been redeemed. Lord Davey held that the maxim 'once a mortgage, always a mortgage' was applicable and that a mortgagee could not make any stipulation which prevented a mortgagor from getting back his property when he redeemed in the condition it was in when he had mortgaged it. The term (collateral advantage) he explained is part of the mortgage, and necessarily comes to an end when the loan is repaid.

However, Bob may have a counter argument. He could argue that, although the term was included in the mortgage document, it was nevertheless a separate and independent transaction with the result that it continued to bind Ken even after the mortgage had been redeemed. This was successfully argued in *Kreglinger* v *New Patagonia Meat and Cold Storage Co Ltd*. In that case, there was a mortgage for five years, but with the provision that it could be redeemed before that period had elapsed. Contained in the mortgage was another term under which the mortgagors would, for a five-year period, offer their sheep skins (a by-product of the business) to the mortgagees for purchase at the market price. The mortgagors redeemed after two years and then claimed that the option ended with the mortgage. The House of Lords held that, as a matter of construction, the granting of the option was a separate contract independent of the mortgage, and in consequence remained binding after redemption for the full five-year period. Without knowing the wording of the term in this case, which would have to be read in the context of the mortgage as a whole, it is impossible to say if Bob would be successful in this contention.

It is possible that this covenant is one that could be construed at common law as contrary to public policy, because it amounts to an unreasonable restraint of trade. It must be noted that the common law test is not concerned with unconscionable or oppressive behaviour, but with the reasonableness of the covenant. In *Alec Lobb (Garages) Ltd* v *Total Oil (GB) Ltd* [1985] 1 WLR 173 the court laid down guidelines: if the restraint was to apply for a period not longer than five years, it is presumed to be reasonable. If it is for a longer period, then it is presumed to be unreasonable. Each case, however, is to be considered on its merits. Again, there are not enough facts in the question to discuss the issue further, but it is an avenue which Ken should be advised to explore.

Chapter 11

Adverse Possession

11.1 Introduction

11.2 Key points

11.3 Key cases and statutes

11.4 Questions and suggested solutions

11.1 Introduction

It is always important for students to be fully conversant with the land law syllabus they are studying and, where relevant, the particular emphasis of the tutorial programme they are undertaking. This is particularly pertinent so far as adverse possession is concerned since it tends not to be a major feature of a number of internal undergraduate degree programmes. However, it is more prominent in land law courses run by external examining bodies. Accordingly, it is advisable for students to determine, if possible, what weight is given to this topic in their land law syllabus. Some understanding of adverse possession will be required in most courses. The key recent development in this area is the Land Registration Act 2002. The pre-Act law on adverse posession was deemed to be unsatisfactory and it has been replaced with an entirely new substantive system applicable only to registered land.

11.2 Key points

Pre-Land Registration Act 2002

Below is a summary of the law which applied prior to the coming into force of the Land Registration Act 2002 on 13 October 2003. This law still applies, as appropriate, to unregistered land.

a) i) Effect – s15(1) of the Limitation Act 1980: 'No action shall be brought ... to recover land after the expiration of 12 years from the date on which the right of action accrued'.

   ii) Time runs from when another person takes adverse possession: see Sch 1, para 1 of the 1980 Act – 'Date of the dispossession or discontinuance'.

b) i) Meaning of adverse possession – takes away but does not give. Possession inconsistent with the title of the true owner.

ii) *Wallis's Cayton Bay Holiday Camp Ltd* v *Shell-Mex & BP Ltd* [1974] 3 WLR 387.

iii) Leaseholds – time only runs against reversioner when lease ends. Unregistered land.

iv) *Fairweather* v *St Marylebone Property Co Ltd* [1963] AC 510. But surrender lease then landlord may evict squatter: cf *Spectrum* below – in registered land.

c) i) Title acquired by adverse possessor.

ii) Title of former owner extinguished but not transferred to squatter. Possession must be adverse and not under a contract. *Hyde* v *Pearce* [1982] 1 All ER 1029.

iii) Thus remedy barred and owner cannot recover through legal proceedings. Section 17 LA 1980. But no transfer of title.

iv) Exception – registered land: title not extinguished but proprietor deemed to hold on trust for adverse possessor. Section 75 LRA 1925. Cf *Fairweather* above; *Spectrum Investment Co* v *Holmes* [1981] 1 All ER 6.

(If squatter registers his rights not defeated by subsequent surrender of lease by original tenant to landlord.)

d) i) No hypothetical licence

ii) Licence suggested by Lord Denning MR in *Wallis's* case (above) but now denied by s15(6) and Sch 1, Part 1, para 8(4) LA 1980.

iii) Effect: does adverse possession = trespass to land? Presume yes.

e) Proof of intention: *Powell* v *McFarlane* (1979) 38 P & CR 452, *Buckinghamshire County Council* v *Moran* [1989] 2 All ER 225

Note the potential comparison between the effects of adverse possession in registered and unregistered land.

f) i) Effect of registered land

ii) s70(1)(f) LRA 1925 – overriding interest

iii) s75 LRA 1925 – rectification of the register s82 LRA 1925

iv) *Re Chowood's Registered Land* [1933] Ch 574

Land Registration Act 2002

a) The former law on adverse possession has been replaced with an entirely new substantive system applicable only to registered land.

b) The effect of the new arrangements is to make it much more difficult for a squatter to obtain title to registered land than it was under the pre-Act law.

c) A registered proprietor's title is not lost through mere lapse of time.

d) Onus is on the squatter to take action if he wants to obtain title to registered land.

e) New regime follows the principle that registration should confer title rather than possession.

f) An application to be registered as proprietor can be made after a period of ten years' adverse possession (ie there is a separate limitation period of ten years for registered land).

g) Upon receipt of such an application, the Land Registry will notify the registered proprietor and other interested parties of it and they can object by serving a counter-notice within a prescribed period.

h) If no counter-notice is served the squatter is registered as proprietor.

i) If a counter-notice is served, the squatter's application is dismissed unless he can establish one of the three limited grounds that could entitle him to be registered.

j) The three grounds are set out in para 5 of Sch 6 to the Act. They are as follows:

   i) It would be unconscionable because of an equity by estoppel for the proprietor to seek to dispossess the applicant and the circumstances are such that the applicant ought to be registered as proprietor.

   ii) The applicant is for some other reason entitled to be registered as proprietor.

   iii) The land to which the application relates is adjacent to land belonging to the applicant, the exact boundary line has not been determined and for at least ten years the applicant or a predecessor reasonably believed the land belonged to him and the land was registered more than a year before the application.

k) Where an application is rejected a further application can be made if the applicant is in adverse possession for a further period of two years.

l) The law relating to unregistered land is not affected by the Act.

11.3 Key cases and statutes

* *Buckinghamshire County Council* v *Moran* [1989] 2 All ER 225
  Intention to possess essential to acquire title by adverse possession – such an intention could usually be inferred from acts of physical possession

* *Earnshaw* v *Hartley* (1999) The Times 29 April
  Para 9 of Sch 1 to the 1980 Act was not to be given a literal interpretation

* *J A Pye (Oxford) Ltd* v *Graham* [2002] 3 WLR 221
  The House of Lords concluded that two requirements had to be satisfied in order to establish adverse possession: first, a squatter had to exercise a sufficient degree of physical custody and control (ie factual possession); second, the squatter had to have an intention to possess the land – the requisite intention was to possess on his

own behalf and to exclude the world at large, including the paper title owner, so far as was reasonably practicable – clarified meaning of 'action' in s15(1) of the 1980 Act

- *James* v *Williams* (1999) The Times 13 April
  An executor de son tort could be a constructive trustee for the purposes of s21(1)(b) of the 1980 Act

- *Wallis's Cayton Bay Holiday Camp Ltd* v *Shell-Mex & BP Ltd* [1975] QB 94
  Possession by itself was not enough to give title – it had to be adverse possession – there had to be something in the form of an ouster of the true owner by the wrongful possessor

- Land Registration Act 2002, Part IX

- Limitation Act 1980, ss5, 15, 17, 18, 21 and 29

11.4 Questions and suggested solutions

Analysis of questions

In those courses where adverse possession is part of the syllabus the students may encounter adverse possession in two types of question. First, where it is a tailpiece to a question dealing primarily with another area of land law. Secondly, a question on adverse possession in its own right (only likely in courses where it is given sufficient weight in the syllabus to justify a full question). In this regard the possibilities could include inviting candidates to look at the fundamental reason for its existence by asking: 'Why do we need adverse possession?' The answer will be found in an article of the same title by Martin Dockray in the Conveyancer and Property Lawyer for July/August 1985 at p272.

QUESTION ONE

In 1979 Miss Sprigg purchased Oaktree Cottage (registered land). The garden of the cottage backed on to a field from which it was separated by an old wooden fence. The field formed part of the Blackacre Estate whose owner, Lord Blacktown, intended to develop it as a caravan site for summer tourists. In 1980 Miss Sprigg removed part of the fence and began cultivating vegetables on part of the field; in 1981 she built a chicken coop on the field and reared chickens there; in 1982 she fenced in that part of the field that she was using to protect her chickens and vegetables from thieves and animals. In 1984 Miss Sprigg died leaving the cottage to her sister, Maud. Maud continued to grow vegetables and keep chickens on the enclosed part of the field. In 1991 Lord Blacktown sold the field to Sunshine Caravans and they wrote to Maud informing her that they proposed to develop the field as a caravan site and requiring her to vacate the field. Maud ignored the letter and in 1994 Sunshine Caravans commenced proceedings for possession.

Advise Maud.

University of London LLB Examination
(for External Students) Land Law June 1994 Q3

General Comment

This question was probably not one of the more popular ones on the paper as adverse possession (with which the question is concerned) is an area of land law which tends not to feature significantly in student revision schedules.

Skeleton Solution

Meaning of adverse possession – s15 Limitation Act 1980 – significance of fencing – successive squatters: aggregation of periods of adverse possession by different owners – significance of communication from paper owner: *Buckinghamshire County Council* v *Moran* – registering a caution: s70(1)(f) Land Registration Act 1925 – what action should squatter take in face of possession proceedings?

Suggested Solution

Adverse possession, with which this question is concerned, means possession inconsistent with the title of the true owner. Section 15 of the Limitation Act 1980 sets a 12-year period for the recovery of land. It provides that 'No action shall be brought to recover land after the expiration of 12 years from the date on which the right of action accrued'. Here it will be necessary to consider the following main issues: (a) when did adverse possession by Miss Sprigg commence? (b) successive periods of adverse possession, ie that of Miss Sprigg first and then Maud; (c) the significance of the communication from Sunshine Caravans who bought the field from Lord Blacktown; and (d) what action Maud can take in the face of possession proceedings commenced by Sunshine Caravans? Each of these issues will be considered in turn.

In 1979, Miss Sprigg purchased Oaktree Cottage which is registered land. Evidence of title takes the form of a register and filed plan issued by the Land Registry which will mirror the documentary title prior to first registration. On the facts given, the registered title will include the back garden up to the adjoining field. When, in 1980, Miss Sprigg removed part of the fence and went onto part of the field to cultivate vegetables she went onto land beyond her registered title and began to treat it as her own. As previously mentioned, s15 Limitation Act 1980 provides that no action can be brought by the true owner to recover any land after the expiration of 12 years from the date on which the right of action accrued to the plaintiff or the person through whom he claims. Time begins to run as soon as (a) the owner has been dispossessed or has discontinued his possession; and (b) adverse possession has been taken by some other person. Miss Sprigg must have had an intention to exclude the owner as well as other people: see *Powell* v *McFarlane* (1979) 38 P & CR 452. Adverse possession is a question of fact in which circumstances such as the nature of the land and the way in which the land is enjoyed must be taken into account. In *Wallis's Cayton Bay Holiday Camp* v *Shell-Mex &*

BP Ltd [1975] QB 94 Lord Denning said that just because some other person enters onto land and uses it for some seasonal purpose like growing vegetables was not adverse to the owner. Accordingly, on the facts it is doubtful, before the fencing in 1982, that acts sufficient to show and establish factual possession and an intention to possess to the exclusion of all others exist. Enclosure is the strongest possible evidence of adverse possession but it is not indispensable: see *Seddon v Smith* (1877) 36 LT 168. It is submitted therefore that on the facts time began to run in 1982.

In 1984, Miss Sprigg died leaving Oaktree Cottage to her sister Maud. If a squatter who has not barred the true owner sells the land he can give the purchaser a right to the land which is as good as his own. This rule also applies to devises or gifts of the land by the squatter. In each case the person taking the squatter's interest can add the squatter's period of possession to his own. Here, Maud can add Miss Sprigg's two-year adverse possession to her own.

Turning to the position of the paper owner, it would seem that 12 years have elapsed since 1982 when the fencing was carried out by Miss Sprigg. However, in 1991 – before 12 years had elapsed – Maud received a letter from Sunshine Caravans informing her that they propose to develop the field as a caravan site and requiring her to vacate the field. It must be shown that the claimant has accepted the assertion of the right by the paper owner and the mere assertion alone by the true paper owner of a claim to possession in land, contained in a letter sent to the squatter, is not sufficient to prevent the squatter obtaining title by adverse possession. Accordingly, if Maud continued to use the land in spite of her knowledge of Sunshine Caravans' intentions this would not be a bar to her continuing to acquire title by adverse possession, provided she maintained her intention to possess the land: see *Buckinghamshire County Council v Moran* [1989] 2 All ER 225.

What action should Maud take in the face of the possession proceedings? If Maud is confident that she has established factual possession and intention she could defend the possession proceedings and assert her squatter's title. She is in possession and should not move off the land unless she is willing to do so. Sunshine Caravans may wish to settle the proceedings and purchase her interest in the land. Maud could consider registering a caution against first registration in respect of the additional land which is undoubtedly an unregistered title. If it were in fact registered her occupation would be an overriding interest protected by s70(1)(f) Land Registration Act 1925. Maud could make application to the Land Registry for title to the land on the basis of her adverse possession. However, in view of the commencement of proceedings by Sunshine Caravans the Land Registry would not proceed with her application until the outcome of the court proceedings were known.

Finally, it is important to note the raison d'etre of the Limitation Act 1980. It is that those who go to sleep upon their claims should not be helped by the courts in recovering their property and that there should be an end to litigation.

Note: candidates had to consider this question in June 1994.

QUESTION TWO

In 1985 Len granted a twenty-year lease of Greenacre (registered land) to Thomas, Thomas covenanting inter alia to pay a quarterly rent of UKP5,000 and not to use the land for business purposes. The lease contains a right of re-entry for breach of covenant. What remedies does Len have and against whom if (i) in 1999 Thomas assigned his lease to Alfred and Len has received no rent since mid 1998, or (ii) in 1999 Thomas granted a sub-lease of Greenacre to Steve and Steve has started operating a mail-order business from the land, or (iii) in 1986 Sid went into adverse possession of a small part of Greenacre where he is now proposing to open a garage?

University of London LLB Examination
(for External Students) Land Law June 1999 Q4

General Comment

The date that the lease was granted is significant because in this case the date (1985) means that the Landlord and Tenant (Covenants) Act 1995 (LT(C)A) does not apply, but nevertheless there are two provisions in the Act which operate retrospectively and do therefore apply here. The question is based on leasehold law, but unexpectedly requires the candidate to discuss another part of the syllabus, namely adverse possession. Candidates should be prepared for this approach by the examiner.

Skeleton Solution

i) Passing of the burden of the covenant to Alfred – privity of estate between Len and Alfred – Len's remedies against Alfred – retrospective provisions of LT(C)A 1995.

ii) No privity of estate between Len and sub-tenant Steve – Len may invoke *Tulk* v *Moxhay* against Steve – Steve bound by the covenant: s23(1)(a) LRA 1925 – Len could forfeit the head lease: s146 LPA 1925.

iii) Limitation Act 1980 – registered title: s75(1) LRA 1925 – *Central London Commercial Estates Ltd* v *Kato Kagaku Ltd*.

Suggested Solution

The lease in this case was granted in 1985 and therefore the Landlord and Tenant (Covenants) Act 1995, apart from certain retrospective provisions, does not apply. We are asked to advise Len in the following situations.

i) In 1999 Thomas assigned his lease to Alfred and the rent has been in arrears since mid 1998.

    The first question to consider is whether the burden of the rental covenant passed to Alfred when Thomas assigned the lease to him. It was established in *Spencer's Case* (1583) 5 Co Rep 16a that the benefit and burden of a tenant's covenant will pass to an assignee of the lease providing they touch and concern the land. A covenant to pay rent is such a covenant: *Parker* v *Webb* (1693) 3 Salk 5 and its burden will have passed to Alfred on assignment.

Len has the benefit of the covenant since he is the original covenantee, and in order to enforce the covenant against Alfred he must show that the relationship of privity of estate exists between them. Privity of estate exists between those parties who enjoy the same estates as were held by the original parties. Since the lease was assigned to Alfred he now enjoys the estate once held by Thomas, and accordingly the relationship exists between Len and Alfred, with Alfred being the tenant in place of Thomas. Alfred will only be responsible for the arrears which has accumulated since he became the tenant. He will not be liable for any arrears accumulated prior to assignment.

The next step is to examine Len's remedies against Alfred, and they are as follows:

a) he may sue Alfred: the Limitation Act 1980 states that not more than six years' arrears can be recoverable but the prohibition is not applicable here;

b) he may levy distress on Alfred's chattels, but this is not a very effective remedy;

c) he may forfeit the lease. This remedy is only available if there is a forfeiture clause in the lease; this lease does contain such a clause and accordingly this remedy is available to Len. However, Len must be advised that a measure of relief is available to Alfred under the Common Law Procedure Act 1852, which provides that if the tenant pays all the arrears and costs before judgment, the forfeiture proceedings initiated by Len will be automatically stayed. Relief is also available to Alfred after judgment, but only if he pays all the arrears and costs within six months of the judgment date. If he does so, then he may apply to the court to re-instate him as tenant. This, however, is at the court's discretion and if Len has re-let the property in the meantime this will not be possible. Alfred can only take advantage of the Act if at least six month's rent is in arrears. It must be remembered that the provisions of s146 LPA 1925 relating to the preliminary service of a notice before forfeiture proceedings do not apply to rental covenants: s146(11) LPA. We do not know if that is the case here.

Len may also sue Thomas not only for his arrears (which had accumulated up to the time of assignment) but also for Alfred's arrears. This is because when the lease was granted the relationship of privity of contract was created between Len and Thomas for the duration of the lease. The effect of this contractual relationship is that Thomas remains liable to Len for all rental payments until the termination of the lease, even after he has assigned the lease. The LT(C)A 1995 has remedied this unsatisfactory state of affairs, but it is not applicable in this case because this lease was created before the Act came into force. However, although Thomas remains exposed to proceedings by Len, there are two retrospective provisions in the Act which provide him with a measure of relief.

Section 17(2) provides that an original tenant shall not be liable under a covenant to pay any amount due in respect of a fixed charge payable under the covenant unless, within six months of the charge becoming due, the landlord serves upon the tenant a notice informing him that the charge is due and specifying the amount the landlord intends to recover from him. The notice must be in the prescribed form and the expression 'fixed charge' includes rent and any service charges.

If the landlord does not serve the notice within the prescribed time limit he loses his right to recover. Accordingly, if Len does not observe the time limit he will lose his right to recover Alfred's arrears from Thomas. He will still of course be able to recover Thomas' arrears subject to the Limitation Act 1980.

The other retrospective provision available to Thomas confers upon him the right to an overriding lease. Previously, if a tenant in Thomas' position was successfully sued by the original landlord for an assignee's arrears of rent, he was in the unfortunate position of having to pay rent for a lease he no longer had. Now, however, if Thomas pays Alfred's arrears, he is entitled to a grant from Len of an overriding lease: s19. This is a lease of Len's reversion, containing the same covenants as the lease, which must be for the same length of time as the lease with an added three days. On the grant of the overriding lease, Thomas will in effect become Alfred's landlord and be able to sue him for Alfred's arrears and even forfeit the lease. If he forfeits the lease he will be able to take possession himself or assign it. Apart from the statutory provisions, if Thomas is compelled to pay Len for Alfred's arrears he may sue Alfred in quasi-contract under the rule in *Moule v Garrett* (1872) LR 7 Ex 101.

ii) During the time that he was the tenant Thomas granted a sub-lease of Greenacre to Steve, and Steve has commenced operating a business therefrom. There is a covenant in the lease under which Thomas covenanted not to use the land for business purposes.

Can Len take proceedings against Steve? The conditions necessary for the passing of the burden of a tenant's covenant have already been discussed. Applying those conditions here, although this is a covenant which touches and concerns the land, the result is that there is no privity of estate between Len and Steve, because Steve does not hold the same estate as Thomas. Thomas still retains his estate – the lease. What Thomas had done is to carve a sub-lease out of that lease for Steve. He has not transferred or assigned the lease. The burden has not therefore passed to Steve under the rules discussed.

However, it is possible for Len to proceed against Steve by another route, namely the principle confirmed in *Tulk v Moxhay* (1848) 2 Ph 774 and as developed in subsequent cases. It would be inappropriate to examine its application here in detail, but one or two points should be mentioned. Len's reversion would constitute sufficient interest in the land to satisfy the requirement that the covenantee (Len) must own land capable of benefiting from the covenant: *Hall v Ewin* (1887) 37 Ch D 74. Normally, the enforcement of restrictive covenants depends on notice: in the case of unregistered land post 1925 restrictive covenants are registrable as a land charge class D(ii) under the Land Charges Act (LCA) 1972. However, restrictive covenants made between a landlord and tenant are not so registrable: s2(5) LCA 1972.

In the case of registered title, which is what we are dealing with here, restrictive covenants made between landlord and tenant cannot be protected by a notice entered on the landlord's register of title: s50(1) Land Registration Act (LRA) 1925. However, Steve will nevertheless be bound by the covenant because under s23(1)(a) LRA a sub-tenant takes the land subject to express and implied covenants in the lease. That being the case Len could apply to the court for an injunction against Steve prohibiting him from operating the mail order business.

As an alternative Len could consider forfeiting Thomas' lease, which would result in the extinction of Steve's sub-lease. This is only available if there is a forfeiture clause in the lease and this requirement is satisfied in this case.

Before commencing forfeiture proceedings Len must first serve on Thomas a notice under s146 LPA 1925:

a) specifying the breach; and

b) requiring it to be remedied if it is capable of remedy; and

c) requiring compensation.

If the breach is not thereafter remedied within a reasonable time, Len may then commence forfeiture proceedings against Thomas. At the hearing Thomas may apply to the court for relief, which the court may grant on such terms as it thinks fit: s146(2). There is a similar provision for sub-leasees in s146(4).

iii) Len granted a lease of Greenacre to Thomas in 1985 and in 1986 Sid went into adverse possession of the demised land. Under the Limitation Act 1980 he became entitled to register a possessory title after 12 years in 1998. There is nothing in the facts to indicate that he has effected registration.

In the case of unregistered land, at the end of the statutory period of 12 years the owner's title is extinguished and the squatter is the new title owner. To quote Lord Radcliffe in *Fairweather v St Marylebone Property Co Ltd* [1963] AC 510 'his title, therefore, is never derived through but arises always in spite of the dispossessed owner'.

In registered land the position at the end of the 12-year period is different. The owner's title is not extinguished but instead is held by him on trust for the squatter: s75(1) LRA 1925. The squatter will then become entitled to register a possessory title at the land registry in place of the owner. He will then acquire the paper owner's estate: *Central London Commercial Estates Ltd v Kato Kagaku Ltd* [1998] 4 All ER 948. It is sometimes said that the squatter acquires the estate by means of a 'parliamentary conveyance'.

The word 'trust' in s75 seems to imply that during the interim the squatter's rights are equitable, but Sedley J in the *Central London Commercial Estates* case described that as 'surely wrong' and the more probable view is that he has a legal fee simple.

Since 1998 Thomas has been holding the lease on the trust imposed on him by s75 in favour of Sid. It must be emphasised that there is no adverse possession against Len. Sid's adverse possession would only commence against Len at the termination of the lease, when Len became entitled to possession.

Is Sid bound by the user covenant in the lease in favour of Len? The answer would appear to be in the affirmative. To quote Sedley J 'in relation to a registered leasehold, however, s75 lifts the extinguishing effect of the Limitation Act and substitutes a trust of the leasehold interest, benefits and burdens alike, from the moment of the extinction of the leasehold title.' (This is rather unfortunate phrasing because under s75 the leasehold title is not extinguished, but remains vested in the leaseholder and is held on trust for the squatter.)

He continued: 'The squatter becomes entitled without regard to merits, to be placed in the same relationship with the freeholder as had been previously enjoyed by the leaseholder.'

On this view Sid therefore stands in the shoes of Thomas and is bound by the user covenant in the lease, which Len can enforce by an injunction or threat of forfeiture.

QUESTION THREE

In 1985 Alice, the registered owner of 'The Gables', granted Tina a 20-year lease of the land. In 1986, Jack, an adjoining landowner, extended his market-garden on to an unused piece of 'The Gables' land, planting fruit and vegetables and, in 1987, he enclosed the piece of land to protect it from Tina's dogs. In 1999 Tina surrendered her lease to Alice, who has now told Jack to leave her land.

Advise Jack. Would your advice differ if 'The Gables' had been unregistered land?

University of London LLB Examination
(for External Students) Land Law June 2000 Q6

General Comment

The first part of the question requires an examination of the conditions which must be satisfied before a claim to a possessory title can be established. The second part is more complex and candidates must be prepared to discuss the position in registered land at the conclusion of the statutory period: s75 Land Registration Act (LRA) 1925; *Central London Commercial Estates Ltd* v *Kato Kagaku Ltd*. Candidates must contrast that position with that pertaining in the case of unregistered land.

Skeleton Solution

Conditions for acquisition of land by adverse possession: when does time begin to run?; the three essential ingredients as applicable to this case; physical control; intention to possess; adverse possession; Jack's position at the end of the statutory period; ss75(1) and 70(1)(f) LRA 1925 – Tina's surrender: after Jack had registered his title; before Jack had registered his title; *Central London Commercial Estates Ltd* v *Kato Kagaku Ltd* – position if the land is unregistered: at the end of the statutory period, adverse possessor acquires title to the land (contrast with the position in registered land) – Jack acquires a new title, not Tina's title – Tina's surrender: *Fairweather* v *St Marylebone Property Co Ltd*; on surrender lease and reversion merged; Alice entitled to possession against Jack.

Suggested Solution

Jack encroached upon The Gables when it was leased to Tina. Has he acquired title by adverse possession to the piece of land in question as against Tina the tenant?

It is necessary, first, to examine the basic principles behind adverse possession claims. Section 15(1) Limitation Act 1980 provides:

> 'No action shall be brought by any person to recover any land after the expiration of 12 years from the date on which the right of action accrued to him or, if it first accrued to some person through whom he claims, to that person.'

Time begins to run against the paper owner when the right of action accrues to him and the statute contains provisions for determining the date of accrual of the right of action to recover the land. Part 1 of Schedule 1 provides:

> 'Where the person bringing an action to recover land, or some person through whom he claims, has been in possession of the land, and has while entitled to the land been dispossessed or discontinued his possession, the right of action shall be treated as having accrued on the date of the dispossession or discontinuance.'

A person claiming a title by adverse possession under the statute, must prove:

a) factual possession of the land; and

b) that in enjoying factual possession he intended to possess it (animus possidendi); and

c) that his possession is 'adverse'.

Before discussing the application of the three requirements to Jack's case, the date from which time began to run against Tina must be ascertained. Time begins to run when the person who was in possession is either dispossessed or discontinues possession. On the facts of this case that was in 1986, when Jack began to encroach upon the land which was part of the lease of The Gables. That date having been ascertained, the next question is: did Jack acquire factual possession of the land?

In answering that question assistance can be derived from the Court of Appeal's decision in *Buckinghamshire County Council* v *Moran* [1989] 2 All ER 225. In that case the council purchased a plot of land in 1955 with the intention that it should be developed to provide a road diversion, but it did not proceed with the plan. In 1967 the defendant's predecessors in title bought adjoining land (Dolphin Place) and treated the council's land as an annex of their own property. They cultivated the plot from time to time and parked a horse box there. No-one challenged their activities.

In 1971 the defendant purchased Dolphin Place and he too treated the council's land as an annex of Dolphin Place. The evidence was that by October 1973 the defendant had enclosed the plot so that access to it could only be gained through Dolphin Place. There was a gate to the plot fronting the highway and the defendant had secured it with a lock and chain. The defendant treated the land as a garden of Dolphin Place and planted daffodils there and trimmed the hedges. Slade LJ quoted his own previous judgment in *Powell* v *McFarlane* (1977) 38 P & CR 452:

> 'Factual possession signifies an appropriate degree of physical control. It must be single and exclusive possession ... The question what acts constitute a sufficient degree of exclusive physical control must depend on the circumstances, in particular the nature of the land and the manner in which land of that nature is commonly used or enjoyed.'

Slade LJ had no difficulty in concluding that by October 1973 the defendant had acquired physical possession of the land. In dealing with animus possidendi, Slade LJ again referred to his judgment in *Powell* v *McFarlane*:

> '... the animus possidendi involves the intention, in one's own name and on one's own behalf, to exclude the world at large, including the owner with the proper title.'

Quoting too from *Seddon* v *Smith* (1877) 36 LT 168 that 'enclosure is the strongest possible evidence of adverse possession' (per Cockburn LJ), he concluded that the defendant had the necessary animus possidendi. In the result Moran's claim to title by adverse possession succeeded.

In applying Slade LJ's observations, attention must be turned to the nature of the land upon which Jack had encroached. We are simply told that it was unused land and its nature is not indicated. In *Hounslow London Borough Council* v *Minchinton* (1997) 74 P & CR 221, Millett LJ assessed the acts in that case as 'not substantial' but 'that was the only available use for the land given its rough nature'. The more derelict or neglected the land, the less the adverse possessor has to prove in order to establish that he has taken physical control. Here, Jack's encroachment commenced with the planting of fruit and vegetables.

We may assume, at lease for the purposes of the question, that given these activities and the fact that the land was unused that Jack would be able to prove the necessary degree of control of the land. However, physical control is of itself not enough. There must also be the requisite intention and the possession must be adverse.

Did Jack have the requisite intention to possess? In *Powell* v *McFarlane* Slade LJ explained that 'the animus possidendi (the intention to possess) involves the intention, in one's own name and on one's own behalf, to exclude the world at large, including the owner with the paper title'. In *Buckinghamshire County Council* v *Moran*, as Slade LJ elaborated further:

'... what is required ... is not an intention to own or even an intention to acquire ownership but an intention to possess ... that is to say an intention for the time being to possess the land to the exclusion of all other persons, including the owner with the paper title.'

This intention has to be deduced from the facts of the case. If the adverse possessor is treating the land as though he was its owner, this is good evidence to support the presence of the intention. Enclosing the land with a fence strengthens Jack's case, since 'enclosure is the strongest possible evidence of adverse possession': *Seddon* v *Smith* (1877) 36 LT 168, per Cockburn LJ. The fencing is evidence of all three elements.

The third element of adverse possession, that the possession be 'adverse', means that the possession must be of such a nature so as to be inconsistent with the paper owner's title. Again, whether the acts in question are sufficient to constitute adverse possession depends on the nature of the land. Trivial acts will not be enough: *Tecbuild* v *Chamberlain* (1969) 209 EG 1069. In *Buckinghamshire County Council* v *Moran* the claimant treated the plot as though it was his own garden. We may conclude that probably, on such facts as we have, Jack will succeed in establishing the three necessary elements.

Adverse possession may well have commenced in 1986, and almost certainly in 1987 when the land was enclosed. Twelve years from those dates takes us up to 1998 or 1999. By those dates the 12-year period had elapsed.

Before discussing Tina's surrender of the lease we must examine Jack's position at the conclusion of the period. This is registered land. At the conclusion of the period, Tina's leasehold title to the land was not extinguished. She remained on the register, but from that point she held the title on trust for Jack. This is the effect of s75(1) Land Registration Act (LRA) 1925. Jack, however, became entitled to apply for registration of himself as registered proprietor with possessory title, but until he does so he will have no legal title in the land. However, in the meantime his rights will be protected as an overriding interest under s70(1)(f) LRA 1925: 'rights acquired, or in the course of being acquired, under the Limitation Acts'. Once Jack is registered with possessory title then Tina's title to the land is extinguished, but not until then. On registration, Jack acquires Tina's title, and it is sometimes said that an adverse possessor has acquired the paper owner's title by 'a parliamentary conveyance'. It must be emphasised that Alice's title is in no way affected. Jack's adverse possession is against Tina and not Alice. Time would not have run against Alice, because she was not in possession of the land.

Jack does not seem to have taken advantage of his right to register a possessory title, but what would be the position if he had done so before Tina had surrendered her lease? The point arose in *Spectrum Investment Co* v *Holmes* [1981] 1 WLR 221.

In that case an adverse possessor acquired title to a registered lease and became its registered proprietor. The dispossessed tenant then purported to surrender the lease to the freeholder. The freeholder applied to have the adverse possessor's title removed from the register. His reasoning was based on the decision in *Fairweather v St Marylebone Property Co Ltd* [1963] AC 510, which was an unregistered land case. The adverse possessor in that case had acquired a possessory title after the 12-year period as against the tenant. The tenant then surrendered the lease to the freeholder. The freeholder argued that the lease and reversion then merged, which entitled the freeholder to immediate possession. The House of Lords agreed and held that the freeholder was entitled to evict the adverse possessor forthwith. It will be appreciated that since the land was unregistered, no question of registration arose.

The freeholders in *Spectrum Investment Co v Holmes* did not meet with the same success. The court held that when the adverse possessor's title was registered, the dispossessed tenant's title to the lease was transferred to the adverse possessor and consequently the tenant has no lease to surrender. The process of a merger of the lease and the reversion could not therefore take place and the freeholder was not entitled to have the adverse possessor's title removed from the register.

Thus, if Tina attempted to surrender the lease after Jack had registered, that surrender would be ineffective. There would have been no merger of lease and reversion, because Tina had no lease to surrender. In consequence, Alice would be powerless to evict Jack or have his title removed from the register.

Suppose, in the alternative, Tina had surrendered her lease to Alice before Jack had secured registration for himself. At that point, she would still have been the registered proprietor of the lease, and would still have had a lease to surrender, unlike the tenant in *Spectrum Investment Co v Holmes*. As has been stated before, in the case of registered land, after the 12-year period has elapsed, the adverse possessor does not automatically acquire title. He does not do so until he registers himself with a possessory title. In the meantime, s75 LRA 1925 applies and the dispossessed owner holds the title upon trust for the adverse possessor. Further, the rights of the adverse possessor are protected as an overriding interest under s70(1)(f) LRA 1925.

If Tina surrendered the lease to Alice before Jack's registration, although its surrender would have been effective, it was held in *Central London Commercial Estates Ltd v Kato Kagaku Ltd* [1998] 4 All ER 148 that, if a lease was surrendered to the freeholder before the adverse possessor's registration of title, the trusteeship imposed by s75 LRA 1925 on the dispossessed tenant was transferred to the freeholder.

Thus, if Tina surrendered the lease before Jack's registration, the trusteeship imposed on her by s75 LRA 1925 would have passed to Alice. To quote Sedley J: 'the squatter becomes entitled, without regard to merits, to be placed in the same relationship with the freeholder as had been previously enjoyed by the leaseholder'. Alice, therefore, would still be powerless to proceed against Jack. She could not obtain possession until the lease terminated. Nor could she obtain deletion of his title from the register.

Would the advice to Jack be different if the land was unregistered? The law relating to acquisition of title by adverse possession is the same until one reaches the end of the statutory period. In the case of unregistered land, the adverse possessor acquires title immediately at the end of that period, albeit without any documentation. This contrasts with registered land where the adverse possessor does not acquire title until his title is registered. In unregistered land there is, of course, no provision for registration of title. Thus at the end of 12 years adverse possession, Jack would have obtained a possessory title to that part of Tina's leasehold land which was subject to his adverse possession.

However, he would not have obtained Tina's title. He would acquire a new title; not Tina's. In the *Fairweather* case, Lord Radcliffe said: 'this (the adverse possessor's) title therefore is never derived through but always arises in spite of the dispossessed owner'. In that case the House of Lords held that in the case of the acquisition of a leasehold title by adverse possession, the leaseholder title, as against the adverse possessor, is extinguished: s17 LRA 1925, but it remains good as against the freeholder. Since the tenant's title as against the freeholder has not been extinguished, the tenant could still surrender that title to the freeholder. Accordingly, the Lords held that the freeholder could evict the adverse possessor with immediate effect because, at the point of effective surrender, the freeholder became entitled to possession of the land.

That would be the position here. When Tina surrendered the lease, which according to *Fairweather* she was still able to do, the lease and reversion merged, giving Alice the immediate right to possession of the land against Jack.

Revision Aids

Designed for the undergraduate, the 101 Questions & Answers series and the Suggested Solutions series are for all those who have a positive commitment to passing their law examinations. Each series covers a different examinable topic and comprises a selection of answers to examination questions and, in the case of the 101 Questions and Answers, interrograms. The majority of questions represent examination 'bankers' and are supported by full-length essay solutions. These titles will undoubtedly assist you with your research and further your understanding of the subject in question.

101 Questions & Answers Series

Only £7.95 Published December 2003

Constitutional Law
ISBN: 1 85836 522 8

Criminal Law
ISBN: 1 85836 432 9

Land Law
ISBN: 1 85836 515 5

Law of Contract
ISBN: 1 85836 517 1

Law of Tort
ISBN: 1 85836 516 3

Suggested Solutions to Past Examination Questions 2001–2002 Series

Only £6.95 Published December 2003

Company Law
ISBN: 1 85836 519 8

Employment Law
ISBN: 1 85836 520 1

European Union Law
ISBN: 1 85836 524 4

Evidence
ISBN: 1 85836 521 X

Family Law
ISBN: 1 85836 525 2

For further information or to place an order, please contact:

Mail Order
Old Bailey Press at Holborn College
Woolwich Road
Charlton
London
SE7 8LN

Telephone: 020 8317 6039
Fax: 020 8317 6004
Website: www.oldbaileypress.co.uk
E-Mail: mailorder@oldbaileypress.co.uk

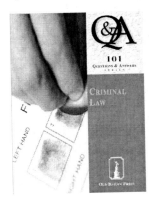

Unannotated Cracknell's Statutes for Use in Examinations

New Editions of Cracknell's Statutes

Only £11.95 Due 2004

Cracknell's Statutes provide a comprehensive series of essential statutory provisions for each subject. Amendments are consolidated, avoiding the need to cross-refer to amending legislation. Unannotated, they are suitable for use in examinations, and provide the precise wording of vital Acts of Parliament for the diligent student.

Commercial Law
ISBN: 1 85836 562 7

Family Law
ISBN: 1 85836 566 X

Company Law
ISBN: 1 85836 563 5

Medical Law
ISBN: 1 85836 567 8

Conflict of Laws
ISBN: 1 85836 564 3

Public International Law
ISBN: 1 85836 568 6

Evidence
ISBN: 1 85836 565 1

Revenue Law
ISBN: 1 85836 569 4

Succession
ISBN: 1 85836 570 8

For further information or to place an order, please contact:

Mail Order
Old Bailey Press at Holborn College
Woolwich Road
Charlton
London
SE7 8LN

Telephone: 020 8317 6039
Fax: 020 8317 6004
Website: www.oldbaileypress.co.uk
E-Mail: mailorder@oldbaileypress.co.uk

Old Bailey Press

The Old Bailey Press Integrated Student Law Library is tailor-made to help you at every stage of your studies, from the preliminaries of each subject through to the final examination. The series of Textbooks, Revision WorkBooks, 150 Leading Cases and Cracknell's Statutes are interrelated to provide you with a comprehensive set of study materials.

You can buy Old Bailey Press books from your University Bookshop, your local Bookshop, directly using this form, or you can order a free catalogue of our titles from the address shown overleaf.

The following subjects each have a Textbook, 150 Leading Cases, Revision WorkBook and Cracknell's Statutes unless otherwise stated.

Administrative Law
Commercial Law
Company Law
Conflict of Laws
Constitutional Law
Conveyancing (Textbook and 150 Leading Cases)
Criminal Law
Criminology (Textbook and Sourcebook)
Employment Law (Textbook and Cracknell's Statutes)
English and European Legal Systems
Equity and Trusts
Evidence
Family Law
Jurisprudence: The Philosophy of Law (Textbook, Sourcebook and Revision WorkBook)
Land: The Law of Real Property
Law of International Trade
Law of the European Union
Legal Skills and System (Textbook)
Obligations: Contract Law
Obligations: The Law of Tort
Public International Law
Revenue Law (Textbook, Revision WorkBook and Cracknell's Statutes)
Succession (Textbook, Revision WorkBook and Cracknell's Statutes)

Mail order prices:	
Textbook	£15.95
150 Leading Cases	£12.95
Revision WorkBook	£10.95
Cracknell's Statutes	£11.95
Suggested Solutions 1999–2000	£6.95
Suggested Solutions 2000–2001	£6.95
Suggested Solutions 2001–2002	£6.95
101 Questions and Answers	£7.95
Law Update 2004	£10.95

Please note details and prices are subject to alteration.

To complete your order, please fill in the form below:

Module	Books required	Quantity	Price	Cost
		Postage		
		TOTAL		

For the UK and Europe, add £4.95 for the first book ordered, then add £1.00 for each subsequent book ordered for postage and packing.

For the rest of the world, add 50% for airmail.

ORDERING

By telephone to Mail Order at 020 8317 6039, with your credit card to hand.

By fax to 020 8317 6004 (giving your credit card details).

Website: www.oldbaileypress.co.uk

E-Mail: mailorder@oldbaileypress.co.uk

By post to: Mail Order, Old Bailey Press at Holborn College, Woolwich Road, Charlton, London, SE7 8LN.

When ordering by post, please enclose full payment by cheque or banker's draft, or complete the credit card details below. You may also order a free catalogue of our complete range of titles from this address.

We aim to despatch your books within 3 working days of receiving your order. All parts of the form must be completed.

Name

Address

Postcode

E-Mail

Telephone

Total value of order, including postage: £

I enclose a cheque/banker's draft for the above sum, or

charge my ☐ Access/Mastercard ☐ Visa ☐ American Express

Cardholder: ....

Card number

☐☐☐☐ ☐☐☐☐ ☐☐☐☐ ☐☐☐☐

Expiry date ☐☐☐☐

Signature: ....Date: ....